CIVIL SOCIETY IN WALES

Civil Society in Wales:

Policy, Politics and People

Edited by
Graham Day, David Dunkerley
and Andrew Thompson

UNIVERSITY OF WALES PRESS
CARDIFF
2006

Published by the University of Wales Press

University of Wales Press
10 Columbus Walk
Brigantine Place
Cardiff
CF10 4UP

www.wales.ac.uk/press

ISBN-10 0-7083-1850-9 (paperback)
ISBN-13 978-0-7083-1850-8 (paperback)

ISBN-10 0-7083-1851-7 (hardback)
ISBN-13 978-0-7083-1851-5 (hardback)

British Library Cataloguing-in-Publication Data.
A catalogue record for this book is available from the British Library.

Printed in Great Britain by Antony Rowe Ltd, Wiltshire

Contents

Figures

Contributors

David Adamson	University of Glamorgan
David Barlow	University of Glamorgan
Sarah Batterbury	University of Bristol
Sandra L. Betts	University of Wales, Bangor
Paul Chambers	University of Glamorgan
Catherine Davies	formerly University of Glamorgan
Graham Day	University of Wales, Bangor
Mark Drakeford	Cardiff University and Welsh Assembly Government
David Dunkerley	University of Glamorgan
Lesley Hodgson	University of Glamorgan
David Jones	formerly University of Wales, Bangor
Isobel Lindsay	University of Strathclyde
Robin Mann	University of Bristol
Philip Mitchell	University of Glamorgan
Anna Nicholl	Welsh Refugee Council
Tom O'Malley	University of Wales, Aberystwyth
Gerald Taylor	University of Glamorgan
Alys Thomas	Welsh Assembly Government
Andrew Thompson	University of Glamorgan
Charlotte Williams	University of Keele

Foreword

RT. HON. RHODRI MORGAN AM, FIRST MINISTER, NATIONAL ASSEMBLY FOR WALES

I regard it as a pleasure to contribute this foreword to a book which, I am sure, will be widely welcomed and equally widely read in Welsh civil society.

For Welsh devolution to succeed it has to mean a transfer of power from Cardiff to the rest of Wales as well as from London to Cardiff. And even this spatial sense of devolution does not capture the whole of what our changed arrangements must come to mean. As well as horizontal devolution – spreading power and responsibility more widely – we have to have vertical devolution as well. I have sometimes tried to sum up this dimension by describing our devolution settlement as a shift from *crachach* to *gwerin*, from government by a self-replicating elite to a new engagement with a far wider and more representative group of people, women and men, people from north and south Wales, Welsh speakers and not, black people as well as white, and so on.

The contributions contained in this book illustrate the emerging strength of this deepening devolution. It has often been said that civil society in Wales has been less developed than in Scotland and some other parts of the United Kingdom, and that the path to the Assembly was strewn with more rocks and minefields as a result. Devolution itself has stimulated a renaissance of voluntary and civil organizations and activity in Wales, just as the Assembly Government, in turn, is able to draw on the powerful contribution which the sector has to offer.

This volume's subtitle, *Policy, Politics and People*, highlights another dimension which I have tried to bring to the fore in discussions of the way in which devolution has developed in Wales. The idea which I have been keen to get across is that devolution and responsibility have to go hand in hand. Now that we have new powers to direct our own affairs, we have to show that we are willing and able to take on the responsibility. For a very long period indeed it was always possible to suggest that things had not worked out in Wales because decisions had been taken elsewhere – to lay the blame, in effect, for failure at another door. That is no longer a viable excuse. New rights of participation in politics have to be matched with a new willingness to share in the hard decisions which have to be faced and made. One of the themes which runs through this volume is the debate which rightly surrounds the terms of engagement between different dimensions of civil society in Wales and our new political structures. Contributions to a maturing of our civil society like this, are as timely as they are welcome.

1. Introduction

GRAHAM DAY, DAVID DUNKERLEY AND ANDREW THOMPSON

It is not unusual for works on civil society to begin by noting how hard it is to define the term. In the opening lines of *Toward a Global Civil Society* (1995: 1) the American political theorist Michael Walzer remarks that there are 'many definitions . . . and there is considerable disagreement at the margins about what the concept includes and excludes'. A precise and accepted definition of 'civil society' is elusive. Often civil society is treated as being synonymous with the voluntary or not-for-profit sector. Both voluntarism and the absence of a profit motivation are, indeed, important considerations for how we think about civil society. Yet, the notion of a *civil* society suggests a sphere that is distinguished by more than the fact that it is inhabited by people and organizations that come together voluntarily and are not characteristically engaged in the exchange of goods and services for profit. Wuthnow, who writes widely on civil society and religion, argues that the 'voluntary sector' itself is conceptualized too often in terms of the services it provides. In arguing for a more normative understanding of the voluntary sector as contributing to the process of 'shaping of collective values' (1991: 22), he brings it more fully into line with the idea of civil society.

Seligman (2002) suggests that civil society is both an idea and an ideal. There is no straightforward objective definition of civil society; neither is there a specific set of institutions that definitively constitute it. The power of the concept lies in how variously it is employed to understand the form and consequences of the relationship between the state and citizens in *actual* societies, how people voluntarily organize themselves into groups, and what the effects of this activity are, both for the individuals involved and for society in general. These issues are not unique to the present time and a preoccupation with the nature of civil society is not a merely voguish phenomenon. Nonetheless, in the context of Wales a focus on civil society may seem just that. After all, Wales can hardly be characterized as a society within which citizens are lacking a public space of free association and in which the shadow of the state looms darkly over private lives. Since the advent of the National Assembly for Wales (NAW), however, there has been a flurry of commentary in which claims, and anxieties, about civil society have been deployed. As an idea that is invoked to think about the relationship between government and the citizen, the significance of market values within contemporary societies and their impact upon individuals, and about how societies voluntarily organize themselves beyond the state, then 'civil society' holds a universal appeal. As many of the chapters in this volume illustrate, it is an idea used – by the contributors, and more typically, by the subjects to whom they refer – to explain a society like Wales both as it is now and as it *might* be.

There is an argument that civil society in Wales is comparatively weak because key institutions in the country do not wield the same clout as equivalent organizations elsewhere, or fail to speak adequately as Welsh institutions. Such an argument can serve to detract from the level of activity, diversity and impact of the civil society that actually exists in Wales. Furthermore, it obscures just how much of social life in Wales is managed and organized through civil society. Some of the contributions that follow advocate a strengthening of the role of certain aspects of civil society or allied areas such as the media (for instance, see the chapter by Barlow et al.) through the intervention of the Assembly and/or the British state. Other chapters highlight how the organizations of civil society are hoping themselves that devolution will help them to advance their interests in a manner not possible hitherto, such as in the case of bodies involved in community regeneration (discussed by Adamson and Hodgson in their respective chapters) or faith groups (considered by Chambers and Thompson). Yet, by any measure, the amount of activity that goes on already within civil society – such as the work done by ethnic minority associations, through inter-faith dialogue or the remarkable energy being invested in community development, to take just three of the examples discussed below – makes a phenomenal contribution to Welsh society, which remains remarkably poorly understood.

In what follows, we will look in much greater detail at what constitutes civil society in Wales and particularly in post-devolution

Wales. All the contributors work with the notion that civil society is best thought of as the realm of non-governmental activity. In addition, the following chapters do not, by and large, address the role of and connections between public bodies in Wales. The matter of Wales's evolving 'civic infrastructure' (B. Jones and J. Osmond, 2002: xx) raises another set of questions. To be sure, the associational life that characterizes civil society makes its own contribution to a civic culture, by which we mean the practice of engaging in and the commitment to the value of public life. Yet, most of the organizations addressed below could not be described as 'civic' to the extent that this implies that they are formally charged with discharging public functions.

Nonetheless, the relationship between the Assembly and *civil* society is a recurring theme in the following chapters. Before, during and after the establishment of the Assembly the notion of 'inclusivity' has been pervasive in both political rhetoric and the emerging new political culture of Wales. Part of the inclusiveness has been a determined effort by the Assembly to work more closely with the voluntary sector in Wales in an attempt realistically to engage with civil society. Drakeford, in his contribution to this volume, traces the development of this aim since 1999 and explores the changing nature of the relationship between the voluntary sector and the Assembly.

Other contributions, such as those by Adamson and Hodgson, point to the problems that arise when the boundaries between state and civil society become too blurred. Most also use the idea of civil society to understand how individuals come together through voluntary association to realize ends that are social rather than individual, or at least are not characterized by the overt pursuit of narrow personal self-interest. There are areas, activities or types of organizations that some will see as characteristic of civil society that are not addressed below, such as education or the environmental lobby. Interestingly, the definition provided by the Welsh voluntary sector itself (WCVA, 2003) sees the voluntary sector as those organizations and individuals to be found between the family, the state and the market where they exist to advance common interests. In this way religious organizations, trade unions, professional associations and the like are included. Drakeford, in this volume, also makes the point that the fact that a voluntary organization does not directly interact with the state (possibly because of its being so small) does not rule it out from being a part of civil society itself.

In the meetings that led to this book the issue of what the contributors understood by 'civil society' was a recurrent feature of our discussions. More specifically, the debates centred on three matters: the relationship between state and civil society; the relationship between market and civil society; and the normative role of civil society.

Within the wider literature in this field there is broad agreement that civil society has to be differentiated in some way from the state. To return to Walzer, civil society, for him, 'incorporates many of the associations and identities that we value outside of, prior to or in the shadow of state and citizenship' (1995: 1). John Keane, a leading contemporary interpreter of and advocate for civil society, also stresses the separation of state and civil society. As he argues in the course of his analysis of the notion of a 'global' civil society, one of the markers of the organizations typically thought of as constitutive of it is that 'they deliberately organize themselves and conduct their cross-border social activities, business and politics outside the boundaries of governmental structures' (2003: 9).

By these terms, then, civil society refers to forms of voluntary social interaction – Walzer speaks of 'uncoerced human association' (1995: 1) – and the networks and exchanges arising therefrom that are relatively independent of the state. However, there is considerable disagreement about the exact relationship between the state and civil society. Moreover, the suggestion that organizations might be part of, or activities typical of, civil society solely because they are non-governmental raises yet more difficult questions about just what civil society *is*, not least of which is the issue of whether or not civil society includes economic institutions. Francis Fukuyama, whose books *Trust* (1995) and *The Great Disruption* (2000) are concerned with the social bonds and moral commitments that link individuals together in society, clearly identifies business as part of civil society. As he chooses to define it, civil society is a 'complex welter of intermediate institutions, including businesses, voluntary associations, educational institutions, clubs, unions, media, charities, and churches' (1995: 4). Such a reading, however, is not to everyone's taste. For Cohen and Arato (1992), the economy is very clearly located outside civil society, quite as much as the state. For them, a crucial feature of civil society is its 'critical potential', and this means that the actors within it should not be constrained by commercial or economic interests, any more than they should be limited by political obligations and restraints.

Why is the differentiation of civil society from the state, as well as, for some, separating civil society and the economy, such a key issue? Keane (2003) points out that the early modern notion of a '*civill society*' referred to a society governed by the rule of law. No distinction was made between society and the state; indeed, it is the state that makes a civil, ordered and comparatively secure society possible, and which, in the work of Thomas Hobbes, the seventeenth-century English philosopher, moves us beyond a 'state of nature' characterized by unrestrained competition and lacking even a basic level of trust between individuals. This rendering of 'civil society' could not be further from the way in which the concept is commonly employed today, where the capacity of actors within civil society to be critical of the state – because they have the autonomy (usually underpinned by legal rights) to do so – defines this sphere of activity.

Countering Hobbes, later writers argued for checks on the power of the state and saw difficulties in the theory that the only alternative to the 'state of nature' was a *Leviathan* (the title of Hobbes's classic account of the state) with unlimited powers. Thus, for John Locke, as John Dunn suggests, in a 'state which was not a civil society, concentrated coercive power confronted individuals with an overwhelming danger. It did so, too, under conditions which gave them no effective means to restrain it or to hold it responsible' (Dunn, 2001: 52). Adam Ferguson, a leading luminary of the Scottish Enlightenment and author of *An Essay on the History of Civil Society* (1767), also held that the associations of civil society would foster a sense of civic virtue and duty that would help keep despotism at bay. Alexis de Tocqueville, the early nineteenth-century French author of *Democracy in America* (1998), argued similarly that political associations – a term that, in the case of the USA, he used to describe town meetings and community groups as well as political parties – train individuals in the workings and meaning of democracy and thus help to constrain any encroachment by the state on their liberty. He remarks that if 'men living in democratic countries had no right and no inclination to associate for political purposes, their independence would be in great jeopardy' (1998: 216). One finds these sentiments repeated today, in the writings of John Keane. A key theme of his work on civil society is the 'fundamental importance of cultivating public spheres as democratic instruments of power-sharing and of keeping power humble' (2000: 11).

Central to many discussions of the civil society concept, then, is an emphasis on the necessity of preserving a realm occupied by associations that represent the plurality of interests that ought to be able to exist – relatively – independent of the state. Cast in this way, civil society serves to defend individual liberty. For some it is the nature of the relationship between state and civil society that defines liberty, rather than a commitment to the existence, in any objective sense, of particular institutions. For example, Pietrzyk suggests that what 'makes civil society "civil" is the fact that it is a sphere within which citizens may freely organize themselves into groups at various levels in order to make the formal bodies of state authority adopt policies consonant with their perceived interests' (2003: 38–9). Thus a good deal of work on civil society focuses generally on its significance for democracy, conceived as a process rather than simply as a system of representative government. Writers from de Tocqueville through to Robert Putnam, perhaps the best-known contemporary figure in this debate (with an influence that extends beyond the academic community), posit that a vibrant, pluralistic civil society, contributing to engagement in public affairs, contributes greatly to good government.

Others maintain that the principal benefit of participation in civil society is that it makes us more aware of, and thereby engenders tolerance for, alternative perspectives and values. Thus, for Walzer 'it may well be that the most important thing people learn in civil society is how to live with the many different forms of social conflict' (2002: 38). This point is also made by Putnam, who marshals evidence from the USA to argue that those who participate in civic activities are 'as a rule *more* tolerant of dissent and unconventional behaviour than social isolates are' (2000: 355). Nevertheless the relationship between civil society, democracy and tolerance is complex. Civil society is not a single, undifferentiated sphere; some organizations, enjoying the protection of the state or working in alliance with the state, may act to prevent others from mobilizing in ways that could advance democracy. With regard to the interaction between voluntary organizations and democracy, for example, Deakin writes that 'some of their interventions can obstruct its operation, or their activities can be marginal or irrelevant' (2001: 110).

Civil society as much as political society is informed by issues of power: some groups are better able to advance their interests because they possess greater organizational resources, as well as more developed connections with the political and economic spheres. As Hodgson argues in this volume, one of the important ways in which civil society functions *as a society* is through networks of personal contacts. In their analysis of the public role of faith groups, Chambers and Thompson note that while the Assembly has recently demonstrated a commitment to working with all the faith groups in Wales, mainstream Christian faiths have the advantage of organizational structures that enable them to communicate better with the Assembly, and also have the services of a full-time National Assembly Liaison Officer. In their chapter on the relationship between the media and civil society Barlow et al. argue that access for civil society to express and question opinions via the media is limited, as is the representation of diversity. These discussions caution against any simplistic understanding of the relationship between an active civil society and democracy.

Civil society can never stand apart wholly from the state, since the state is able to determine the conditions under which civil society can exist. However, for those concerned with issues of democracy, perhaps the key question is how far the state permits dissent and allows expression of critical public opinion through organized civil society. Some would contend that even the relative autonomy of civil society is compromised in ways other than through direct coercive state action. De Tocqueville, for example, argued that a fear of civil disorder stemming from conditions actually created or exacerbated by democracy, notably materialism and individualism – the 'habit' among citizens of 'always considering themselves as standing alone' (1998: 206) – predisposed people to turn to the state to guard against such a development. More particularly, he suggested that the 'love of equality' by which democracies are marked fosters a 'hatred' of privilege that may, in turn, lead the majority towards the state to guarantee uniformity and equality of conditions. For these reasons, he saw the centralization of political power as a natural tendency of democratic societies, a development which would lead populations along a 'longer, more secret, but more certain road to servitude' (1998: 341–2). The upshot of this centralization, according to de Tocqueville, is the gradual loss of liberty, understood not so much in terms of the removal of formal political rights, but more as the erosion of general individual autonomy and self-motivation. Civil society, whose very existence depends upon the desire of humans to interact and to work to achieve common ends, is therefore gradually sapped of its lifeblood. Centralization of power in democracies 'does not tyrannise' but 'stupefies a people, till each nation is reduced to nothing more than a flock of timid and industrious animals, of which the government is the shepherd' (1998: 359). De Tocqueville believed that a vibrant civil society was one of the principal factors that headed off such potential despotism in the nineteenth-century USA. Citizens were committed to forming associations to fulfil functions that, in other democratic societies, such as his native France, he believed, people were only too willing to see performed by the state.

The view is increasingly expressed today that the situation de Tocqueville feared is now manifest not in only in the USA but in many liberal democracies across the world. Amitai Etzioni, one of the leading figures in the communitarian movement, has maintained for some time that people in America are too preoccupied with individual rights, and show scant concern for personal and social responsibility as well as for civic activity. He argues, for example, that the influence of special interest groups over government has happened because of the 'fact that most people, most of the time, are politically inactive' (1994: 227). Elsewhere, to differing degrees, others attribute the weakness of civil society to the growth of 'big government' and especially to the welfare state. In Britain, David Green, director of Civitas and formerly of the Institute of Economic Affairs, holds that the state has assumed progressively functions that were once performed by 'free associations', to use de Tocqueville's phrase, such as charitable organizations, and also by the family. The result, for Green, is a decline in liberty and personal responsibility. Thus, in language that echoes de Tocqueville, he writes that the real problem with regard to education is that 'the welfare state has stripped parents of a major part of the responsibility for raising their children and thus helped to undermine the family, the main building block of a free society' (1993: 133).

Not surprisingly, the effects of 'big government' on civil society are sharply contested. Putnam considers that this has not been a major factor in accounting for the decline of social capital and civic participation in the USA since the mid-twentieth century. While Fukuyama acknowledges that the welfare state has contributed to the demise of extant organizations that partly fulfilled the roles it has subsequently assumed, much more systematically, he maintains that 'the rise of the welfare state cannot be more than a partial explanation for the decline of community' (1995: 314). As a response to perceptions of declining participation and weakening civic engagement, Britain has been experiencing greater movement towards, and experimentation with, the involvement in service delivery of private and 'third' sector organizations. A key concern for many is how far this will permit such bodies to continue to exercise independence and authority, rather than act merely as an extension of the state. Anthony Giddens, perhaps the pivotal intellectual figure in the development of 'third way' thinking in Britain, makes the point that the revitalization of civil society needs to happen in partnership with the state, stressing that the former should not be 'swamped' by the latter (1998: 85).

In contemporary Wales, many organizations, from faith groups to community groups, are keen to work with the Assembly and to promote civic activity and local involvement in public life. However, as our contributors highlight, the issue of the autonomy of civil society remains an important one, given the currency of ideas of political inclusiveness. The nature of the relationship between the voluntary sector and the Assembly is considered in the chapters in this volume by Drakeford and Adamson. Adamson examines especially the part played by the voluntary and community sector in community regeneration partnerships. This issue also runs through other chapters, including those by Day, Hodgson and Williams.

The relationship between civil society and the economy, or more precisely business organizations and market values, also often rests on the issue of the extent to which the autonomy of civil society can be maintained. In early discussions of civil society, such as the writings of Ferguson and Hegel, economic life and organizations are emphatically part of civil society. As we have already noted, some contemporary writers, such as Keane and

Fukuyama, agree in not demarcating civil society from the economy. In *Trust* (1995) Fukuyama proposes that one cannot separate economic prosperity from cultural and social life, an argument that was advanced earlier in Max Weber's *The Protestant Ethic and the Spirit of Capitalism* (1904/1930). The creation of prosperity depends on the existence of a fund of social capital, itself produced by the inculcation of shared values learned and reinforced through social relationships and, in particular, through life in civil society. In a more recent book, *The Great Disruption* (2000), Fukuyama acknowledges that organizations lobbying on behalf of business interests might not share the same motivations as organizations viewed by others as being more typically part of civil society, such as not-for-profit housing organizations. Indeed, he comments that 'our view of the health of civil society would be very different if it were populated exclusively by commercial interest groups rather than by charitable voluntary organizations' (2000: 53). Even so, he treats both as part of civil society. Others do not share this view. Another American writer, Benjamin Barber, who in one celebrated study (*Jihad Vs. McWorld*, 2003) has attacked the spread of American corporate values across the globe, argues for a civil society that stands guard against both state and market (Barber, 1998).

In practice, as discussed by Day and Jones in this volume, separating economic and civil society is difficult. Are not trades unions, often clearly located within civil society, as much economic organizations as the businesses with which they are connected so intimately? What about community regeneration ventures that, to all intents and purposes, look and behave like businesses? Does not the advocacy and practice of corporate social responsibility underline how closely economy and civil society are interwoven? Even the quantification of the fiscal value of work done within the 'third sector', often cited as evidence of the tangible output of civil society, has the effect of framing it in economic terms, itself perhaps an effect of a wider spread of market values within capitalist societies into the public sector and society in general. Several of the following chapters address the relationship between the market and civil society.

As editors, it is our view that both state and market have the capacity to intrude into, and narrow down, the scope for people to exercise control and have *real* choice over their own lives. The state does so through its use of power and authority to regulate and condition individual and collective behaviour; the economy by subjecting everything to the logic of the market and the rule of profit. To this end, we follow writers such as Cohen (1995) who argue that civil society should be able to act as a 'mediating' influence over political and economic processes. Deakin's point that the voluntary sector needs to take care in its relations with economic organizations not so much because of the direct adoption of commercial values but more because otherwise it may come to embrace 'competitive instincts at the basic human level' (2001: 157) also seems to us a useful reminder of the different concerns of market and civil society.

Commonly, analyses of civil society have identified it as a realm in which the transmission of values is central to its wider societal role. Hegel and Ferguson were of the view that civil associations would serve to build bonds between individuals and foster cohesion, effects captured today by the terms 'social capital' and 'trust'. Both philosophers were concerned that modernity, and particularly capitalism, brought with it increasing individualism, raising troubling questions about the prospects for social cohesion and order. For Hegel, civil society provided part of the solution to this new dilemma, for through participation in associations comes the realization that individual interests entwine inextricably with the interests of others. De Tocqueville shared a similar view of the virtue of civil association in balancing tendencies towards increased individualism in democracies, writing that through it the individual 'begins to perceive that he is not so independent of his fellow men as he had first imagined, and that in order to obtain their support he must often lend them his co-operation' (1998: 210). For Putnam, a modern interpreter of de Tocqueville, the concern is with what he reads as declining rates of participation in community-based civil associations in the USA and diminishing levels of political participation. Specifically, Putnam contends that when the generalized trust and reciprocity generated by social networks – 'social capital' – weakens then this has a knock-on effect on civic engagement. This is because 'voluntary associations may serve not only as forums for deliberation, but also as occasions for learning civic virtues, such as active participation in public life' (2000: 339). His objective, pursued though various ventures, is to revitalize civil society. Putnam's most recent book, *Better Together*

(Putnam and Feldstein, 2003), documents the role of those organizations in American public life that serve to strengthen social capital through their local initiatives.

Viewed in this way, it is easy to understand why the concept of civil society should appeal to so many, not least to politicians. The idea of a *civil* society, as the realm in which social virtue and civility is fostered, would seem to be a panacea for many social ills. In a number of the chapters that follow contributors provide illustrations of the 'bonding' and 'bridging' social capital to which Putnam refers; the ethnic minority associations considered by Charlotte Williams are illustrative of the former, and the networks between Cymdeithas yr Iaith Gymraeg (the Welsh Language Society) and environmental organizations described by Robin Mann of the latter. At the same time, the discussions in this book point to a variety of tensions between civil society, government and the market, as well as within civil society itself.

Although this book is able to explore only a limited number of potential areas of investigation, we believe that *Civil Society in Wales* contributes to a debate that is of growing interest among academics, practitioners and policy-makers, and of fundamental importance to the future direction taken by people and society in Wales.

References

Barber, B. (1998). *A Place For Us*, New York: Hill and Wang.

Barber, B. (2003). *Jihad vs. McWorld*, London: Corgi.

Cohen, J. (1995). 'Interpreting the notion of civil society', in M. Walzer (ed.), *Toward a Global Civil Society*, Oxford: Berghahn.

Cohen, J. and Arato, A. (1992). *Civil Society and Political Theory*, London: MIT Press.

Deakin, N. (2001). *In Search of Civil Society*, London: Palgrave.

Dunn, J. (2001). 'The contemporary political significance of John Locke's conception of civil society', in S. Kaviraj and S. Khilnani (eds), *Civil Society: History and Possibilities*, Cambridge: Cambridge University Press.

Etzioni, A. (1994). *The Spirit of Community*, London: Touchstone.

Fukuyama, F. (1995). *Trust*, New York: The Free Press.

Fukuyama, F. (2000). *The Great Disruption*, New York: The Free Press.

Giddens, A. (1998). *The Third Way*, Cambridge: Polity.

Green, D. (1993). *Reinventing Civil Society*, London: Institute of Economic Affairs.

Jones, B. and Osmond, J. (eds) (2002). *Building a Civic Culture: Institutional Change, Policy Development and Politics Dynamics in the National Assembly for Wales*, Cardiff: Wales Governance Centre and Institute for Welsh Affairs.

Keane, J. (2000). 'Keeping tabs on power', *CSD Bulletin*, Centre for the Study of Democracy, 7, 1.

Keane, J. (2003). *Global Civil Society*, Cambridge: Cambridge University Press.

Pietrzyk, D. (2003). 'Democracy or civil society', *Politics*, 23, 1.

Putnam, R. (2000). *Bowling Alone*, New York: Simon & Schuster.

Putnam, R. and Feldstein, L. (2003). *Better Together*, New York: Simon & Schuster.

Seligman, A. (2002). 'Civil society as idea and ideal', in S. Chambers and W. Kymlicka (eds), *Alternative Conceptions of Civil Society*, Princeton, NJ: Princeton University Press.

Tocqueville, A. de (1998). *Democracy in America*, Harmondsworth: Penguin.

Walzer, M. (2002). 'The concept of civil society', in M. Walzer (ed.), *Toward a Global Civil Society*, Oxford: Berghahn.

Weber, M. (1930). *The Protestant Ethic and the Spirit of Capitalism*, London: Unwin.

Welsh Council for Voluntary Action (WCVA) (2003). *Civil Society, Civil Space*, Cardiff: WCVA.

Wuthnow, R. (1991). 'The voluntary sector: legacy of the past, hope for the future?', in R. Wuthnow (ed.), *Between States and Markets*, Princeton: Princeton University Press.

gt fm
106
Community radio f r P

2. The Communicative Dimension of Civil Society: Media and the Public Sphere

DAVID BARLOW, PHILIP MITCHELL AND TOM O'MALLEY

Introduction

Writing prior to the establishment of the National Assembly for Wales (NAW), John Osmond asserts that 'the new Welsh politics is about creating a new democracy and a new civil society to make the democracy work' (1998: 15). This is a plea for a *Welsh* civil society, with the NAW seen as the key to achieving such a goal (see also Day et al., 2000; Paterson and Wyn Jones, 1999: 175). The NAW responded by articulating its vision for a 'new' Wales, prioritizing – amongst a raft of initiatives – the promotion of active citizenship, social inclusion and a general rejuvenation of democracy (NAW, 2000, 2001).

The importance of the media to this 'project' is foreshadowed in 'Broadcasting in Wales and the National Assembly' (Welsh Affairs Select Committee, 1999). This report reiterates the central role played by the media in the processes of citizenship and democracy through the provision of information, education and, to a lesser extent, entertainment. However, the report also prompts questions about the extent to which the media in Wales fulfils this role. It thus echoes more widely held concerns that the media in Wales is an important, but 'weak', element of Welsh civil society (Paterson and Wyn Jones, 1999: 176). Assertions such as these are based on two interrelated arguments. One, that the ownership, allegiances and orientation of the media in Wales continue to be unduly influenced from beyond its borders.[1] The second posits that as 'civil society in Wales developed within a British context . . . its

"Welshness" . . . has remained a matter of doubt' (Paterson and Wyn Jones, 1999: 173).

This chapter begins by exploring the ways in which civil society and the media are associated and understood in contemporary society, before invoking the 'public sphere' as a way of exploring the *communicative dimension* of civil society. Here, three principles of the public sphere – independence, access and diversity – are suggested as 'benchmarks', in order to examine the relationship between the media and civil society in Wales. By focusing on the communicative dimension of civil society, this allows 'voice' to take centre stage. 'Voice' is significant because this dimension of civil society is often overshadowed by the more popularly promoted characteristics of loyalty, trust and virtue, which contribute to the notion of 'social capital' associated with traditional forms of 'third sector' voluntary bodies (Cohen, 1999: 56–7).

'Unpacking' media and civil society

Interest in the relationship between civil society and the media has been invigorated by the post-1997 Labour government's revisions to communications policies, most notably by the debates leading up to – and following – the Communications Act 2003. One publication, *Culture and Communications* (Higdon, 2001), includes a specific section on 'Broadcasting and Civil Society'. Here, a range of topics are addressed, such as the potential of new media for democracy, media representation of ethnic diversity, the 'threats' and promises of the new communications environment for young people, and the future of public service broadcasting. Essentially, the relationship between civil society and the media is imagined as symbiotic and central to the democratic health of contemporary society.

However, the same publication overlooks some key issues. For instance, no consideration is given to whether the information and communication needs of civil society in Wales may differ from those of other parts of the UK. There is also ambivalence over whether media audiences in this 'new' era are to be understood primarily as citizens or consumers. When used by the government, 'civil society' tends to frame the public as a passive entity to be consulted when necessary, but not actively involved in the formation of policy. In such instances, Cohen's (1999: 57) observation is apposite: 'no conception of civil society . . . is neutral, but is always part of a project to shape the social relations, cultural forms, and modes of thought of society'. This conception of civil society has its origins in the work of Gramsci (1971).

Gramsci envisaged civil society as a site of struggle where a dominant group, or class, 'organises consent and hegemony', and where subordinate groupings, with opposing or alternative views, build alliances with the aim of constructing a counter-hegemony (Forgacs, 1988: 224; Simon, 1991: 27). Not surprisingly, certain institutions are considered core elements of civil society because of their role in the formation of public opinion. Included here are the education system, churches, trade unions, voluntary associations, and, of course, the media. It is through such institutions 'that a particular order is legitimated or becomes de-legitimated: it is in civil society that the struggle for hegemony takes place' (Paterson and Wyn Jones, 1999: 171). However, the process of enabling normative concerns to emerge requires attention to the communicative dimension of civil society, here suggested as the public sphere.

Habermas (1974, 1989, 1992) envisaged the public sphere as a social-cultural space between the realm of the state and the private domain. It provided an opportunity for private citizens to debate issues of public concern and thereby participate in critical discussion of the state. The public sphere made claims to universalism, enabling a 'public view' on matters discussed. Today, newspapers, magazines, radio, television and the Internet comprise the major media of the public sphere. However, paradoxically, this 'media-rich' environment exercises limits on the ability of members of civil society to 'talk back'. For Habermas, the key issue is

> whether, and to what extent, a public sphere dominated by mass media provides a realistic chance for the members of civil society, in their competition with the political and economic invaders' media power, to bring about changes in the spectrum of values, topics, and reasons channelled by external influences, to open it up in an innovative way, and to screen it critically. (Habermas, 1992: 455)

While Habermas's conception of the public sphere has been criticized, detractors and advocates alike agree that the concept retains significant potential (see, for example, Boyd-Barrett, 1995;

Stevenson, 2002). It provides a model, vision, or 'ideal type' for a public communications system (Golding and Murdock, 2000: 76–7), in which 'public good' takes priority over private gain, and where listeners, readers and viewers are imagined, first and foremost, as citizens.

Illuminating the communicative dimension of civil society

This section considers the extent to which the media in Wales can be seen as embodying the core principles of this 'ideal' public sphere – independent, accessible and diverse – and thereby facilitating and enabling an active and inclusive *Welsh* civil society.

Independence and accountability

Public debate on the media's 'independence' often centres on the degree of supposed freedom of a given media outlet from political control and regulatory constraints. Seen in this light, arguments that the media can serve the public interest only if independent of the state automatically cast doubt on public service broadcasters such as BBC Wales and S4C. A renowned exponent of such views is Rupert Murdoch: 'Public service broadcasters in this country have paid a price for their state sponsored privileges. The price has been their freedom' (cited in Curran, 1996: 84). However, free-market ideologues tend to overlook the fact that commercially funded media are equally flawed when claiming the mantle of independence. Here, reliance on advertising and sponsorship revenue and the inevitable relationships between media owners and wider (and now global) corporate structures combine to undermine the ability of such institutions to provide a critical surveillance – or 'watchdog' – role on behalf of the public (Curran, 2000: 121).

It is hard to deny that BBC Wales remains firmly anchored to London. The BBC's broad policy guidelines are decided centrally by the Board of Governors, of which the national governor for Wales is a member. The Board of Governors is appointed by the queen on the advice of the prime minister. The national governor for Wales chairs the Broadcasting Council for Wales (BCW), whose members are also appointed by the Board of Governors. The BCW is charged with advising on programmes, overseeing

Welsh interests and 'hold[ing] BBC Wales to account on behalf of Welsh audiences' (BBC Cymru Wales, 2002). However, doubts have been raised about the BCW's independence, in that the chair's dual roles of management and scrutiny are seen as incompatible (Welsh Affairs Select Committee, 1999, para. 22).[2]

Similar concerns have been aired about S4C. This channel is directly accountable to the S4C Authority, a self-regulating body whose members are appointed by the secretary of state for Culture, Media and Sport. Furthermore, S4C is under no obligation to consult on changes to its services, neither is it required to undergo a ten-yearly review as with the BBC charter, and nor does it have a local advisory body similar to the Broadcasting Council for Wales (Welsh Affairs Select Committee, 1999, para. 20).[3]

Before the advent of the Office of Communications (OfCom),[4] HTV Wales and the West of England was regulated by the Independent Television Commission (ITC). The ITC appointed a national member for Wales to its Board. Any notion about HTV's local accountability and independence has long gone, however, with ownership passing from United News and Media to Carlton Communications in recent years, followed by a 're-branding' after the Granada/Carlton digital television fiasco in 2002. This resulted in the 'HTV' identity logo being removed from all but local programmes and replaced by 'ITV1 Wales' (Wells, 2002).

The credentials of independent local radio (ILR) in terms of any genuine locality and independence have long been questioned (Local Radio Workshop, 1983). Commercial imperatives clearly take precedence over public service goals. Today, the majority of the fourteen ILR services in Wales are owned and operated by companies beyond its borders, most with other radio or media interests (Barlow, 2003: 79–80, and 2005). There has also been further consolidation since the Communications Act 2003. As a result of a merger between the UK's major radio companies, GWR and Capital, to form G-Cap, Red Dragon in Cardiff and the Champion, Coast and Marcher stations on the north Wales coast are now under the same ownership (Shah, 2005a: 56).[5] In south and south-west Wales, Ulster TV gained control of the Wireless Group and, in doing so, became the latest owner of Swansea Sound, The Wave and Valleys Radio (Shah, 2005b: 62; Snoddy, 2005: 4–5). OfCom now oversees the regulation and licensing of all ILR stations throughout the UK, a function previously carried out by the Radio Authority, a body based in London and whose members, including the national member for Wales, were appointed by the secretary of state for Culture, Media and Sport, as opposed to the NAW.[6]

A similar pattern is discernible with regard to the press. Here too the relevant self-regulatory body – the Press Complaints Commission (PCC) – functions on a UK-wide basis. Moreover, the fact that the PCC has no formal Wales-specific representation arguably exacerbates the commission's existing shortcomings, there being widespread criticism that it is not subject to any authentic public control, and that it acts as defender and mediator rather than as regulator (Curran and Seaton, 2003; Hutchison, 1999; O'Malley and Soley, 2000).

In the nineteenth century the press was linked to Welsh society in complex ways, often through ownership by nonconformist organizations, allowing it actively to engage with the range of political issues that dominated Welsh national politics (Jones, 1993). By the beginning of the twenty-first century, the overall contribution that the press in Wales is able to make to Welsh civil society is hampered by its structurally weak position. First, the ownership of the press in Wales is heavily integrated into UK-wide business interests. Second, it is a declining part of the daily lives of the population. Third, the press produced in Wales for Welsh people continues to compete with one produced in England for a UK readership within the borders of Wales (Barlow et al., 2005; Mackay and Powell, 1997). Finally, the intrinsic localism of the Welsh press calls into question the idea that it can reasonably be described as a regional, let alone a 'national' press (Williams, 1997b).

The Internet is often assumed to be unaffected by the constraints affecting broadcasting and the press, in that its relative freedom of operation is frequently taken as self-evident. In Wales, as elsewhere, however, there are fears about the extent to which the technology may be developing as a corporate-driven rather than citizen-based phenomenon (see Mitchell, 2005). A degree of optimism is nevertheless focused on the increasingly interactive nature of the usage of Internet-related technologies by public bodies and elected representatives (though this remains under-exploited in some areas, notably by the elected AMs, see Greenough, 2002). The hope, therefore, is that such initiatives in accountability will help to bridge what Hagemann (2002: 61) identifies as 'the gap between institutionalised public discussion that exists within the party élite and the uninstitutionalised, informal public discussion that transpires in other public and private domains'.

Access and participation

Critics argue that the media should reflect – and thereby represent – the plurality of different groups, politics and lifestyles that comprise civil society. However, whether at the level of decision-making, production, or occasional participation in the role of interviewee, public access to the media remains limited and partial.

For instance, in relation to the BCW, concerns are voiced about the lack of transparency over appointments, the preference for selection over election, and doubts about the 'representativeness' of appointees (Williams, 1997a: 62). S4C, moreover, operates without any equivalent body – despite its public service remit – and relies primarily on opinions aired at 'viewers' evenings' held around Wales. Unsurprisingly, ILR services in Wales, their prime accountability being to shareholders, keep the public at a distance, relying on ratings as their principal means of feedback.

Public access to the media is further curtailed by means of the occupational ideology of professionalism. This ensures 'professionals' determine what is to be produced, when, and by whom, relegating much of civil society to 'bit parts'. This is particularly so for groups labelled as 'minority' or 'radical'. Such practices are aptly described by Keane (1995: 263) as the media 'distribut[ing] entitlements to speak'.

Such exclusivity is a denial of communication rights in two senses. Firstly, some groups in civil society are denied expression of their views directly through the media to the wider public. Secondly, a logical consequence of this is that citizens are deprived of access to the full range of opinions expressed by their peers, and are thereby reliant on the 'filtered' versions of public opinion provided daily by mass media.

Community media are seen by some as a counterbalance to the gradual displacement of public service ideals by market ideology and the hegemony of professional codes of practice. Wales's first community radio station, GTFM 106.9, in Pontypridd, is a noteworthy example of a community media outlet (Everitt, 2003).[7] A comparable role is played by a set of non-commercial, Welsh-language community newspapers which began circulating in the 1970s and which continue to thrive (Huws, 1996). These voluntarily staffed papers are known as the *papurau bro*. Thirty-eight were established between 1973 and 1978, and this figure reached fifty-four in the early 1990s, with average sales of around 70,000 per month. In addition, there exists an even smaller sector of left, republican and environmental publications such as *Y Faner Goch* and *Seren*.[8]

Such organizations are established on a non-profit basis, have emerged through 'grass-roots' community initiatives, and pursue goals concerned with 'public good' rather than private gain. Furthermore, they eschew the exclusivity of 'professional' media organizations by using volunteers alongside paid staff. Not only is this an illustration of active citizenship, it also helps develop skills and may enhance employment opportunities. These media also seek to build and develop the horizontal linkages of civil society, in contrast to the 'top-down' communication flows of 'mainstream' media, which are tending to prioritise consumerism over representation (see, for example, Downing, 1995: 241; Curran, 2000: 140).[9]

The fact that publications like *Y Faner Goch* are also published electronically confirms that the Internet's role here is potentially beneficial, since there are initial signs that online journalism is increasingly seen as a means for overcoming ownership constraints, and it is already showing signs of augmenting existing publishing initiatives in 'alternative' and community-based journalism and information provision (see, for example, Dahlgren, 1996). Nevertheless, hopes regarding the Internet's emancipatory potential have been tempered in the Welsh context by constraints on citizens' physical access to the relevant resources. UK government statistics show that Internet penetration in 2002 in both homes and businesses in Wales was among the lowest anywhere in the UK.[10] The financial barrier to equality of user access has been a very tangible one, and it is arguably exacerbated by other barriers to full participation: cultural, educational, gender-related, generational and linguistic.

In response to such constraints, the flagship of the NAW's ICT Strategy, launched in 2001, is *Cymru Ar-Lein* – Online for a Better Wales. Building on the WDA's late-1990s 'Wales Information Society' project, this consists of community regeneration programmes via a whole battery of 'e-initiatives'. The framework makes explicit claims that the investment will foster cultural and linguistic diversity and enhance active participation in local communities, 'where the voice of local people is heard' (NAW, 2002). Clearly, these initiatives will be a key priority for any critically informed monitoring of devolved democracy in Wales, given the large claims they stake towards empowering local activism and enhancing public accountability. Against these claims must be set the scepticism expressed by Haywood (1998) regarding the Internet's real capacity for alleviating social exclusion, and the specific caveats voiced by Mackay and Powell (1998: 204) regarding the technology's future development in Wales.

Diversity and plurality

The third principle of the public sphere invokes ideas about diversity and plurality, alongside issues of representation. Ideally, the media should be sufficiently open to ensure that 'all groups in society can recognise themselves and their aspirations as being fairly represented' and to foster the widest possible debate – including dissent – on matters of public interest that entail 'political choices' (Golding and Murdock, 2000: 77).

The dominance in Wales of London-based newspapers is exacerbated by the absence of any single indigenous daily newspaper that covers the whole of Wales (Jones and Wilford, 1983: 227).[11] This particular 'information deficit' is seen by Wyn Jones et al. (2000: 172) as having 'implications for the future legitimacy of the National Assembly', in that this limitation constitutes 'a basic deficiency in the country's political infrastructure'.

In parallel with developments in the UK, the twentieth century saw a decline in the numbers of newspapers produced in Wales, and an increase in the concentration of ownership. With regard to the latter, for example, since 1995, Trinity International, which became Trinity Mirror in 1999, has been the dominant owner of newspapers in Wales (Mackay and Powell, 1997: 14–16). In 2003 it owned the two major dailies, the *Western Mail* in the south and the *Daily Post* in the north; it also controls *Wales on Sunday*, and a large number of other papers across Wales and the UK. Its Welsh publications are therefore firmly locked into a UK-wide business, and exemplify the long-term trend towards concentration in both the Welsh and the UK press.

Linked to this is a clear pattern of decline in the circulations of Welsh newspapers. Figure 2.1 shows that there has been a downward trend across all three types of paper, most markedly in the daily morning sector. This decline needs to be set against the continued significance of the circulation in Wales of newspapers produced in England, an important factor since the nineteenth century (Barlow et al., 2005; Jones, 1993; O'Malley, 2005).

The opportunities afforded by web-based publishing may potentially help Wales to overcome some of the economic and geographic problems which have restricted the setting up of a wider variety of news outlets. Prominent among these problems have been notoriously high distribution costs, tight profit margins and the lack of the substantial AB audience which is crucial to newspaper advertising revenue (see Talfan Davies, 1999: 19). More difficult to overcome will be the cultural and demographic difficulties presented by entrenched readership patterns.

The web-based public service provision offers a useful indicator of the authenticity of diversity in content, particularly as to whether a sufficient Wales-specific differentiation is being incorporated. In this context, BBC Wales's launch of online bilingual news sites is clearly intended as a key exponent of public service

Figure 2.1. The decline in circulation of Welsh newspapers 1999–2004

	1999	2004	% Change
Daily morning papers[12]			
Western Mail	57,035	43,247	–24.2
Daily Post Wales	46,233	40,835	–11.6
Subtotal	103,268	84,082	–18.6
Daily evening papers[13]			
SW Echo (Cardiff)	73,129	57,852	–20.9
SW Evening Post	67,185	56,487	–15.9
SW Argus	30,936	30,788	–0.9
Subtotal	171,250	145,127	–15.3
Weekly papers[14]			
Yr Herald	1,862	1,311	–30
Y Cymro	4,355	5,000	+15[15]
Subtotal	6,217	6,311	+1.5
Overall total	280,735	235,520	–16.1

broadcasting's response to the post-devolutionary situation (see Talfan Davies, 1999: 28–9 and 49).

As regards television, widespread pessimism about achieving the relevant public sphere goals in Wales is encapsulated by one commentator's observation that Wales is subject to a 'surging mass of English/American culture channelled overwhelmingly through centralised London-based television' (Osmond, 1992: 26). In this context, Williams's examination of the range and quality of analogue television services provided by ITV1 Wales (previously HTV), S4C and BBC Wales for Welsh speakers and English speakers led to the conclusion that the former are 'full and comprehensive', and the latter 'patchy and dotted' (1997b: 19–20). A representative sample of the analogue TV output in 2003 provides a 'snapshot' of the quantity of weekly provision of Wales-specific output (figure 2.2) and of the nature of its diversity (figure 2.3).[16]

Among points which might be emphasized here is the neglect of minority interests such as women's sports, as acknowledged by S4C (2003: 1), because they fail to attract sufficient viewers and, one might add, advertisers.[17] There is every likelihood that this situation will be exacerbated as in 2005 OfCom controversially recommended that ITV companies should reduce the amount of Welsh produced programming after digital switchover (NUJ, 2004; OfCom, 2004: 11; OfCom, 2005: 13; O'Malley and Birtwistle, 2004).

This limited amount of Wales-specific 'space' on analogue television underpins concerns about the reflection and representation of Wales and Welshness in television drama (see, for example, Berry, 2000). This trend has its counterpart in the Welsh press in the growth of entertainment and lifestyle content in papers like *Wales on Sunday* (Williams, 1994: 250–1), and, whilst this can be seen as part of an arguable downgrading of news across newspapers in the UK, little is known about the long-term impact on public knowledge of such developments.

Turning to radio, the most popular services in Wales originate in London, with BBC Radio 2 and BBC Radio 1 easily out-rating Radio Wales and Radio Cymru (Rajar, 2003). The latter two stations also face problems in dealing with the growing competition provided by a fast-developing ILR sector within Wales. As a result, Radio Cymru has adopted a more populist approach to its programming, while Radio Wales has recast itself as a service for the

Figure 2.2. 'Snapshot' of average weekly differentiated analogue TV output in Wales via S4C, BBC Wales, BBC 2 and ITV1 Wales (previously HTV)

	Total	% of total air-time
BBC Wales	7 hours 5 minutes	6
BBC 2	2 hours 10 minutes	2
ITV1 Wales	8 hours 25 minutes	7
S4C	32 hours 45 minutes	26

Figure 2.3. Locally derived programmes by genre (weekly hours averaged over survey period)

	BBC Wales	BBC 2	ITV1 Wales	S4C	TOTAL
Children's programmes				8' 45"	8' 45"
News bulletins	2' 55"		2' 55"	2' 25"	8' 15"
Documentary	1' 30"	10"	1' 0"	1' 35"	4' 15"
Politics	30"	1' 30"	30"	1' 30"	4' 0"
Drama	30"			3' 0"	3' 30"
Consumer affairs			1' 0"	2' 30"	3' 30"
Arts	30"		30"	2' 15"	3' 15"
Sports (male)		55"		2' 0"	2' 55"
Comedy			30"		30"
Welsh-learning				30"	30"
Music			30"		30"
Religion				30"	30"

whole of Wales rather than the south Wales valleys, its traditional heartland (Ellis, 2000). As a *quid pro quo* for access to the radio spectrum, ILR is expected to provide services in the public interest. However, most of these services offer little in the way of speech programming, depending almost entirely on a diet of popular music. Reliance on revenue from advertising and sponsorship ensures that listeners are envisaged as active consumers, rather than active citizens.

A listening environment aimed at fostering consumption and maximizing listeners is not conducive to the inclusion of critical discussion about local issues. Nor is it likely to reflect the full diversity of local communities. This is apparent in the reluctance of some stations to provide adequate programming in Welsh. It is further evidenced in the virtual absence of Wales's ethnic minorities from the 'airwaves' (Ellis, 2000: 197). This is also the case with television (Williams, 1997b: 24), an issue recognized by BBC Wales in their appointment of a Diversity Adviser (BBC Cymru Wales, 2002). Other segments of the community are also 'missing' on-air. As most ILR services aim to attract listeners between their late teens and early fifties, the needs and interests of younger and older citizens are simply disregarded.

A further shift is evident in the way audiences and services are viewed. In common with its commercial counterparts, BBC Wales has recast its listeners and viewers as 'consumers' and 'stakeholders', and its television and radio services as 'brands' and 'brand-identities' (BBC Cymru Wales, 2001). Furthermore, the ever-pervasive predilection of broadcasters to 'chase' ratings shapes the type and range of programmes being broadcast. In so doing, it marginalizes significant elements of civil society and the issues they wish to see addressed in the public domain. In such an environment, notions of 'public good' and 'public interest' are displaced by the mantra of 'consumer choice', leading to a situation where '[c]onsiderations of what [people] need and what is needed to build a healthy and vibrant citizenship and community are downplayed' (Williams, 1997b: 29).

Exposé! Whose media, whose interests, whose voices?

Judgements about the 'quality' of the communicative dimension of civil society in Wales rest on the extent to which its media constitute an ideal public sphere. To what extent are they independent, diverse and accessible? Posing this question not only directs attention to the individual media outlets, but also encompasses the structure and organization of the public sphere. For, as Calhoun (1993: 276) observes, the critical issue is how civil society is organized, not simply that it exists. In Wales, the ramifications of this assertion are clearly illustrated when focusing on issues related to media and communications.

Developments in the Welsh media have been influenced by the Communications Act 2003, with the new competitive environment calling into question the future of commercial public service television, S4C and the BBC in Wales (Balsom, 2005; OfCom, 2004, 2005; O'Malley, 2002, 2005; S4C, 2004, 2005). OfCom is designed to promote economic efficiency in the industry and to encourage cross-media ownership and concentration across the commercial media. Whilst its predecessors had Welsh representatives, OfCom has no formal Welsh representation at board level (OfCom, 2003–4: 64). Members of the Advisory Committee for Wales are appointed by OfCom, as are Wales's sole representatives on the Content Board and the Consumer Panel, both of which have a UK-wide remit. The National Assembly for Wales (NAW) has no formal role here, but is expected to be consulted on appointments such as these (Department of Culture, Media and Sport, 2000).

Concentration of ownership in the newspaper press and in commercial broadcasting means that power in these sectors is vested in elites, driven by commercial imperatives and generally based outside of Wales. Power over the BBC and S4C resides, ultimately, in Westminster, not in Wales. It is in Westminster that the final decisions over appointments to the boards that run these bodies are made. Thus, the independence of the Welsh media is compromised by commercial power and political centralization. However, it is the case that the BBC, HTV and S4C contribute to the maintenance of a diverse broadcasting system. In particular S4C, Radio Cymru, the BBC online bilingual news service and a small number of ILR services add linguistic diversity to the national media. Nonetheless, there is an increasing tendency for both the press and broadcasting in Wales – and the UK as a whole – to be driven by an entertainment-orientated agenda (Barnett and Seymour, 1999; Hodgson, 2002: 30).

Evidence that the media in Wales provide unmediated access for the public is sparse. Whilst the experience of other countries shows that community media can provide a voice for habitually marginalized groups (Jankowski, 2002; Lewis and Booth, 1989), there is no fully fledged independent community media sector in Wales. Initiatives like *Cymru Ar-Lein* and the National Assembly website, plus the host of other Welsh-based community, pressure group and public body websites are of real interest. Yet these operate on the margins of mass communications, linking the interested with the interested, rather than with the public at large. Both the newspaper press and broadcasting organizations in Wales are organized to select, filter, repackage and represent the views and cultural interests of the people in Wales back to the public. This is not access.

There are, however, some grounds for optimism. In spite of the colonization of the newspaper press in Wales by large corporations and the expansion of commercial imperatives in broadcasting, the power of the British state has historically been exercised to promote institutions in Wales, especially public service broadcasting, which defend values that stimulate cultural independence and diversity. In addition there still exists in Wales small-scale media which survive, precariously, outside a commercial framework. Yet, given the developments associated with the Communications Act 2003, the institutions of public service broadcasting in Wales, especially the ITV sector, are becoming severely compromised in the more intense competitive environment (O'Malley, 2005; OfCom, 2004, 2005).

Following Gramsci, civil society is the arena in which key arguments about the direction of society are developed and won, thus influencing the disposition of power (Paterson and Wyn Jones, 1999: 171). Significantly, power over the framing of issues for debate in Welsh civil society rests, ultimately, with small numbers of people, whose practice as owners, civil servants and regulators is framed by the demands of profit maximization and the political imperatives of the British state. Thus the ability of autonomous groups within civil society to determine the agenda of the media in Wales, and thereby engage meaningfully in the 'struggle for hegemony' is heavily circumscribed.

Furthermore, Welsh civil society has been described as a 'fragile plant', due in part to the weakness of certain elements, of which the media is one (Paterson and Wyn Jones, 1999: 176).[18] The material surveyed in this contribution does support a view of the media in Wales as a weak element within civil society. There is a strong case for public intervention in order to invigorate this important element of Welsh civil society. Regrettably, discussions about democracy and the oft-heard calls for 'active citizenship' rarely make connection with the need for greater media accountability and genuine citizen participation (see, for example, Hain, 2000; Labour Party 1999; NAW, 2000, 2001). In this respect, it is noteworthy that while decisions were being made in Westminster to consolidate and centralize regulatory arrangements in the form of a London-based OfCom, a similarly exclusive and barely publicized process was occurring in Wales to decide on the nature of the relationship between the new regulator and the NAW. It was a five-person and hardly representative body – the 'OfCom Advisory Group' – appointed by the minister for Culture, Sport and the Welsh Language that recommended an 'advisory structure' for Wales, rather than 'a structured relationship' between an OfCom Wales Office and the National Assembly (OfCom Advisory Group, 2003: 2). Exactly who was consulted, how and when remains unclear, as the OfCom Advisory Group err towards the opaque rather than the transparent, simply identifying their sources as 'broadcasters, regulators and other stakeholders' (OfCom Advisory Group, 2003: 4).

Conclusion

The bilingual nature of the media in Wales, plus the increasing influence of commercial imperatives in broadcast content and regulation, militate against the development of a powerful Welsh 'voice' in mass communications. Furthermore, the debate over public policy and the media in Wales is, with notable exceptions (Andrews, 2005; Williams, 1997b), underdeveloped. The NAW has the opportunity to promote such a debate. Indeed, being a body that stands for the devolution of political power to Wales, the NAW is well placed to engage critically with the centralizing drive of the Communications Act 2003.

After full public consultation and drawing on some of the positive traditions that exist within the Welsh media, the NAW can engage with the government on various issues. These include the lack of elected Welsh representatives on the boards of the BBC and OfCom, the possibility of replacing unelected and unrepresentative advisory committees with citizens' juries (Stewart et al., 1994), and the need to develop a distinctively Welsh press and to encourage a diverse media. It can argue for a much greater role for the Assembly on questions of media mergers, on the allocation of radio licences and on the regulation of standards. It can set up structures to promote continuous public involvement in the Welsh media.

These measures will go some way towards bolstering the media as an instrument of genuine diversity, independence and access in Wales. They will also help provide an environment within civil society where people who lack the economic and political power of large media organizations can make their views heard. In so doing, the NAW will also be contributing towards the growth of a strong, autonomous and *Welsh* civil society.

Notes

1. See, for example, Allan and O'Malley (1999), Barlow et al. (2005), Mackay and Powell (1997), Talfan Davies (1999) and Williams (1997b).
2. In a Green Paper on the review of the BBC's Royal Charter, *A Strong BBC, Independent of Government*, the Department of Culture, Media and Sport canvass the idea of electing, rather than appointing, members of the BBC Broadcasting Councils (Department of Culture, Media and Sport, 2005: para. 5.56). In their response to the Green Paper, the BBC Governors reject this idea (BBC, 2005: 58–9).
3. S4C did, however, conduct an internal review as part of the policy in 2004: *S4C Review: A Welsh Language Television Service Fit for the 21st Century* (S4C, 2004).
4. OfCom combines the functions of five previous regulatory bodies: the Independent Television Commission, the Broadcasting Standards Commission, OfTel, the Radio Authority and the Radiocommunications Agency. OfCom became fully operational on 28 December 2003 (OfCom, 2003–4: 2).
5. It is noteworthy that the OfCom Advisory Committee for Wales did not provide advice on this matter to OfCom 'central', as 'it was not identified as a priority by the Committee' (email response to author, Barlow, on 9 May 2005).
6. It is worth noting that several ILR licences in Wales were allocated during the 1990s before the appointment of a national member for Wales to the Radio Authority Board.
7. This station was one of fourteen pilot broadcasters originally licensed in the UK under the Access Radio project. GTFM was awarded a community radio licence on 20 April 2005. A further station, AfanFM, has also been awarded a community radio licence to broadcast a music-based information service to young people in Neath and Port Talbot. Three other groups in Wales are yet to receive adjudications on their applications for community radio licences (see *http://www.ofcom.org.uk* for further information). It should be noted that community-based groups in Wales, notably in Cardiff, Aberystwyth and Newtown, established local radio stations during the 1980s and 1990s, under the ILR licensing regime, all of which have since become commercial operations. See Lewis and Booth (1989: 108–14) on the rise and demise of Cardiff Broadcasting Company.
8. The absence of a Welsh-language daily paper led in 2001 to the Mercator Project at the University of Wales, Aberystwyth embarking on a feasibility study and establishing a small company to develop the project by 2003 (Philpot, 2003).

9. See Barlow (1999, 2002) for illustrations of how community media organizations in Australia provide opportunities for citizens to own, manage and operate their own local communications medium.
10. Within the UK only Northern Ireland has a lower domestic take-up of Internet connections than Wales (*http://www.statistics.gov*).
11. In 2005 plans were well advanced for an all-Wales, Welsh-language daily (see Philpott, 2003, and Thomas, 2003/4).
12. Source: Talfan Davies, 1999; ABC, July–December 2002.
13. Source: Talfan Davies, 1999; Newspaper Society, July–December 2004.
14. Source: Talfan Davies, 1999; Newspaper Society, July–December 2004.
15. This increase in circulation recorded by *Y Cymro* may be an encouraging indication of the potential for growth in Welsh-language newspaper publishing (see note 8).
16. These figures are derived from a representative sample of six weeks' programming for all four channels, between May and July 2003.
17. While proponents of the digital era promise more choice, others are less convinced. Gardam (2003: 8) encapsulates the views of many in arguing that 'digital channels almost universally trade in pre-sold products – sport, films, repeats, pre-branded programmes, or in a narrow range of surefire genres: sex, Nazis and pyramids'. This is not to forget S4C's provision of Welsh-language programmes on S4C–1 and live coverage of proceedings at the NAW on S4C-2.
18. In contrast, Paterson and Wyn Jones (1999: 178), drawing on the work of MacInnes (1992, 1993), note both the 'distinctiveness of the Scottish media' and its 'cultural self-confidence'.

References

Allan, S. and O'Malley, T. (1999). 'The media in Wales', in D. Dunkerley and A. Thompson (eds), *Wales Today*, Cardiff: University of Wales Press.

Andrews, L. (2005). 'Wales and the UK's communication legislation', *Cyfrwng*, 2.

Audit Bureau of Circulations (2002). Report of the National Newspapers Circulation (July 2002 to December 2002), *www.abc.org.uk*, accessed 14 April 2003.

Balsom, S. (2005). 'Broadcasting Barricades', *Agenda*, Cardiff: Institute of Welsh Affairs, Spring Issue.

Barlow, D. M. (1999). 'By the people for the people: a rural community radio station', in L. Briskman, M. Lynn with H. La Nauze (eds), *Challenging Rural Practice: Human Services in Australia*, Geelong: Deacon University Press.

Barlow, D. M. (2002). 'Conceptions of access and participation in Australian community radio stations', in N. W. Jankowski (ed.), *Community Media in the Information Age: Perspectives and Practice*, New Jersey: Hampton Press.

Barlow, D. M. (2003). 'Who controls local radio?', *Planet*, 158.

Barlow, D. M. (2005). 'Re-assessing radio: role, scope and accountability', *Contemporary Wales*, 18.

Barlow, D. M., Mitchell, P. and O'Malley T. (2005). *The Media in Wales: Voices of a Small Nation*, Cardiff: University of Wales Press.

Barnett, S. and Seymour, E. (1999). *A Shrinking Iceberg Travelling South: Changing Trends in British Television*, London: Campaign for Quality Television.

BBC (2005). *Review of the BBC's Royal Charter. BBC Response to 'A Strong BBC, Independent of Government'*, London: BBC.

BBC Cymru Wales (2001). *Annual Review 2001/2002* (http://*www.bbc.co.uk/wales/review*).

Berry, D. (2000). 'Unearthing the present: television drama in Wales', in S. Blandford (ed.), *Wales on Screen*. Bridgend: Seren.

Boyd-Barrett, O. (1995). 'Conceptualising the public sphere', in O. Boyd-Barrett and C. Newbold (eds), *Approaches to Media*, London: Arnold.

Calhoun, C. (1993). 'Civil society and the public sphere', *Public Culture*, 5.

Cohen, J. L. (1999). 'American civil society talk', in R. K. Fullinwider (ed.), *Civil Society, Democracy, and Civic Renewal*, New York: Rowman and Littlefield.

Curran, J. (1996). 'Mass media and democracy revisited', in J. Curran and M. Gurevitch (eds), *Mass Media and Society*, 2nd edn, London: Arnold.

Curran, J. (2000). 'Rethinking media and democracy', in J. Curran and M. Gurevitch (eds), *Mass Media and Society*, 3rd edn, London: Arnold.

Curran, J. and Seaton, J. (2003). *Power without Responsibility*, 6th edn, London: Routledge.

Dahlgren, P. (1996). 'Media logic in cyberspace: repositioning journalism and its publics', *Javnost/The Public*, 3, 3.

Davies, J. (1994). *Broadcasting and the BBC in Wales*, Cardiff: University of Wales Press.

Day, G., Dunkerley, D. and Thompson, A. (2000). 'Evaluating the "new politics": civil society and the National Assembly for Wales', *Public Policy and Administration*, 15, 2.

Department of Culture, Media and Sport (2000). *Concordat between the Department for Culture, Media and Sport and the Cabinet of the National Assembly for Wales*, London: DCMS.

Department of Culture, Media and Sport (2005). *Review of the BBC's Royal Charter. A Strong BBC, Independent of Government*, London: DCMS.

Downing, J. (1995). 'Alternative media and the Boston Tea Party', in J. Downing, A. Mohammadi and A. Sreberny-Mohammadi (eds), *Questioning the Media: A Critical Introduction*, 2nd edn, London: Sage.

Ellis, G. (2000). 'Stereophonic nation: the bilingual sounds of Cool Cymru FM', *International Journal of Cultural Studies*, 3, 2.

Everitt, A. (2003). *New Voices: An Evaluation of 15 Access Radio Projects*, London: Radio Authority.

Forgacs, D. (ed.) (1988). *A Gramsci Reader*, London: Lawrence and Wishart.

Gardam, T. (2003). 'For whom the Bill tolls', *Independent Review*, 1 July.

Golding, P., and Murdock, G. (2000). 'Culture, communications and political economy', in J. Curran and M. Gurevitch (eds), *Mass Media in Society*, 3rd edn, London: Arnold.

Gramsci, A. (1971). *Selections from the Prison Notebooks*, London: Lawrence and Wishart.

Greenough, M. (2002). 'Spinning the web', *Planet*, 154.

Habermas, J. (1974). *Theory and Practice*, London: Heinemann.

Habermas, J. (1989). *The Structural Transformation of the Public Sphere*, Cambridge: Polity.

Habermas, J. (1992). 'Further reflections on the public sphere', in C. Calhoun (ed.), *Habermas and the Public Sphere*, Cambridge, MA: MIT Press.

Hagemann, C. (2002). 'Participation in and contents of two Dutch political party discussion lists on the internet', *Javnost/The Public*, 9, 2.

Hain, P. (2000). 'Casting out false gods', *Agenda*, Winter.

Haywood, T. (1998). 'Global networks and the myth of equality: trickle down or trickle away', in D. B. Loader (ed.), *Cyberspace Divide: Equality, Agency and Policy in the Information Society*, London: Routledge.

Higdon, S. (ed.) (2001). *Culture and Communications: Perspectives on Broadcasting and the Information Society*, London: ITC.

Hodgson, P. (2002). 'Priorities for quality television', in Westminster Media Forum, *New Future or Missed Opportunity? Reaction to the draft Communications Bill 2002*, London: WMF.

Hutchison, D. (1999). *Media Policy*, Oxford: Blackwell.

Huws, G. (1996). 'The success of the local: Wales', *Mercator Media Forum*, Cardiff: University of Wales Press.

Jankowski, N. W. (ed.) (2002). *Community Media in the Information Age: Perspectives and Practice*, New Jersey: Hampton Press.

Jones, A. (1993). *Press, Politics and Society: A History of Journalism in Wales*, Cardiff: University of Wales Press.

Jones, J. and Wilford, R. A. (1983). 'Implications: two salient issues', in D. Foulkes, J. Jones and R. A. Wilford (eds), *The Welsh Veto: The Wales Act 1978 and the Referendum*, Cardiff: University of Wales Press.

Keane, J. (1995). 'Democracy and media: without foundations', in O. Boyd-Barrett and C. Newbold (eds), *Approaches to Media*, London: Arnold.

Labour Party (1999). *Democracy and Citizenship – Consultation Paper*, London: Labour Party.

Lewis, P. M. and Booth, J. (1989). *The Invisible Medium: Public, Commercial and Community Radio*, London: Macmillan.

Local Radio Workshop (1983). *Capital: Local Radio and Private Profit*, London: Comedia.

MacInnes, J. (1992). 'The press in Scotland', *Scottish Affairs*, 1.

MacInnes, J. (1993). 'The broadcast media in Scotland', *Scottish Affairs*, 2.

Mackay, H. and Powell, A. (1997). 'Wales and its media: production, consumption and regulation', *Contemporary Wales*, 9.

Mackay, H. and Powell, T. (1998). 'Connecting Wales: the Internet and national identity', in B. D. Loader (ed.), *Cyberspace Divide: Equality, Agency and Policy in the Information Society*, London: Routledge.

Medhurst, J. (1998). 'Mass media in 20th century Wales', in P. H. Jones (ed.), *A Nation and its Books*, Aberystwyth: National Library of Wales.

Mitchell, P. (2006). 'Constructing the e-nation: the Internet in Wales', *Contemporary Wales*, 18.

National Assembly for Wales (2000). *Better Wales* (*http://www.wales.gov.uk*).

National Assembly for Wales (2001). *Strategic Statement on the Preparation of 'Plan for Wales 2001'* (*http://www.wales.gov.uk*).

National Assembly for Wales (2002). *Cymru Ar-Lein* (*http://www.wales.gov.uk*).

Newspaper Society (2003a). *http://www.newspapersoc.org.uk/facts-figures/ top20_table.html*, accessed 14 April 2003.

Newspaper Society (2003b). *http://www.newspapersoc.org.uk/database/reports/newspaperdetail* accessed 14 and 17 April 2003.

National Union of Journalists (NUJ) (2004). *The Response of the National Union of Journalists to: 'Phase 2 – Meeting the Digital Age OfCom Review of Public Service Television Broadcasting*, London: NUJ.

OfCom (2003). *http://www.ofcom.org.uk/about/csg/adv-cmmt-nations/acw/*

OfCom (2003–4). *Annual Report 2003–4*, London: Office of Communications.

OfCom (2004). *Phase 2 – Meeting the Digital Age OfCom Review of Public Service Television Broadcasting*, London: OfCom.

OfCom (2005). *OfCom Review of Public Service Television Broadcasting Phase 3 – Competition for Quality*, London: OfCom, February.

O'Malley, T. (2002). *Why the Communications Bill is Bad News*, London: Campaign for Press and Broadcasting Freedom.

O'Malley, T. (2005). *Keeping Broadcasting Public: The BBC and the 2006 Charter Review,* London: Campaign for Press and Broadcasting Freedom.

O'Malley, T. (2006). 'The Newspaper Press in Wales', *Contemporary Wales*, 18.

O'Malley, T. and Birtwistle, M. (2004). 'We must act now to keep Wales on TV in a new age', *Western Mail*, 8 December.

O'Malley, T. and Soley, C. (2000). *Regulating the Press*, London: Pluto.

Osmond, J. (1992). *The Democratic Challenge*, Llandysul: Gomer Press.

Osmond, J. (1998). 'Introduction', in J. Osmond (ed.), *The National Assembly Agenda*, Cardiff: Institute of Welsh Affairs.

Paterson, L. and Wyn Jones, R. (1999). 'Does civil society drive constitutional change?', in B. Taylor and K. Thomson (eds), *Scotland and Wales: Nations Again?*, Cardiff: University of Wales Press.

Philpott, A. (2003). 'Tuag at bapur newydd dyddiol yn y Gymraeg', paper presented at the First Mercator International Symposium on Minority Languages and Research, 8–9 April, University of Wales, Aberystwyth.

Rajar (2003). *Quarterly Summary of Radio Listening* (*March*) (*http://www.rajar.co.uk*).

S4C (2003). *Annual Report, 2002* (*http://www.s4c.co.uk*).

S4C (2004). *S4C Review: A Welsh Language Television Service Fit for the 21st Century*, Cardiff: S4C.

S4C (2005). *Review of the BBC's Royal Charter – S4C's Response*, Cardiff: S4C.

Shah, S. (2005a). 'Daily Mail group mulls £700m bid for merged Capital Radio–GWR', *Independent*, 18 April.

Shah, S. (2005b). 'MacKenzie could make £6.4m from Wireless Group sale to Ulster TV', *Independent*, 20 April.

Simon, R. (1991). *Gramsci's Political Thought: An Introduction*, London: Lawrence and Wishart.

Snoddy, R. (2005). 'Radio silence? No chance', *Independent* (Media Weekly), 13 June.

Stevenson, N. (2002). *Understanding Media Cultures: Social Theory and Mass Communication*, 2nd edn, London: Sage.

Stewart, J., Kendall, E. and Coote, A. (1994). *Citizens' Juries*, London: Institute for Public Policy Research.

Talfan Davies, G. (1999). *Not by Bread Alone: Information, Media and the National Assembly*, Cardiff: Wales Media Forum.

Thomas, N. (2003/4). 'Y Byd. Papur dyddiol cenedlaethol', *Agenda*, Cardiff: Institute of Welsh Affairs, Winter Issue.

Wells, M. (2002). 'ITV buries regional identity in £100m network facelift', *Guardian*, 10 June (*http://www://media.guardian.co.uk*).

Welsh Affairs Select Committee (1999). *Broadcasting in Wales and the National Assembly* (*http://www.parliament.the-stationery-office.co.uk*).

Williams, K. (1994). 'Are we being served? The press, broadcasting and a Welsh Parliament', in J. Osmond (ed.), *A Parliament for Wales*, Llandysul: Gomer Press.

Williams, K. (1997a). 'Dear Ron', *Planet*, 123.

Williams, K. (1997b). *Shadows and Substance: The Development of a Media Policy for Wales*, Llandysul: Gomer Press.

Wyn Jones, R. Trystan, D. and Taylor, B. (2000). 'Voting patterns in the referendum', in J. Jones and D. Balsom (eds), *The Road to the National Assembly*, Cardiff: University of Wales Press.

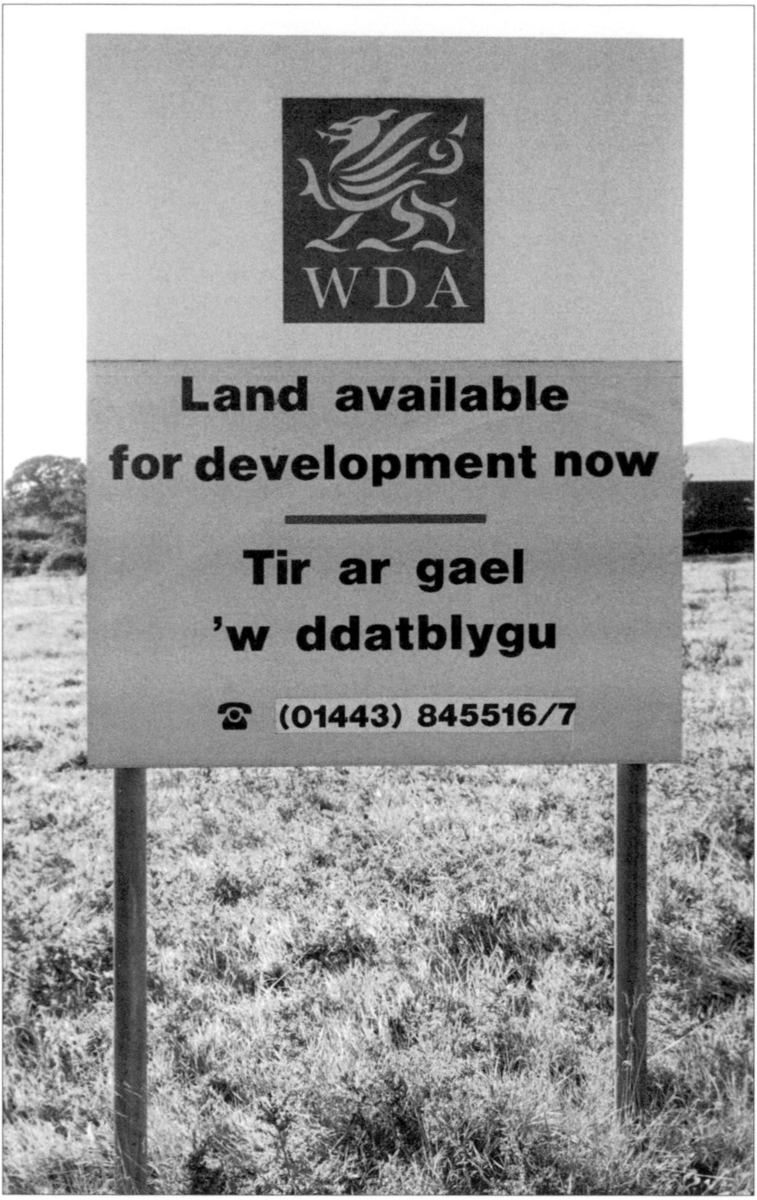
WDA
Land available
for development now
Tir ar gael
'w ddatblygu
(01443) 845516/7

3. Civil Society and the Institutions of Economic Development

GRAHAM DAY AND DAVID JONES

Introduction

According to Morgan and Mungham,

> of all the challenges facing the Welsh Assembly none will be as important, or as difficult, as the task of raising the level of economic well-being in Wales, particularly in the west and the valleys . . . In the fullness of time the Assembly will be judged on this economic development test before all others. (2000: 217–18)

The test includes the Assembly's ability to bring about a more balanced pattern of economic development between the Welsh regions. Likewise J. Barry Jones (1998: 66) has suggested that the success of devolution will be judged according to the Assembly's record in spreading wealth and economic activity more evenly across Wales. These claims place economic renewal and revitalization at the heart of the devolution process. The limitations of Wales's past economic performance are seen as among the main driving forces which have brought devolution about, and hence the constitutional changes surrounding the creation of an Assembly are to be evaluated in terms of the extent to which they are able to transcend these problems. Obviously this is not the only way in which the Assembly and its role have been interpreted and appraised. It is also seen as a major vehicle of democratization in Welsh society. However, there is an intimate connection between arguments to do with democracy and expectations in relation to economic improvement. Greater democratic participation and involvement within Wales has been viewed as a necessary condition for a more innovative, enterprising and successful economy. Such arguments imply a need for the mobilization, and transformation, of Welsh civil society. This chapter will seek to explore some of the threads of these arguments.

To some, a discussion of the Welsh economy might seem to sit oddly within an analysis of civil society. Yet, at the same time, no account of civil society would be complete without a consideration of the economic context in which it operates. Indeed, much of the recent social science debate around questions of comparative economic development and performance has been concerned to bring these different aspects together, and to demonstrate that the boundaries between the economic and the social, never very precise, have now become extremely blurred. This might suggest some problems for those who wish to keep these areas distinct. A common way of defining civil society, for example, is to see it as occupying a space somehow between the economy and the state. It is that area of non-economic, non-governmental activity, in which people participate 'freely' as members of groups, associations and communities. Indeed, on some accounts it forms an important buffer between the economy and the state, a domain where different values, and different modes of conduct, prevail, such as those of 'sociality' and 'civility'. The role of civil society is to stave off the intrusions of political and economic pressures into those areas where they do not belong, such as neighbourliness, voluntary cooperation, and conviviality. In the approach adopted by the WCVA/Civicus study (see Nicholl in this volume, and WCVA, 2002), civil society is located 'between the family, the state and the market' and consists of a range of groups, organizations and networks where people come together voluntarily to advance their common interests.

However, in reality some of these interests may be economic – for instance, the bodies within civil society are said to include trade unions and professional associations, many of whose objectives are very firmly economic in nature, to do with jobs, wages, working conditions and advancing the status of their members. Likewise, organization and lobbying conducted within the workplace is counted as part of the activity of civil society, although civil society does not extend to include business organizations as such, presumably because these are situated within the market. Yet the world of business and commerce also throws up organizations and associations, such as chambers of commerce, Rotary and Inner Wheel, where membership is voluntary, common goals are pursued and people seek out their own solutions to problems. These organizations may pursue business interests, but they also engage with various other civic tasks and functions, such as charitable works and providing civic leadership. Thus, as has been apparent ever since Weber's classic studies of the Protestant sects in America (Gerth and Mills, 1948), it is far from easy to disentangle the 'economic' from other spheres and dimensions of society. Economic organizations such as businesses, unions and various economic development and planning agencies do not exist in a hermetically sealed sphere of their own, but have to interact with the other parts of society, and do so through a wide variety of channels. Similarly, individuals do not cease to be part of their communities of interest and association when they enter the place of work or behave as economic actors.

The connection between economy and civil society is made very directly by Morgan and Mungham when they refer to another of the daunting tasks faced by the Assembly – that of building civic capacity. This is justified in terms of its likely economic as well as political yield: a more informed, intelligent society will be capable of pressing for better performance. Civic capacity is spelled out in terms which others might refer to as 'social capital', namely the presence within a population of norms of trust, reciprocity and civic engagement. Theorists of social capital contend that these are amongst the conditions making for an effective and dynamic economic performance (Fine, 2000; Field, 2003). The point is repeated by Morgan and Rees, in their treatment of civil society as itself possibly the most significant of all development resources (Morgan and Rees, 2001: 169). In other words, the suggestion is that civil society crucially influences and underpins the working of any economy. Here too the boundaries between the civic and the economic become unclear in that, alongside community groups and voluntary organizations, civil society's foundations are said to encompass networks of business connections. Hence the social relationships which develop among economic actors as they go about their business form part of civil society.

The very popularity of the term 'social capital' itself shows how concepts previously associated with the realm of economics ('capital') have become melded into social analysis. That this has been happening across a number of linked conceptual fields suggests that something highly significant is taking place in the way in which we understand and organize our societies. The emergence of new sorts of skills and capacities, the formation of new types of economic groupings and divisions, and the continual reorganization of economic spaces have all imposed a need for changing attempts to modulate economic activity, and this is reflected in the rethinking of old distinctions (for examples, see Miller and Rose, 1990; Rose, 1996; Walters, 2002). A similar convergence between the economic and the social can be observed with respect to new approaches to governance, to institutional analysis and to frameworks of regional development. Among the attempts of social scientists to capture these changes we find references to the 'new regionalism' and the 'new institutionalism' (Cooke and Morgan, 1998: Lovering, 1999). The latter signifies an approach in which the success or failure of an economy is seen to depend increasingly upon the institutional framework which regulates the relationships among firms, organizations and the associations of civil society. An institutionalist perspective on regional development recognizes the importance of the collective or social foundations of economic behaviour, the way in which an economy consists of activity that is socially embedded (Amin, 1999).

Such wide-ranging forces are bound to exert an influence on the reshaping of economic and social relationships in contemporary Wales, and in the literature which has appeared to deal with these issues we can detect themes which will be familiar from the discussion in a number of other chapters in this volume. They relate to the assumed limitations and weaknesses of civil society in its existing form and the need to bring about in it those changes which will revitalize Welsh society, politics and economic life. There is a long-standing perspective on Wales in which the defects of civil society and social organization are seen as weakening and undermining efforts to improve economic performance. This has been expressed in a variety of ways, including references to economic 'backwardness', dependency, colonization and marginalization (Day, 2002). Conversely, more recent measures to tackle the economic needs of Wales show a concern with reconstructing aspects of civil society, and modifying the values and behaviours of its members.

New economy, new civil society?

The economic changes undergone by Wales in recent years are a palimpsest of wider transformations: over a period of twenty or thirty years, a wholly new economy has risen on the ruins of the old. From a situation in which economic and social life was dominated by a triumvirate of basic industries – coal, steel and agriculture – the Welsh workforce has witnessed tremendous diversification and complication (Bryan and Jones, 2000; Day, 2002). The new economy is centred on the service sector, on a range of new industries, and in a radically different industrial geography. This economic upheaval has brought with it dramatic social and political effects. Arguably, to a greater extent than most of the rest of Britain, the 'old' Wales had been formed around collectivist institutions of community and solidarity. Even if there were profound differences between them, the working classes of industrial Wales and the farming communities of rural Wales shared some important commonalities of experience and living conditions, which unified them into significant and relatively highly organized social blocs. Within each of these, despite recurrent economic deprivation and uncertainty, individuals and families experienced a certain security grounded in a well-defined sense of identity, common interests and established ways of living. These conditions have been shattered by economic change, leaving a familiar legacy of serious economic and social problems – unemployment, adjustment and adaptation (Adamson, 1995) – in parts of Wales, and a more generalized feeling of disruption and fragmentation. While not peculiar to Wales, these alterations have met with some distinctively Welsh responses.

In retrospect, it is difficult to regard these historic social patterns simply as evidence of a 'weak' civil society, since they clearly involved strong institutions of collaboration and support, infused with extensive normative agreement and conventions of loyalty and trust. However, measured in the purely instrumental terms of their economic pay-off, they were not necessarily conducive to a dynamic, outward-looking adaptability. Rich in social capital, their 'traditionalism' was nevertheless a hindrance to economic development. They were built defensively, to provide individuals and families with communal support, and to minimize risk, in conditions of adversity. At the same time, they upheld visions of a future in which the main outlines of economic and social life would be safeguarded and strengthened by collective organization and state intervention. It was envisaged that the task of the state was to protect and improve the conditions of people, predominantly within their existing jobs and occupations, and to raise their standards of living and quality of life while preserving the outlines of their existing communities. In the south Wales coalfield, for example, the primary rationale which lay behind economic intervention was 'the unquestioned social benefit of preserving the "communities" of the Valleys' (Rees, 1997: 102). Despite their independent-mindedness, the small farmers of rural Wales were as ready to seek government subsidy and support for their 'way of life' as the miners and steelworkers.

From the perspective of the agencies of economic regeneration, however, past strengths quickly became identified as present handicaps. Social relationships and attitudes built around mutual defence and cooperation were criticized for breeding dependence and lack of initiative. Perceived motivational problems were matched by structural shortcomings: the lack of a Welsh business class and an entrepreneurial tradition were seen as producing an unreadiness to take risks, a social unadventurousness and conservatism. These traits were said to be encouraged by the size and composition of the dominant industries in Wales: a pattern of very large organizations, exercising considerable market control, relying upon external management and skills, and extensive state public ownership. Indeed, Wales was referred to as a 'nationalized region', populated by individuals who were over-reliant on union power and state welfare. This made Wales a prime target for the Thatcherite revolution of the 1980s, although analyses produced from a range of positions, on both the political right and the left, were pervaded by surprisingly similar assumptions.

An incoming chief executive of the Welsh Development Agency captured this viewpoint when he wrote in 1990 of the 'defeatist' and 'subservient' attitudes he encountered in Wales, and which he contrasted with the greater confidence of his native Scotland. Never had he met 'a people so apparently intent on talking themselves down into terminal disaster' or more prepared to look to 'them' (governments, outsiders) to produce solutions (Waterstone, 1990). Ten years later, a senior local government official drew attention to what he regarded as the crucial limitation of Welsh political culture, that it had not 'developed a capacity to tolerate and take advantage of differences within itself . . . Within parties, chapels, councils and unions the dominant expectation is one of solidarity; opposition is regarded as illegitimate; dissent is not tolerated; discussion is regarded with deep suspicion' (Morgan and Mungham, 2000: 210). In other words, a pervasive rhetoric of unity set the framework within which action could occur, a 'regionalist consensus' extending much further than the valleys of south Wales, a proposition borne out by the promotion of 'Team Wales', and the idea that everyone involved in economic development in Wales should 'sing from the same hymn sheet'. According to Morgan and Henderson (1997) Wales remains at bottom a corporatist society, with a prevailing culture which sets a high premium on collaboration between labour and management and between public and private sectors.

The implied diagnosis behind such comments was that the form of civil society which had grown up in Wales, in understandable response to historic circumstances, was in need of a thorough overhaul if the country was to move forward, economically and socially. Economic change alone would not suffice: institutional reform had to revitalize and reshape civil society as well. In part, accomplishing this has involved the planned renewal and replacement of existing forms of social capital, in a Schumpeterian process of would-be creative destruction. Moribund communities which had lost their economic purpose needed to be replaced, or at least regenerated, through deliberate intervention, rather than perpetuated. Over the years Wales has seen numerous initiatives for reconstruction and renewal, of the Valleys, the slate communities and the rural areas. While these were justified primarily in terms of the economic needs they would serve, invariably they required a simultaneous transformation of local social relationships and cultures. New towns have been created, in Cwmbran and in Newtown in mid Wales, and major projects have been designed to reorganize economic and social space (the Cardiff Bay development, Swansea Marina and the M4 and A55 road projects). This regrouping of community and social relationships to suit economic purposes has been brutal at times, and has earned justifiable criticism for its disregard for earlier values and achievements (Williams, 1979; Rees, 1997). The most obvious example is the wiping away of the mining communities of south and north Wales through the virtual elimination of the industry which created and sustained them. The steel towns have more or less followed suit, while the basis of existence in the agricultural communities has been precarious for generations.

More important still perhaps have been the unplanned processes through which individuals have migrated with their families to new areas and new places, usually in search of better economic opportunities. Very few of the Welsh population are now living in the same places, with the same neighbours and the same relationships, as they did even ten or fifteen years ago. Those who are tend to represent islands of stability, or stagnation, in a sea of change. In a context where it is widely recognized that attachment to place, with a sense of local distinctiveness, has been a fundamental social characteristic (Harris, 1990: 232), this has left people struggling where possible to rebuild their connections and identities, in the face of fragmentation and individualization. Emphasis during the 1980s and 1990s on the power of the market and competitive individualism as the basis for growth and development accentuated these tendencies.

Some have hailed these changes as essential 'modernization'. More than once, the emergence of a 'new Wales' has been celebrated. As early as 1977 it was suggested that 'devolution of decision making from Westminster has become a reality . . . sure to cause administrative (if no other) upheaval that will change the patterns of life of all Welshmen [*sic*] in the future' (Thomas, 1977: 7). This referred to the setting up of the Welsh Office in 1964. By 1990 it was being claimed that there was now 'an effectiveness about many aspects of life . . . that was lacking in the past' (Cole, 1990: 3). This was attributed to the existence of new channels enabling people to transmit their aspirations to, and pressurize, the 'powers that be', while also receiving better indications of the 'standards' that were required to make those powers actually respond to pressure. Interestingly, this hints at the two-way nature of the process: changes in institutions allowed new forms of communication, but also involved an educative process, in which people were asked to take on board new conceptions of 'appropriate' attitudes and action. The result was said to be greater optimism and confidence, and a general sense of revival. However, in the same period others were criticizing the 'raj' nature of the Welsh Office, the inordinate power accrued by the quangos and the resultant 'democratic deficit' in decision-making (Morgan and

Roberts, 1993). They insisted that further action was required to close the gap that had grown up between the 'powers that be' and the mass of the Welsh population. It was the latter viewpoint which eventually won out in the creation of the Assembly, to assume its role as the key institution which would mediate between the wishes of the people and government action, and in doing so help to reconfigure the institutional terrain, hopefully in ways that would set Wales on the path to new economic achievements. In the next section we will outline some of the main institutional changes which have accompanied this stage in the devolutionary process.

The enterprising economy and the learning country

Following the uncertain early months in the Assembly, the economic objectives of the new government for Wales were set out in the partnership agreement *Putting Wales First*, which contained a commitment to promote a strong, modern, knowledge-based, enterprise economy (NAW, 2000). This was seen as the route to high employment, wealth generation and provision of high-quality public services. In order to achieve this, the Assembly government undertook to create a 'vibrant indigenous business sector' which would help bridge the prosperity gap between Wales and the rest of the UK, and put Wales in a position where it could lead, rather than lag behind, in economic development. Accordingly, the first three objectives of the National Economic Development Strategy, *A Winning Wales* (NAW, 2002), are to encourage innovation, encourage entrepreneurship, and to make Wales a learning country. Particular emphasis is placed upon education and training, and raising the standards of skills and initiative amongst the Welsh population.

Endorsement for these aims is contained in the Wales Management Council's *Agenda for Action* (2003), which recognizes that in a modern economy greater value must be placed upon the knowledge and skills of the workers, and the positive ways in which they can be embedded and utilized within work organizations. Consequently, the employee is no longer viewed as a passive 'consumer' of training, but becomes an active agent in the learning process. Likewise trainers are transformed into 'facilitators', and managers from 'commanders' into 'leaders'. Above all, we are told, 'Wales must be a place where good managers and leaders are admired, talked about, and valued' (Wales Management Council, 2003: 42). All this implies some major reconstruction of the social relationships between 'leaders' and 'led'. However, the Council's first chief executive was stimulated to question whether Wales was 'hungry enough' yet to create a genuine culture of enterprise, even though its merits seemed self-evident, because: 'who wouldn't want to see lots of home grown Welsh entrepreneurs making their mark by setting up businesses which grow to become household names?' (Jones, 2002). He conceded that a more energetic encouragement of native entrepreneurship would require 'a completely new attitude throughout society which encourages and respects competition and risk taking – an attitude, nurtured from early on at school, that life is about competing and that there are winners and losers' (Jones, 2002). To build this would entail dealing with a cultural legacy which is risk averse, and treats risk-taking capitalism 'with some suspicion'. In short, Wales is represented as still facing the need for an overhaul of its existing legacy of industrial and communal values.

The Assembly has at its disposal a number of policy instruments with which to try to achieve this. Some impression of the complexity involved can be gained from the matrix of bodies and organizations potentially involved in providing management and leadership training in Wales, reproduced from the Wales Management Council's *Agenda for Action* (p. 69) (see figure 3.1). This morass of organizations and acronyms represents only a small part of a much larger field. The report notes that the interaction within and between these four groupings should be 'continuous and productive', but that inability to ensure this is one of the failings of the current arrangements. Given the limitations of space, we will restrict ourselves here to considering a few of the main relationships in this crowded field, and especially the role played by two of the key economic agencies now under direct Assembly control, the Welsh Development Agency (WDA) and the more recently formed National Council for Education and Learning Wales (ELWa). Traditionally, the former has represented the main vehicle for the management of the demand side of economic policy in Wales, whereas the latter deals more with supply side responses. However, as the aforementioned emphasis

Figure 3.1. Management and leadership supply matrix in Wales

Influencers	**Funders**
Welsh Assembly Government	Welsh Assembly Government
NC-ELWa	NC-ELWa
HEFCW	HEFCW
WEFO	European Structural Funds
Local authorities/WLGA	Local authorities
WCVA	WDA
Universities/business schools	Finance Wales
FE colleges/Fforwm	Knowledge Exploitation Fund
CCETs	Skills Development Fund
SSCs	Welsh Funders Forum
SSDA	Individuals
CBI	
FSB	
IOD	
CIPD	
CMI	
ILM	
ACAS	
Trade/professional bodies	
Structural Fund Partnerships	
Regional Economic Fora	
Industry Fora	
Regional Technology Plan	
Entrepreneurship Action Plan	
Managers	
Employers	**Deliverers**
Private sector	HE institutions
Public sector	Business schools
Voluntary sector	FE colleges
Community groups	Private sector training orgs
Individuals	CMI
	CIPD
	IOD
	ILM
	Learn Direct
	Mentor Wales
	Business Connect
	Voluntary and community sector
	Individual consultants and trainers

Source: Wales Management Council, 2003: 69.

on 'learning' and 'enterprise' indicates, there has been a notable convergence between the two fields of action. In relation to economic development, the aims and objectives of the bodies are clearly intended to be complementary.

The role of the Welsh Development Agency

In existence since 1976, the WDA has operated chiefly as an investment bank and brokerage service for inward investment. Although not directly charged with a social agenda, its activities have had a number of important indirect effects upon the formations of Welsh civil society. Apart from the overall change in economic climate that it has helped to bring about, specific actions to encourage economic diversification and to shift the balance between different industrial sectors have resulted in significant alterations in the social and occupational composition of local labour markets. Thus the development of factory units and industrial estates, together with related infrastructural investments, has encouraged movements of employers and workers to new locations, whilst depriving other places of their relative attractiveness. These movements have included the importation of key managerial, professional and skilled personnel, who have tended to be under-represented within the Welsh workforce, and whose backgrounds and values often differ markedly from those already present in local communities. At the local level, this has produced a chequerboard pattern of growth and decline, associated with shifting alignments of interest and competition. Typically, the WDA has been accused of intervening from above, as a remote agency, without being answerable for such local consequences.

The WDA is known best for its record in stimulating inward investment, and especially its role in bringing foreign companies into Wales. The successes Wales has enjoyed in this respect have been widely publicized, and inward investors have been seen as leading by example, creating changes in industrial attitudes, workplace cultures and technological efficiencies that have helped Wales compete more effectively not just within the British context, but across Europe and internationally. Until recently, the major part of this development has taken place in a geographically limited zone, along the border regions of south-east and north-east Wales. By definition, it has remained virtually entirely under the control of interests located beyond Wales. The relative growth of places like Newport and Cardiff in the south and Deeside in the north and the decline of the older industrial areas have widened the gap in living conditions between different localities. Disparities in economic conditions and lifestyles between 'post-modern' and 'traditional' or 'redundant' communities put new strains on the cohesiveness of Welsh society. The relative failure of west Wales and the Valleys, which has qualified them for European Objective One status, has tended to split Wales along east–west lines, rather than the older north–south polarization.

More recent years have seen an increasing awareness on the part of the WDA that it needs to focus more on the generation of indigenous business, and to encourage the expansion and spread of small and medium-sized enterprises (SMEs). The vast majority of businesses in Wales have fewer than 250 employees; indeed, 98 per cent have fewer than 20 employees. Businesses with under 250 employees employ two-thirds of the workforce, and produce 57 per cent of the turnover (Wales Management Council, 2003). By comparison with inward investors, these small and micro businesses are viewed as potentially less vulnerable to external economic fluctuations, better rooted in local conditions, and more likely to form effective relationships with each other. Encouraged by innovations in theories of regional development, emphasis has been put on the relevance of 'clustering' and networking activity among such businesses as the crucial condition for stability and reliable expansion. According to Cooke and Morgan, this represents a 'third way' to economic development, in which civil society to some extent displaces both market and state, since:

> High trust, learning capacity and networking competence are now widely perceived to be associated with relative economic and social success. Each of these is founded upon high capability in social interaction and communication rather than either individualistic competition or strong state-led economic development programmes. (Cooke and Morgan, 1998: 5)

In other words, economic performance reflects the virtues, or shortcomings, of the type of civil society into which firms and other economic actors are embedded. For reasons of size and ease of communication, Cooke and Morgan see this consideration as most pertinent at a 'regional' level. In European terms, Wales is just such a region, able to compete on terms with other 'motor' areas such as parts of Italy, Spain and Germany. Even before the Assembly appeared, they argue, Wales had already benefited considerably from its devolved economic institutions: the WDA plus the Welsh Office represented an 'unparalleled governance capacity' denied to other parts of Britain. However, the logic of the newer focus on growth from within clearly sets an imperative to work more closely with other parts of the social system, given that the interactive and communicative structures of local society will help determine the eventual outcomes. 'Intelligence' therefore does not consist solely of the 'people' having a better, more informed, idea of what is needed from them; it also requires agencies to maintain effective contact with local opinion and conditions. This necessitates the creation of effective, and multiple, conduits of information, decision-making and control, that can work to mobilize the power of collective intelligence, pooling the knowledge and understanding distributed through society (Brown and Lauder, 2001). As Amin (1999) notes, attempts to unlock the 'wealth of regions' as the prime source of development and renewal tend to favour policy actions that are bottom-up, region-specific, more long term and able to engage with a plurality of actors. The mobilization of endogenous potential also involves efforts to upgrade the local supply-side infrastructure for enterprise and entrepreneurship.

While agencies like the WDA can make a difference by working on some of the macro parameters, it is evident that there are limits to what can be achieved by a single agency operating with a restricted economic remit. In fact, arguably, things have gone backwards in this respect, since the WDA absorbed into itself the former Development Board for Rural Wales (DBRW), which used to oversee the economic development of mid Wales, and which possessed some explicit powers to carry out 'social' and 'community' tasks, such as funding local community centres, subsidizing cultural and artistic events, and even supporting local play schemes. In this way, the DBRW could be seen as intervening directly into local civil society, and as consciously seeking to repair some of the damage done by rural decline and depopulation. While not necessarily a popular organization, even among recipients of its largesse, the DBRW was not considered to be quite so remote and 'top-down' as the WDA. Indeed, the lack of democratic oversight of the operations of the WDA, and its ability to elude accountability for its actions, played a significant part in the mounting pressure for reform of 'quangoland' which helped win over public support for the creation of the Assembly (Morgan and Mungham, 2000). Subsequent developments, discussed below, might suggest that there is an awareness still of the need for greater democratization of control over the agency.

The WDA's current strategy is to pursue a more balanced mixture of inward investment and the consolidation of local business, aimed at fewer big 'hits' and a more diffuse influence throughout the Welsh economy. This is implemented through the formation of partnerships of various kinds. Naturally, the main thrust of its work continues to be directed towards creating relationships between firms and economic organizations, such as union and employers' associations, in the form of supply chains and training consortia. While it has achieved a degree of success in this respect, the networks and linkages it has built have proved to be quite vulnerable to economic contingencies (Cooke, 2003), possibly because they remain confined to the level of economic relationships and have not penetrated more deeply into civil society. As a government agency, albeit with close to 1,000 employees, the WDA does not have the capacity to work closely with local groups and communities. It maintains regional offices in north and mid Wales, but is still seen by many as a south-Wales-oriented, Cardiff-centric body, with the interests of the south Wales economy closest to its heart.

However, WDA officials serve on a host of committees and partnership organizations through which they seek to exercise some control over the direction of local developments, and are thereby brought into contact with a wider range of representatives of civil society. The WDA tends to be the senior partner in such bodies. Organizations and agencies seeking support and funding from the agency have to produce business plans and development strategies which comply with its strategic objectives and regulations. If they lack the ability to do so themselves, then they must resort to experts and consultants who can do so in a 'professional' fashion. In this way, the WDA contributes to the infiltration of an economic rationality into wider community and social relationships (Walters, 2002); but it cannot do so entirely on its own terms. The move towards a more 'bottom-up' reliance on indigenous growth imposes some constraints of its own. Nurturing local initiative and enterprise requires a readiness to adopt a more flexible approach, with a larger role for local participation and involvement (McKenna and Thomas, 1988). There have to be elements of consultation and consensus building, not least because success is dependent upon sensitivity to local knowledge. At a minimal level, this requires responsiveness to regional variations within Wales.

The regionalization of economic policy instruments

The pattern of regional governance within Wales continues the pattern established before the creation of the Assembly. The shape of the administrative regions, and the extent to which they correspond to any meaningful distinctions within Wales, has been questioned (Rees, 1998). Despite hopes that they might be used to engage productively with the demands of emerging policy communities across Wales (Jones and Osmond, 2001: 164) the Assembly's four Regional Committees (for north, mid, south-west and south-east Wales) have been reckoned generally to be among the more ineffectual of the new institutions. Their role is advisory and consultative, their brief ranges widely across policy areas, and attendance by Assembly Members (AMs) has sometimes been poor. Complaints from north and mid Wales that regional interests within Wales are poorly represented as compared to those of the south are echoed lower down the institutional framework.

The regional pattern is mirrored in the divisionalization of both the WDA and the National Council – ELWa, as well as in the formation of the four Regional Economic Fora. These are voluntary partnerships whose role is to help coordinate regional strategies and policies for economic growth and development, and to secure the commitment of relevant partners in their region, across the public and private sectors. The fora exchange examples of best practice, and try to minimize duplication of activity. Their purpose is to provide a strategic voice for the regions, with which to influence and lobby the National Assembly for Wales, the UK and EU governments and others. Thus the Mid Wales Partnership states that its goal is to 'promote and develop coherent and inclusive policies in response to issues of common interest across the region' (*http://www.mwp.ruralwales.org*), while the North Wales Economic Forum was set up in 1996 to 'speak with a clear and unified voice' on behalf of north Wales on economic and related issues (*http://www.llandrillo.ac.uk/host/nwef*). At the same time, the forum can not claim to be the sole voice of the business community in north Wales. Its membership consists of representatives of the six local authorities, the Wales Tourist Board, CBI, ELWa, JobCentre Plus, TUC, further and higher education and the North Wales Chambers of Commerce. Meetings are attended by observers from the Federation of Small Business, Snowdonia National Park Authority and Business North Wales. The chair of the Assembly's North Wales Regional Committee sits 'at the table' as of right, and the forum is chaired by the chair of the WDA.

With a membership of some forty-plus representatives of these key organizations, the forum has to be seen as a gathering of the 'regional elite', considerably removed from the groups and associations of civil society. The partnership does not include members of community organizations or the voluntary sector. The forum meets three or four times a year, and sponsors a series of working groups dealing with such specialist topics as rural issues, competitive business, skills, transportation, energy, the Territorial Employment Pact, Information Communications Technology (ICT) and the Local Employment Observatory. These groups issue a stream of reports and studies. Like the other fora, the North Wales Economic Forum lists among its aims the promotion of investment in people and communities, raising the image of north Wales and investing in intellectual capital. It commissions research and monitors economic trends. Obviously its work extends beyond simply interacting with local business and enterprise. In terms of its involvement with people, for instance, it states that

> People are at the heart of the Forum's mission. A skilled, adaptable workforce is a prerequisite for economic success. But this is not enough: North Wales needs a vibrant society, maintaining its cultural heritage, in which economic benefit extends to all, wherever they live and whatever their status in society. (*http://www.llandrillo.ac.uk/host/nwef*)

Similarly, in terms of promoting intellectual capital, the importance of stimulating a flow of information commensurate with a 'learning region' is acknowledged:

> Intellectual capital is the source of growth: new ideas and technologies lead to new processes, new products and services, and new, profitable markets. New knowledge-based activities must be encouraged within the North Wales economy. The Forum must also ensure that its activities are continually refined and developed by better intelligence. (*http://www.llandrillo.ac.uk/host/nwef*)

As well as operating at an all-Wales level, the 'rhetoric of unity' evidently also has its regional impact. As partnerships, the regional economic fora operate by consensus. They do not have powers of direction, nor are they delivery vehicles for policy. This means that they seek to avoid 'divisive' issues and controversy. An argument in one subgroup of the North Wales Forum led to the resignation of a CBI representative, who complained that the private sector was given only a token role in such discussions. Responding to this complaint, the forum coordinator confirmed that in circumstances where a consensus view could not be achieved, voting was permissible, but that 'this had never proved necessary at any sub-group meeting of the Forum in the past' (Forum minutes, 2000). Experiences like this can only reinforce a common perception among business that such groupings are no more than 'talking shops' in which discussions are stage-managed to avoid contentious matters (Morgan and Rees, 2001: 148), a view which leads to a search for other, more direct, but less transparent channels of influence.

The issue of ensuring reasonable communication with and responsiveness to local (that is, regional) interests has been aired within the forum. It has been pointed out that the relocation of Assembly and other government offices to north Wales would help the private sector engage more effectively with Objective One and other European programmes, and therefore that spatial as well as gender and ethnic balance should be sought on committees and partnerships. For example, an Interreg programme with Ireland had been run from an office in Cwm Cynon, described as 'possibly the most distant point in Wales from Ireland', rather than from Colwyn Bay in north Wales. Unsuccessful attempts to arrange a transfer of responsibility (and personnel) were explained in terms of adverse effects on career development among Assembly officials and civil servants.

The challenge of cultural change: enterprise, education and training

As the policy perspective driving the activities of the WDA has changed over the years, so the rhetoric has put more stress on working with the 'community' and the importance of 'listening' and 'enabling local people to become genuine partners in the regeneration process' (Annual Report, 2003). The agency has been identifying itself more closely with people and communities, through projects like Dynamo and Potentia, which focus on the individual, or the Community Regeneration Toolkit and various other 'local' initiatives, including the Small Towns and Villages Enterprise Initiative. This moves it distinctly towards supply-side intervention. An obvious aspect of the agency's work is a focus on 'enterprise'. The agency manages the Assembly's Entrepreneurship Action Plan (EAP), which aims to produce wide-scale cultural change in Wales by developing new models of entrepreneurship that the general public will view more favourably. As well as new business start-ups and growth of existing businesses, the EAP seeks to encourage entrepreneurship in the public sector and the social economy. A promotional campaign is supported by a website, *http://www.becauseyoucan.com*, which aims to be 'the first comprehensive online community of Welsh entrepreneurs'. Approximately £65m of European grant money has been made available under the Objective 1 programme for west Wales and the Valleys to fund entrepreneurship initiatives over the period 2000–6. Approved projects include: Promoting an Entrepreneurial Culture, The Business Birth Rate Strategy, Enterprise Factory, Developing Social Entrepreneurs and Women's Enterprise. 'Potentia' is a programme for social inclusion which aims to 'unlock the enterprise potential' amongst groups not traditionally associated with business – young people, the over-50s, disabled people, black and minority ethnic groups, Welsh speakers and single parents. 'Dynamo' is a more mainstream vehicle aimed at pupils aged 14–16, who are given the opportunity to meet local role models who have succeeded in 'navigating the entrepreneurial journey'. As part of a move to embed entrepreneurship in the school curriculum, the programme is being extended to younger groups.

Such programmes have brought the agency closer to the education and training world of ELWa. Whereas the WDA relates to the

Economic Development Committee of the National Assembly, ELWa mirrors the role played during its early years by the Post-16 Education and Training Committee, which started out with a remit that included aspects of employment policy (New Deal and the role of the Employment Service). The committee's scrutiny of an action plan prepared by the Education and Training Action Group (ETAG) was said to be the most significant piece of early work undertaken by an Assembly subject committee (Egan and James, 2001) and resulted in the development of the current framework of provision for post-16 education, intended to meet employers' local skills needs. That there are still problems with this framework is suggested by the Wales Management Council:

> The supply side is very fragmented. There seems to be relatively little contact between different types of provider – for example further education and higher education, or public and private sector provision. Frequently each operates in their own world. Providers of formal education often do not relate to learning which takes place in the work place. (Wales Management Council, 2003: 70)

ELWa was designed to remedy this situation. Established in 2001 from a merger of the four Welsh Training and Enterprise Councils (TECs), the Council of Welsh TECs and the Further Education Funding Council for Wales, it is responsible for planning and promoting sixth-form and further education, work-based training, adult and continuing education. Apart from a small team covering all-Wales corporate functions, it has four regional offices, which, as noted previously, are partners in the regional Economic Fora. ELWa also works with local authorities, and with partnerships implementing European Structural Fund Local Action Plans. It participates in drawing up community regeneration strategies, making sure that they pay attention to investment in learning and skills capabilities. ELWa also works in partnership with a network of twenty-three Community Consortia for Education and Training (CCETs) across Wales. CCETs are intended to form the essential link with the 'local learning market'. Their role is to achieve more efficient delivery of education and training, and to promote collaboration between schools, further education and training providers and others so as to meet the needs of individuals and employers more effectively and coherently. CCETs develop local plans and strategies in response to local needs.

Higher education in Wales (funded through HEFCW) also has as part of its mission an economic responsibility in relation to wealth and job creation and the commercial exploitation of knowledge. The 'third mission' assigned to universities (apart from teaching and research) relates to their contribution to local economy and community. As well as the work of departments of 'lifelong learning', various forms of 'community university' have been set up in Wales, following Swansea's example, catering for outreach and vocational skills activities. These initiatives represent efforts to realize the ambition of making Wales a 'learning country' – a place where 'high quality, lifelong learning provides the skills people need to prosper in the new economy, liberates talent, extends opportunities and empowers communities' (NAW, 2001). With these attributes, it is claimed, Wales will be able to 'vault the barriers to social progress and prosperity'. Accordingly, ELWa's corporate strategy document outlines a vision for a competitive knowledge-based economy and an inclusive society, based on high skill levels, achievement of personal potential, openness to change and willingness to innovate and take risks. It also warns that failure to achieve this will result in Wales's getting caught in a low-skills, low-growth trap, with a stagnant labour market, the threat of a breakdown of social cohesion and movement of people away from many areas.

Conclusion

Since the advent of the Welsh Assembly, some strenuous efforts have been made to enlarge the connections between the institutional framework for economic development, and society 'on the ground'. There is an explicit desire to raise the level of engagement with communities and localities, and to mobilize the energies and commitments of individuals. Beneath the very large institutional structures we have been describing, there exists, of course, a massive, and growing, jumble of local partnerships, Objective 1 projects, regeneration schemes and renewal strategies, within which particular local communities, organized groups and voluntary agencies are involved (see Adamson in this volume). These constitute a set of intermediate institutions between the market and the state, and draw at least parts of civil society more firmly into the economic arena. They have the potential to contribute to the growth of a 'thick' foundation of institutions, which, in accordance with the maxims of institutionalist governance (Amin, 1999), could encourage the emergence of a multiplicity of voices, active within a number of decentralized centres of decision-making. These could play a vital role in disseminating information, knowledge and learning for economic adaptability. Yet the gap between the potential and its realization remains very large. An idea of its dimensions is evident in a recent survey and analysis of 'community development' work in south Wales (Clarke et al., 2002). The book is full of examples of the gulf between 'top-down' programmes and directives, and the perspective from the grassroots. Forging links between national strategies for economic and social renewal, and the interests and aspirations of people in their various communities, is acknowledged to be extraordinarily difficult. Interestingly, there is only passing reference to the importance of bodies like the WDA or ELWa in setting the broad parameters to which community-level activity has to respond. As the authors warn, without a process which changes the nature of the relationship between the participants, we risk being stuck with a model of regeneration and development in which local people remain always on the periphery of the decision making process (Clarke et al., 2002: 222) and there is only a token gesture towards 'listening' and learning from civil society. Without more work to close the gap, the likelihood is that those who construct the policies and programmes will continue to play a 'preemptive and determining role'. Expressions of frustration with the slowness of attainment of aims under the Objective One Programme, and the difficulties of working with bureaucracies in Cardiff and Brussels, provide further illustration of the problems. Yet at the same time, whenever measures are taken to improve the connections between local needs and awareness and larger economic purposes, the risk is run that the spontaneous interests of civil society will be subordinated to economic pressures and governmental control.

In 2004 the first minister, Rhodri Morgan, announced his intention that WDA and ELWa, together with the Wales Tourist Board, should be brought directly within the framework of the Welsh Assembly Government, as part of the promised 'bonfire of the quangos'. With 1,600 staff and an annual budget of around £1 billion, these three organizations account for the bulk (70 per cent) of Welsh quango funding. The organizations would cease to exist as from April 2006. The decision was justified in terms of making the Assembly 'more governmental', with greater 'firepower' and the ability to generate more distinctively Wales-oriented policies (Thomas, 2004). It was also said to be a further step towards democratization and improved scrutiny. However, concerns have been expressed as to whether this signifies instead a move towards added centralization. For example, the Welsh Local Government Association has argued that some of the responsibilities of the quangos could be devolved to local authorities, or vested in new regional bodies, able to oversee local community strategies. The fear is that a rolling back of the quango state in Wales will enhance greatly the Assembly's ability to determine a regional economic policy, but at the cost of a bureaucratic straitjacket, that takes away some of the independence of action which was a strength of the former organizations, and serves to aggravate the perceived prosperity divide between south-east Wales and the rest of the country.

References

Adamson, D. (1995). *Living on the Edge: Poverty and Deprivation in Wales*, Llandysul: Gomer Press.

Amin, A. (1999). 'An institutionalist perspective on regional development', *International Journal of Urban and Regional Development*, 23, 2.

Brown, P. and Lauder, H. (2001). *Capitalism and Social Progress: The Future of Society in a Global Economy*, Basingstoke: Palgrave.

Bryan, J. and Jones, C. (2000). *Wales in the Twenty-First Century*, Basingstoke: Macmillan.

Chaney, P., Hall, T., and Pithouse, A. (2001). *New Governance, New Democracy? Post Devolution Wales*, Cardiff: University of Wales Press.

Clarke S., Byatt, A. M., Hoban, M. and Powell, D. (2002). *Community Development in South Wales*, Cardiff: University of Wales Press.

Cole, D. (ed.) (1990). *The New Wales*, Cardiff: University of Wales Press.

Cooke, P. (2003). 'The regional innovation system in Wales: evolution or eclipse?', in P. Cooke, M. Heidenreich and H. Braczyk (eds), *Regional Innovation Systems*, London: Routledge.

Cooke, P. and Morgan, K. (1998). *The Associational Economy*, Oxford: Oxford University Press.

Day, G. (2002). *Making Sense of Wales: A Sociological Perspective*, Cardiff: University of Wales Press.

Egan, D. and James, R. (2001). 'Driving a policy agenda: the post-16 education and training committee', in J. Barry Jones and J. Osmond (eds), *Inclusive Government and Party Management: The National Assembly For Wales and the Work of its Committees*, Cardiff: Institute of Welsh Affairs.

Field, J. (2003). *Social Capital*, London: Routledge.

Fine, B. (2000). *Social Capital Versus Social Theory: Political Economy and Social Science at the Turn of the Millenium*, London: Routledge.

Gerth, H. and Mills, C.W. (1948). *From Max Weber: Essays in Sociology*, London: Routledge and Kegan Paul.

Harris, C. C. (1990). 'Changing social conditions', in Cole (ed.), *The New Wales*, Cardiff: University of Wales Press.

Jones, A. (2002). 'Entrepreneurship – are we hungry enough?', *Insight*, Journal of the Wales Management Council (available from *http://www.crc-wmc.org.uk/hungryenough.asp*)

Jones, J. Barry (1998). 'The committees', in J. Osmond (ed.), *The National Assembly Agenda*, Cardiff: Institute of Welsh Affairs.

Jones, J. Barry and Osmond, J. (eds) (2001). *Inclusive Government and Party Management: the National Assembly For Wales and the Work of its Committees*, Cardiff: Institute of Welsh Affairs.

Lovering, J. (1999). 'Theory led by policy: the inadequacies of the "new regionalism" illustrated from the case of Wales', *International Journal of Urban and Regional Research*, 23, 2.

McKenna, C. J. and Thomas, D. (1988). 'Regional policy', in K. D. George and L. Mainwaring (eds), *The Welsh Economy*, Cardiff: University of Wales Press, pp. 263–90.

Miller, P. and Rose, N. (1990). 'Governing economic life', *Economy and Society*, 19, 1.

Morgan, K. and Henderson, D. (1997). 'The fallible servant: evaluating the Welsh development agency', in R. Macdonald and H. Thomas (eds), *Nationality and Planning in Scotland and Wales*, Cardiff: University of Wales Press.

Morgan, K. and Mungham, G. (2000). *Redesigning Democracy: the Making of the Welsh Assembly*, Bridgend: Seren.

Morgan, K. and Rees, G. (2001). 'Learning by doing: devolution and the governance of economic development in Wales', in P. Chaney, T. Hall and A. Pithouse (eds), *New Governance, New Democracy? Post Devolution Wales*, Cardiff: University of Wales Press.

Morgan K. and Roberts E. (1993). *The Democratic Deficit: A Guide to Quangoland*, Papers in Planning Research 144, Cardiff: Department of City and Regional Planning.

National Assembly for Wales (NAW) (2000). *Putting Wales First: A Partnership for the People of Wales*, The First Partnership Agreement of the National Assembly for Wales, Progress Report. Cardiff: NAW.

NAW (2001). *The Learning Country – Paving Document*, Cardiff: NAW.

NAW (2002). *A Winning Wales* – the National Economic Development Strategy of the Welsh Assembly Government.

Osmond, J. (ed.) (1998). *The National Assembly Agenda*, Cardiff: Institute of Welsh Affairs.

Rees, G. (1997). 'The politics of regional development strategy: the programme for the valleys', in R. Macdonald and H. Thomas (eds), *Nationality and Planning in Scotland and Wales*, Cardiff: University of Wales Press.

Rees, I. B. (1998). 'The regions of Wales', in J. Osmond (ed.), *The National Assembly Agenda*, Cardiff: Institute of Welsh Affairs.

Rose, N. (1996). 'The death of the social?', *Economy and Society*, 25, 3.

Thomas, A. (2004). *The Reform of Assembly Sponsored Public Bodies*, Cardiff: National Assembly for Wales (Members Research Service).

Thomas, D. (1977). *Wales: A New Study*, Newton Abbot: David and Charles.

Wales Council for Voluntary Action (WCVA) (2002). 'A civil society diamond for Wales', Cardiff: WCVA.

Wales Management Council (2003). *Management and Leadership Development and Training in Wales: An Agenda for Action.*

Walters, W. (2002). 'Social capital and political sociology: re-imagining politics?', *Sociology*, 36, 2.

Waterstone, D. (1990). 'The incomer's view', in D. Cole (ed.), *The New Wales*, Cardiff: University of Wales Press.

Welsh Development Agency (2003). Annual Report, Cardiff: WDA.

Williams, R. (1979). *The Fight For Manod*, London: Chatto and Windus.

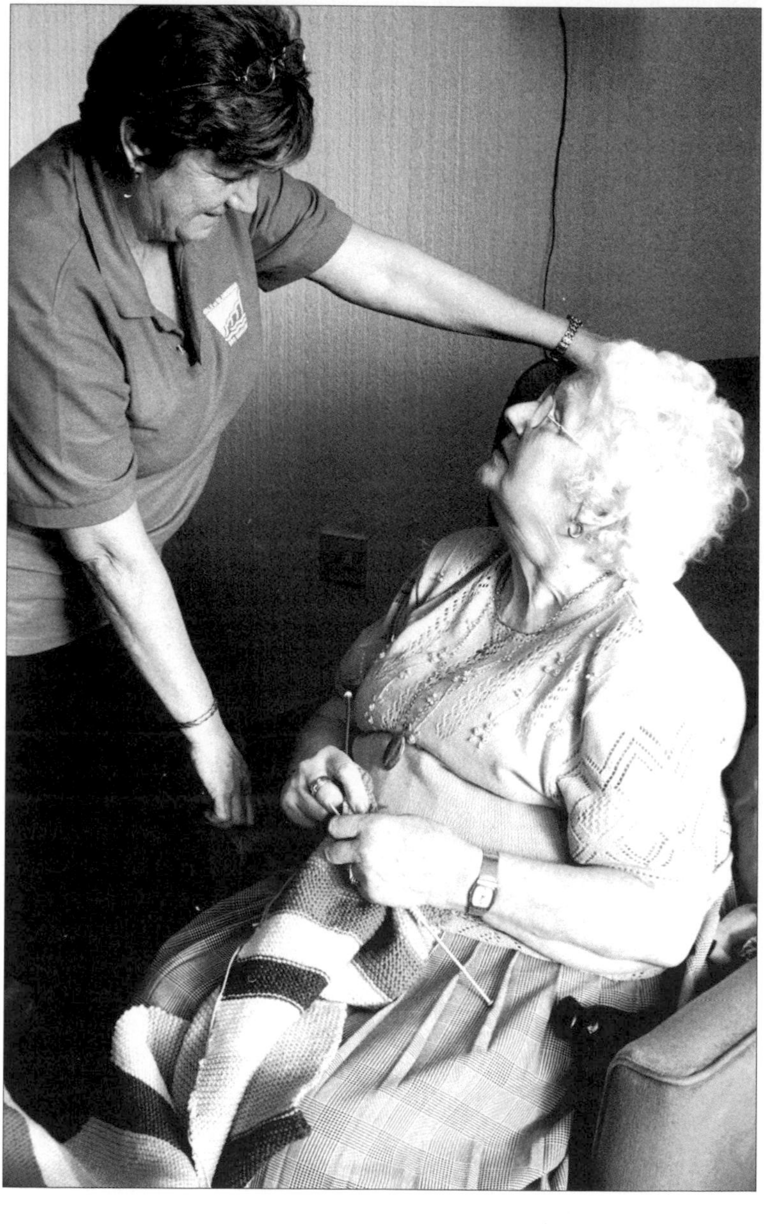

4. The Civil Society Index for Wales

ANNA NICHOLL

Wales Council for Voluntary Action (WCVA), together with a steering group made up of a cross-section of civil society organizations (CSOs) and interested partners in Wales, implemented a pilot Civil Society Index for Wales in 2001–2. The project was led by CIVICUS – an international alliance dedicated to strengthening citizen action and civil society throughout the world – which has developed the project to assess and strengthen the health of civil society internationally. The Civil Society Index for Wales was one of fourteen pilot projects conducted internationally. This chapter is based on the report of the project.[1]

The CIVICUS project

CIVICUS developed this project in response to the increasing awareness of the enormous role that civil society plays today, whether it be local groups coming together to find ways of improving their communities, or the global movement against neo-liberal globalization.[2] Whilst our recognition of the vital role that civil society plays in public life is increasing, there remains a lack of knowledge about what civil society is and how it operates compared with the public and private sectors. There is certainly little way of measuring how civil society is faring, compared with the many well-established economic and government indicators, such as GDP.

In response to this, CIVICUS developed a project attempting to capture this information in an index and to empower civil society practitioners in the process. The project attempts to increase understanding of civil society but not simply through providing a greater body of research. Crucially, it is also intended to act as a tool for practitioners and strengthen civil society by bringing practitioners together to consider what they can do to improve civil society's state – based on the information assembled through the project. CIVICUS outlines how they anticipate the Civil Society Index (CSI) project will strengthen civil society in a threefold process:

- by increasing the knowledge and understanding of civil society through reflecting on and assessing the health and nature of the sector;
- by empowering civil society stakeholders through promoting dialogue, alliances and networks;
- by providing stakeholders with a tool for developing a vision of civil society in the future, and an agenda to achieve this vision.

The pilot Civil Society Index assessed four key dimensions of civil society in order to assess the overall health of civil society:[3]

1. the **structure** of civil society with regard to its basic components, their size and relationship and the resources they command;
2. the legal, political and socio-cultural **space** that civil society occupies within the regulatory, legal and social environment;
3. the **values** that civil society represents and advocates;
4. the **impact** of civil society on social and community well-being.

In Wales, WCVA acted as the lead national body and worked closely with a steering group comprising a cross-section of civil society organizations in Wales and partners, including: Wales TUC, the Chartered Society of Physiotherapy, Oxfam Wales/Cymru, CYTÛN – Churches Together in Wales, Torfaen Voluntary Alliance and the Department of Voluntary Sector Studies, University of Wales, Lampeter.

Central to the implementation was a survey targeted at those with a broad knowledge of civil society in Wales, whether they worked within CSOs or not. Participants were asked to assess the strength of civil society in Wales on a number of issues within the four dimensions. The outcomes were analysed by CIVICUS and translated into 'scores' from 0–100, where 100 represents a perfectly 'healthy' civil society.

Objectives and approach of the Wales study

The objectives of the Civil Society Index for Wales were to:

- increase understanding of the strengths, development needs, challenges and opportunities for civil society in Wales;
- promote dialogue and alliances among civil society organizations;
- raise awareness about civil society in Wales and its potential;
- feed into setting agendas and goals for action to strengthen civil society, including a Manifesto for Civil Society used to campaign for positive change in the run-up to the 2003 National Assembly for Wales elections;
- provide some basis for comparison and sharing information about civil society in Wales and civil society in the other countries which have participated in the project.

What/who is civil society in Wales?

Civil society is made up of a broad variety of groups, organizations and networks through which people come together voluntarily to advance their common interests. It encompasses the huge range of organized activity outside the public or private sectors, including trade unions, professional associations, religious organizations, voluntary and community organizations. It is different from the private and public sectors – and it operates with or without their support. Civil society reflects the fundamental right of people to organize and cooperate. It is about people, consumers and communities taking action and taking responsibility for finding solutions to their own problems, initiating and managing their own services and facilities, organizing in their workplaces, and lobbying the public and private sector alike for change and improvements.

> Civil society is the sphere of institutions, organizations and individuals located between the family, the state and the market, in which people associate voluntarily to advance common interests.

The steering group agreed to use the above as the working definition for the project in Wales, whilst recognizing that existing definitions vary both within and beyond Wales. This definition includes the voluntary sector, trade unions and professional associations but excludes political parties, the media and universities. It recognizes that civil society can be 'uncivil', and the indicators for civil society's values underline this. Civil society is not a term commonly used by researchers, practitioners or their partners in Wales. Indeed, confusion as to the definition of 'civil society' was a regular comment in the responses to the survey and was also given as a reason for not replying to the survey at all. However, one of the aims of conducting the project and survey was to increase understanding of and discussion around the term.

History of civil society in Wales

Civil society in Wales stems from different foundations from its UK counterparts. In all parts of the UK it has developed alongside industrialization, political and social change and democratization. In Wales, however, the roots of civil society can be found in the Nonconformist religious revival of the early nineteenth century. Arising from the heartlands of rural Wales the Nonconformist movement capitalized on existing kinship ties, a significant feature of social cohesion historically, and stimulated not only a religious, but also a political and national consciousness. This underpinned the organization of many social and educational institutions that provided a new route to participation in society. Towards the end of the century in the rapidly expanding urban areas of industrial south Wales civil society developed around the institutions that bound the mining communities together.

The increasing secularization and latent decline in trade union membership that characterized the second half of the twentieth century reduced the role of these two main influences and paved the way for the enormous growth in the voluntary sector. Today, although there is still evidence of rural/urban differences in the structure of civil society in Wales, across the whole country it comprises a diverse set of organizations that represent a far broader range of interests, thus reflecting other less communalistic, more individualist trends in society.

Roles and characteristics of contemporary civil society in Wales

Civil society in Wales is diverse and various and does not organize itself under one umbrella. It is worth looking at some of the different dimensions that make up civil society in Wales.

The voluntary sector

The voluntary sector in Wales is made up of some 30,000 organizations, including community groups, volunteers, self-help groups, community cooperatives and enterprises, religious organizations and other not-for-profit organizations of benefit to communities and people in Wales. It is extremely diverse and operates at a variety of levels from informal community groups to large international organizations. WCVA has an extensive database of 26,000 voluntary organizations, divided into forty-six different areas of activity.

WCVA acts as an umbrella body for national organizations and has over 1,300 member organizations. WCVA Volunteering Unit works closely with volunteering bureaux and advocates policies to promote volunteering at a national level. There are several national umbrella bodies working within specific areas in Wales from advice and advocacy to youth.

At a local level, each county has an umbrella body for the voluntary sector – county voluntary councils. These differ widely in size and resources but they all provide core services to support the local voluntary sector. Each county has a volunteer bureau which promotes volunteering in the area. There is a wide range of local networks that vary between areas.

The voluntary sector also has formal links with the National Assembly for Wales (NAW), which has a statutory duty to publish a scheme setting out how it will promote the voluntary sector in its work and monitor implementation. The Voluntary Sector Scheme includes two key mechanisms for regular dialogue and cooperation between government and the sector: the Voluntary Sector Partnership Council and regular meetings with ministers.

Trade unions

At a national level Wales TUC (Trade Union Congress) operates as an umbrella body for trade unions in Wales. It has a membership of fifty trade unions, which in turn represent just under half a million union members or about 45 per cent of all employees in

Wales. Trade union membership as a percentage of all employees is significantly higher in Wales than in other parts of Great Britain and this has enabled Wales TUC to exercise a significant level of influence in public affairs throughout Wales. Wales TUC sits on the National Assembly for Wales's Business Partnership Council, alongside other individual trade unions. Wales TUC has a regional structure which reflects the four economic regions of Wales and matches the regional committee areas of the National Assembly. There are also twenty-seven regional Trade Union Councils working in tandem with Wales TUC across Wales.

Faith groups[4]

The various strands of Christian faith have been a very important area of civil society traditionally within Wales and have developed a strong network at a national level in CYTÛN – Churches Together in Wales. CYTÛN has twelve member organizations which in turn represent 85 per cent of the Christian faith in Wales and 10 per cent of the whole population. CYTÛN also has several local networks active across Wales. It runs a Churches' National Assembly Centre and represented religious groups for the first two years of the Voluntary Sector Partnership Council. There is also an Evangelical Alliance in Wales, which represents churches across the nation from some thirty different denominations.

Historically, there has not been a well-established umbrella body or single point of contact for the several non-Christian faiths in Wales. However, in April 2002 the Interfaith Council for Wales met for the first time. It was established by (and as part of) the National Assembly for Wales in the wake of the 11 September terrorist attacks, following an alarming rise in racially motivated attacks in Wales. A range of faith groups are represented including Baha'i, Christian Evangelical, Christian Free Church, Christian Church in Wales, Christian Roman Catholic, Hindu, Jewish, Muslim and Sikh communities. The council provides a forum to address issues of common interest that have an impact on religious communities in Wales and was the nominated network for faith groups on the Voluntary Sector Partnership Council for 2002–5 (see Chambers and Thompson in this volume).

Professional associations

Professional associations in Wales have the least degree of unity and joint working to promote common interests. There is no umbrella body for professional associations in Wales and no single point of contact to access further information about what associations are operating. The most comprehensive point of information is the Yellow Pages telephone directory. Further research could be undertaken to establish why this is the case and whether forming closer alliances could strengthen the work of professional associations.

Some individual professional associations are developing their profile in Wales in terms of membership, advocacy and relationships with the Assembly. For example, the Chartered Society of Physiotherapy has 1,500 members in Wales. They work closely with other professions in the health, social care and education sectors in which their members work. They also work collaboratively with a number of voluntary organizations, for example, Arthritis Care in Wales. A couple of the larger professional associations – the Institute of Directors and the Engineering Employers' Federation – have a place on the National Assembly's Business Partnership Council.

Research on civil society in Wales

Some research has been conducted on civil society in Wales by academic institutions, consultants, government and perhaps most of all by civil society organizations themselves. It was not possible within the project to collate a list of the research that has been and is being undertaken in relation to aspects of civil society across Wales.

It is difficult to assess the total amount of academic research that has been undertaken on or including various aspects of civil society in Wales, although this has certainly been done in several academic institutions.[5] Whilst there has been little academic research to date on civil society as a whole in Wales, this is now changing and this volume itself represents the first publication to provide a systematic analysis and focus on civil society in Wales. This may reflect a new tendency for these separate areas of research to be brought under the umbrella term of 'civil society'.

Civil society organizations undertake significant research including a range of one-off and specific research projects. Both

Wales TUC and WCVA have full-time research officers and WCVA produces a Wales voluntary sector almanac.

The Welsh Assembly Government collects a range of statistical information regarding civil society in Wales, albeit under separate areas within civil society. It is committed to providing an annual statement of direct and indirect Assembly spending on the voluntary sector.

The Civil Society Diamond for Wales: what is a 'healthy' civil society?

In developing the CSI project, CIVICUS has drawn on existing research into what a 'healthy' civil society might look like. Based largely on information provided by CIVICUS, the steering group decided that a very strong structure for civil society would include an active membership base with sufficient and effective umbrella bodies, cooperation within civil society and with other sectors and secure funding. A strong space for civil society would be one where regulations and taxes support civil society, the right to dissent and the independence of civil society is fully recognized and employers actively support staff in their work with civil society. A civil society that actively promotes good race relations, equal opportunities and sustainable development within its work and in wider society would have strong values. A civil society with strong impact would improve the lives of the people with whom it works through successfully promoting the interests of its constituents in public policy and providing goods and services that meet people's needs.

Civil society in Wales

Summary

The Civil Society Diamond for Wales depicts a civil society that is overall of 'medium health' although the rather strong impact rating is particularly noteworthy. The diamond shape itself, however, is less interesting than a more detailed look at individual factors within these dimensions.

Structure

Survey respondents regarded the structure of civil society as in a good condition overall and the broad and active membership base was identified as a particular strength. Civil society organizations were also seen to be good at engaging with politicians to express their interests in public life. However, the survey identified a perceived lack of regional distribution of civil society organizations and low cooperation with the private sector as two problematic areas that needed to be addressed.

Space

Civil society in Wales was seen to operate in a rather enabling environment and overall the state was seen to play a positive role by requesting civil society organizations to be involved in policy formulation (particularly at a national level), respecting civil society's independence and recognizing people who have shown great public service in civil society. However, employers were not seen to be very active in supporting their employees' activities in civil society and the regulations for registering a civil society organization were regarded as somewhat burdensome.

Figure 4.1. The Wales Diamond

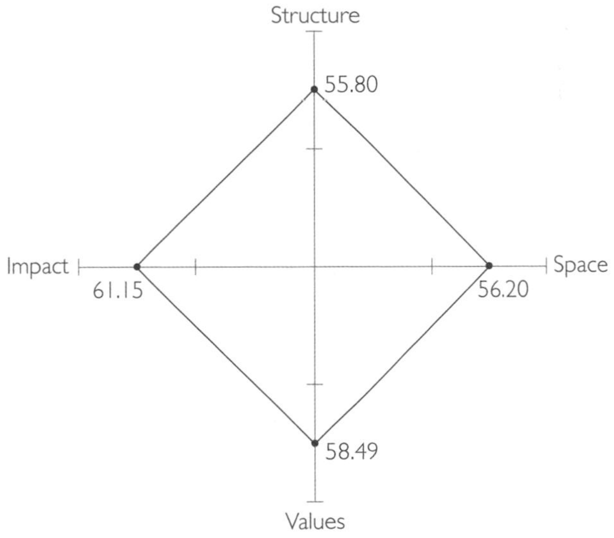

Values

Civil society in Wales was seen as active in expressing, practising and promoting positive values. According to respondents, civil society has rather good systems of financial transparency in place and promotes internal democracy in the way it selects leadership and makes decisions. However, only slightly more than 10 per cent of respondents agreed that many CSOs are promoting the sustainable use of natural resources. Likewise, civil society was not seen to mirror the cultural diversity of Welsh society – two areas of concern that need to be addressed (see Williams in this volume).

Impact

Civil society's contribution towards solving specific social, economic and political problems received the highest rating among the four dimensions. Civil society organizations were seen as able to provide their services in a way that would not be possible for the statutory or private sectors and to produce goods and services that reflect the needs and priorities of their constituents and communities. Compared with other organizations, civil society's media image and coverage was seen as rather strong. Civil society organizations were seen to contribute to a positive national identity and, most importantly, to improve the lives of the people they work with. They were also seen to be good at putting these issues on the public agenda but, notably, far less able to influence government policies in favour of their constituents. Neither was civil society seen as particularly effective at mobilizing excluded groups to take part in public life. These are two very important areas that the National Assembly and civil society should address.

Professional background

It is perhaps unsurprising to see that those working in civil society organizations perceived the values of civil society organizations and the way they structure themselves as being stronger than representatives from other institutions. In contrast, government perceived civil society organizations as having a greater space within which to operate than CSOs indicated. Similarly, those respondents who did not belong to civil society organizations or government saw civil society as being weaker in three out of the four dimensions. The different interpretations point to the need for a debate across the different sectors in society as to the role that civil society plays in Wales. However, the differences are not very large and do not call into question the general tendency of the results.

Strengths

Civil society organizations in Wales are seen to make a positive contribution to solving specific social, economic and political problems and play a role in the public policy process. Particular strengths of CSOs are seen to be their ability to:

- provide their services in a way which would not be possible for the statutory or private sectors;
- produce goods and services that reflect the needs and priorities of their constituents and communities;
- improve the lives of the people with whom they are working;
- contribute towards a positive national identity;
- engage positively with the media.

The values by which civil society organizations promote and work are regarded as relatively strong. Particular strengths of CSOs are seen to be their ability to:

- make their accounts publicly available;
- promote internal democracy through using elections to select their leadership and involving their members and stakeholders in their decision-making;

Particular strengths in the composition of civil society in Wales and the way in which it organizes itself are seen to be that it has:

- an active membership base and
- engages with politicians to express their interest in public life.

Civil society organizations are also seen to operate in a moderately enabling environment in Wales. Government and political parties in Wales are seen to support civil society organizations by:

- requesting CSOs to be involved in policy formulation by national government;
- showing recognition to people who have shown great public service in CSOs.

These are all positive findings about civil society in Wales and should be used to promote the work of civil society organizations.

Weaknesses and points for further action

The survey highlighted a number of areas that are either seen as weaknesses or that merit action to ensure that they are strengthened. Particular issues that the civil society organizations need to tackle are:

- ensuring that civil society organizations reflect the cultural diversity of Wales;
- achieving a more even distribution of CSOs across the country;
- supporting the growth of local umbrella bodies;
- promoting the sustainable use of natural resources;
- tackling conflicts between civil society organizations that prevent them from joining alliances to strengthen their work.

Civil society organizations also need to work with partners to address perceived weaknesses identified in the survey. Key issues include:

1. Working with the businesses, statutory organizations and CSOs to promote the benefits of employees' involvement with CSOs in the workplace.
2. Working with government and statutory bodies to:
   - introduce regulations that make it easier for CSOs to establish themselves;
   - ensure that government policies take greater account of the agendas that civil society organizations put forward and reflect the interests of civil society's constituents;
   - mobilize excluded groups in society to take part in public life.
3. Working with the private sector to create greater cooperation between civil society and the private sector.

Overall comments

Several people commented on the questionnaire that they were not comfortable with answering on behalf of 'civil society'. Many reasons were given for this. One respondent noted that whilst he or she had a good knowledge of their own area within civil society, they were not able to comment on other areas of civil society and so their answers were only in relation to some areas of civil society in Wales. Another commented that the questions demanded different responses according to different types of organizations within civil society. One respondent commented that she had asked several managers within the voluntary sector what a 'civil society organization' was but that none of them understood what this meant.

It is clear that the term 'civil society' is not widely understood in Wales or is not a term widely used by practitioners to describe their work. Hopefully, this project will go some way towards increasing knowledge around what civil society is in Wales and the enormous role it plays.

Impact of devolution on civil society in Wales

As the Civil Society Index in Wales acted as a snapshot of civil society, it did not give any indication of whether various aspects have improved or weakened, and it is not possible to draw any conclusions about the impact of devolution from the study. Ideally, the project should be implemented every two to four years to allow an analysis of how civil society has changed over time.

As the project was conducted post-devolution, the secondary research regularly reflected developments affecting civil society post-devolution. For example, civil society organizations are involved in the National Assembly's Business Partnership Council and Voluntary Sector Partnership Council and the establishment of the Interfaith Council for Wales by the Assembly is a clear example of where devolution has had a significant impact on the structure of civil society.

If the project is repeated, stakeholders may well want it to be adapted to include specific consideration of the impact of devolution on civil society.

A comparative perspective

The pilot implementation also took place in Pakistan, Croatia, Estonia, Romania, Belarus, Ukraine, Indonesia, Canada, Mexico,

Uruguay, Ghana, South Africa and New Zealand. An illustration of comparative Civil Society Index results are given in figure 4.2.

It should be stressed that there is limited value in simply comparing the index figures. The findings are subjective as they rely heavily on the stakeholder survey and there is a lack of benchmarks for comparison. However, it is still interesting to see how civil society stakeholders *perceive* the state of civil society in different countries:

Structure: there was not a great deal of difference between countries, but Wales appeared more at the lower end.

Space: Wales came at the top, together with other OECD countries and South Africa, which may indicate that the more democratic the state, the better the environment for civil society.

Values: Wales came in the middle, but higher than countries with problems of political, ethnic, or religious violence such as South Africa and Pakistan. Croatia scored surprisingly highly in this category given the deep divisions within Croatian society.

Impact: Wales was again in the top group with other OECD countries and South Africa, which may indicate the more democratic the state, the greater the impact of civil society.

Looking at specific strengths and weaknesses reveals the most interesting comparative information. Within 'structure', civil society in Wales appears to be more membership based than in most other pilot countries but the regional distribution is more

Figure 4.2. Comparative Civil Society Index results

	Structure	Space	Values	Impact
Wales	56	56	58	61
Canada	55	55	67	68
New Zealand	66	53	58	56
South Africa	65	56	53	60
Pakistan	52	43	50	41
Croatia	54	35	61	48

unbalanced. Wales scored the highest rating for 'space' and within this the lowest indicators related to the role of business in strengthening civil society – something reflected in other country reports. Within 'values', Wales scored higher on accountability and transparency than most other pilot countries. However, Wales has weak indicators in relation to the cultural diversity within civil society and to the role of civil society in promoting environmental sustainability. As in other countries, civil society's impact on policy-making was perceived to be low. However, its impact at least to influence the public agenda and gain access to the policy-drafting process was perceived to be higher than in most other countries.

The projects found that civil society as a term is widely used and understood by grass-roots organizations in some countries, whilst in others, such as Wales, it is an emerging concept. Respondents' concerns about their ability to comment on the whole of civil society in their country, rather than the area of civil society in which they work, was common across the pilot countries.

Limitations of the project

The project report did not provide an exhaustive analysis of civil society in Wales, but rather a snapshot. The results are based on a survey targeted at a relatively small number of selected organizations within civil society and partners with some knowledge of civil society. As the majority of the responses were from CSOs, this makes the responses from organizations interacting with civil society notably small and may not necessarily represent the views of others working with CSOs. As the responses came mainly from civil society, the survey may have yielded an overtly positive response to some questions. The steering group recognizes that a more accurate reflection of civil society in Wales could be achieved if a similar survey were to target a broader range of individuals and organizations.

Time and resource limitations meant that working groups were not established to agree a common understanding of civil society in Wales before the survey was issued. For similar reasons, but also because of a low response to invitations, no focus groups were held following the survey to put the results in context and to facilitate greater alliances between different strands within civil society. Cynefin y Werin/ Common Ground, a network of groups concerned with international issues, invited WCVA to give a presentation on the survey results and their comments fed into the final report.

Both of these factors mean that interpretation of the results must be made with caution. In many instances, the results are pointers for areas where further research or discussion might be facilitated, rather than presenting firm conclusions.

Next steps for the Civil Society Index

CIVICUS undertook an evaluation of the pilot phase of the project in order to develop a stronger project design in the next phase of implementation. The detailed evaluation found that the Index project is an innovative, contextually flexible, empowering and uniquely participatory tool for self-assessment by civil society stakeholders of the state of civil society in their countries. However, it also identified some fundamental flaws in concept and design. Much work has been done to redesign the project and develop a more accurate methodology.

A key development in the new design is in the data collection. The new methodology has less dependence on the stakeholder survey and instead introduces a range of research methods including a variety of surveys. The indicators themselves are more clearly defined with an innovative and transparent method for scoring. This provides better benchmarks to make international comparisons. The new CSI does not refer to the 'health' of civil society, but rather aims to assess the 'state' of civil society. However, as the CSI seeks to measure and compare the state of civil society, it remains normative.

CIVICUS is now working with civil society in sixty countries, including Wales, to implement the CIVICUS Civil Society Index with the new methodology.[6]

Conclusion

The key finding of the project was that civil society in Wales is perceived to be of medium strength. This in itself is significant and challenges some recent discussions around civil society in Wales that conclude that civil society is in a state of relative weakness.[7] This overall conclusion has been reached through exploring the four key dimensions of civil society – its structure, the legal, political and socio-cultural space that it occupies, the values that it represents and advocates and its impact on social and community well-being. Significant weaknesses have been revealed in each of these dimensions and it is perhaps by focusing on some of these areas that previous research has concluded that civil society in Wales is such a 'fragile plant'.[8] Civil society organizations and their partners in government and business need to work together to address these weaknesses.

It is equally important to recognize the real strengths of civil society, not only to give confidence to civil society organizations and underline the value of their work, but also to highlight to partners in government and business the important role that civil society plays in Wales and the potential benefits of increased cooperation between these areas in society.

The report did not attempt to provide an exhaustive analysis of civil society in Wales, but rather a snapshot and to act as a catalyst for further discussion and debate. It is hoped that this chapter will be another step in doing this.

The pilot Civil Society Index in Wales enabled debate around and greater understanding of the state of civil society in Wales and indeed the concept of civil society in Wales. Since the report's publication, a number of organizations have expressed an interest in the project and it has engaged some key stakeholders in dialogue around civil society in Wales. The project fed into WCVA's manifesto for the 2003 Assembly elections, *Civil Society: Civil Space* (WCVA, 2003), which highlights positive actions that the government could take to strengthen civil society. The project has also been useful in highlighting what unites the different areas of civil society and will hopefully lead to more joint action to promote common agendas. It is hoped that this can be built upon through future CSI projects in Wales, using the new methodology and with greater engagement of civil society organizations and their partners.

Acknowledgements

The pilot CIVICUS Civil Society Index for Wales was only possible with the input of the steering group in Wales including Nina Finnigan, Jan Jones, Philippa Ford, Darron Dupre, Keith Roberts, Bryan Collis and Graham Benfield, as well as the close guidance of Volkhart Finn Heinrich who manages the Civil Society Index Project in CIVICUS.

Notes

1. 'Civil society diamond for Wales', WCVA, October 2002 (available on WCVA website: *http://*www.wcva.org.uk).
2. See Volkhart Finn Heinrich & Kumi Naidoo, 'From impossibility to reality: a reflection and position paper on the CIVICUS Index on Civil Society project 1999–2001'.
3. For more information on the Diamond Tool, see Anheier, Helmut K., 2001, 'The Civil Society Diamond: a primer,' CIVICUS Occasional Paper No. 2, and Helmut Anheier and Lisa Carlson (2004), *Civil Society: Measurement and Policy Dialogue*, London: Earthscan.
4. Faith groups are formally part of the voluntary sector but only where they promote activities for public benefit that are not faith specific and so they were also included as a separate category within this project.
5. Department of Voluntary Sector Studies, University of Wales, Lampeter; Centre for Social Policy Research and Development at University of Wales, Bangor; Institute of Welsh Politics, University of Wales, Aberystwyth; National Centre for Public Policy Research, University of Wales Swansea; School of Social Sciences, Cardiff University; Centre for Civil Society, University of Glamorgan.
6. For up-to-date information please see the CIVICUS website at *http://www.civicus.org.uk*.
7. For a summary of this debate see Day, Dunkerley and Thompson, 2000.
8. See Paterson and Wyn Jones, 1999.

References

Anheier, H. with Carlson, L. (2001). 'The Civil Society Diamond: a Primer', in *CIVICUS Index on Civil Society Occasional Paper Series,* Volume 1, Issue 2.

Anheier, H. with Carlson, L. (2004). *Civil Society: Measurement and Policy Dialogue*, London: Earthscan.

Day, G., Dunkerley, D. and Thompson, A. (2000). 'Evaluating the "new politics": civil society and the National Assembly for Wales', *Public Policy and Administration,* 15, 2, Summer.

Heinrich, V. and Naidoo, K. (2001). 'From impossibility to reality: a reflection and position paper on the CIVICUS Index on Civil Society project 1999–2001', in *CIVICUS Index on Civil Society Occasional Paper Series*, Volume 1, Issue 1.

Nicholl, A. (2002). *Civil Society Diamond for Wales*, Cardiff: WCVA.

Paterson, L. and Wyn Jones, R. (1999). 'Does civil society drive constitutional change?', in Bridget Taylor and Katarina Thomson (eds), *Scotland and Wales: Nations Again?*, Cardiff: University of Wales Press.
WCVA (2003). *Civil Society: Civil Space*, Cardiff: WCVA.

5. Political Culture and Civil Society in Wales

ALYS THOMAS AND GERALD TAYLOR[1]

Introduction

Political culture can be defined as the beliefs, attitudes and feelings of citizens towards their system of government and the political environment. It is a key determinant in lending systems of government legitimacy, trust and, consequently, stability. The creation of a new political institution such as the National Assembly for Wales (NAW), therefore, raises important questions about political culture. While several studies have argued for the existence of a Welsh political culture (or cultures), it overlaps with a UK context. Citizens within Wales will experience beliefs, attitudes and feelings not only with regard to the new political environment but also with regard to the old. While people are increasingly cynical about politicians, many will still assert that Westminster as 'the mother of parliaments' is superior as a legislature to its foreign counterparts, its legitimacy grounded in antiquity.

The Welsh political elite is acutely aware of the need to legitimize the Assembly in the eyes of the Welsh population and it is clear that civil society can be considered as an agent of socialization. This chapter will consider the definitions of Welsh political culture and consider the impact of civil society on post-devolution political culture.

Defining concepts

Political culture is understood as a pattern of values, expectations and attitudes to authority, society and politics which are shared by a substantial part of the country's population and make up the unwritten 'rules of the game' about political life. Academic studies of political culture have tended to focus on its importance as a guarantor of democratic stability (Almond and Verba, 1963), its significance with regard to group engagement to the extent that it determines whether interests are seen as *legitimate* or *illegitimate actors* and the willingness of people to join organized interests or the prevalence of 'association' (Putnam, 1993). Studies have also focused on *socialization*, the process through which political culture is transmitted or how the 'rules of the game' are learned. In this context debate has focused on the relative importance of the pre-existence of a strong civil society and 'civic' roots in relation to the establishment of democratic political institutions.

Political culture theory is concerned with the political behaviour of individuals and groups but assumes a national political system as its overall framework. The national definition is taken as self-evident and natural and values and attitudes are measured by the extent to which they bind the national community together. Societies characterized by polarization and lack of cross-cutting cleavages are thus considered prone to instability and disorder. Associations are considered important but only to the extent that they are defined in relations to the prior existence of the national system. Political culture theory is a 'systemic image of politics in which the behaviour of associations and actors is assessed in terms of their relationship with a formal structure of political authority' and is focused on the activities of elites (Walters, 2002).

Putnam's work on social capital theory shifted the focus from strong orientation towards the governing centre. It is less concerned with the ideological legitimacy and stability of liberal democratic regimes than the performance of democratic institutions. Putnam emphasizes political culture rather than institutional structures as drivers for collective action (Casey, 2002). Networks of association via civic and cultural organizations instil in the populace bonds of trust, cooperation and social solidarity which provide a foundation for stable democracy and, moreover, responsive and effective government. Research was carried out in selected Italian regions over a twenty-year period. There were three premises for the study:

1. Institutions shape politics 'because they shape actors' identities, power and strategies';

2. Institutions are shaped by history and 'therefore embody historical trajectories and turning points';
3. 'the practical performance of institutions is shaped by the social context in which they operate'.

Consideration of historical difference between northern and southern Italy concluded that the historic existence of 'civic roots' accounted for the relative success of regional governments in the north in comparison with the south. However, critics argue that Putnam makes politics and state institutions the *resulting expression* of a prior civil society and that *institutional design* needs to be considered as a variable alongside social capital in explaining government performance (Lowndes and Wilson, 2001).

Civil society can be seen as a 'natural' condition of human freedom. As a concept, it cannot be identified with the existence of plural institutions as a counterbalance to the state alone but must be accompanied by two factors: *civic spirit*, which binds citizens to their obligations and responsibilities, and economic prosperity (Gellner, 1991). Historical examples suggest that 'it is not a high level of associationism but the virtue of civility, responsible citizenship, and strong political institutions that are the measure of a well ordered democratic civil society'. Thus civil society and democracy overlap in that 'democracy presupposes the existence of civil society and civic culture which precede politics in its institutionalised aspect' (Pietrzyk, 2003: 40–1).

'Civil' and 'civic' societies

Paterson and Jones noted that 'in recent times the concept "civil society", along with its apparent extension "civic society" has played a prominent role in political discourse not only in Scotland and Wales, but more generally' (1999: 169). The relationship between political culture and civil society in Wales raises the question of civil society in the wider sense of the relationships between associations and the state, but also the more specific notion of 'civic society' or 'civic' identity which has a more overt political significance in defining attitudes and dictating relationships to political institutions. As seen above, Gellner (1991) sees 'civic spirit' as a separate but related precondition of a stable democratic society.

A crucial difference between Wales and Scotland, with regard to the devolution issue, is the strength of 'civic society' in Scotland

and the relative weakness of such a thing in Wales given its long-standing historical entanglement with England (Patterson and Wyn Jones, 1999: 173). Harvie (1977) identified the institutions of civic society in Scotland as the Kirk, law, local government and education, bolstered by a Scottish press and through which national consciousness was channelled (see also Lindsay, chapter 15 in this volume). Implicit in Harvie's 'civil society' in Scotland and Putnam's 'civic community' in Italy is the behaviour of national and regional elites. Furthermore, the presence of a nationalist dynamic can add complexity to the understanding of these concepts. Economic, cultural and political elites exist, each of which can be anticipated to have different relationships with nationalism and with the state. Where there is a discernible nationalist presence the political elite might be fragmented, the cultural elite strong and the economic elite the least 'nationalist' (Kellas, 1991). In terms of 'civic community' Harvie (1993) stresses the importance of the economic elite as the 'organic intelligentsia of capitalism', in that it must remain physically rooted in the region, whereas cultural elites can exist in exile.

The issue of Welsh autonomy has represented a faultline across the political landscape. The fragmented nature of Welsh society and its elites has militated against the existence of a 'civic community'. The roots of historical development in Wales were overwhelmingly rural until the nineteenth century but the Industrial Revolution transformed and fragmented society. The process of institution building in Wales from the late nineteenth century onwards, from the creation of cultural institutions such as the university to the establishing of administrative institutions in the twentieth century which could have fostered a stronger civic identity, came at a time when any cohesion in Welsh society had already disappeared. Welsh Nonconformity, dominant as it was in the nineteenth century, by its very nature was fragmented into denominations. Moreover, Edinburgh, with its ancient heritage, is accepted as a capital city whereas Cardiff is a brash newcomer viewed with suspicion by many in Wales. A key question, therefore, is the extent to which the existence of the NAW can foster a sense of civic engagement and civic spirit amongst the elites and the Welsh population at large.

Welsh political culture before devolution

The evolution of 'British' political culture has been linked with the emergence of English nationalism. It emerged at a time when Parliament was established as a component of English government, with widespread support amongst different groups within society and which saw the English people as free and equal individuals under the law, with a right to participate in politics and government (Greenfeld, 1992). However, the very fact of devolution testifies to the imperfect integration of the United Kingdom as a nation-state. Attempts to explain the 'persistence of difference' and national identity in Wales and Scotland inevitably raise the issue of political culture. Given differing experiences of the nation-building process it might be expected that attitudes, beliefs and feelings about the political system would manifest themselves differently. Moreover, in Northern Ireland there is a highly distinctive political culture shaped by a divided and conflictual society.

Attempts to define political culture in Wales have inevitably been bound up with the definition of Welsh identity which itself is bound up with the issue of language. Madgewick observed:

> It is not at all clear how far there is a Welsh political culture (one or several) and how this might relate to the British culture. The latter is no doubt powerful in Wales, and brings with it the integrating and stabilising forces of British nationalism, national experience (especially war), and symbols (the monarchy, parliament, Downing Street). But it also brings the majoritarian and centralist outlook which is insensitive to cultural cleavages and the inassimilable minority. (1978: 236)

The question of multiple political identities in Wales reflects the recent history of Wales with its concentrated industrialization and subsequent anglicization in linguistic terms and the persistence of a Welsh-speaking society focused on the rural areas. The latter, for most of the twentieth century, were dominated by a strand of Liberalism that was closely associated with an agenda related to the concerns of Nonconformist religion and a manifestation of linguistic and cultural identity. Industrial Wales became a Labour heartland, yet one which nevertheless saw itself as distinctively Welsh. In 'Welsh' Wales voting Labour was seen as an expression of Welsh identity (Balsom, 1985). However, the question of multiple identities has been used to cast Wales as an unmanageable political entity, peopled by warring factions:

> Welsh political culture is . . . shot through with Welsh cultural and national values and is thus inherently conducive to antagonism, anger and conflict, especially when there is no external threat (Madgewick, 1978: 237).

Of course, as seen above, political culture is about more than partisanship, it is also about attitudes to politics generally. Political culture in Wales may also be deemed 'bifocal' in that people's attitudes and feelings may differ according to a particular framework and there will be a crossover with the broader 'British' political culture.

Political culture in a devolved Wales

In May 2003 the second elections to the NAW were held. Turnout was 38 per cent, significantly down on the 46 per cent in the first elections in 1999. This raises concerns for a new institution seeking to embed itself and an emergent political system. Putnam identified new institutionalists as being agreed on two points: that institutions shape politics 'because they shape actors' identities, power and strategies'; and that institutions are shaped by history and 'therefore embody historical trajectories and turning points'. He added a third: 'the practical performance of institutions is shaped by the social context in which they operate' (1993: 7–8).

An institution shaped by history

The devolution settlements in Wales and Scotland and Northern Ireland differ for historic reasons. Wales has a form of executive devolution where primary legislative powers remain in Westminster. The proposals received a narrow endorsement in the 1997 referendum, causing Welsh devolution to continue to be contested and its legitimacy questioned by some actors. A sensitivity to this informed the architects of devolution and the word 'inclusivity' became an emblematic word in both the design and the process of designing the Assembly.

The Government of Wales Act (1998) erected the 'external architecture' of the National Assembly which reflected a new institutional and political ethos. Cross-party representation was built into the Act. The presiding officer and deputy presiding officer must be from different parties, there is party balance on subject committees and regional committees, specifically for north Wales, reflecting concerns about geographical inclusivity. The Act flagged up some of the driving values of inclusivity, by requiring the Assembly to observe and monitor equal opportunities in the context of its functions and in having an equal basis for the conduct of business in Welsh or English. The 'golden threads' – with local government, the voluntary sector and business – carried forward the notions of openness and inclusivity but could also be seen as adding value. Furthermore, explicit references to openness and integrity signalled a commitment to basing the new institution on the post-Nolan values.

The Welsh Assembly, therefore, was shaped by historic concerns about geographic, linguistic and cultural divisions in Welsh society and politics. However, the question remains to what extent institutional design of this nature can have a wider impact on political culture.

Policy actors

So, to what extent has the NAW shaped actors' identities, power and strategies? Perhaps the first thing to note is that the Assembly itself created new policy actors, specifically sixty new professional politicians situated in Cardiff Bay who had to find their feet in the context of existing political institutions and political power both within local government and amongst Welsh MPs. In addition the selection of Assembly members was self-consciously different, seeking to create a new 'meritocracy' following the political priorities of the Westminster-based leadership of the Labour government and Labour Party (Laffin et al., 2004: 59–60).

The face of the first National Assembly reflected a break with traditional Welsh political representation. In the first term twenty-four of the sixty members were women and following the 2003 election the Assembly is exactly gender balanced. Although the twinning process which was used to boost female representation caused internal difficulties for Labour (Edwards and Chapman, 2000), there is no doubt that it achieved its objective and provided the first minister with the raw material to promote women into the Assembly Cabinet. Furthermore, as a new institution, there was no ready-made male-dominated hierarchy with its 'favoured sons' (although those who had been MPs assumed a mantle of seniority).

However, the 2005 general election provided a dramatic twist and challenge to this erosion of Labour Party localism and 'favoured sons'. Perhaps bolstered by their achievements in the National Assembly and the selection in some safe Labour seats, such as the Rhondda and Ogmore, of Labour parliamentary candidates who certainly did not fit the traditional mould of local activists with important mentors within the local or regional party, Labour decided to push ahead with an attempt to increase the selection of women candidates and, thus, the proportion of Labour women MPs in Wales, at the 2005 general election. Whilst this was accepted by most constituencies, it was dramatically challenged in one, Blaenau Gwent. Here the sitting Labour Assembly member, Peter Law, a candidate with a strong local background, decided to stand as an independent candidate against Labour's selected candidate for Blaenau Gwent, NEC member Maggie Jones, who had been selected from an all-woman shortlist in line with UK party policy. Law provides the appearance of a classic 'favoured son' candidate, and in overturning a Labour majority of 19,000 brings into question the extent to which the Assembly has established a new political culture within the Labour Party, based on merit and UK party interests, or whether the political culture of localism is being re-established. At present the full ramifications of Law's victory, not only in denying Labour one of its safest parliamentary seats, but also in eroding Labour's position within the National Assembly, are unclear and its effects on Welsh political culture are yet to be established.

In the Assembly business style has aspired to the consensual and tended towards informality. These can be double-edged swords. Consensual working was supposed to represent a move away from Westminster adversarialism but, as many commentators have pointed out, consensus can be rather dull as a spectacle. The main piece of high drama of the first term was the motion of no confidence in Alun Michael and his pre-emptive resignation which was a highly partisan affair.

However, aside from presentational matters, critics argue that the limited nature of Assembly powers necessarily makes the conduct of business dull. The Assembly is unlikely to witness a debate on the momentous scale of, for example, the Commons debate on the Iraq war. On the other hand, such occasions are not frequent and much House of Commons business is conducted in a sparsely attended chamber. Moreover, much of the real work of Parliament and the Assembly takes place in their respective committees. In the case of the Assembly the subject committees have formed a crucial nexus with other policy actors in Wales and it is in this interface that some useful observations can be made regarding a changing political culture based on early research projects.

The replacement of a secretary of state and two ministers with a Cabinet of nine and sixty members interested in scrutinizing, influencing and debating policy has been felt strongly by policy actors and organizations including local government, the voluntary sector and business which all have formal partnerships with the Assembly. The partnership between local government and the Assembly is a statutory Partnership Council that provides a 'necessary symbolism' to the conduct of Assembly–local government relations. However, the reality of partnership exists in day-to-day contacts between Assembly officials and local authorities, internal party relationships between elected members at both levels, professional associations, assorted working groups and local authorities' exploitation of multiple channels of access into the Assembly (Laffin et al., 2002; Thomas, 2002).

With regard to the voluntary sector, a voluntary sector scheme is required by the Government of Wales Act and a non-statutory Partnership Council has been set up. Early research indicated that 'the creation of a National Assembly for Wales has already altered the relationship between the voluntary sector and government in Wales' (Dicks et al., 2001: 122). Voluntary organizations were well organized and prompt in gearing themselves up for devolution, although concerns were expressed that the formalized dialogue would be dominated by larger organizations and those bodies without capacity and resources would lose out. One view is that the Communities First policy succeeded in focusing on the centrality of community in Welsh society to the extent that: 'That traditional way of life may be based on a golden age, but nonetheless it has mobilised a process of policy development and provided a consensus that would be hard to replicate in any other policy area' (Adamson and Johnson, 2003: 161).

However, of the three 'golden threads', the partnership with business has been the most difficult. Morgan and Rees observed, in the case of the proposals for post-16 education, 'that the political influences on the policy-making process were so significant emphasizes the greater openness of the new system of governance in Wales; quite simply, things could not have happened as they have done under the Welsh Office regime of administrative devolution'. Furthermore, this was an environment for which the business community was unprepared, bringing with them 'a historical baggage which reflects their particular place in the Welsh social structure and in relation to political processes' (2001: 162–3).

More broadly, Morgan and Rees argued that participants in the new system of governance continued to occupy 'assumptive worlds' reflecting the priorities of the old Welsh Office system of administrative devolution (2001: 166–7) The impact of the change was summed up by a political adviser:

> The Assembly was a very rapid learning curve for the civil servants. The Welsh Office was very sheltered from politics – particularly with ministers who weren't from Welsh constituencies – and there was a sudden exposure to a political hothouse. In Whitehall you'd get back-benchers from your own party coming to lobby and the ministers would then pressure the civil servants, whereas in Wales it didn't arise because there weren't any Tory backbenchers. (Quoted in Laffin and Thomas, 2001)

However, there is evidence that the civil servants are adapting to the new environment not least because, as Laffin observed, 'the new politics of the Assembly Administration are more immediate than those of central government' (2002: 38). The work of subject committees, in particular, has robbed civil servants of their anonymity and the unusual 'geography' of the committee sessions sees them seated around the table with the politicians.

Early evidence, therefore, points to a clear change in the conduct of government in Wales in the sense that it is more open and more politicized, thereby requiring different policy actors to adapt culturally. Some appear to be dealing with this better than others. However, these policy actors are people directly engaged with the process and often in contact with the Assembly on a daily basis. The question still remains to what extent the new political environment is impacting of the attitudes, feelings and beliefs of the wider Welsh population.

Civic participation

The most basic form of political participation is voting. Recent UK general elections have seen a significant dip in turnout (71.5 per cent in 1997, 59.4 per cent in 2001, 61.3 per cent in 2005), and this fall has been even more marked in Wales (Taylor, 2004: 116). In local government and European elections turnout has traditionally been low with just 24 per cent turning out for the latter in 1999. Against this backdrop Wales has consistently recorded higher electoral turnout than England (as does Scotland) at all levels. In the 2001 election Welsh turnout was 61.6 per cent, but it only improved to 62.4 per cent in 2005. Turnout in the devolution referendum turnout was just 51.3 per cent and the first Assembly elections saw a turnout of just 46 per cent which fell to 38 per cent in 2003. This is a cause of concern to the political elite as for a new institution low turnout implies that the Assembly is seen as irrelevant and lacking political legitimacy.

To explain what low turnout means in the case of the NAW and what it reveals about Welsh political culture it needs to be recalled that political culture is about people's attitudes, not necessarily what they do. One view is that the referendum and Assembly elections are 'second order' elections in which turnout is affected by how much is considered to be at stake.

Jones and Trystan surveyed people on reasons for not voting in the first Assembly elections in 1999 and found that hostility to devolution accounted for about 8 per cent of non-voters. Most explanations were practical, involving absence or work or just apathy. However, they observed 'that voters are apparently more willing to make the effort to overcome such practical barriers in the context of UK general elections' (2001: 29–30). The Electoral Commission report on public opinion research of the 2003 Assembly election found:

> Interest in politics shows little evidence of a decline over recent years, even while turnout has dropped in all elections. There is also little evidence that the rise in electoral abstention reflects substantial public antipathy to the devolved institution. Public support for devolution in Wales has grown since 1999, and relatively few voters believe that devolution has made the governance of Wales or the provision of public services worse. Furthermore, there is also some evidence in our findings that significant numbers of people may be more inclined to vote if the process of voting were made easier and they could be persuaded that the elections were more likely to make a difference to their lives.

> Nonetheless, this optimism must not be taken too far: a significant number of people indicate an unwillingness to vote in almost all circumstances. (Electoral Commission, 2003: 8)

Trust and legitimacy

The extent to which the Assembly is *trusted* as a political institution and the extent to which it is seen as *legitimate* are of crucial importance in establishing its authority. There is a difference between social trust, where people are inclined to trust others in the community, and political trust which is an explicit trust of political institutions and government. However, there are some unique factors in the Welsh settlement which can be said to militate against trust.

An important element of distrust is geographic. Despite the design of the institution it is still widely perceived as south-Wales dominated, especially in the north. Before the 2003 Assembly election this perception was even stronger, with no north Wales AM in the Cabinet. People in north-east Wales in particular stress a greater closeness and integration with north-west England. Numerous commentators have pointed out that this is exacerbated by the fact that many people watch television news from north-west England. In the 2003 Assembly election, the Electoral Commission found that:

> Only one person in four felt that newspapers gave enough coverage to the election while a plurality (41%) said that there was insufficient information. Fluent Welsh-speakers, the youngest respondents and those living in the North were most likely to claim under-coverage by newspapers. (Electoral Commission, 2003: 14)

Supporters of a Welsh Parliament argue that the Assembly's lack of powers means that it is seen as trivial and lacking competence and legitimacy. This can be countered by evidence that the Welsh Assembly Government has succeeded in carving out distinct Welsh policies using the powers it has, for example, in education. However, the nature of settlement clouds transparency and clear lines of accountability. For example, it is only in the last two years that a procedure for the scrutiny of primary legislation involving the Assembly and Welsh MPs has been put in place for Wales-only bills. Moreover, some MPs feel that England-and-Wales legislation remains under-scrutinized from a Welsh point of view (Laffin, Thomas and Thomas, 2003: 25). This is exacerbated by the type and location of the medium from which people receive their information. Head teachers, for example, found themselves being asked why their schools were not receiving cash straight from the Treasury like their English colleagues across the border. This was because the Welsh Assembly Government takes a different approach to its funding arrangements but all people were hearing were reports relating to policy in England. This is not a 'bifocal' political culture but a culture where the focus on one polity is absent altogether and this remains a significant challenge for those who wish to engage the electorate with the Assembly and a Welsh political context. The Electoral Commission report on the 2003 election revealed that only a little over a third of survey respondents claimed to 'know a great deal or a fair amount' about the work of the Assembly (Electoral Commission, 2003: 17).

Another problem remains the *contested* nature of the settlement. The *petit oui* of 1997 led to the view that devolution is not the 'settled will' of the Welsh electorate. It is here that gaps open up between political elites, or more correctly policy actors, who are engaged on the 'business end' of the new institution, and the wider population who are concerned with *outcomes* of the National Assembly's work, for example, with the standards of the services they receive, but are less interested in the *process*. Those engaged with policy formulation and delivery in different sectors understand that devolution has arrived and that it is necessary to work with the new system to achieve desired objectives. Naturally, the new reality takes longer to filter through to the wider populace, which is why policies such as free bus travel for pensioners and Assembly Learning Grants for students were cited as key achievements of the first term as they represent direct benefits to sectors of the electorate for which the 'Assembly' can be credited (although in fact it was the ruling administration which formulated these policies).

However, while 'good news stories' might be used to sell a positive view of devolution generally this presents a problem when people are *complaining* about the actions of the 'Assembly' when they mean the ruling administration. Opposition parties do not want to be held responsible for growing hospital waiting lists. The branding of the executive as the 'Welsh Assembly Government' with a distinct logo in 2002 was aimed at this problem. A measure of a shift in political culture will be when people routinely talk of 'the Assembly' and the 'Assembly Government' as they do with Parliament and the government.

Better governance for Wales

The Assembly's reaction to some of these criticisms was the creation of the Richard Commission which was to examine the scope of the Assembly's powers and the election of Assembly members (National Assembly for Wales, 2004). The Richard Commission led first to a Labour Party policy document (Welsh Labour Party, 2004), and then to the publication of a White Paper *Better Governance for Wales* following the 2005 General Election. This White Paper focuses on three issues: following the Richard Commission there are proposals on improved legislative powers and changes to the electoral system for the National Assembly, and following the rebranding of the Welsh Assembly Government there are proposals formally to separate the executive and legislative branches of the Assembly (Cm. 6582). Whilst increased legislative powers might be seen as an endorsement of the Assembly's legitimacy the White Paper stops well short of the full legislative powers: proposing 'maximum discretion' within the Assembly's secondary powers in future legislation; creating a new procedure which, on the request of the Assembly, would allow the government of the day to introduce Orders in Council to provide powers to the Assembly to modify legislation or make new provision in specific areas; and finally, in the long term, giving the Assembly 'general powers to make primary legislation in those areas where functions have already been devolved' (Cm. 6582: 12). The tentative nature of the proposals is illustrated in the tenor of the Report's proposals: 'We are therefore proposing to give the Assembly, gradually over a number of years, enhanced legislative powers in defined policy areas where it already has executive functions.' (Cm. 6582: 12)

The limitations of these proposals were also explored in evidence to the Assembly's committee on the *Better Governance for Wales* White Paper (National Assembly for Wales, 2005). With respect to the electoral system the White Paper seeks to defend the relationship between elected members and their constituencies by preventing those who have failed to win a constituency seat from standing successfully in the regional lists under their party banners. Interestingly, no connection is made between the party control over the names on the regional lists put forward for the election and any erosion of accountability to constituencies and their voters, nor is the role of list members addressed. Instead the problem is seen as one of Assembly member legitimacy rather than of democratic accountability. Finally, it is proposed that the corporate nature of the Assembly is ended, giving statutory emphasis to the separation of the Welsh Assembly Government mentioned above. Once again this is seen in terms of legitimacy and is, perhaps ironically, equated to the reforms of local government which have created executives in local authorities (Cm. 6582: 9ff). The focus on the perceived lack of trust, accountability and legitimacy of the Assembly was also a major focus, from across the political spectrum, in the subsequent Commons debate on the White Paper (HC Deb 2005a, see also HC Deb 2005 b). On the surface this may be seen as confirmation of the Assembly's failing to inspire trust and command authority within Welsh civil society, but it can also be read as an attempt by MPs, concerned about the erosion of their lack of authority and legitimacy by the arrival of the Assembly, to reassert their dominant position. Again it is too early to provide any definitive analysis of such events in the fledgling life of the Assembly.

Conclusion

Any discussion of political culture in post-devolution Wales must be underpinned by caveats. Firstly, that cultural change is a slow process and six years is too short a period in which to make definitive assertions about a transformed political culture. Secondly, the Assembly has come into being when there is a widespread disengagement with politics and politicians, not just in the UK but across many democratic systems. However, it is valid to ask whether the presence of the Assembly has produced any evidence of a burgeoning 'civic spirit' or positive engagement with the new political institution.

As stated in the introduction, the Welsh political elite is profoundly aware of the need to engage with the Welsh public in order to come to be seen as legitimate. Indeed, the Assembly is engaged with a very direct project of political socialization (for example, subsidizing school children's visits to its building and visitors' centre in Cardiff Bay). It also has a 'Location Strategy' which is relocating some functions in offices around Wales. The regional committees have also been an attempt to bring the proceedings of the Assembly to other areas of Wales. However, political socialization is more than a top-down process. It is transmitted through family, peer groups and the workplace. The media also plays a key role and the fragmented character of the modern media means a diffused message. So a key challenge for the Assembly is how it communicates to the Welsh electorate what it does and how its decisions affect life in Wales and, in terms of partisan politics, that the political parties have alternative programmes for the future of Welsh government. It is perhaps here that engagement with civil society represents a vital conduit between the governed and the governing. The routine contact the Assembly establishes with the agencies of civil society should go some way to strengthening the elusive civic identity and culture which many argue Wales has lacked. What effect the formal ending of the Assembly as a corporate body might have remains to be seen.

The Electoral Commission report on the 2003 election ended on an optimistic note: 'Despite the evidence of lack of awareness of the Assembly and its activities, far more people said that it had had improved things in terms of how Wales is governed (46 per cent) than thought it had made these matters worse (11%)' (Electoral Commission, 2003: 24). Nevertheless, political culture in Wales will remain 'bifocal' even if the focus on Wales shifts. People will continue to engage with Westminster and world politics on one level and local/Welsh politics on another. However, as the *Better Governance for Wales* White Paper itself appears to exemplify, the new political landscape still lacks clarity and the new rules for political engagement are not fully understood.

Note

1. The original draft for this chapter was completed by Alys Thomas then substantially revised and updated by Gerald Taylor.

References

Adamson, D. and Johnson, E. (2003). 'Communities first', in Osmond and Jones (eds), *Birth of Welsh Democracy*.

Almond, G. and Verba, S. (1963). *The Civic Culture*, Boston: Little Brown.

Balsom, D. (1985). 'Three Wales Model', in J. Osmond (ed.), *The National Question Again*, Llandysul: Gwasg Gomer.

Chaney, P., Hall. T. and Pithouse, A. (eds) (2001). *New Governance – New Democracy? Post-Devolution Wales*, Cardiff: University of Wales Press.

Cm. 6582 (2005). *Better Governance for Wales*, Norwich: TSO.

Casey, T. (2002). 'Devolution and social capital in the British regions', *Regional and Federal Studies*, 12, 3.

Dicks, B., Hall, T. and Pithouse, A. (2001). 'The National Assembly and the voluntary sector: an equal partnership?', in Chaney et al. (eds), *New Governance – New Democracy?*.

Edwards, J. and Chapman, C. (2000). 'Women's political representation in Wales: waving or drowning?, *Contemporary Politics*, 6, 4.

Electoral Commission (2003). *National Assembly for Wales Election 2003*, Cardiff: Opinion Research Report.

Gellner, E. (1991). 'Civil society in historical context', *International Social Science Journal*, 43.

Greenfeld, L. (1992). *Nationalism: Five Roads to Modernity*, Cambridge, Mass.: Harvard University Press.

Harvie, C. (1977). *Scotland and Nationalism: Scottish Society and Politics 1707–1977*, London: George Allen & Unwin.

Harvie, C. (1993). *Regional Government in Europe*, London: Routledge.

HC Deb (2005a) 435, cols 263–77.

HC Deb (2005b)435, cols 781–3 and 788–9.

Jones, J. B. and Osmond, J. (eds) (2002). *Building a Civic Culture: Institutional Change, Policy Development and Politics Dynamics in the National Assembly for Wales*, Cardiff: Wales Governance Centre and Institute for Welsh Affairs.

Jones, J. B. and Osmond, J. (eds) (2003). B*irth of Welsh Democracy: The First Term of the National Assembly for Wales*, Cardiff: Institute of Welsh Affairs and Wales Governance Centre.

Jones, R. W. and Trystan, D. (2001). 'Turnout, participation and legitimacy in the politics of post devolution Wales', in Chaney et al. (eds), *New Governance – New Democracy?*.

Jones, R. W. and Scully, R. (2003). 'Public engagement', in Osmond and Jones (eds), *Birth of Welsh Democracy*.

Kellas, J. (1991). *The Politics of Nationalism and Ethnicity*, Basingstoke: Macmillan.

Laffin, M. (2003). 'The engine room: the Civil Service and the National Assembly', in J. B. Jones and J. Osmond (eds), *Birth of Welsh Democracy*, Cardiff: Institute of Welsh Affairs and Wales Governance Centre.

Laffin, M. and Thomas, A. (2000). 'Designing the Welsh Assembly', *Parliamentary Affairs*, 53, 3.

Laffin, M. and Thomas, A. (2001). 'New ways of working: political-bureaucratic relationships in the National Assembly for Wales', *Public Money and Management*, 21, 2.

Laffin. M., Taylor, G. and Thomas, A. (2002). *A New Partnership: The National Assembly for Wales and Local Government*, York: Joseph Rowntree.

Laffin, M., Thomas, A. and Thomas, I. (2003). *Future Options for the Welsh Assembly: An Assessment of the Powers of the National Assembly for Wales*, Submission to the Richard Commission, Pontypridd: University of Glamorgan.

Laffin, M., Taylor, G. and Thomas, A. (2004). 'Devolution and party organization: the case of the Wales Labour Party', *Contemporary Wales*, 16.

Lowndes, V. and Wilson, D. (2001). 'Social capital and local governance: exploring the institutional design variable', *Political Studies*, 49.

Madgewick, P. (1978). 'Linguistic conflict in Wales: a problem in the design of government', in G. Williams (ed.), *Social and Cultural Change*, London: Routledge and Kegan Paul.

Morgan, R. and Rees, G. (2001). 'Learning by doing: devolution and the governance of economic development in Wales', in Chaney et al. (eds), *New Governance – New Democracy?*.

National Assembly for Wales (2004). *The Report of the Richard Commission*, Cardiff: National Assembly for Wales.

National Assembly for Wales (2005), *Record of Proceedings*, Cardiff: National Assembly for Wales. Available at *http://www.wales.gov.uk/keypubrecordproceedings/content/bgw-e.htm*.

Osmond, J. (ed.) (1985). *The National Question Again: Welsh Political Identity in the 1980s*, Llandysul: Gwasg Gomer.

Paterson, L. and Jones, R. W. (1999). 'Does civil society drive constitutional change?', in K. Taylor and B. Thomson (eds), *Scotland and Wales: Nations Again?*, Cardiff: University of Wales Press.

Pietrzyk, D. (2003). 'Democracy or civil society?', *Politics*, 23, 1.

Putnam, R. (1993). *Making Democracy Work: Civic Traditions in Modern Italy*, Princeton, NJ: Princeton University Press.

Taylor, G. (2004). 'Disaster? Whose disaster? The National Assembly election 2003', *Contemporary Wales*, 17.

Taylor, K. and Thomson, B. (eds) (1999). *Scotland and Wales: Nations Again?*, Cardiff: University of Wales Press.

Thomas, A. (2002). 'Realising partnership: relations between the Assembly and local government', in Jones and Osmond (eds), *Birth of Welsh Democracy*.

Walters, W. (2002). 'Social capital and political sociology: re-imagining politics?', *Sociology*, 36, 2.

Welsh Labour Party (2004). *Better Governance for Wales*, Cardiff: Welsh Labour Party.

Williams, G. (ed.) (1978). *Social and Cultural Change in Contemporary Wales,* London: Routlege & Kegan Paul.

IV

6. Infiltration or Incorporation? The Voluntary Sector and Civil Society in Post-devolution Wales

MARK DRAKEFORD

Much of this volume has been concerned to explore the potential usefulness, as well as the limitations, of the concept of 'civil society' as a way of understanding some basic relationships in a complex, post-devolution society such as Wales. This chapter concentrates upon one fundamental dimension of that relationship: the development of social policy and civil society since 1999. It aims to explore four main themes: the formation of the National Assembly and the institutional framework of its relationship with the voluntary sector; the state of the Welsh voluntary sector; social policy-making and the Welsh Assembly Government; and, finally, the relationship between the sector and social policy-making.

As with most contributions to this volume, it is as well to begin with some clarification of terms. Apparently straightforward at first glance, definitions of 'civil society' vary between contexts and contenders (see, for example, Morris, 2000; Deakin, 2000; and Anheier with Carlson, 2002, for accounts of these debates). Adamson, in chapter 14 of this volume, illustrates very directly the way in which – like its close cousin, 'community' – the term is capable of being used by commentators and policy-makers of very different ideological persuasions. This chapter, concerned as it is with that strand within civil society represented by the voluntary sector, utilizes the definition recognized by the Welsh voluntary sector itself:

> the sphere of institutions, organisations and individuals located between the family, the state and the market, in which people associate voluntarily to advance common interests. It encompasses the huge

> range of organised activity outside the public or private sectors – trade unions, professional associations, religious organisations, voluntary and community organisations. (WCVA 2003a)

Beneath this essentially descriptive account lies a view of civil society as a place apart from the conventional political arena, where individual participation and collective effort meet in pursuit of agreed goals. Even so, in reporting the results of a substantial survey of the sector (considered in more detail by Nicholl in chapter 4 of this volume), published to coincide with the manifesto published by voluntary organizations in the run-up to the National Assembly elections of 2003 – *Civil Society, Civil Space* – the authors concluded: 'confusion as to the definition of "civil society" was a regular comment in the responses to the survey and was also given as a reason for not replying to the survey at all' (WCVA, 2003a: 1).

One key to this confusion lies in the attempt to differentiate, conceptually, between 'civil society' on the one hand, and the 'voluntary sector' on the other. For the most part, this chapter is concerned with those voluntary bodies and organizations which are identifiably engaged with government. Yet, many such groups are too small to feature in such a relationship, or are concerned with activities which lie outside the remit of the state. As Deakin (2002: 2) suggests, however, 'those smaller community based groups said to operate "below the radar screen" [have a] future [which] is quite rightly seen as crucial to the continued health of civil society'. The result is, as far as this chapter is concerned, that the permeability of the relationship between the two concepts has to be accepted rather than resisted, and factored into any discussion – as the WCVA definition suggests – rather than defined out of it. Indeed, the fluidity of the relationship between government and the voluntary sector, and of relationships within the sector itself, was part of the inheritance of the National Assembly in its earliest days. An understanding of the ways in which these relationships have developed over the seven years since 1999 depends upon an awareness of some basic intellectual and ideological frameworks which were in the process of being established during the same period (see Osmond, 1998, for an account of a number of these themes). It is to these debates which this chapter now turns.

Setting up the Assembly

One of the most vaunted claims which surrounded the establishment of the National Assembly was that it would pave the way to a new and 'inclusive' form of political culture in Wales. In the gestation period which preceded the establishment of the new institution, there were pragmatic as well as principled reasons for emphasizing such an approach. Devolutionists in Wales faced the mountain of the 1979 referendum defeat. Reversing that decision demanded as united a front as possible between all parties in favour of a Welsh political institution. Yet, if the history of almost a century was to be any guide, the outcome of elections to a new Assembly would, in all likelihood, deliver a regular and reliable majority for one party – and, in modern times, the Labour Party. Securing the support of a range of other political groups, in this context, required a practical series of measures designed to ensure that the day-to-day workings of the new institution would deliver a sufficient level of involvement – or 'inclusivity' – to maintain the engagement of those who could look forward only to long periods of opposition.

A set of solutions to this central problem fashioned the central approach of the Government of Wales Act (1998), and the set of Assembly Standing Orders which were crafted from the report of the National Assembly Review Group (NARG). The National Assembly was to be elected by a form of proportional representation in which all four main political parties would be reasonably sure of a clutch of elected members. The institution itself was to be a 'body corporate', in which the Westminster fault-line between 'government' and 'legislature' would be blurred and eroded. In what supporters claimed to be the best of both models, the Assembly would include both the decision-making clarity of a Cabinet, and the policy-involvement of a series of committees drawn more from a local authority model. Within this structure, the rules of political engagement were designed to place a series of levers in the hands of those members outside any governing majority. If Labour were to enjoy the sort of sustained period in office which its electoral performance in Wales would indicate, then the checks and balances inside the new body would ensure that it could not become impervious to a wider range of views and voices. The final formula preserved an essential distinction between 'process', in which all would have a proper and protected part to play, and 'outcome' which rested with the ruling majority. Thus the demands of political participation and performance of government were to be balanced and preserved.

It is as well to remind ourselves that, amongst the range of supporters of devolution themselves, the achievement of such an arrangement was by no means uncontroversial or uncontested. The major battles were those fought within the Labour Party. Other chapters in this volume (see Taylor and Thomas and Lindsey) set out in more detail the contrast between the long-standing Constitutional Convention through which Scottish devolution had been shaped and shepherded to success and the absence of such a formal cross-party mechanism in Wales. In its place, the Wales Labour Party itself established a commission, ostensibly designed to take evidence from a range of interested individuals and organizations, as a contribution to shaping party policy. In practice, the commission appears to have operated mainly as a device for securing agreement to some basic elements of the 'inclusive' agenda – particularly on proportional representation – which remained fiercely opposed by a range of fundamental interests inside the labour movement, including a depth of baffled hostility amongst party loyalists at the prospect of voluntarily making the return of a Labour majority more difficult. Whereas in Scotland proportional representation delivered a key, if defensive, advantage to Labour in consigning the SNP to perpetual opposition in a Scottish Parliament, in Wales the case for PR rested upon a more principled appeal to democratic values and the advantages of participation – even if, as argued earlier, this approach was grounded in a very practical purpose of building up the devolution coalition. For the politically partisan Labour member such arguments were very often not compelling. It remains one of the major achievements of the political management of the whole process that the final arrangement was as broadly based as it turned out.

Election aftermath

And then the voters decided to pose quite a different dilemma. The Labour Party entered the first National Assembly elections in May 1999 in a state of disarray. The precipitate fall from grace of Ron

Davies, the consequence of the first of his 'moments of madness', was followed by a bleak period in which the fabled Millbank election machine had secured victory for its favourite candidate to succeed him, only to find that this success hung like a ball and chain around Labour candidates in the elections to the Assembly itself. Plaid Cymru, by contrast, had the advantages of a leader, Dafydd Wigley, who combined personal popularity and an ability to communicate a sense of political gravitas, with the electoral windfall which was thought to be the established legacy of regionally based parties in regionally based elections (see Wyn Jones et al., 2003, for a developed account of this thesis). The Labour Party's decision to demonize Plaid Cymru – from the publication of its core attack script *The A–Z of Nationalist Madness* onwards – provided the unlooked-for bonus of a regular supply of the oxygen of publicity which elevated their rivals from minor and peripheral players to serious competitors for power.

The result thus provided for the unforeseen outcome of a minority Labour administration. Without a majority, the conditions for inclusive government might have been regarded as necessary, even to those who were not in favour of such an approach. As described by its more enthusiastic proponents, of whom Ron Davies continued to be the most prominent (see Chaney and Fevre, 2002), inclusivity appeared to prefigure a new form of political alignment, in which 'progressive' forces in all political parties would combine around specific issues to create majorities in favour of policies in tune with Welsh needs and preferences. All political parties are coalitions in themselves, sheltering within their boundaries individuals of very different views who may be bound together by beliefs of only a very general persuasion. This was certainly true of parties at the Assembly, particularly those for whom the elections provided a new point of entry into Welsh politics (as was true of the Conservative Party) or those whose unexpected success had brought into membership individuals who might not usually have been considered electable (as was the case for Plaid Cymru). Weak government was thus joined by weak party boundaries which might have been expected to add still further to the prospects of a new politics.

In practice, however, the experience of the first year of the Assembly was one which proved highly damaging, rather than enhancing, to the sort of inclusivity which had been promoted.

Without a secure majority, the distinction between 'process' and 'outcome' in the basic settlement could not hold. Minority parties not only enjoyed all the advantages which had been written into their participation in scrutiny and policy development, but now, without the agreement of at least one other party, the minority Labour administration could not secure the passage of government measures through the Assembly. The result was very far from grand coalitions on matters of high principle. The business of the Assembly depended upon a succession of daily deals, usually constructed in secret and over which parties scrambled to claim the credit.

Effect of the voluntary sector

Against this background, engagement between the Assembly as an institution and the wider world outside was inevitably fragile. Some commentators (see, for example, Loughlin, 2003) have suggested that the whole of the first Assembly term was characterized by an unsuccessful struggle to engage the interest of the wider Welsh public in the work of the institution. Others, such as Davies and Dunkerley in chapter 8 of this volume, have noted the 'top-down' nature of much contemporary policy-making, even after devolution. In such circumstances, interaction between the proxy-public of civil society and elected politicians took on a new importance. On the positive side, the key individuals within the Assembly turned out to be people with established track records of engagement with the voluntary sector. Alun Michael, the Assembly's first first minister had been responsible for designing Labour's policy towards the voluntary sector during the long years of opposition (see Plowden, 2002, for a more general discussion). Under his influence, the Government of Wales Act 1998 contained a requirement that the Assembly 'make a scheme setting out how it proposes, in the exercise of its functions, to promote the interests of relevant voluntary organisations'.

Once in office, he brought direct experience of the sector and an ideological preference for the politics of cooperation rather than competition. In an early speech as first secretary he suggested that arrangements in Wales were the culmination of 'many years in which I have been seeking ways to overcome barriers – real and perceived – between government and the voluntary sector' (NAW, 1999). New arrangements would, he said, mean that 'the voluntary sector is assured a meaningful and important role in the development of the policies of the National Assembly' (NAW, 2000).

In the run-up to the first devolved elections, the Cardiff-based think-tank, the Institute of Welsh Affairs, published an influential handbook, *The National Assembly Agenda,* which aimed to cover all the main policy and sectoral interests in which the new body would have an interest. The chapter dealing with the voluntary sector was co-written by Jane Hutt (Bryant and Hutt, 1998) who, as the new Cabinet member for Health and Social Services, took the chair of the Assembly's Voluntary Sector Partnership Council. The council comprises eleven Assembly members, reflecting the balance of political parties within the institution, the WCVA and representatives of twenty-one voluntary sector networks in Wales. It meets quarterly and provides an interface between all twenty-one voluntary sector networks in Wales and elected politicians. The Voluntary Sector Scheme, adopted by the Assembly in July 2000, and which underpins the work of the council, sets out commitments to designate a named minister to have specific responsibility for the interests of the voluntary sector, while expecting every part of the Assembly – Cabinet, committees and officials – to promote the interests of the voluntary sector in its work and decision-making. It sets out arrangements for contact between the sector and government in Wales and includes a series of aims which seek to strengthen its work by encouraging volunteering amongst all sectors of society.

Many of these themes were picked up by the minister from her earliest speeches. Speaking, for example, at the first all-Wales convention on volunteering on St David's Day 2000, she declared:

> Volunteering, doing things for others, freely and by choice, is part of good citizenship, an essential ingredient of a healthy democracy and an indispensable part of creating an inclusive and supportive society. Strong communities are those which help individuals to realise their full potential. It is therefore a key element of the Assembly's social inclusion policies. (Hutt, 2000)

All this stands in contrast to the Scottish experience where, as Burt and Taylor (2002) put it, 'crucially, the Scottish Compact does not commit the voluntary sector to a "partnership" with government

. . . it recognises that from time to time voluntary organisations may need to 'bite the hand that feeds them' – and, moreover, that it is not only acceptable, but vital in a healthy democracy that they should do so'. We return to the tension between being both agent and antagonist of government in a later section.

One final point needs to be made, in order to put the developing relationship between government and the voluntary sector into perspective in post-devolution Wales. The experience of minority administration reached its nadir in February 2000, when opposition parties combined to effect the removal from office of the first first minister, Alun Michael. His successor, Rhodri Morgan, was more convinced of the need to bring stability to the operation of the institution and, for that key purpose, entered into a 'partnership agreement' with the Liberal Democrats at the Assembly, in order to provide for secure majority government. On that basis, First Minister Morgan also embarked upon one of the most radical strands in his administration – and very much one which he himself drove to fruition – in the increasing separation between the 'governmental' and the 'parliamentary' aspects of the institution. By the end of the first four-year term, the Assembly itself had endorsed the 'greatest possible separation' between the two branches, as might be consistent with the original Government of Wales Act (1998). The term 'Welsh Assembly Government' had also gained common currency, as a shorthand way of referring to the administration, rather than the Assembly as a whole.

With the election of a majority Labour Assembly Government in May 2003, albeit one with the narrowest of working majorities, the days of 'inclusivity' were firmly at an end. From the perspective of civil and voluntary organizations the development had mixed results. On the one hand, it had the effect of devaluing some of the contacts with Assembly committees and non-ministerial Assembly members, which had been held out in early days as one of the distinguishing features of the institution. On the other hand, the clear emergence of 'government' and 'opposition' positions simplified some of the interaction between the sector and the Assembly. In terms of funding, policy-making and manifesto implementation, the government had emerged unambiguously as the dimension of the Assembly with which serious business had to be conducted. Alongside this development, as a part of the policy agreement on which the Labour/Liberal Democrat government had been created, the new administration set up the Richard Commission to review the experience of the first four years of devolution in Wales and to make recommendations for the future. The important implication of the aftermath of Richard for the relationship between civil society, the voluntary sector and government are explored in the final section of this chapter.

Civil society in Wales

The Assembly inherited a voluntary sector made up of some 23,000 organizations, involving one in three of the population (Pithouse et al., 2001). The 1999 *Voluntary Sector Almanac*, published by the Wales Council for Voluntary Action, estimated that there were some 25,000 voluntary groups in Wales. It suggested that

> over 80% of the adult population in Wales are volunteers, contributing nearly 4 hours per week of voluntary time. Of these, 1.1 million are formal volunteers, and 1.7 million are informal volunteers assisting neighbours and their communities outside of formal organizations. The value of this volunteering is estimated at £3.4 million. By 2003, the WCVA's *Almanac* estimated that the sector had grown to 30,000 voluntary organizations, 7,000 of which are registered charities, engaging some 150,000 individuals as trustees or management group members and employing almost 23,000 people. (WCVA, 2003b)

These figures are particularly impressive when set against the WCVA's own assessment of the sector some fifteen years previously when Hunt (1984) had described a weak, fragmented, poorly resourced and indifferently regarded sector.

Financially, the sector also appears to be in relatively good heart, with a growth in income of £60 million between 1998 and 2002 when annual income totalled some £430 million, excluding the £200 million raised by housing associations. Public giving remains by far the single most important income stream, contributing £210 million of that total. The National Lottery contributed £29 million to voluntary organizations in Wales in 2001. Significantly, in terms of the main concern of this chapter, the Welsh Assembly Government is also a substantial financial contributor to the sector. Analysis of the Assembly budget for

2003/4 shows five funding strands directly available for support of voluntary organizations.

Grants to Local Voluntary Services	£2,629,000
Volunteering in Wales Fund	£912,000
Millennium Volunteers Programme	£307,000
Partnership Capacity Building	£186,000
Core funding of WCVA	£656,000

Of course, such figures exclude major sources of funding which the Assembly makes available to the voluntary sector for specific purposes, such as the Carers' Grant, the unified children's fund, Cymorth and, as discussed in more detail below, the Communities First fund which, taken together, amount to substantially more than £100 million.

Policy engagement

A newly active engagement between civil society and the Assembly, at a policy level, is one of the more prominent claims made by the proponents of devolution. Some contextual understanding of the arena within which this engagement takes place is necessary and may best be gleaned from two keynote lectures which First Minister Rhodri Morgan provided in the run-up to the National Assembly elections in May 2003. The first, widely cited thereafter as the 'clear red water' lecture, was delivered in Swansea in October 2002 and set out the case for distinctiveness in the social policy-making of the Assembly Government. The second, delivered in Newport in March 2003, set out four key priority areas for any returned Labour administration.

In his Swansea speech, the first minister (Morgan, 2002) drew attention to what he called 'those ideological fault-lines in the approaches to social welfare in post-war social policy in Britain – universalism against means-testing and the pursuit of equity against pursuit of consumer choice'. Positioning the Assembly Government clearly on the side of 'a new set of citizenship rights', he argued for a 'continuing stake in social welfare services for the widest possible range of our citizens'. In doing so, he drew particular attention to what he admitted to being 'a rather grand-sounding claim to have created a *new pluralism*, in policy-making in Wales'.

That pluralism included a stronger sense of engagement between the voluntary sector and government in Wales 'than ever before', a 'new and closer engagement between policy-makers and front-line practitioners' and participation in policy-making on a scale 'that would have been quite inconceivable in the days before devolution'.

In Newport (Morgan, 2003), the four themes which Morgan outlined as priorities for any second Labour administration were tackling economic inactivity, preventing crime, creating a healthy future and building communities. The basis of all four dimensions was to be an effort to 'harness the willingness which is so apparent in such communities to bring about improvements in their own lives by providing them with the means of doing so'. The combination of collaborative approaches and individual advancement remained the cornerstone of the approach both to social policy and economic development which Morgan summarized as 'securing individual progress as a result of collective effort'.

Against this background, it is unsurprising to find that the direct engagement of voluntary organizations is to be found across a wide range of Assembly functions, of which only four brief examples can be cited here. The Objective One programme, for example, involves the sector as both contributor (through mobilization of match funding) and as beneficiary from the single most important economic programme which will operate in Wales over a seven-year period. In the health field, the new Local Health Boards, through which three-quarters of funding for the health service in Wales now flows, include two voluntary sector representatives, and two lay members, amongst those guaranteed places at board level. In a more controversial area, the special inquiry conducted by the Assembly's Environment, Transport and Planning Committee into the Nantygwiddon refuse tip was precipitated by the actions of a civil society grouping which lay outside the respectable mainstream of most Welsh voluntary effort. RANT, as its name implies, was a campaigning group with a willingness to take direct action and an impatience for some of the more established routes of engagement. The ability of the Assembly to devise and implement a novel means of connecting both with the issue and with the range of local organizations and players was a clear demonstration of its capacity to respond resourcefully and effectively in a difficult policy arena.

The Communities First initiative (discussed at greater length by Adamson in chapter 14 of this volume) is a flagship programme of the Labour-led administration which aims to provide long-term funding to some of the most disadvantaged communities in Wales in a way which is genuinely community led. The engagement of civil society in those parts of Wales where voluntary activity is low and local networks fragile poses a new range of challenges to those who regard devolution as a process in which power was not simply to be shifted from London to Cardiff, but transmitted onwards to the different communities of Wales.

The inputs into Communities First are considerable, even if measured only in financial terms. The outputs, in terms, for example, of projects generated will be carefully tracked. For civil society, however, the challenge is likely to be felt more in terms of *outcomes* – the longer-term, more deeply rooted changes in local cultures and confidences which the programme is designed to generate.

The view from inside

If these are some of the themes and prospects for civil society in a devolved Wales, then how does the sector itself view the history of the first four years of the National Assembly? A number of independent research efforts have explored this question. The discussion here draws upon research conducted for a national review of voluntary sector developments in the post-devolution era (for a fuller account see Drakeford and Green, 2002) and which involved analysis of key documents, a postal questionnaire and a number of focus group discussions. Returns and participation covered all strands represented at the National Assembly's Partnership Council and reflected the geographical spread of voluntary sector organizations within Wales. In addition, the results included observations from bodies at the largest and more formal end of the voluntary sector spectrum, as well as and some far smaller organizations.

To begin with the most positive findings, respondents were upbeat in their assessment of the sector's strengthened influence upon government policy-making and in the engagement of the sector with policy-makers. Without exception respondents expressed the view that, in the years since devolution, the voluntary sector in Wales now found itself more in tune with government policy, more engaged in the policy-making process and better placed to have an impact upon policy development.

One of the most striking features of the questionnaire lies in the sense of optimism and confidence which the sector reports about its own internal health. The balance of opinion lay firmly in favour of propositions which suggested that the sector was better and more professionally managed, more effective in delivering key policies, more cohesive in its relationships with other sector members and better at involving users in a meaningful way. The same sense of confidence extended to reported relationships with the outside world. Plowden (2002) has, elsewhere, reflected upon the tendency of voluntary sector members to display a 'certainty of the rightness of their own motives' and a secure 'belief in their own altruism'.

The questionnaire dimension of the research ended with an overall assessment of comparative optimism. Were they, respondents were asked, more or less optimistic about the future of the sector, and their own organization, now, in comparison with five years earlier? Once again, and particularly in relation to respondents' own organization, responses were very positive. Consolidating all answers, no reply reported a strong feeling of pessimism, 16 per cent reported feeling mildly pessimistic about the future, 63 per cent reported themselves as mildly optimistic and 21 per cent strongly optimistic.

Against these strongly positive views, a number of reservations and dangers were also identified. Respondents were ambivalent in relation to some dimensions of the improved sense of involvement and influence which were widely reported. It appeared almost as a quid pro quo that, in the minds of Welsh respondents, greater proximity to policy-makers and politicians brought with it additional pressures to take on more public sector duties and to substitute for, rather than complement, public services themselves.

The need to pay particular attention to the potential conflict of interest which exists for any independent sector when both carrying out work on behalf of government and attempting to remain at a critical distance from some of that same government's actions and activities was strongly in the minds of research participants. There is ample evidence of such a history in south Wales, in particular Clarke et al. (2002) and especially from the community development field. Conflicts between entrenched representative democratic voices and the participative democracy of community development has produced a series of more or less spectacular clashes in which more heat and light has often been generated. These dangers occur more widely across the boundary of engagement between civil and political society. The role of dissent remains fundamental to the contribution which the sector makes. In the mid-1990s Deakin (1996) spoke of the concern that the sector was 'at risk of being captured by the state's fiscal, regulatory and policy agenda'. The partnership model, both in the funding-for-service model and in the participation-in-policy model bring with it what Plowden (2002) describes as the inevitable enmeshment 'in the formal mechanisms and burdens of public accountability, and the informal mechanisms of political accountability'. In this whole process a series of essential qualities are put at risk – innovation, advocacy, spontaneity, risk-taking and challenge.

Quite certainly, the dangers for the sector in its closer relationship with the Assembly are well documented. Chaney et al. (2001: 216) put it in this way: 'Claiming partnership with the "voluntary sector" as a whole, the Assembly may find it all too easy in fact to cherry-pick a (relatively) small number of organizations with which to work closely.' Were that to be the case then the previous relationship between parts of the sector and the former Welsh Office – cosy and exclusive according to Kendall and Knapp (1996) – would be in danger of being recreated.

How far are such criticisms true of the sector in contemporary Wales? Quite certainly a long tradition exists in Wales in which dissent is expressed through collective campaigning in voluntary associations. Over the past thirty years the most visible examples of such opposition have tended to coalesce around issues of language and identity. The National Assembly provides a paradoxical focus for such dissent because the political goal of devolution (or independence) has been closely associated with the same linguistic and cultural ends. In that sense the dissenters of the language movement are, in large number, to be found inside rather than outside the new political institution. On the other hand, voluntary organizations in the social welfare field have generally found some degree of political co-alignment with those left-of-centre forces which have dominated Welsh local government. The relationships may be difficult and funding questions fraught, but at an ideological level voluntary sector campaigns around issues such as homelessness, poverty and health improvement are more likely to find themselves on ground shared by government in Wales than might be the case outside.

A second main strand in reservations expressed by respondents lay in a nagging anxiety about the extent to which global terms, such as voluntary sector and civil society, conceal as much as they reveal about the state of the different bodies which are encompassed within them. Plowden's (2002) summary of the imbalance within the English voluntary sector between the size and financial significance of the larger charities and the far greater number of much smaller bodies is reflected in Wales, although with the additional complexity that a number of the more substantially resourced bodies in Wales are themselves offshoots of English parent bodies.

There is, too, an inevitable tension between different elements in the sector. The Wales Council for Voluntary Action is, itself, a substantial body with, inescapably, interests of its own to protect. In some quarters the complaint can be heard that the ear of government has been captured by this, and a small number of other well-resourced bodies, to the exclusion of smaller and less well-off organizations. Reviewing the early experience of the post-1999 Assembly, Chaney et al. (2001: 217) were already warning that, while relying on the WCVA as 'a single, easily identifiable representative of the sector as a whole would make a certain amount of sense, it would not be entirely unproblematic'. The scale of that difficulty is well illustrated by Day et al. (1998) when describing the range of civic society and voluntary bodies with an interest in policy-making in Wales. The position is further complicated by the fact that the council is both a substantial recipient of Assembly funding, and a channel for dispersing further funding to the sector on the Assembly's behalf. Chaney et al. (2001) conclude their review by putting some of these tensions within the context of the 'complex and differentiated' nature of civic society and voluntary organizations in Wales. If the relationship between the Assembly and the sector is to be a genuinely iterative one, when finding a way of engaging which avoids over-reliance upon 'a voluntary sector elite, or *crachach*, enjoying a privileged relationship with government' (Chaney et al. 2001: 216) will be a continuing necessity.

Looking ahead

The election of May 2003 brought with it some important changes for the voluntary sector and its relationship with the Assembly Government. In particular, it saw the return of a single-party, Labour administration and the formation of a new portfolio, that of Social Justice within which responsibility for the voluntary sector was now located. The same section of the Government of Wales Act 1998 which requires the National Assembly to establish a Voluntary Sector Scheme also requires the Assembly to keep the scheme under review and in the year following each ordinary election to consider whether it should be remade or revised. In the autumn of 2003, in pursuance of that obligation, the new Social Justice minister, Edwina Hart, announced the establishment of an independently chaired commission to undertake the review and to report to her by the end of March 2004. The commission concluded that the scheme to date had worked well, but included a series of recommendations for its further development. In particular, it looked to ways in which funding regimes could be simplified and stabilized and at how a more level playing field might be created between larger and smaller voluntary organizations, in their interface with government.

At the same time as the Voluntary Sector Scheme was being reformed, however, larger changes were looming. The Richard Commission *Report* (Richard, 2004), referred to above, led (in a process too complex to be outlined here) to a White Paper, published by the newly returned Blair government, at the start of its third term in office. The White Paper, *Better Governance for Wales* (Wales Office, 2005), contained three key areas of reform. It proposed to make *de jure* the de facto separation between the 'parliamentary' and 'executive' arms of the Assembly; it set out ways in which the legislative powers of the Assembly could be enhanced; and it suggested ways in which anomalies in the 1999 electoral system might be reformed. For the purposes of this chapter, the first of these changes, although the least controversial in political circles, is the most important. The Bill which will follow the White Paper is likely to reform section 114 of the 1998 Government of Wales Act in a way which will make the Welsh Assembly Government, rather than the Assembly itself, responsible for making a Voluntary Sector Scheme. The obligation to have such a scheme will not be removed, but the design and delivery of it will be firmly a governmental obligation. It seems likely, at the time of writing, that the Bill will propose a less restrictive set of ground-rules for such a scheme – for example, in abolishing the obligation to review it according to the electoral cycle – while continuing the requirement to consult the sector itself, and secure the support of a majority of Assembly members, for any proposed changes. Taken together, the changes mean major developments in the National Assembly as an institution, with inevitable and consequential changes in the relationship between the voluntary sector, civil society and government. Whether this is likely to lead to greater pressure towards incorporation remains to be seen, but the new arrangements do seem likely, to least, to make such a process more transparent than under the former 'corporate' arrangement.

Conclusion

The first half of the second Assembly term has seen the relationship between the voluntary sector, as representative of civil society, and the Assembly at important new junctures. The first four years were largely successful in establishing a way of working in which the major players on both sides were able to engage together across a wide range of policy issues and to make practical progress in a series of priority areas. It can be argued that, in order to achieve development at this rate, and with such a reach, it has been inevitable that those involved have had to concentrate upon those areas in which agreement was most possible, rather than tackling more contentious territory. In the second term, the challenge has been to build upon these foundations to take in a wider range of actors, at both the political level and within the voluntary sector, as well as moving to address some more controversial questions. It may be that such a new variety of voices and issues will produce a new level of discord and dissent in the relationship between the sector and the state than has been apparent over the first four years. Put positively, however, this may be sign of a maturing relationship, in which both sides continue to draw an important dividend from the investment which both are making. What now seems clear is that, with a new Government of Wales Act pending, the foundations laid down in the first two terms will be particularly important in negotiating a refreshed relationship within the new set of circumstances in which Welsh devolution will operate from 2007 onwards.

References

Anheier, H. K. with Carlson, L. (2002). *Civil Society: Measurement and Policy Dialogue*, London: Earthscan.

Burt, E. and Taylor, J. (2002). 'Parliaments and politics: the voluntary sector in Scotland', in *Next Steps in Voluntary Action: An Analysis of Five Years of Developments in the Voluntary Sector in England, Northern Ireland, Scotland and Wales*, London: National Council for Voluntary Organisations/Centre for Civil Society, pp. 71–96.

Bryant, P. and Hutt, J. (1998). 'The voluntary sector', in J. Osmond, (ed.), *The National Assembly Agenda*, Cardiff: Institute of Welsh Affairs.

Chaney, P. and Fevre, R. (2002). 'Ron Davies and the cult of "inclusiveness": devolution and participation in Wales', *Contemporary Wales*, 14.

Chaney, P., Hall, T. and Dicks, B. (2001). 'Inclusive governance? The case of "minority" and voluntary sector groups and the National Assembly for Wales', *Contemporary Wales*, 13.

Clarke, S., Byatt, A., Hoban, M. and Powell, D. (2002). *Community Development in South Wales*, Cardiff: University of Wales Press.

Day, G., Fitton, M. and Minhinnick, M. (1998). 'Finding our voices', in J. Osmond (ed.), *The National Assembly Agenda*, Cardiff: Institute of Welsh Affairs.

Deakin, N. (1996). *Report of the Independent Commission on the Future of the Voluntary Sector in England*, London: National Council Voluntary Organisations.

Deakin, N. (2000). *'Putting Narrow-mindedness Out of Countenance': the UK Voluntary Sector in the New Millennium*, Civil Society Working Paper 4, London: Centre for Civil Society, London School of Economics.

Deakin, N. (2002). 'Five years after: a brief commentary', in *Next Steps in Voluntary Action: An Analysis of Five Years of Developments in the Voluntary Sector in England, Northern Ireland, Scotland and Wales*, London: National Council for Voluntary Organisations/Centre for Civil Society.

Drakeford, M. and Green, C. (2002). 'Wales – assemblies and action', in *Next Steps in Voluntary Action: An Analysis of Five Years of Developments in the Voluntary Sector in England, Northern Ireland, Scotland and Wales*, London: National Council for Voluntary Organisations/Centre for Civil Society.

Hunt, R. C. (1984). *The Shape of Voluntary Action in Wales*, Caerphilly: Wales Council for Voluntary Action.

Hutt, J. (2000). 'Voluntary sector at the heart of policy making', Welsh Assembly Government Press release, 00202, 1 March.

Kendall, J. and Knapp, M. (1996). *The Voluntary Sector in the UK*, Manchester: Manchester University Press.

Loughlin, J. (2003). 'Effective decentralisation: international lessons for Wales', School of European Studies, Cardiff: University of Wales, Cardiff.

Morgan, R. (2002). 'Making social policy in Wales', Third Anniversary Lecture, National Centre for Public Policy Research, Swansea: University of Wales Swansea.

Morgan, R. (2003). 'Change and the economy', Annual HSBC Lecture, Newport: University of Wales, Newport.

Morris, S. (2000). *Defining the Non-profit Sector: Some Lessons from History*, Civil Society Working Paper 3, London: Centre for Civil Society, London School of Economics.

National Assembly for Wales (NAW) (1999). Press release, 14 September.

NAW (2000). Press release, 29 January 2000.

Osmond, J. (ed.) (1998). *The National Assembly Agenda*, Cardiff: Institute of Welsh Affairs.

Pithouse, A., Butler, I. and Drakeford, M. (2001). 'Social services', in J. Osmond (ed.), *The National Assembly Agenda*, Cardiff: Institute of Welsh Affairs.

Plowden, W. (2002). 'Next steps in voluntary action', in *Next Steps in Voluntary Action: An Analysis of Five Years of Developments in the Voluntary Sector in England, Northern Ireland, Scotland and Wales*, London: National Council for Voluntary Organisations/Centre for Civil Society.

Richard, I. (2004). *Report of the Richard Commission*, Cardiff: National Assembly for Wales.

Wales Office (2005). *Better Governance for Wales*, London: HMSO.

Welsh Council for Voluntary Action (WCVA) (2003a). *Civil Society, Civil Space*, Cardiff: WCVA.

WCVA (2003b). *Wales Voluntary Sector Almanac 2003: Key Facts and Figures*, Cardiff: WCVA.

Wyn Jones, R., Scully, R. and Trystan, D. (2003). 'Explaining the "quiet earthquake": voting behaviour in the first election to the National Assembly for Wales', *Electoral Studies*, 22, 4.

Tapes 50p

7. 'A Few Hours a Week': Charity Shop Volunteering, Social Capital and Civil Society in Wales

SANDRA L. BETTS

In recent years the term civil society has experienced something of a theoretical rebirth. It has acquired a pivotal role in modern democratic theory and is seen as a foundation for current analyses of citizenship. Politicians and academics have embraced it as a prescription for the organization of society. Civil society refers to that sphere of voluntary associations and informal networks in which individuals and groups engage in activities of public consequence. Such activities are distinguished from the public activities of government because they are voluntary and from the private activities of markets because they seek common ground and public good. Civil society, often referred to as the 'third sector', is thus a mediating space between the private and public spheres where individuals and groups are free to form organizations that function independently and that can mediate between citizens and the state (Wedel, 1994). Civil society is concerned with the values of civility and morality, with compassion, trust and participation. In civil society people and communities take action and take responsibility for finding solutions to problems. The intermediate institutions of civil society such as communities, neighbourhoods, voluntary associations and churches teach the civic virtues of trust and cooperation (Etzioni, 1994; Fukuyama, 1995; Putnam, 1993), which are the source of moral and social cohesion in the globalized market society. Civil society institutions provide the 'means for people to transcend pure individual self interest in the name of the public good' (Landry and Mulgan, 1995).

The development of social capital is an integral part of civil society at both the macro and micro levels. Trust and willingness to cooperate allow people to form groups and associations which facilitate the realization of shared goals. Social capital is a resource inherent in the structure of relationships in interpersonal and organizational social networks; it refers to those stocks of social trust, norms and networks that people can draw upon to solve common problems (Putnam 1995). Putnam argues that the touchstone of social capital is the principle of generalized reciprocity. Reciprocity, a close cousin of civility, broadly refers to our sense of fair play towards a 'generalised other' (Putnam, 2000). Attention is thus directed to our treatment of people with whom we have no personal relationship. The notions of civility and reciprocity incorporate ideas which explain a trusting attitude and a willingness to do things for people we do not actually know. In this context the notion of active citizenship acquires much importance. The 'active citizen' is one 'who has embraced a form of solidary individualism that addresses the imperative of the common good' (Marquand, 1996). He or she achieves a moral commitment through involvement in the community and achieves empowerment through participation in the decision-making process (Etzioni, 1994).

The growth of interest in and the debates surrounding active citizenship, social capital and civil society have led to an increased focus on volunteering. Volunteering is seen as a major component in building social capital – that is building social relationships, trust and 'connectedness' within a community. 'If we have a vision of an inclusive society based on equality of opportunity and a participatory democracy based on active citizenship, then volunteering is crucial to our society. This needs to be actively acknowledged at all levels of government' (New Zealand Ministry of Social Development, 2003). In the United Kingdom these themes of social capital, civil society and active citizenship have been high on both national and devolved government agendas. The realization that volunteering has the potential to be a powerful force for social change and can help build social capital has produced a range of policies and initiatives designed to promote volunteering and give it a wider appeal.

The Home Office Active Communities Agenda focuses on increasing the number and diversity of people who participate in their communities and the range of opportunities open to them. The Active Communities Unit (relaunched in May 2002) has as its aim that of creating a step change in voluntary and community involvement. It is responsible for the achievement of the government's target of increasing voluntary and community sector activity, including increasing community participation by 5 per cent by 2006.

In Wales the voluntary sector is at the heart of National Assembly policy. The 1998 Government of Wales Act required the Welsh Assembly to show how in the exercise of its functions it would promote the interests of relevant voluntary organizations. The resultant Voluntary Sector Scheme involves the Voluntary Sector Partnership Council, the Wales Council for Voluntary Action (WCVA) and nineteen County Voluntary Councils. The Assembly places high value on volunteering. It is seen as fundamental to the fostering of civil society and the development of inclusivity. Through the Voluntary Sector Scheme the Welsh Assembly Government aims to 'improve access to volunteering for people from all sectors of society; make it easier for people to participate in volunteering; encourage the more effective involvement of volunteers; improve the organisation and infrastructure of volunteering and raise the status and improve the image of volunteering' (NAW 2000).

Volunteering has a central role to play in the development of civil society and in the building of both economic and social capital. Volunteering in Britain has been estimated to be valued at £12 billion per year. In Wales it is valued at £1.1 billion (WCVA, 2003). It contributes to the national economy, helps to create a stable, cohesive society and brings personal benefits to the volunteers themselves (Davis Smith, 2000). Volunteering builds social capital – the trust and 'connectedness' that strengthens the fabric of society and can serve to reconcile divided communities.

The nature and extent of volunteering

Volunteering encompasses a diverse range of activities. Most researchers would agree with Davis Smith (1998) that there are four key elements to volunteering. It is unpaid, without compulsion, done for the benefit of others or the environment, and is regular, reliable or organized. Voluntary activity may be undertaken on an informal, individual basis or more formally through a group or organization. Informal volunteering is giving unpaid help to an individual who is not a member of the volunteer's family. Formal volunteering is giving unpaid help to groups, clubs or organizations. The regularity and reliability of either form of voluntary activity will, of course, vary. Help may be given regularly and reliably on a daily, weekly, monthly or even yearly basis. Alternatively it may be given as and when required. Statistics on volunteering are used as key indicators of social capital and the strength of civil society, but the picture is far from clear. Differences in methodology and context between surveys make comparisons difficult, and consequently estimates of the extent of voluntary activity, both UK-wide and in Wales, vary considerably.[1]

The 1997 UK survey of volunteering estimated that 82 per cent of the UK adult population had been involved in some form of volunteering over the past year (48 per cent in formal volunteering and 74 per cent in informal volunteering) (Davis Smith, 1998). However, only 29 per cent were 'regular' volunteers, involved with one or more organizations on at least a monthly basis. These figures represented a slight decline in levels of volunteering from the 1991 position, but remaining volunteers were devoting more hours per week to volunteering than in 1991. Mean hours per week undertaken in formal voluntary activity had risen from 2.7 to 4.05. According to the 1997 survey volunteering in Wales was not as strong as in some other parts of the UK. In Wales, only 44 per cent of the adult population were formal volunteers compared to 48 per cent in England, 50 per cent in Scotland and 33 per cent in Northern Ireland. However, only 74 Welsh respondents were included in the survey and there was no 1991 figure for Wales available to provide a comparison.

The *Home Office Citizenship Survey* (Home Office, 2001) sampled people aged sixteen and over living in private households in England and Wales. Of these, 67 per cent had volunteered informally at least once in the past twelve months and over the same time period 39 per cent had volunteered formally at least once. On a more regular basis, 34 per cent had volunteered informally at least once a month over the past year and 26 per cent formally. No separate Welsh data is available from this survey.

In 1999 Wales Council for Voluntary Action estimated that there were '1.86 million volunteers, over 80 per cent of the adult population, contributing nearly four hours per week each of voluntary time' (WCVA, 1999: 4) This estimate was based on its own analysis of the 1997 UK survey (WCVA, 1998). However, the most recent attempt to quantify the amount and value of volunteering in Wales presents a rather different picture and the data from this research is cited in the most recent WCVA *Voluntary Sector Almanac* (2003). The 'Volunteering in Wales 2001' survey was commissioned by the Assembly in order to inform the implementation of the Active Community Strategy in Wales. Two studies of involvement in volunteering were undertaken: one of young people and the other of adults (16 years plus). With respect to adults the results suggest a much lower involvement in voluntary activity in Wales than in other parts of the UK. Only 48 per cent of the adult population (1.12 million people) had taken part in some form of volunteering (formal or informal) in the past twelve months. The researchers point out that differences in definition and in questionnaire design as well as the decision not to emphasize the difference between formal and informal volunteering may account in part for the differences between this survey and other findings. Nevertheless the research concludes that large numbers of people in Wales take no part in voluntary activity.

The 2001 survey does, however, suggest that the profile of those who do volunteer in Wales is very similar to that of volunteers in the UK as a whole. People aged 45 to 59 years are the most likely to volunteer. Of this group 55 per cent are involved in volunteering. Participation is below average among 25 to 34 year olds (41 per cent) and among those aged 74 plus (36 per cent). Nevertheless, retired people make up 24 per cent of all volunteers and 47 per cent of the retired do volunteer. Men and women are equally likely to volunteer, although men are more involved in tackling local issues and women in collecting or raising money and visiting people with special problems. Those from higher socio-economic groups are more likely to volunteer as are those who stayed in education up to and after the age of 21 and those who are in employment. Additionally, the Wales 2001 survey found that volunteering was above average in north and mid Wales (57 per cent) and below average in south-east and south-west Wales (45 per cent). Although 48 per cent of the adult population live in the south-east, only 43 per cent of volunteers reside there. Those who spoke at least some Welsh were more likely to participate in voluntary activity than other respondents.

The most common voluntary task was helping one's neighbour and/or those living nearby but nearly half (48 per cent) of all voluntary activities were undertaken as part of a group, club or organization. Where involvement was as part of an organization it was mostly with voluntary and charity groups rather than religious organizations or education bodies.

Volunteering is a wide and diverse activity. People engage with and participate in their communities through voluntary action in a variety of ways both formally and informally. Research suggests that some people are more likely than others to be volunteers and some groups are under-represented, particularly in formal volunteering, mirroring their exclusion from society in other respects. The young, the elderly, unemployed people, disabled people and those from black and minority ethnic communities are all under-represented in formal volunteering (Institute for Volunteering Research, 2003). Many of the recent and current volunteering initiatives aim to broaden the base of volunteering and make it available to all people in society. The Assembly's policy on volunteering states that volunteering 'should be available to all people in society and special measures should be taken to include those who are vulnerable to social exclusion such as those from ethnic communities, those who are disabled and those with learning difficulties' (NAW, 2000: ch. 5). In particular, the Assembly seeks to 'encourage a growth in the contribution of different age groups to ensure that voluntary activity is seen as part of active citizenship irrespective of age or other circumstances' (ch. 2). These aims are central to the development of civil society and the fostering of inclusivity. However, there is one group of volunteers who already 'buck the trend' of typical charity volunteers. The investigation of this group may provide lessons for the future expansion of the volunteering base and a better understanding of the ways in which people engage with society. The group in question are charity shop volunteers and the remainder of this chapter considers the roles of the charity shop and charity shop volunteers in civil society today.

Charity shop volunteering

The charity retail sector has grown significantly in recent years and the charity shop has developed its own particular presence on the high streets of most towns and cities. Income from shops is now an important source of charity funding. It is estimated that there are between 6,500 and 7,000 charity shops in the UK with an annual combined turnover of £400 million (*http://www.charityshops.org.uk*). Whithear (1999a) predicts that the number could reach 10,000 in the next few years. Whilst exact figures for the number of charity retail outlets in Wales are not available, contact with the major national charities revealed that most had between 17 and 25 shops operating in Wales. In addition, there are many individual shops that identify with local issues and causes. According to the WCVA, buying in a charity shop accounts for 5.9 per cent of charity income in Wales. This amounts to £14 million per year (WCVA, 1999). Recent research by the Charities Advisory Trust (2000) suggested that charity shops are the most popular fund-raising method; 94 per cent of the population think that charity shops are a good way of raising money for charity; 90 per cent believed that unwanted clothes should be given to a charity and 78 per cent had donated to a charity shop.

Charity shops are more than just retail outlets. They are supported by thousands of volunteers and can provide training and rehabilitation opportunities for those returning to work and to the socially excluded. They offer a vital service to those on low incomes, selling good quality clothing and other items at low prices. In addition they publicize the charity, providing information about it in an easily accessible way. The appeal of charity shopping is not, however, restricted to a particular group of the population. According to the report *Volunteering in Wales* (Beaufort Research, 2001), 26 per cent of the population buy goods from charity shops. Women, particularly those aged 45 years and over, are the most frequent shoppers, 33 per cent of this age group buy in charity shops (Beaufort Research, 2001).

It is the volunteer workforce that makes the charity shop unique within the retail sector. The use of volunteers confers a 'legitimacy' on the process of turning donated goods into charity funds (Whithear, 1999a). All the main charities contacted considered their volunteer workforce to be extremely important, 'the lifeblood of the organisation' and something without which they would not be able to operate. However, whilst investigation into charity volunteering more generally has been the focus of much research, specific reference to those working in charity shops is negligible (Humble,

1982; Hatch, 1978; Field and Hedges, 1984; Schleglmilch and Tynan, 1989; Matheson, 1990; Davis Smith, 1998). Little is known about the numbers of people volunteering in charity shops but estimates suggest that each shop has on average 30–40 volunteers. Across the UK as a whole this would imply approximately 210,000 to 280,000 volunteers (7,000 shops) (Corporate Intelligence, 1989; Horne and Broadbridge, 1992). There is also a relative lack of knowledge about the characteristics of people who volunteer to work in charity shops. Research undertaken by Horne and Broadbridge (1992, 1994) in Scotland and Whithear (1999a, 1999b) in Ruislip, England, suggests that the general profile of volunteers in charity shops differs from that of the typical charity volunteer identified in UK and Welsh surveys (Davis Smith, 1998; Beaufort Research, 2001). Whereas the typical charity volunteer is equally likely to be male or female, aged between 35 and 59 years, educationally well qualified, in paid employment and of high socio-economic status, the vast majority of charity shop volunteers are women, married or widowed, retired, over the age of 55 and with few, if any, educational qualifications.

The charity shop is one area of volunteer activity which does display a very pronounced gender and age bias. This raises a series of questions concerning the role and indeed the future of such volunteers in contemporary civil society. The research reported on in this chapter explores some of these issues. Questionnaires were sent to the head offices of the national charities which operate shops in Wales. Information was sought concerning the number of shops, the number and recruitment of volunteers and attitudes and policies towards volunteering. Some charities were unable to provide data specific to Wales, others gave best estimates. Research was also undertaken in charity shops in two locations in north-west Wales. Ten shops were surveyed and a total of eleven interviews were carried out with volunteers on duty at the time of visiting. In most cases the interviews were tape recorded (with the respondents' agreement), and later transcribed. Observation of the day-to-day activities of the shops was also carried out.

All of the shops visited were situated in primary high-street locations. Most trade between 9 a.m. and 5 p.m. six days a week. None closes for lunch or half day and none opens on a Sunday. All have other charity shops trading in the area which they consider to be their main competitors. Most have a paid manageress and in a minority of cases there is also a paid deputy manageress. Volunteers are organized on a shift basis. They are encouraged to volunteer for a particular shift or shifts each week which is likely to comprise of a morning or an afternoon. This results in a different group of volunteers being responsible for the operation of the shop each day. As well as traditional retailing activities, volunteers are involved in a variety of other activities within the shop. Donated goods need to be sorted, some may require repair, ironing and/or cleaning. In certain circumstances, where donors are unable to take the goods to the shops, the donated goods need to be collected from the donor's home. Other tasks involve pricing, window display and accounting.

The profile of the Welsh charity shop volunteer is similar to that identified by Horne and Broadbridge (1994) in Scotland and Whithear (1999a) in Ruislip. In this study 94 per cent of shop volunteers were female and the majority of these (70 per cent) were 60 years of age and over, with 30 per cent being over 70; 60 per cent were married or widowed, 40 per cent were Welsh-speaking, none had educational qualifications beyond school-leaving age and none were in paid employment. The majority (70 per cent) were involved in other volunteering activities as well as charity shop work. Charity shop volunteering also appears to be relatively stable and long term. Volunteers in this study had been working in their shops for between one and sixteen years. The average length of service was 6.5 years.

A more detailed picture of the charity shop volunteer workforce was gained from the series of semi-structured interviews conducted during which respondents were asked about how they got involved, why they volunteered, other voluntary activities they were engaged in and what they perceived to be the benefits of volunteering.

Among the older volunteers – those aged 60 and above (70 per cent of the sample) – there was remarkable consensus. The following two vignettes illustrate the main issues. Names have been changed to protect the identity of respondents.

> Mrs Williams is 63 years old, married and resident in north Wales. She left school at 17 and has no further educational qualifications. She is of Welsh nationality, but her first language is English. She has been a shop volunteer for nearly 7 years. She works in the shop once a week for a 4–5-hour shift. Her initial involvement was through her mother who

had also been a shop volunteer. Mrs Williams used to go with her mother on occasions to help out. The tradition is being continued because Mrs Williams's daughter is also now involved with the shop.

As well as her charity shop work, Mrs Williams also volunteers with the WRVS and with the Air Training Corps for which she is an unpaid secretary and helps out on flag days for the Air Services.

Mrs Williams believes that 'helping out' is a way of putting something back into society. Giving her time in the shop enables the charity to raise funds that may not have been possible to raise any other way. She believes that this particular charity is a 'good cause' that will benefit the local population (this was a local hospice charity shop). She says that she gets 'much pleasure from helping' as well as 'the satisfaction of knowing I have done something positive and am spending my time usefully'.

In terms of the social aspects of volunteering, Mrs Williams gets to meet many people through the shop, especially the 'regulars' who come in on certain days, or at regular times. The shop presents a 'social opportunity', particularly for elderly customers, to meet each other and pass the time. Most customers do have knowledge of this particular charity and what it is trying to do and they use the shop as a way of helping it. For those who do not know about the cause, Mrs Williams is happy and able to provide information.

Mrs Green and Mrs Evans, both now widowed, are long-standing friends who volunteer together in another charity shop in north Wales. Both are over 70, but did not wish to state their exact age! They live locally, but neither speaks Welsh. Both have been volunteers in this particular shop since it first opened 6 years previously. It was, in fact, started by Mrs Evans's daughter. Mrs Green's involvement with the shop began when she was invited to help out by an acquaintance from her local church. Mrs Evans previously volunteered in another charity shop. She has also been involved with the WI (Women's Institute) and the British Red Cross and she is currently involved in the running of a flower club in her village, for which she has been the chair and secretary.

Both ladies expressed a feeling of gratitude that they were 'relatively' fortunate in their circumstances compared to many of the people they saw coming into the shop. They noted that many of the customers were 'regulars' and suggested that the shop was seen by these as a 'refuge' where they could spend time and meet other people without being hassled, or feeling in the way. Being older ladies themselves, they felt that they understood the problems faced by many other older people and that they could offer moral as well as practical support. They felt that many customers came into the shop for reasons of boredom, loneliness and social need, and they saw themselves as providing a service that could alleviate some of these problems. In the words of Mrs Green 'sometimes you need to be a psychiatrist to work here'.

Strong religious and moral overtones were apparent in talking about their reasons for volunteering. They commented that they had been brought up in an era where you learned to appreciate what you have, and take the time to look out for others – 'there but for the grace of God' was the comment voiced.

Mrs Evans stressed the importance of being able to help others who are less fortunate than themselves, and despite her own limitations due to her disability (limited use of one arm) she was happy to be able to do all she could.

Both ladies said that volunteering was 'fun' as well as being a way of keeping occupied. They felt that volunteering was of great benefit to them in the sense that they were people who had always led busy lives and were used to working and to helping others. They needed their volunteering as an activity to keep them going – 'a reason to live', said Mrs Green. In discussing what they thought they contributed to society through their volunteering, both felt that it was their 'duty to do for others' as long as they were able to. They referred to a previous era of community spirit and social networking in which people knew each other and looked out for each other, they felt that these values should still be maintained and volunteering was their way of expressing them.

These case studies highlight a number of important themes pertaining to charity shop volunteering which were also apparent in the responses of other interviewees.

Recruitment

The most common route to involvement with charity shop volunteering was through personal contact and invitation. Nine out of the eleven interviewees were recruited in this way via friends, neighbours and relatives who were already volunteers. Whithear (1999b) refers to this as 'concentric' volunteering. In his study 78 per cent of shop volunteers were recruited in this manner. Information from charity headquarters indicated that a variety of recruitment methods were used – posters in shop windows, adverts in the local press and leaflets in carrier bags. However, all agreed that 'word of mouth' was the most effective form of volunteer recruitment. Charity shop volunteering tends therefore to be network, rather than skill based. Volunteers recruit others from within their existing networks, thus the resultant homogeneity and stability of charity shop volunteers is not surprising.

Multi-volunteering

The majority of charity shop volunteers were busy, active citizens. Eighty per cent were involved in other voluntary activities in addition to their shop work. These included other charity work as well as voluntary activity within their local communities. Mrs Evans helped run a village flower club, others were involved in 'meals on wheels', WRVS shop work, Age Concern, church groups and organizations and helping friends and neighbours who were unable to get around.

Perceptions of volunteering

As evidenced in the case studies above, interviewees saw volunteering as some sort of moral or civic duty. They spoke about the duty 'to put something back into society', 'to help others who are less fortunate', 'to give what you can' and the need to do your best and help by giving your time. Two other respondents echoed similar sentiments. One spoke of helping others being her 'aim in life' and another suggested that by volunteering she was 'doing her little bit for the country'. However, all of the volunteers recognized that the commitment they were making brought great benefits for themselves as well as for the charity. According to one volunteer: 'it helps me as well as I help them. It's both sided.' They spoke enthusiastically about the 'fun' and 'enjoyment' they had working in the shop and the new friends they had made among other volunteers and customers. Volunteering got them 'out of the house', kept them busy and gave 'a reason to live'. Many of the sentiments expressed are summed up in the words of the oldest volunteer (75 years): 'I come here and hopefully I do my best . . . I help by giving my time. It takes me out of the house . . . I enjoy it and the people are all lovely, we all get on well with each other . . . I'll stick with it while I've got my health'.

These findings reinforce those of the 1997 *National Survey of Volunteering* and the results of the Carnegie 3rd Age Programme

(Carnegie Trust, 2000). Davis Smith (1998) found that 92 per cent of the 55 plus age group saw meeting people and making friends as an important benefit of volunteering. Learning new skills was not important, but, for 75 per cent the important thing was that volunteering 'gets me out of myself'. The Carnegie programme also identified the social aspects of volunteering as highly significant. 'Asked what they would miss most when they stopped volunteering, 59 per cent identified the social aspects including contact with other volunteers, staff and service users. The social aspects were more likely to be missed than the task-related aspects or the satisfaction of feeling useful' (Carnegie Trust, 2000). Volunteering, and charity volunteering in particular, has the potential to reduce social isolation and expand social networks. The charity shop is a site of reciprocity (Putnam, 2000) and social well-being, particularly for older volunteers.

Not all the respondents in this study were 'third age citizens'; a minority were young or middle-aged. Nevertheless they shared some experiences in common with the older group of volunteers. Mrs Wilson who was in her mid-forties had a history of volunteering. The mother of a handicapped child, she had been active in the charity associated with his disability for many years and continued to contribute to their newsletter and telephone link. She came to work in the charity shop through her mother who had also been a volunteer there. Charity shop work got her 'out of the house', she enjoyed meeting different people and being able to publicize the cause of this particular charity. Miss Mason and Miss Parsons (working in different shops) did more shifts than any of the other volunteers. One worked a full week and the other four days. Both ladies had learning difficulties. It was clear that they took a great pride in their work and enjoyed it. They had made many friends through their volunteering as well as gaining skills. Both viewed it as work experience. Miss Mason who was in her twenties saw volunteering as a step towards paid work: 'I find in a way I'm working, I know it's not a wage but I am still in the work environment and so doing this while I'm looking for work is keeping me busy and the training gets me more confident in looking for that type of job.' Miss Parsons, a middle-aged volunteer, had worked in several charity shops previously. In her view other shops had 'fobbed her off' and the training schemes and placements she had been on had not been to her liking. She was, however, extremely happy in her present post. She had made a number of friends among the other volunteers, some of whom she met up with outside the shop setting. She spoke highly of the shop manager whom she viewed as her friend and mentor.

The charity shop was clearly a source of networking, help and support for both groups of volunteers, but the network extended further than just the volunteers and staff; it also included the regular customers. There was a social network of people around each charity which produced a 'club' atmosphere and a 'club' affiliation (Whithear, 1999a). Club membership includes long-serving volunteers and 'regular' customers. All of the interviewees were aware of the 'regulars'. 'You get your regulars coming in . . . socially . . . a lot of people do come in and just have a chat.' The regulars come in on certain days or at a regular time, many of them are elderly customers who treat their visit to the shop as a social opportunity. It was suggested by some respondents that these regular customers came in because of 'boredom, loneliness or social need' and that the shop was seen by some as a 'refuge'. The shop was a club house, somewhere people could go to meet with others, discuss problems and receive advice within the 'legitimate' framework of shopping and helping the charity. As Mrs Green and Mrs Evans suggested, customers could spend time without being 'hassled', or feeling in the way. This is not to imply that these 'regulars' did not purchase items from the shop, many did, but they were also able to 'purchase' social contact. The volunteers recognized this important function of the shop and saw themselves as providing a counselling and friendship service as well as providing goods for sale. They offered moral as well as practical support.

The findings of this study present a very positive picture of charity shop volunteers which accords with those of Whithear (1999a and 1999b) and Horne and Broadbridge (1994). Charity shop volunteers are a strongly motivated, dedicated and loyal group who tend to be older and female dominated. Their volunteering contributes much to them and to civil society as well as to the charity they serve. Volunteering benefits both the individual and the wider community. For people facing social exclusion in other aspects of their lives, volunteering helps them to establish new networks, gain a feeling of belonging and to find a purpose in their lives. Volunteering also has wider social benefits. By fostering notions of trust and reciprocity volunteering helps in the development of social capital (IVR, 2003a). Charity shop volunteering demonstrates both 'bridging' and 'bonding' social capital (Putnam, 2000). It has the capacity to build bridges between strangers (bridging social capital) as well as bonding or cementing links between people with some commonality. Furthermore, the charity shop provides evidence of what Putnam (2000) refers to as the 'externalities' of social capital. He notes that the stock of social connectedness stored in social capital 'can have externalities in the wider community, so that not all the cost and benefits accrue to the person making the contact' (Putnam, 2000: 20). In the case of the charity shop, externalities accrue for the beneficiaries of the charity and for the shop customers, in particular for the 'regulars' who themselves develop social capital through the operation of the shop and the work of the volunteers. The charity shop is social capital in action, civil society in microcosm. It fosters trust, shared norms and rewarding social networks. The charity shop provides an opportunity for many who might otherwise be socially excluded to build social contacts to develop social networks and thus increase social capital. The shop is a base upon which social capital and therefore an active civil society can be built.

There is, however, some cause for concern with respect to future trends in the charity shop sector. Until recently the majority of charities were entirely dependent on volunteers for the operation and management of their shops, but increasingly, as shops are being seen as important income generators, the trend is towards professionalism and managerialism. Increasingly this involves the use of paid staff. The rationale behind this is that paid staff bring in more income and so providing their costs are more than covered, the decision to employ them makes economic sense. Conclusive evidence of a correlation between more pay and more revenue is provided by the *Charity Shop Survey* (NGO Finance, 1997).

Most of the national charities contacted in the course of this study had made a policy decision to have paid shop managers and some had extended this to an assistant or deputy manager, and even to some shop assistants, although this had not yet reached Welsh shops. The use of paid staff is predicated on a desire for professionalism rather than a shortage of volunteers. According to the charities, volunteers are still an essential component of the charity shop scene, but increasingly they will work alongside paid workers. This finding suggests that the trend identified by Whithear (1999a) is continuing apace. His study of national charities operating shops in Ruislip concluded that volunteers would increasingly provide a support role and most shops would have a core staff that is paid in order to guarantee that the shop can function as a commercial unit. Nevertheless, he too found that the charities were committed to the continuing use of volunteers. 'They all predicted that their shops would continue to involve volunteers for other reasons. For instance, more than one suggested that, in marketing terms, volunteers were a unique selling point. It was also said that a lack of volunteer involvement might lead to fewer donated goods to sell and/or fewer customers willing to buy' (Whithear, 1999a: 7). These trends could have longer-term implications for the nature of charity shop volunteering, in particular for the profile of volunteers. Whithear's research (1999a) showed that paid managers many of whom are ex-retailers, are looking for greater commitment in the shape of full working shifts, as opposed to occasional hours, and for some retail experience or other skills. Shop volunteers who can offer a contribution in terms of effort or skill, or both, are likely to replace those that 'just lend a hand'. Such developments may extend the trend, noted in volunteering generally, toward 'short-term volunteering'. According to McCurley and Lynch (1998) the 'long-term' volunteer is dedicated to a cause or group, whereas the 'short-term' volunteer wants a well-defined job, is actively recruited and has a general interest in the cause, but not necessarily a deep one. As Whithear (1999b: 114) notes, 'paid managers tend to want to target their recruits; they are less interested in "warm bodies" than in individuals with talent and time'. But 'warm bodies' are, according to the evidence of this research, those which produce the social capital that is critical to building a healthy civil society. Economic rationality, the 'contract culture', increasing professionalism and the 'new managerialism' may seriously undermine the present volunteering role in charity shops and indeed the nature of the shops themselves. The social networks, the 'club' affiliation character and the 'refuge' nature of the charity shop may be under threat.

As Deakin (2001) has argued, in practice some voluntary activities overlap with other spheres, in this case, the market. This can have the effect of diluting the civil society dimensions of such activities. Whilst the present study did not find much evidence of this occurring to any great extent in north Wales, nevertheless the warning of Russell and Scott (1997) that the contract culture could squeeze out volunteers needs to be heeded. Similarly, the signals apparent in other research must be noted. Trends in volunteering in the Netherlands and the USA show a shift in volunteering from 'active membership' and 'active citizenship' to 'unpaid work' (Dekker, 2003). Such a shift poses a serious threat to the benefits of volunteering for civil society and the formation of social capital. The challenge is to find ways to combine the openness of modern volunteering with the associative and discursive qualities of traditional volunteering. The needs of the organization and the wants of the volunteers must be balanced.

A minority of shops in this study were not linked to national charities but identified with local issues and causes, for example, a local hospice. These tended not to be as affected by managerialism as national charity shops. They remained volunteer driven and volunteer managed. The sample was not large enough to identify any clear differences between types of charity shop but there were some indications that in volunteer-managed shops volunteers were generally older and longer serving, more committed to the group they work with and had a stronger 'club' affiliation (Whithear, 1999a). Further study of community volunteering by profiling and contrasting volunteers in different types of shops may throw more light on this section of the volunteer community.

Conclusion

The benefits of volunteering for civil society and for the formation of social capital are well documented. This chapter has focused on charity shop volunteers and has drawn attention to the traditional and 'associative' nature of this form of volunteering and to the social, personal and economic needs that the charity shop serves. The charity shop is far more than just a retail outlet providing goods for sale, it is a microcosm of civil society generating trust, associations and networks.

Currently, the majority of shop volunteers are older females. In the light of economic retrenchment and adverse demographic trends the propensity of a growing number of older people to be involved in volunteering represents promising opportunities. However, the influence of the market on the charity shop sector may close or restrict what are important avenues for many third-age citizens to develop social capital and contribute to civil society in Wales. Such developments could, potentially, exacerbate social exclusion among volunteers and local citizens alike. As Dekker (2003) notes, whilst modern voluntary work may be becoming more business like and functional, the challenge is to find ways to combine the openness of modern volunteering with the associative and discursive qualities of traditional volunteering if the civil society and social capital benefits of the charity shop are not to be lost.

Note

1. Some surveys do not distinguish between formal and informal volunteering. Some report on voluntary activities undertaken by respondents over the past year, others focus on more frequent activities, for example, over the past month.

References

Association of Charity Shops (2002). *Response to the Strategy Unit Report 'Private Action, Public Benefit'*, *http://www.charityshops.org.uk*.

Beaufort Research (2001). *Volunteering in Wales 2001*, report commissioned by the Welsh Assembly Government.

Carnegie Trust (2000). *A Decade of Progress and Change*, Dunfermline: Carnegie Trust.

Charities Advisory Trust (2000). *The Public Perception of Charity Shops*, London: Charities Advisory Trust.

Corporate Intelligence (1989). *Retail Research Report*, London: Corporate Intelligence Research Publications Ltd.

Davis Smith, J. (1998). *The 1997 National Survey of Volunteering*, London: National Centre for Volunteering.

Davis Smith, J. (2000). 'Volunteering and social development', *Journal of the Institute for Volunteering Research*, 3, 1.

Deakin, N. (2001). *In Search of Civil Society*. Basingstoke: Palgrave.

Dekker, P. (2003). 'On the prospects of volunteering in civil society', *Journal of the Institute of Volunteering Research*, 4, 3.

Etzioni, A. (1994). *The Spirit of Community*, New York: Touchstone.

Field, J. and Hedges, B. (1984). *A National Survey of Volunteering*, London: Social and Community Planning Research Centre.

Fukuyama, F. (1995). *Trust: The Social Virtues and the Creation of Prosperity*. New York: Free Press.

Fukuyama, F. (1999). *Social Capital and Civil Society*, available from *http://www.imf.org/external/pubs/ft/seminar/1999/reforms/fukuyama.htm*, 13.6.03.

Hatch, S. (1978). *Voluntary Work: A Report of a Survey*, Occasional Papers Series, Berkhampstead: The Volunteer Centre UK.

Home Office (2001). *Active Communities 2001 – Home Office Citizenship Survey*, London: HMSO.

Horne, S. and Broadbridge, A. (1992). *From Rags to Riches: A Classification of Charity Shops*, IRS Working Paper 9302, Stirling University.

Horne, S. and Broadbridge, A. (1994). 'The Charity Shop Volunteer in Scotland: Greatest Asset or Biggest Headache', in *Voluntas*, 5, 2.

Humble, S. (1982). *Voluntary Action in the 1990's – A Summary of the Findings of a National Survey*, Berkhampstead: The Volunteer Centre UK: SCPR.

Institute for Volunteering Research (IVR) (2003a). *Volunteering and Social Exclusion*, available from *http://www.ivr.org.uk/social exclusion/about.htm*.

Institute for Volunteering Research (2003b). *Study of Older Volunteers in 25 Organisations*, Available from *http://www.ivr.org.uk/socialexclusion/about.htm*.

Landry, C. and Mulgan, G. (1995). *The Other Invisible Hand: Remaking Charity for the 21st Century*, London: DEMOS.

Marquand, D. (1996). 'Victorian values, modern strife', *Guardian*, 28 October.

Matheson, J. (1990). *Voluntary Work – A Study Carried Out on Behalf of the Home Office as Part of the 1987 General Household Survey – OPCS Social Survey Division Series GHS*, No. 17, supplement A, London: HMSO.

McCurley, S. and Lynch, R. (1998). *Essential Volunteer Management*, Directory of Social Change.

New Zealand Ministry of Social Development (2003). *Valuing Volunteering*, available from *http:/www.dsw.govt.NZ/voluntary/summary_of_submissions/3-valuing-volunteering*, 17.6.03.

National Assembly for Wales (NAW) (2000). *Voluntary Sector Scheme*.

NGO Finance (1997). *Charity Shop Survey*, July/August.

Putnam, R. D. (1993). *Making Democracy Work: Civic Traditions in Modern Italy*, Princeton, NJ: Princeton University Press.

Putnam, R. D. (1995). 'Tuning in, tuning out: the strange disappearance of civic America', *Political Science and Politics*, Winter (December) 1995.

Putnam, R. D. (2000). *Bowling Alone: The Collapse and Revival of American Community*, New York: Simon & Schuster.

Russell, L. and Scott, D. (1997). *Very Active Citizens: The Impact of Contracts on Volunteers*, Manchester: University of Manchester.

Schleglmich, B. B. and Tynan, C. (1989). 'Who volunteers? An investigation into the characteristics of charity volunteers', *Journal of Marketing Management*, 5, 2, 133–51.

WCVA Wales Voluntary Sector Almanac (1998). *Wales Volunteering Statistics, WCVA Analysis of the 1997 Survey*, Cardiff: WCVA.

WCVA (1999). *Wales Voluntary Sector Almanac 1999*, Cardiff: WCVA.

WCVA (2003). *Wales Voluntary Sector Almanac 2003. Facts and Figures*, available from *http://www.wcva.org.uk/content/all//dsp_text.cfm?0=0&display_sitetexid=185*, 25.6.03.

Wedel, J. (1994). *US Aid to Central and Eastern Europe in East-Central Europe Economies in Transition,* Congress of the United States, Washington: US Government Printing Office.

Whithear, R. (1999a). 'Charity shop volunteers: a "no-cost" option?', *Journal of the Institute for Volunteering Research*, 1, 3.

Whithear, R. (1999b). Charity shop volunteers: a case for 'tender loving care', *International Journal of Non-profit and Voluntary Sector Marketing*, 4, 2.

Zappala, G. (2000). *'How many people volunteer in Australia and who do they do it'*, The Smith Family Research and Advocacy Briefing Paper No.4, Sydney: Smith Family.

comma
exclamation mark
question mark
semicolon
apostrophe
A Legionary's Day
History
Roman Times
Lloyds TSB
BOBATH
THREE
POUNDS
13/01/05
KINGS
SCHOOL

8. Young People, Identity and Citizenship

CATHERINE DAVIES AND DAVID DUNKERLEY

Introduction

Numerous aspects of the lives and experiences of children and young people have come to the fore in recent times both in Wales and in the UK more generally. Legislation emanating from the National Assembly for Wales (NAW), the UK Parliament and from the European Parliament has had profound effects on how we perceive young people and how they themselves have challenged accepted views of their role in society. Possibly the most influential change that has occurred results from debates over the nature of citizenship – again, in Wales, the UK and the EU – and the ensuing attempts to instill notions of citizenship into young people almost in the form of social engineering to produce 'the good citizen'. This chapter shows that much of what is being proposed and implemented is of a 'top-down' nature from the various legislative bodies and the question remains as to the extent to which such imposed measures are welcomed by their recipients – young people themselves. The data on young people presented in this chapter provide fascinating insights into the perceptions young people in Wales have of their own identities and of being active citizens in a changing world.

Recently published official statistics from the 2001 census and other national surveys suggest that in some ways life for children and young people in Wales is different from those in other parts of the UK (see figure 8.1 below). It is not the aim of the chapter to explore why it is that Wales comes out as 'the bottom of this' or the 'highest of that' – a picture that in many respects is more bleak than elsewhere in the UK. But this bleakness is being systematically addressed by a variety of measures originating from civil society organizations and the NAW itself so that Wales can pride itself on being the first to introduce innovative enquiries, new posts and imaginative action programmes all designed to improve the position of children and young people. As shown below, however, these programmes have yet to make a significant impact on young people themselves.

Young people, citizenship and politics

Within the UK there is currently considerable research focusing on all aspects of the devolution process. Both the ESRC and the Leverhulme Trust have recognized the importance of continuing to monitor and evaluate the impact of devolution by establishing research programmes on devolution. Projects within these programmes show a commitment to the changing nature of constitutional change within the UK and within that is to be found research on young people, devolution and politics.

While there may be debates being raised over citizenship there is more worrying evidence about the apathy and lack of participation in party politics among young people. Evidence suggests that young people in Britain have developed a negative attitude to the process of elections and politics over the last decade or so. Furthermore, young people tend to be more cynical and less supportive of the political process than their counterparts in the 1990s and there is some evidence that the cynicism of young people is directed at party politics rather than political issues (Electoral Commission, 2002).

A recent study by the Electoral Commission claimed that young people in Wales were 'too busy' to vote in the Assembly's elections in 2003. The Electoral Commission commissioned the survey after it was found that turnout in the under-25 age group was at a low of just 16 per cent. And only a fifth of voters in the next age group of 25- to 34-years-olds voted, while voters in these two age groups were found to be least informed about the Assembly's achievements (BBC News, 2003).

All of this has resulted in one of the most influential changes that has occurred in debates over young people in Wales and beyond – the assumption that a new kind of political generation is emerging, with young people rejecting conventional politics and engaging with other issues such as human rights and the environment.

On the whole, most of the research carried out has concluded that young people are disengaged from politics and that they feel disassociated from it. Young people have been found to be engaged with other issues such as education, leisure interests and the environment. When they think about politics they have difficulty in conceptualizing political life and the various political processes. They feel alienated from and dissatisfied with the political system. Moreover, research has been unable to ascertain clearly why it is that young people are not engaged in political activities although a consistent finding is that young people feel politicians are not interested in their opinions. According to White et al. (2000: 9) young people felt politicians were 'out of touch' with 'ordinary' people from different backgrounds and were not always aware of 'real' problems and 'real circumstances'. Furthermore, social changes have created a new social mobility for young people involving partner search, moving house and climbing the job ladder. To accommodate these changes a coalition of pressure groups, political parties and charities have launched a campaign for the lowering of the voting age to 16. According to Matthew Green MP, the Liberal Democrat youth affairs spokesperson: 'young people are passionately interested in political issues, but they feel politicians are out of touch and unresponsive to their needs' (*Guardian*, 15 January 2003).

The image of young people as dissociated from and disaffected with political life can be challenged as seen in events associated with the 2003 Iraq War. 'Schoolchildren lead the way in protests' was the *Western Mail* headline at the beginning of the war when over 300 peace protesters, most of whom were schoolchildren, staged a demonstration in Cardiff. A 17-year-old said: 'We want to make sure our voice is heard. Tony Blair is ignoring us so far, but we want to move the peace movement forward' (*Western Mail*, 20 March 2003). Another 300 schoolchildren from Powys staged a 30-minute protest. Events such as these show that there are young people currently taking part in political activities and who clearly have a political voice.

The National Centre for Social Research (NCSR) (2000) has explored in detail young people's political interests and behaviour. On the whole, evidence suggests that young people have low levels of political interest and poor opinions of politicians. One of the aims of the investigation was to explore why young people are disengaged from politics. Those interviewed were more concerned with activities other than politics. When asked about how they felt about politics their responses were largely linked to a lack of trust in politicians. Overall, the young people identified the lack of opportunities for them to engage in political life. This and their mistrust of politicians contributed to low levels of political interests. The results of the findings demonstrated a negative perception of young people and political life.

However, the findings did show that a number of young people interviewed had a high level of political interest and that as they grew older they found a greater interest in politics and, once having reached the voting age, their interest became activated.

The NCSR study found young people taking part in a range of political activities even if they do not regard them as political. They were generally disengaged from political life and yet were able to identify the core aims of the government's agenda, with issues such as education, jobs, qualifications and discrimination being highlighted. The researchers conclude that perhaps too much emphasis is focused on young people's apathy towards politics and political life and that more attention should concentrate on the role of politicians and teachers to engage and represent the benefits of young people.

The problem is that there is no generic 'young person' but rather many young people who are keen on politics and political issues and who are less apathetic and more interested in public issues and current affairs than is commonly supposed. But politicians – along with the word 'politics' – are widely seen as boring and irrelevant. The picture painted is not one of apathetic youth but of serious disengagement from the political system, particularly among economically marginalized young people who have little knowledge about or confidence in the formal democratic process. This does not make them cynics. Instead, politicians in particular might wish to think seriously about how they can make the political process more relevant to young people. Similarly, schools might use citizenship education to help develop young people's political literacy and encourage a sense of political efficacy in both the formal and informal political arenas.

Figure 8.1. Relevant facts and figures for Wales[1]

- There were 772,000 children and young people under the age of 21 years living in Wales from a total population of 2.9 million in 2001.
- There are around half a million school-aged children in Wales.
- In 2000, 10% of 16–18 year olds left school with no qualifications – the highest rate in the UK.
- Wales has the highest rate of child poverty in Britain with 1 in 3 children living in households where the mean income was below 50% of the average in 1999/2000.
- In 1999/2001 21% of primary school and 18% of secondary school pupils were entitled to free school meals.
- 2,126 children were on the Child Protection Register in Wales in 2001, most of whom were at risk of neglect.
- 3,849 children were looked after by Local Authorities in March 2000.
- In 1998, 20% of children lived in households with a lone parent.
- Wales has the highest rate of teenage pregnancy in the UK.
- 10% of baby teeth in children are decayed – double the rate for England.
- 4,000 young people under the age of 18 were homeless in Wales at some time during 2000.
- Suicide accounts for 20% of all deaths of young people with rates rising for boys and young men.
- In 1998, 40% of boys and girls in Wales said they had tried drugs.

Policy, young people and the National Assembly for Wales

The NAW holds as a core value that 'children and young people are to be treated as valued members of the community whose voices are heard and needs considered across the range of policy-making'. Furthermore, it has stated that it wants to create a Wales which 'values its children and where young people want to live, work and enjoy a high quality of life'. The core aims for children and young people stated by the NAW are to ensure that all children and young people:

- have a flying start in life and the best possible basis for their future growth and development;
- have access to a comprehensive range of education, training and learning opportunities, including acquisition of essential personal and social skills;
- enjoy the best possible physical and mental, social and emotional health, including freedom from abuse, victimization and exploitation;

- have access to play, leisure, sporting and cultural activities;
- are listened to, treated with respect, and are able to have their race and cultural identity recognized;
- have a safe home and a community that supports physical and emotional well-being;
- are not disadvantaged by child poverty.

Since its inception the NAW has made it a high priority to invest in better opportunities and services for children and young people and recognized that if children are to become active and responsible citizens and active members of civil society in Wales, they must be involved from an early age in decision-making. Local authorities, too, are increasingly investing in the development of a children's rights framework and setting up new ways of hearing from children as service-users and local citizens.

A Children's Commissioner for Wales was appointed in November 2000. The commissioner acts as an independent champion for children in Wales by influencing and representing their interests. The commissioner's plans are to consult regularly with children and young people and the overall aim is to give children and young people a voice within Wales and for their voices to be heard. Following the first recommendation of the Waterhouse Report into child abuse in Wales – *Lost in Care* – the office of the independent Children's Commissioner for Wales was established initially under the Care Standards Act 2000. Peter Clarke – formerly the director of Childline Wales – was appointed in November 2000 and has been in post since March 2001, following an inclusive recruitment and selection process that, interestingly, included candidates being interviewed by children and young people themselves. The appointment is for a seven-year non-renewable term. The NAW's policy on introducing the commissioner had all-party support in Wales.

The original functions of the office under the Care Standards Act concentrated on children receiving care:

- reviewing and monitoring arrangements for dealing with complaints, advocacy and whistleblowing;
- examining the cases of particular children where there are general implications. The commissioner can require the production of documents and attendance of witnesses and failure to comply is contempt of court;

- providing assistance and representation in the case of proceedings or disputes;
- providing advice and information;
- making reports (including an Annual Report) to the NAW;
- requiring the provision of information and disclosure of documents.

However, the Children's Commissioner for Wales Act 2001 extended the commissioner's powers and introduced new functions. Thus, the 2001 Act:

- made the principal aim of the commissioner to safeguard and promote the rights and welfare of children;
- gave the commissioner the power to consider, and make representations to the Assembly, about any matter affecting the rights or welfare of children in Wales;
- extended the commissioner's functions to a wide range of public bodies operating in Wales (including the Assembly) where they have or provide statutory functions or services relating to the functional fields devolved to the Assembly;
- conferred a new power to review the effect on children in Wales of any existing or proposed legislation of the Assembly.

These new and extended powers mean that the commissioner's role is as an independent champion for children in Wales by determining and representing their interests.

Listening to children and young people

Another significant development in Wales has been the drawing up of an overall policy for children and young people that includes provision to establish mechanisms for their participation in policy development and service planning in health, education and local government.

The NAW is firmly committed to allowing young people to participate in decision-making as can be seen in *Children and Young People: A Framework for Partnership* (2000). Two interesting developments have been the establishment of Llais Ifanc/Young Voice and Biteback. The former has been a genuine attempt to establish a dialogue with the young people of Wales and aims to establish ways in which children and young people can have a say in decision-making in Wales generally and in the work of the NAW more specifically. Biteback complements the work of Llais Ifanc/Young Voice through having a representative elected panel of young people that, *inter alia*, helped in the recruitment of the Children's Commissioner. The NAW is conscious of the need to follow certain principles if young people really are to participate in decision-making. These include accessibility (making available relevant information), inclusion (participation at all levels), results (acting upon the views and opinions of young people and providing feedback to suggestions for change) and support/training (sometimes necessary to ensure that children and young people can adequately express their views). Furthermore, the NAW has attempted to include as broad a range of young people as possible including those from black, ethnic minority and traveller communities as well as those with disabilities.

An approach has emerged in Wales looking to incorporate children's participation. The NAW has introduced a framework that promotes strategic partnerships in the twenty-two Welsh local authorities as the key planning framework for all policies that impact upon children and young people. This national policy means that many local authorities are increasingly looking to engage young people in their decision-making. Most local authorities in Wales now have local youth forums as a way to enable young people to participate in local government and health groups. Similar forums are being developed in schools, youth clubs, voluntary organizations and community councils. The plan is for these to provide representatives to a General Council with a membership of 60, so that there is representation at an all-Wales level. The General Council's aims are to promote the rights of children and young people, to inform and represent, to review participation in planning, to hold an annual 'gathering' and to represent Wales on bodies elsewhere in the UK and Europe. The overall aim of the framework is to listen to the voices of children and young people, to hear their views and to ensure that services respond to their wishes and their aspirations.

Welsh ministers have also launched a new online attempt to engage children and young people in the policy-making process. The creation of this website – 'Funky Dragon' – promotes the views of young people on topical issues. Funky Dragon comprises a council of representatives from local children and young people's forums, with council members providing Welsh representation on Britain's youth parliament. The website, designed and run by young people, provides up-to-date information on key issues as well as information on policy proposals, local government and health services in Wales.

Young people and the National Assembly for Wales

We report now on an original study that has involved interviewing over 150 16- to 18-year-olds in Cardiff and the south Wales valleys.[2] The research was qualitative in design and employed a combination of 30 focus groups with around five young people in each session.

In general, the young people interviewed were either in favour of the National Assembly or appeared to be indifferent to it. In some cases, indifference resulted from uncertainty or lack of knowledge of the Assembly and what it can and cannot do. Interestingly, there was hardly any opposition to the idea of the NAW. On the whole, it would seem that young people are aware that the National Assembly exists but do not understand what it actually does. They seemed to equate the Assembly with having no real powers but think the answer lies in devolution and looking to Scotland as an example. Views about devolution seemed at the forefront of young people's thinking about the role of the NAW and felt that it does little or nothing to help young people in Wales. A few comments from young people themselves illustrate these points:

> *Wales should not have voted for an Assembly we should have had devolution. Now we have to look at Scotland and say here is what Scotland has to say and look what Wales can have in the future.* (David, 17)

> *I want Wales to have our own Government I want to be away from England and Parliament . . . They've let the Scottish I don't see why they can't let the Welsh break away. We were only allowed an Assembly why weren't we allowed a government?* (Keith, 17)

> *To me we need devolution so Wales can sort out its own problems without going to England.* (Mark, 17)

I don't know that much about it but I don't think it does much. It is not very active, most of the power is controlled by Westminster. In the end it is just creating jobs for your friends really. I don't think it is anything to be proud of. (Bill, 16)

A lot of people or I think people my age don't understand what the Assembly is about. It does not really appeal to us in anyway. It is seen as something for the grown ups. (Tim, 17)

On the whole, then, it would seem that the young people have a range of different views and opinions about the NAW and through the various discussions about the Assembly it would seem that they are in favour of devolution for Wales. They are certainly aware of what devolution is and look to Scotland as an example.

Discussions about the NAW and the extent to which it helps young people revealed that young people felt that it does little or nothing for young people. They felt disengaged with the Assembly because (a) they thought the NAW is not interested in young people, (b) they felt politicians do nothing to help young people, (c) young people are not interested in politics because they know nothing about it and (d) young people, it was suggested, are not taken seriously.

Overall I don't think the National Assembly is appealing to young people. The Assembly needs to target young people if they are going to be the ones who vote for devolution. (Matt, 17)

Our school visited the Assembly and I just thought that's very interesting what does it do for the young people today. Many times on the news and in newspapers you find that young people are bored with nothing to do then why is the National Assembly not doing anything for them? (Helen, 16)

Politicians do not bring voting down to our level. I think they need to target young people 'cos we are the next ones to vote. I am the right age to vote and I don't know anything really about party politics. I know my parents are Labour. I have no clue really. (Jody, 18)

Politicians are not interested in young people. We are not really told about political parties. When we come to vote at 18 we don't know enough about the political life in Wales. It is mostly older people who vote. (Michael, 17)

We don't know enough about voting or well at least none of my friends do anyway. I don't think politicians target or include young people. They do not connect with young people. (Sarah, 17)

> *I think the Assembly and politics on the whole don't take young people serious anyway. So there is no surprise that young people are not interested or don't know a lot about the Assembly. It would be good to have our voices heard 'cos we are not stupid, we have something to say.* (Mark, 17)

> *If all the youngsters in Wales had to vote on the Assembly probably most of them won't have a clue. That's how we are treated . . . anyway nobody cares what the young people think.* (Keith, 17)

The above quotes really get to the heart of why young people do not participate in politics and feel disassociated and isolated. Young people feel they are not taken seriously and they are viewed as irresponsible young adults. For these young people hearing and being listened to would make a difference, they feel they have something to contribute and feel that their current participation within society is non-existent.

Citizenship and a new identity for Wales?

What young people think about the future of Wales, the extent to which a new identity has emerged within Wales and the implications for views on citizenship and civil society are all highly topical and real issues. From the study it would seem that young people understand what citizenship means but have mixed reactions about it. One of the concerns from the young people with regards to citizenship means a dissociation from one's national identity. They feel that applying for citizenship in another country means that you no longer feel an affinity to your national identity that you choose to belong somewhere else. This idea of citizenship was illustrated by the actor Anthony Hopkins in applying for American citizenship. Several young people believe that Anthony Hopkins renounced his Welsh national identity in order to become an American citizen. Conversely, for others the idea of citizenship was embraced so that applying to become a citizen of another nation does not mean a denouncement of national identity but involves becoming an active citizen of another nation. On the whole, while it would seem that young people understand what citizenship means they are sceptical about its application and especially with reference to national identity. Others have a more positive attitude towards the nature of citizenship and its role within social life.

> *I think Anthony Hopkins is critical of being Welsh and he is saying that he wants to be American. You would only apply for citizenship if you felt that you had no pride in where you were brought up so you would seek to get citizenship in another country.* (Tim, 17)

> *There is probably more to citizenship but to me I think it is also about your identity. So many people have different identities they could say they feel Welsh but was born in France just say. I think these people who are not happy with their nation may apply for citizenship elsewhere.* (Sean, 17)

> *We hear of citizenship being introduced among schools throughout the country, I am sure I read that somewhere. You take Anthony Hopkins who has applied for citizenship and I think it has been granted for him. Yes, I think people can have two identities and I have no objections to people becoming citizens of that particular country.* (Caroline, 17)

Furthermore, one of the debates in Wales is whether, through the establishment of the National Assembly, a new stronger identity has emerged. This study asked the young people to what extent they thought a new identity has emerged in Wales and what the future holds for Wales. On the whole, these young people feel no new identity has emerged since the establishment of the Assembly. They believed the NAW has made no real difference to the identities of people in Wales even though they seemed to have a strong sense of Welsh identity.

Young people interviewed generally believed that the NAW has had little or no impact upon the ways in which people think about their national identity. What is interesting are the ways in which they talk about their national identity as something to be proud of and proud of who they are. 'I am proud of who I am – to be Welsh' is a typical and much cited quotation from the young people.

Discussion

Described above is a wide range of actual and intended initiatives in Wales designed for and about young people. All of these new measures are still in their early stages so no real assessment of them can yet be made. Although a lot of work is being done with young people in Wales there is still a long way to go. But if the variety of principles is considered then they should inform the future development of services to support young people in Wales and to map out the changes needed to implement this vision at Assembly and local level. If these succeed then the future of Wales, the National Assembly and young people will begin to make a difference to future young people. At present this has not gone far beyond the rhetoric and planning stages.

When it comes to addressing what young people think of the NAW and, most importantly, how they can become engaged within the social, political and cultural life of Wales, some interesting outcomes are observed. It would seem that young people have mixed reactions about the NAW. They are aware of its existence but are not quite sure what it really does. A number of arguments were made in favour of devolution and the young people interviewed feel they should have had a Scottish-type Parliament not an Assembly. Among these positive views were to be found some scepticism about the NAW having no real powers and feeling that Wales is still governed by Westminster. In spite of the formal initiatives highlighted earlier, the young people in this study feel that the NAW does little or nothing to promote young people and they also believe they are not taken seriously. This has led to young people becoming dissociated from politics, voting and politicians. The results do not show that young people are not interested in politics. Overall, we can argue that young people are political and can contribute widely to topics about political life in Wales. They may be disillusioned about politics and politicians because they feel alienated by these institutions and elites.

Interestingly, then, what young people themselves have had to say is not really out of kilter with the initiatives and measures recently or currently being introduced. Indeed, the latter, when more firmly established, should overcome the negative attitudes young people are currently expressing about politics and political life in Wales. Young people are being given more of a voice and are being taken more seriously and being listened to. Attitudes can take time to change but they will change if what is being promised is actually delivered. Wales is already ahead of the rest of the UK in addressing these issues and there is every reason to think it will remain so. Whether the major social problems affecting young people identified earlier can also be addressed and resolved is more problematic.

Notes

1. These statistics are derived from the 2002 manifesto, *Wales' Children – Our Future* and Bradshaw and Mayhew (2005). The former is a children's manifesto generated jointly by Barnardo's Cymru, Children in Wales, NCH Cymru, NSPCC and Save the Children.
2. The empirical study forms part of Catherine Davies's Ph.D. on National Identity and Young People (2003) undertaken at the University of Glamorgan.

References

BBC News (2003). 'Young People 'too busy' to vote', 8 July, London, BBC, *http://www.bbc.co.uk/go/pr/-/1/hi/wales/3053186.stm*.

Bradshaw, J. and Mayhew, E. (2005). *The Well Being of Children in the UK*, 2nd edn, London: Save the Children.

Chaney, P., Hall, P. and Pithouse, A. (2001). *New Governance – New Democracy? Post-Devolution Wales*, Cardiff: University of Wales Press.

Davies, R. (1998). 'Devolution: a process not an event', *The Gregynog Papers 2*, Cardiff: Institute of Welsh Affairs.

Electoral Commission (2002). *Wales votes? Public attitudes towards Assembly elections*, *http://www.electoralcomission.org.uk*.

Electoral Commission (2003). *National Assembly for Wales Election Opinion Research*, *http://www.electoralcomission.org.uk*.

ESRC (2003). 'Devolution and constitutional change', *http://www.devolution.ac.uk*.

Jones, J. B. and Balsom, D. (eds) (2001). *The Road to the National Assembly for Wales*, Cardiff: University of Wales Press.

Jones, G. and Wallace, C. (1992). *Youth, Family and Citizenship*, Buckingham: Open University Press.

Hain, P. (1999). *The Welsh Third Way?*, London: Tribune.

Laffin. M. (2000). 'Constitutional design: a framework for analysis', *Parliamentary Affairs*, 53, 3.

Laffin, M., Thomas, A. and Webb, A. (2000). 'Intergovernmental relations after devolution: the National Assembly for Wales', *The Political Quarterly*, 71, 2.

Lehn, Sine (2001). 'Carnegie Young People initiative study: ways of promoting youth participation in education in Denmark', *http://www.cefu.dk/upload/application/e7f8effc/b_sine_lehn_-_denmark-.pdf*.

Morgan, K. O. (1999). 'Welsh devolution: past and the future', in B. Taylor and K. Thompson (eds), *Scotland and Wales: Nations Again?*, Cardiff: University of Wales Press.

Nations and Regions website *http://www.ed.ac.uk/usgs/forum/Leverhulme/TOC.html.*

National Assembly for Wales (2000). *Better Wales, http://www.betterwales.com.*

National Assembly for Wales (2001). *Sure Start: A Programme to Increase Opportunity for Very Young Children and their Families in Wales*, Circular, *http://www.wales.gov.uk/subichildren/toc-e.htm.*

National Assembly for Wales (2001). *Children's Commissioner for Wales: Consultation on Assembly regulations*, consultation paper, *http:// www.wales.gov.uk/subichildren/toc-e.htm.*

National Assembly for Wales (2001). *Moving Forward – Listening to Children and Young People in Wales – proposal for consultation*, consultation paper, *http:// www.wales.gov.uk/subichildren/toc-e.htm.*

National Assembly for Wales (2003). *Children and Young People's strategy update: March 2003*, report from the National Assembly, *http:// www.wales.gov.uk/subichildren/toc-e.htm.*

National Assembly for Wales (2000). *Children and Young People: A framework for Partnership*, policy guidance from the National Assembly, *http:// www.wales.gov.uk/subichildren/toc-e.htm.*

National Centre for Social Research (NCSR) (2000), *Political Interest and Engagement among Young People*, York: Joseph Rowntree Foundation.

National Statistics (2001). Census 2001 – Wales, *http://www.statistics.gov.uk.*

Osmond, J. (1998). *The National Assembly Agenda*, Cardiff: Institute of Welsh Affairs.

Parreria, F. (2003). 'New coalition for votes at 16', *Guardian*, 28 January.

Taylor, B. and Thompson, K. (eds) (1999). *Scotland and Wales: Nations Again?*, Cardiff: University of Wales Press.

Treseder, P. (1997). *Empowering Children and Young People. Children's Rights and Save the Children. Promoting involvement in decision making*, London: Save the Children office.

Welsh Local Government Association (1998). *Developing a Strategy for Children in Need in Wales: The Local Government Role*, Cardiff: Zenith Print.

Welsh Local Government Association (2001). *Children's Action Plan: A Children's Action for Local Authorities in Wales*, Cardiff: Zenith Print.

Webb, A. (1999). 'Foreword', in D. Dunkerley and A. Thompson (eds), *Wales Today*, Cardiff: University of Wales Press.

White, C., Bruce, S. and Ritchie, J. (2000). *Young People's Politics – Political Interest and Engagement Amongst 14–24 Year-Olds*, York: Joseph Rowntree Foundation.

White Paper (2002). A New Impetus for European youth, *http:// www.europa.eu.int/comm/education/youth.ywp/index.html.*

Wyn Jones, R. and D. Trystan (1999). 'The 1997 Welsh referendum vote', in B. Taylor and K. Thompson (eds), *Scotland and Wales: Nations Again?*, Cardiff: University of Wales Press.

Yapp, C. (2003). 'Pupils plan to walk out in anti-war protest', *Western Mail*, 15 March.

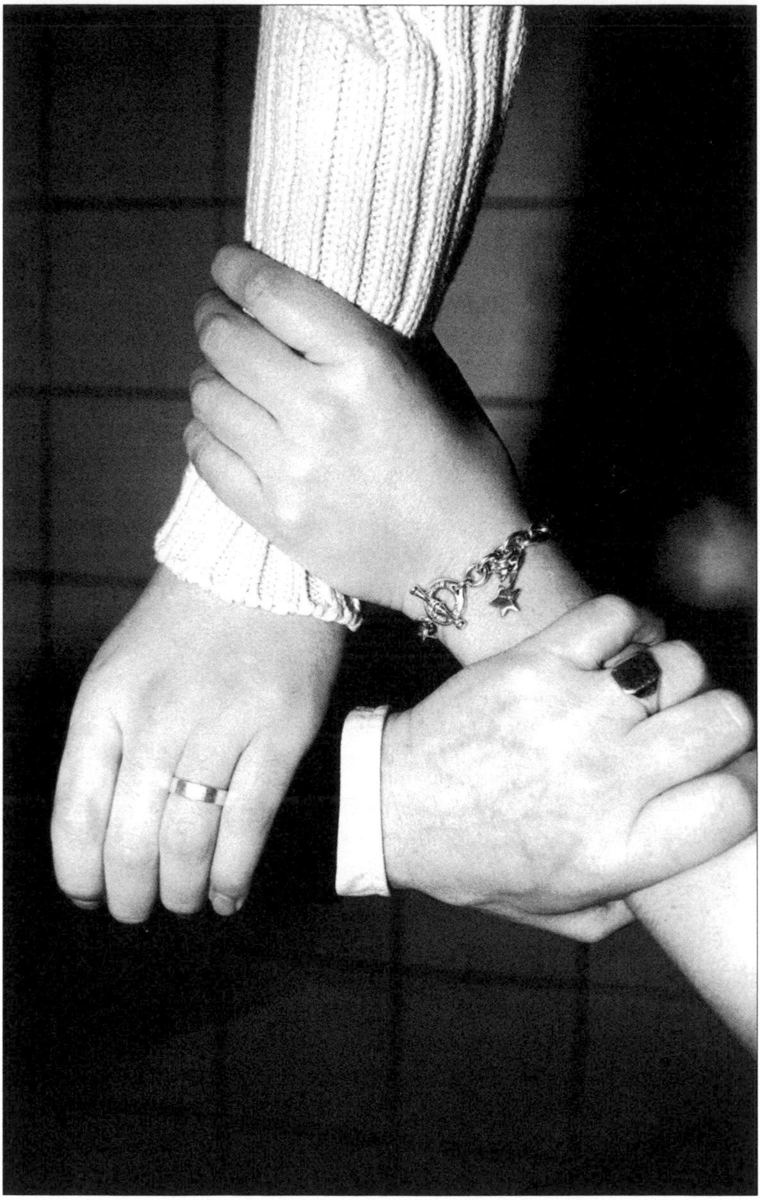

9. Civil Society in Action: Network Building and Partnerships in Wales

LESLEY HODGSON

Introduction

This chapter investigates the way in which civil society organizations in Wales form networks and partnerships. It argues that the contemporary world of civil society is being fundamentally altered by bodies outside the civil society sphere and investigates what impact this is having on the day-to-day operation of civil society.

There can be little doubt that a diverse range of bodies concerned with issues of governance are seeking to draw civil society into a broad range of partnerships and policy networks. The UN secretary general's (2002) programme for 'Strengthening the United Nations', for example, highlights the development of 'improved modalities of interaction' to facilitate partnership with civil society. Similarly, De Schutter suggests (2002: 200) that new 'modes of collaboration' are being developed at a European level, drawing civil society groups into networks and partnerships with various EU institutions. Closer to home, the Labour Party's constitutional reforms have served to realign civil society within the discourse of partnership, joined-up government and a political third way (Blair, 1998; Deakin, 2001; Taylor, 2001). In moving away from the preceding government's contract culture, New Labour has focused on developing a 'partnership culture' in terms of both service delivery and policy deliberation. Henig (2005) suggests that this new involvement can be viewed as two worlds meeting: the world of formal politics and the world of community activism. Taylor (2001: 95) meanwhile sees civil society groups as increasingly being viewed as both 'insiders' and 'outsiders' in policy development: forming an integral part of the consultation process and at the same time operating out there in the 'real world'.

In Wales, the statutory requirement for the National Assembly for Wales (NAW)[1] to enter into a legally binding partnership with civil society groups (Government of Wales Act 1998) has engendered a more formalized consultation process than previously experienced. The Voluntary Sector Scheme published in 2000 set out how this relationship would be developed with 'relevant' organizations.[2] Annual reports (NAW, 2001; WAG, 2002 and 2003 and an Independent Commission Report in 2004) monitor the implementation of the scheme. New networks and partnerships said to benefit both the Assembly and civil society have been instigated. Indeed, the Assembly Government is posited as an instrument that can reinvigorate and strengthen a 'weak', underdeveloped or incoherent civil society (Osmond, 1998; Jones and Osmond, 2002; Osmond and Jones, 2003; Davies, 1998; Paterson and Wyn Jones, 1999; WCVA, 2002). Whilst other writers in this volume focus specifically on investigating some of these partnerships (see, for example, Drakeford and Williams) this chapter examines network and partnership working from within civil society.

One question that needs to asked at the outset is why partnership with civil society is seen as necessary or desirable? It is true to say that various civil society groups have long been involved in service delivery; therefore it may seem logical that they should be increasingly involved in forming policies that affect them (see Harris and Rochester, 2001). Current political thinking in the UK and elsewhere seeks to modernize and redefine political boundaries in a globalized world. Involving civil society in decision-making processes can therefore be seen as part of the development of a 'third way' approach (Giddens, 1998; Newman, 2001). However, recent moves to partner civil society move beyond the confines of service deliverers to a broad range of civil society groups.

When we examine the literature surrounding civil society we find that there is a host of social, political or communal goods said to be derived from voluntary association.[3] Putnam (2001), for example, focuses on the ability of civil society to generate social capital – the idea that our social networks can engender norms, trust and reciprocity, elements that are said to act as the social glue that makes society cohesive. In turn, 'people who trust one another are all-round good citizens' (Putnam, 2001: 137). Thus civil society can engender a civic culture (Almond and Verba, 1965 and 1989) and combat a perceived lack of engagement in the political process. This idea has been promulgated in Wales within the work of the IWA (see Jones and Osmond, 2002; Osmond and Jones, 2003). Civil society and the reciprocity it develops, is also viewed as a means of rejuvenating socially excluded communities (see Adamson, chapter 14 in this volume) and the building of a 'good society' comprising moral citizens (Etzioni, 1996) by developing norms based on 'strong values, socially shared' (Blair 1995). Civil society, then, can engender an 'active citizenry' and deliver a stable social order. Thus civil society has 'political benefits' (NCVO, 2000). Whether these social goods can be generated or transferred through taking a joined-up approach to civil society is questionable. Fukuyama (1995) warns, for example, that social capital is a fragile asset that can be destroyed through government intervention and so the current drive to partner civil society raises specific concerns regarding the autonomy of civil society. If what is different about civil society is its ability to engender social goods, what effect will government intervention in civil society have on those goods and on civil society itself?

Partnership working is not new to civil society (although, for many, partnership working or consultation with governmental bodies may be new). Often, the success or otherwise of a civil society group or organization has depended on the extent to which it facilitates networking or engages in partnership. Indeed, commentators reflect that when investigating civil society as a 'real flesh and blood "thing" – a social realm, consisting a range of actual institutions' (Eberly, 2000: 7) one of its defining features centres on its ability to form 'relational networks' (Walzer, 1995: 7). Salamon et al. suggest that whilst civil society is diverse, reflecting the range of 'cultural, historical, political, and economic forces' that operate, it 'still take(s) *definable shapes* where circumstances are similar' (my italics, Salamon et al., 1999: 24).

This chapter focuses on these 'relational networks'. It examines how networks and partnerships give civil society its 'definable shape': how civil society acts as a 'society'. This is an aspect missing from larger debates. The chapter seeks to address this lacuna. In doing so it is structured as follows. First, some definitional and methodological points are provided. Second, the chapter focuses on the formation of networks, the loose bonds and linkages that groups form between each other. Third, it explores the experience of partnership working, the formal linkages where groups work together in a more structured way. Included in the work is an examination of the impact of the state as and when appropriate. In concluding, the discussion examines the challenges that closer partnership with civil society brings. Throughout the chapter, quotations from civil society group members are inserted to highlight key ideas.

Background

The chapter draws on data derived from a larger study into civil society in Wales (Hodgson, 2002), prompted by the paucity of information concerning the actual experience of belonging to civil society in Wales (see also Day et al., 2000). For the purpose of the study, a broad definition of civil society was adopted, which, based on the work of Walzer (1995) and Deakin (2001), identifies civil society as the sphere of 'uncoerced human association' that is carried on in the arena outside of the state, the market and the private sphere.[4] This association can take the form of membership in both formal (voluntary sector and community activities) and informal groups (leisure, recreational and interest activities). It is, however, somewhat naive to think that this realm of voluntary activity is completely separate from other spheres of life. In practice, they overlap the state, market and private spheres. Deakin (2001) refers to these areas of overlap as the 'borderlands'. It is suggested here that it is the area where the state and the market 'bleeds' into civil society, sometimes strengthening but often diluting and at other times contaminating civil society. This is an important point when we consider that civil society partnerships and networks are increasingly being constructed by state initiatives. There is recognition on the part of government about the importance of the independence of civil society (SEU, 2000; NAW, 2000). The prime minister recognizes the need for government to be 'acutely aware of the need not to stifle . . . the voluntary sector' (Blair, 1998: 4). This chapter suggests, however, that civil society groups are increasingly constrained into forming networks and partnerships that they otherwise would not.

The research findings are based on the transcripts of semi-structured interviews with individuals involved in over forty civil society organizations. These were selected using a snowballing technique designed to reflect the types of civil society groups in the area under study.[5] Groups were involved in a range of what could be termed mainstream activities, yet were as diverse as crochet clubs, housing associations, cycling 'clubs' and national charitable bodies. Triangulation was achieved through participant observation of three groups and an examination of the literature associated with groups, where available. The findings are provided below.

Networking

The data highlight that informal groups most often facilitate ties through their members' involvement in other group activities. That is, group members often belong to other clubs and information about the clubs' activities is passed on to others through individual group members. At times informal groups join forces with other groups to engage in fund-raising activities. Within the study, for example, an informal cycle 'club' joined with other cycling clubs to engage in fund-raising activities within the community. In this way group members are engaged in constructing informal networks; utilizing social capital in the form of friends, family members and local knowledge to locate groups to take part in activities.

In the case of formal groups, networking is more strategic and 'goes with the territory' or is 'part of the job'. Interviews highlighted that networking takes place at a number of levels: national, regional, local and community level and each tier has a range of organizations that facilitate networking. For example, the National Council for Voluntary Action (NCVA) facilitates networking at a national level, the Wales Council for Voluntary Action (WCVA) at regional level and the Community Voluntary Councils (CVCs) at local and community level. In addition, there are a number of umbrella bodies that facilitate networks between groups with similar interests. These latter bodies are more likely to include a range of groups spread across the hierarchical 'span'. To illustrate, one umbrella body concerned with the rights of black and ethnic minority groups facilitates networks between four local authorities, five police forces and a range of voluntary organizations concerned with similar issues, but they also network with community-based groups and employment organizations in their local area that want information on race issues. Interviews highlighted the loose but complex nature of networks, whereby some groups want constant contact and others drift in and out as and when they want. Networking can be as simple as sending a letter, e-mail or making a phone call (indeed some networkers never meet face to face) or as complex as attending regular meetings. One respondent suggested 'It's like a spider's web where everyone links up with everyone else. It becomes so complicated at times that I lose track of all the groups that we network with.'

Whilst civil 'society' is more concrete at the local level there are other tiers to this society. Respondents made reference to being involved in networks at local, regional and national (Wales) level, with some groups being involved in UK, EU and international networks. These latter are often facilitated through the Internet.

Networks may operate at a 'communicate/disseminate' level: sharing ideas, funding information, good practice and problem solving or they may be used to consolidate partnership working. They also ensure that a duplication of services, which could endanger the very existence of a group, does not occur. When initiatives are at the developmental stage, groups come together to see what they can gain from the venture (usually in financial terms) but also what they can specifically 'give' to the project. Respondents suggested that this type of networking was vital, as it was a means of locating the group within the wider sphere. So, for example, respondents spoke about being 'in there', 'keeping your particular focus in the minds of others . . . so that, someone will say "ah, yes, so and so can do with that"' and 'fitting in to the whole picture'. These references portray the idea that group members have a sense of being included in something wider than a single group, a wider civil 'society' that is cognisant of the other groups within it. They have a distinctive place or role within that society and the references to fitting in to the 'whole picture' and accommodating other groups ('so and so could do with that') indicates a societal concern for one's own.

The data also highlight that groups often share a common outlook and common problems. Whilst groups might tackle issues in different ways, recognition is given to the fact that at times they need to show solidarity, especially when coming under threat from state bodies. Thus, when engaged with networks involving the local authority, for example, an informal 'pre-network network' may be formed to discuss strategies for dealing with local authority personnel and bureaucratic structures. The impression given is of a society within a wider society; a society that looks after its own, that faces and combats unique problems, that has a concern for others as well as itself. A society founded upon networking.

On a practical level, networking is time-consuming – involving meeting attendance, sitting on committees, conference attendance, sitting on the board of other groups or, as one respondent put it, 'generally putting yourself about'. Respondents highlighted that there is a certain skill involved in networking; at a most basic level having the 'gift of the gab'. Whilst this skill is not the natural resource of all individuals engaged in voluntary activity, success is often measured by the group's ability to network and so it has 'got to be done if you want to succeed'. This is something that those new to voluntary activity find particularly difficult. One newly appointed manager of a regeneration project when recounting her experience suggested: 'The more you do it, the easier it is because you get to know people and so on, but it's really hard that first couple of times. I think it's hard for anybody who is volunteering, anybody off the street feels very, very intimidated.' This 'intimidation' is more pronounced when individuals from small civil society groups have to be involved in networks involving individuals who are perceived as 'professional' networkers. These, often referred to as 'the suits', are individuals belonging to statutory bodies, the local authority, umbrella bodies or large voluntary agencies. A respondent who had recently taken over a community-based forum suggested that, whilst networking with these people was difficult, 'you need to be "in" there'. The data suggest, however, that those that are 'in' in the true sense are primarily managers, chairpersons and development workers; the elite members of well-established groups. These 'professional networkers' refer to other civil society groups by making reference to the name of the person running the group or the person they network with. There would seem to be an implicit 'Who's Who' of networkers and networks. Many of these individuals have built up 'reputations' as good networkers and there is evidence to suggest that they are being head-hunted by various agencies inside and outside the civil society sphere.

Networking is becoming increasingly formalized and professionalized, largely due to the new partnership culture being developed between the state and civil society. New positions (often termed liaison officers) have been developed that allow individuals to act as intermediaries between groups and state bodies. These roles are often filled by what are seen to be professional people who are being co-opted into, or trained within, the voluntary sector. Thus networking is becoming a specific role in its own right and is being conducted with a wider range of actors than previously, many of these outside the civil society sphere. In recognition of this, various capacity-building schemes, generated through funding provided by the NAW, facilitate the training of grass-roots members and 'ordinary people' in a range of skills conducive to networking with a wide range of actors. Whilst many groups have availed themselves of the training opportunities open to them, some feel that they are being coerced into roles not of their choosing. There is the suggestion that individuals feel they are being alienated from the 'real life' activities of the group to become what one respondent suggested was a 'glorified facilitator'. Respondents were aware that they were increasingly juggling roles and constantly weighing up the benefits of attending a particular network meeting as opposed to being engaged in work/voluntary activity. The dichotomy arises, of course, because of a fear that non-attendance could mean 'missing out on something vital', being 'left out of the loop'.

Traditionally, an important reason for networking has been the access it allows to funding streams and bodies. For many of the small-to-medium-sized groups, this has been at the heart of networking. Increasingly, however, the formation of networks is now a 'requirement' stipulated by funding criteria. One project manager recounted that although networks had always developed naturally as and when they were needed, 'now it's a case of *having to do so, otherwise we wouldn't be fulfilling our funding criteria.* We have to *prove* that we are forging links between other groups and ourselves . . .' (my italics). Thus, rather than 'organic links' being developed, whereby groups come together to fulfil a need within the community, groups are being coerced to forge links because of funding concerns. Whilst the majority of links are formed with similar groups and user participants, sometimes they include networking with actors outside of civil society. This can benefit all parties. Deakin's (2001) suggestion that being involved in a network that includes the local authority enhances a voluntary organization's credibility, for example, was mirrored in this study. Yet questions need to be asked about the effect such forced involvement has on the way individuals network. The study indicated that for the most part networking entails forging loose connections between groups that can be dropped, and picked up again, at a future point – one respondent from a housing association suggested: 'There is no structure to the way we operate, the way we work as groups that is, the way we form alliances and networks, it shouldn't work at all, but it does.' The evidence from this study, however, may point to a change in networking whereby networks are becoming increasingly formalized and aggressively developed through conference attendance, local authority 'open' meetings, NAW meetings, community awareness-raising sessions and so on. It seems that, more than ever, networkers are on the lookout for opportunities to get their group pushed to the forefront of networking activity in order to access funding. Networking is becoming increasingly cut-throat and there is some evidence to suggest that rather than uniting groups, new networking methods threaten to drive a wedge between groups as they try to outdo each other in making new contacts.

Networking therefore comes at a price. One respondent involved in a development trust explains that to 'be a good networker these days is to be very sophisticated, almost machine minded'. Others suggested that it was 'becoming businesslike'. It would seem that the contemporary framework within which civil society groups operate has so altered that networking is becoming increasingly professionalized, with the day-to-day operation of networking becoming formalized and elitist. This may be a cause for concern and questions need to be asked as to the extent of networking activity and the impact of professionalized, aggressive networking on the civil society ethos.

Partnership

Partnerships can be defined as 'networks in action' in that networks often facilitate the building of relationships that generate the mutual trust, shared goals and acceptance that allows groups to engage in some form of long-term co-operative activity. Whilst informal groups are less likely to sustain a long-term relationship with others, there is evidence to suggest that the length of time an informal group exists and the type of activity in which the group is engaged have a bearing on the development of more formal links. Choirs often forge partnerships with other choirs, for example, and whilst at times there is a competitive element there is also a sense that group linkages are more pronounced than loose networks.

Although partnerships are not the sole prerogative of formal groups, they are much more likely to work along with other groups in a sustained way. Even where formal groups show a determination to be independent, there is evidence to show that there comes a time when they find themselves forging stronger links than the loose connections or networks previously discussed.

Networks are looser and can be widespread; partnerships, because they entail a closer working relationship, are more localized. Thus, for example, a group in the Valleys concerned with drug abuse is involved in partnership working with the Welsh Council for Drugs, Drug Aid Wales, the Drugs Hotline and the Toxicology Unit at the local hospital; all organizations can be found in a 20-mile radius. The umbrella organization concerned with ethnic minority issues has widespread networks but 'partners' groups much closer to both their areas of interest and locality. So, although they may have networks with local businesses, partnerships are more likely to be forged with groups more closely concerned with race issues. Similarly, a manager of a large group working with older people explained that although they network with national, regional and local civil society bodies they 'work' with those who have a similar remit – social services, health authorities, local authority housing, solicitors, chiropodists, and a whole range of groups: 'Basically whoever offers a service for older people in the immediate area.' Thus, partnerships operate on a different level from networks and when we talk about the operation of civil society in this regard it is more often at local or regional level that it operates as a society.

Partnerships are of a different quality than networks in that they form the basis of a formal relationship, a 'working' link, that is more likely to be consolidated through written codes between groups, setting out who does what. The numbers of groups involved in networks can be almost infinite but more formal partnerships are usually smaller in number. So, within the discourse of partnership, various civil society 'societies' exist, where groups come together to work on a chosen project.

It is also at this level that the relationships between civil society, the state and the market sector become 'blurred' and the 'borderlands' (the areas between state and civil society) are more pronounced. The local authority (LA) plays a large part in the life of voluntary organizations at this level. A large proportion of groups in the study had what they described as a 'working link' with the LA through funding initiatives. Some groups actively develop and nurture partnerships with LAs, seeing them as sources of power, influence and funding. For these there is a certain 'kudos' in being a 'key partner' alongside the LA. Other groups fear their status as independent groups will be undermined by such involvement.

There are, however, a number of problems with partnerships involving the LA. Resentments arise between groups that are seen as significant players and those that are on the periphery of the partnership. The view is that 'key partners' gain insider information and have first pick of funding opportunities. There is also concern in relation to the perceived imbalance of power. Some group members suggested that partnerships with LAs are in reality little more than a means of bureaucratically and 'administratively . . . keeping a hold on power' and that at times the LA 'drives straight through the partnership'. There is little sense that 'real' partnerships are being formed. A respondent involved with the needs of ex-miners suggested: 'When the council say partnership, they mean we lead and you follow.' Another respondent said: 'they can choose how much to involve us, we *need* them, that's the difference, so the partnership isn't equal.'

Another concern relates to the different operating styles of the various actors involved in partnerships. There are a number of fears here: 'incorporation' – whereby voluntary agencies become integrated within the state and become indistinct from state bodies and what DiMaggio and Powell (1983) term 'isomorphism' – where a certain amount of role-blurring occurs; groups lose their distinctive nature and mirror the mechanics or ways of operating of the organizations they partner. Within the study, both fears were realized. Group members voiced concern that in the minds of the public there is a lack of distinction between civil society and the state (here in the form of the LA), and that involvement with state bodies was channelling or constraining the operation of groups; respondents often suggested they were viewed as an 'arm of the local authority'.[6] This is a real concern for one group (providing drug-counselling services) that works in partnership with the LA. The group finds itself on the brink of physically moving premises alongside a range of statutory agencies and service providers concerned with health issues. The dichotomy for them lies between providing a better level of provision and care (and more secure funding) and being 'squeezed . . . getting sucked into the bureaucracy . . . getting swallowed up and becoming part of the statutory agencies'. The respondent felt there was a real concern regarding trust, which could impact on their user-members:

> People don't trust them [the state] and won't come forward for help. We are trying very hard to keep the ethos of the group together; to keep doing what we set out to do in the beginning, keeping our independence . . . not let the statutory sector dictate to us what's going on.

Partnership working, therefore, not only affects groups involved in the partnership itself but also the wider community.

Isomorphism is a more insidious concept. It is often only from the outside, or with hindsight, that isomorphism can be detected. It could be argued that in many cases capacity building, 'best practice' criteria, and efficiency measures are ways of crafting isomorphism through allowing groups to develop the structures and skills necessary to work within a bureaucratized environment. Within the context of this study, isomorphism was something that was seen to affect larger groups that work closely with state bodies. Many groups, for example, suggested that the WCVA had 'sold out' and was now indistinct in terms of agenda and working methods from the National Assembly.

Increasingly partnerships, like networks, are being formed on an economic basis. The need to develop 'coordinated action plans' in order to access funding has led to the development of what I term 'hybrid' groups. A hybrid group comprises a number of smaller groups based in one community that come together to form a larger partnership that might, or might not, involve the LA. The following interview extract based on the comments of a member of one such partnership explains:

> Several local community groups had gone forward to try and seek funding. The rugby club had gone to get indoor training facilities, another group had gone to get something developed on the old pit site. They all met with the same answers that unless they provided a coordinated plan they weren't going to get anything . . . They had all been

told, coordinate a plan and you will succeed. So, we formed the [X] Regeneration Project. Our aim is to bring together the groups in a partnership and provide one co-ordinated plan for funding. We will act as the distributor . . .

Strategically formed, these groups are often labelled 'regeneration', 'renewal' trusts, forums or projects and are to be found at the heart of government and NAW policies regarding community regeneration and combating social exclusion (NAW, 2000; SEU, 1998 and 2000). These partnerships are said to benefit all involved. For the government, they are a means of gaining a legitimized community view, while groups can not only access funding but also help to 'set the agenda'. Such partnerships are, however, often linked to specific government programmes, meaning that the hybrid group seeks to address aims that are wider, or distinct from, the purposes of individual groups. Within this study, almost one quarter of the groups were 'hybrid' groups.

There is the suggestion that groups that come together in partnerships of this kind suffer specific problems. Discussions with various groups and attendance at group meetings highlighted an often contentious situation whereby individual groups within the 'hybrid' group differed in their approach to combat a specific need. This is particularly evident where groups have suffered some form of historical rift. The data show that while they *have* to come together to secure funding, there is little partnership in any real sense. The coordinator of one regeneration forum provides an insight into one problem area:

> The group was set up to regenerate the area. I know that sounds vague but it's got to be open – I think the focus is about funding, especially for the local authority and it is not something that I feel particularly comfortable with, it's just the way it is though . . . Each group have got ideas of what they want . . . There is still a long way to go before it is to be cohesive. [The community] is divided into two groups that have got substantial differences, so both of them are represented on the board otherwise we will be excluding one angle on the community.

The forum discussed here consists of four groups encompassing three communities (each group has another set of smaller groups within it). Two of the groups are situated in one community. This community has historically been split over territorial lines and friction exists within the community, both groups making claims and counter-claims about the use of funding monies. In recent years the local authority has 'advised' all four groups to access funding they need to work together to form a strategic plan to regenerate the wider community. The groups have done so but there is evidence that the split within one community spills over into the other community groups and bad feelings have been generated. Meetings have to be held in 'neutral territory' and a general air of mistrust and suspicion can be felt in the area. There is little doubt that as individual groups much 'good' is accomplished in the various communities and it may be the case that if differences can be overcome this 'good' could be widened out to the larger community.

Forcing groups to come together in fabricated networks and partnerships, therefore, may serve only to exacerbate any disjuncture. Even where these 'hybrid' partnerships operate smoothly, tensions over the allocation of funding cause heated debate, with arguments about which community or area 'deserves' resources surfacing. Rather than engendering trust and social capital, some partnerships may actually spread distrust and cleavage within communities. It becomes evident that the basis for partnership needs to be deeper than mere economic rationality if these initiatives are to work.

Conclusions

This chapter allows us to develop a perspective on the various linkages that exist between civil society groups and between the civil society sphere and other spheres of society. It suggests that networking and partnership are an integral aspect of civil society. More than that, it is this interaction that allows civil society to operate as a 'society' or 'societies'. The chapter has also highlighted that the framework within which networking and partnership takes place is changing as the state attempts to involve itself in civil society in a more concrete way than previously.

A number of concerns have been raised. Groups increasingly find themselves constrained by funders who dictate the way groups network and increasingly determine the working partnerships, group formation and methods of operating of civil society. State involvement has meant that groups try to become increasingly professionalized and there is increasing evidence to suggest that the emphasis of some groups is changing and moving away from an immediate concern with helping 'the other' to finding some form of secure funding with fewer constraints. There is a growing acceptance that the 'funding chase' is a legitimate activity for civil society groups that want to survive. Individuals within groups bemoan the fact that they are no longer involved in the kinds of activities for which they first became involved in voluntary association: to help others/community. There is some discussion as to whether this really is the way forward for groups but there is also a resigned atmosphere and whilst group members recognize the concern, they are able to rationalize their position in the belief that their existence will in the long term be beneficial to wider society. For informal groups these issues were not of immediate concern. Nevertheless, there is growing evidence to suggest that informal groups are being targeted by umbrella bodies, funding bodies and those who wish to map out civil society.[7] There is, of course, nothing wrong with economic rationality *in the right place* (see Fevre, 2000); however, in the case of civil society, there is a danger that it is undermining the independence of the realm.

There is little doubt that those concerned with issues of governance seek to draw civil society into an ever closer set of relationships, whether this be in policy development or policy implementation. This chapter has highlighted, however, that, although networks and partnerships are at the heart of civil society, these relationships do not always run smoothly. This is especially the case where those from outside the civil society sphere become involved. There is evidence to suggest that the capacity-building, regulation and criteria-setting of the state and other funding bodies are a double-edged sword. On the one hand, these serve to create an open, accountable, skilled professionalized 'team of players' but, on the other, the construction of new ways of working may lead to civil society being 'morphed' or incorporated into unfamiliar and bureaucratized organizational working methods. Questions need to be asked as to whether the Assembly is assisting capacity-building or whether it is in fact moulding a new breed of bureaucrats (Jones, 2005). There is also the question as to whether civil society organizations are becoming more accountable to, and representative of, their own stakeholders or simply to state bodies.

Policy-makers and those who are concerned with creating 'new modalities of interaction' with civil society need to be aware of these concerns when constructing initiatives that bring civil society groups into networks or partnerships. Partnership may not be the panacea for all ills it is promoted to be. Forcing groups to work together in partnership, coalition or networks that do not organically develop may undermine the independence, the ethos and the modus operandi of civil society. The challenge at this time is to find a way whereby such partnerships can be adopted so as to safeguard the independence of civil society, preserving it as a distinct entity. This is an important point. Partnership working has the potential to benefit everyone involved but serious concerns need to be raised about the incorporation of civil society in this way. After all, what will be the 'value' of civil society if it is indistinct from the state or the market?

Notes

1. The National Assembly for Wales separated the legal and executive aspects of the Assembly in November 2001. After this time the executive became known as the Welsh Assembly Government (WAG). For clarity this chapter uses the older title NAW.
2. Despite the VSS making reference to the criteria for defining what is a 'relevant' organization this is still somewhat woolly.
3. It should be noted that most civil society writers are cognisant of the negative aspects of civil society and the 'goods' it is said to generate (see, for example, Deakin, 2001; Putnam 2001).
4. Diverging from Deakin and Walzer's definitions somewhat, I suggest that there is nothing uncoerced or voluntary about family ties. These ties are obligatory, albeit in a different way to other voluntary relationships. Whilst I agree that such relationships might form the basis of group involvement, they do not feature in my definition.
5. The area of study comprises a number of valleys in south-east Wales. Semi-structured interviews were conducted with individuals at different hierarchical levels within the forty groups.
6. Anecdotally, there would seem to be some support for this view. Having lost my way to an interview I stopped to ask directions to the local Residents and Tenants Association. Mystified, the local resident suggested I ask at the local council office further along the street. It did, of course, turn out to be the residents association building.
7. There is also evidence to suggest that funding bodies are increasingly targeting informal groups through umbrella bodies. The increasing numbers of directories and audits of community-based groups facilitates this.

References

Almond, G. and Verba, S. (1965). *The Civic Culture*, Boston: Little Brown.

Almond, G. and Verba, S. (1989). *The Civic Culture Revisited*, London: Sage.

Annan, K. (2001). *Strengthening the United Nations: An Agenda for Change*, UN A/57/387.

Blair, T. (1995). 'The rights we enjoy reflect the duties we owe', *The Spectator Lecture*, 22 March.

Blair, T. (1998). *The Third Way: New Politics for the New Century*, London: The Fabian Society.

Davies, R. (1998). *Devolution: A Process not an Event*, *The Gregynog Papers 2*, Cardiff: Institute of Welsh Affairs (IWA).

Day, G., Dunkerley, D. and Thompson, A. (2000). 'Evaluating the "new politics": civil society and the National Assembly for Wales', *Public Policy and Administration*, 15, 2, 25–37.

Deakin, N. (2001). *In Search of Civil Society*, Basingstoke: Palgrave.

De Schutter, O. (2002). 'Europe in search of its civil society', *European Law Journal*, 8, 2, 198–217.

DiMaggio, P. and Powell, W. (1983). 'The iron cage revisited: institutional isomorphism and collective rationality in organizational fields', *American Sociological Review*, 48, 147–60.

Eberly, D. (2000). *The Essential Civil Society Reader: The Classic Essay*, Maryland: Rowman & Littlefield.

Etzioni, A. (1996). *The New Golden Rule: Community and Morality in a Democratic Society*, New York: Basic Books.

Fevre, R. (2000). *The Demoralisation of Western Culture: Social Theory and the Dilemmas of Modern Living*, London: Continuum.

Fukuyama, F. (1995). *Trust: The Social Virtues and the Creation of Prosperity*, London: Hamish Hamilton.

Giddens, A. (1998). *The Third Way: The Renewal of Social Democracy*, Cambridge: Polity Press.

Government of Wales Act (1998). London, HMSO, also available at *http://www.legislation.hmso.gov.uk/acts/acts1998/19980038.htm*.

Harris, M. and Rochester, C. (eds) (2001). *Voluntary Organisations and Social Policy in Britain: Perspectives on Change and Choice*, London: Palgrave.

Henig, S. (2005). 'Partnership and the English regions', paper given at ESRC Local and Regional Governance: Bringing The Voluntary Sector in, Research Seminar Series 2004–6, University of Bath, 13 May.

Hodgson, L. (2002). 'Experiencing civil society: the reality of civil society in post-devolution Wales', unpublished Ph.D. thesis, University of Glamorgan.

Jones, B. (2005) 'Concluding remarks', *ESRC Local and Regional Governance: Bringing the Voluntary Sector In*. Research Seminar Series 2004–6, University of Bath, 13 May 2005

Jones, B. and Osmond, J. (2002). *Building a Civic Culture: Institutional Change, Policy Development and Political Dynamics in the National Assembly for Wales*. Cardiff: IWA and WGC.

National Assembly for Wales (NAW) (2000). *Voluntary Sector Scheme*, Cardiff: National Assembly for Wales (NAW).

NAW (2001). Voluntary Sector Scheme *First Annual Report*, Cardiff: NAW Communities Directorate.

National Council for Voluntary Organisations (2000). 'Civil society in the new millennium', *Research Quarterly*, 12, 1–4.

Newman, J. (2001). *Modernising Governance: New Labour, Policy and Society*, London: Sage.

Osmond, J. (1998). *The National Assembly Agenda*, Cardiff: IWA.

Osmond, J. and Jones, B. (2003). *Birth of Welsh Democracy: The First Term of the National Assembly for Wales*, Cardiff: IWA and Wales Governance Centre.

Paterson, L. and Wyn Jones, R. (1999). 'Does civil society drive constitutional change?', in B. Taylor and K. Thompson (eds), *Scotland and Wales: Nations Again?* Cardiff: University of Wales Press.

Putnam, R. (2001). *Bowling Alone: The Collapse and Revival of American Community*, London: Schuster & Schuster.

Salamon, L. M., Anheier, H. K. et al. (1999). *Global Civil Society: Dimensions of the Nonprofit Sector*, Baltimore, MD: The John Hopkins Centre for Civil Society.

Social Exclusion Unit (SEU) (1998). *Bringing Britain Together: A National Strategy for Neighbourhood Renewal*, Stationery Office: London Social Exclusion Unit.

SEU (2000). *National Strategy for Neighbourhood Renewal: A Framework for Consultation*, Social Exclusion Unit (SEU): Cabinet Office.

Taylor, M. (2001). 'Partnership: insiders and outsiders', in M. Harris and C. Rochester (eds), *Voluntary Organisations and Social Policy in Britain: Perspectives on Change and Choice*, Basingstoke: Palgrave, pp. 94–107.

Welsh Assembly Government (WAG) (2002). Voluntary Sector Scheme *Second Annual Report*, Cardiff: Welsh Assembly Government (WAG).

WAG (2003). Voluntary Sector Scheme *Third Annual Report*, Cardiff: WAG.

WAG (2004). Independent Commission to Review the Voluntary Sector Scheme – Final Report submitted March 2004.

Walzer, M. (1995). 'The civil society argument', in Beiner, R. (ed.), *Theorizing Citizenship*, Albany: State University of New York Press.

Wales Council for Voluntary Action (WCVA) (2002). *The Civil Society Index*, Cardiff: Wales Council for Voluntary Action (WCVA).

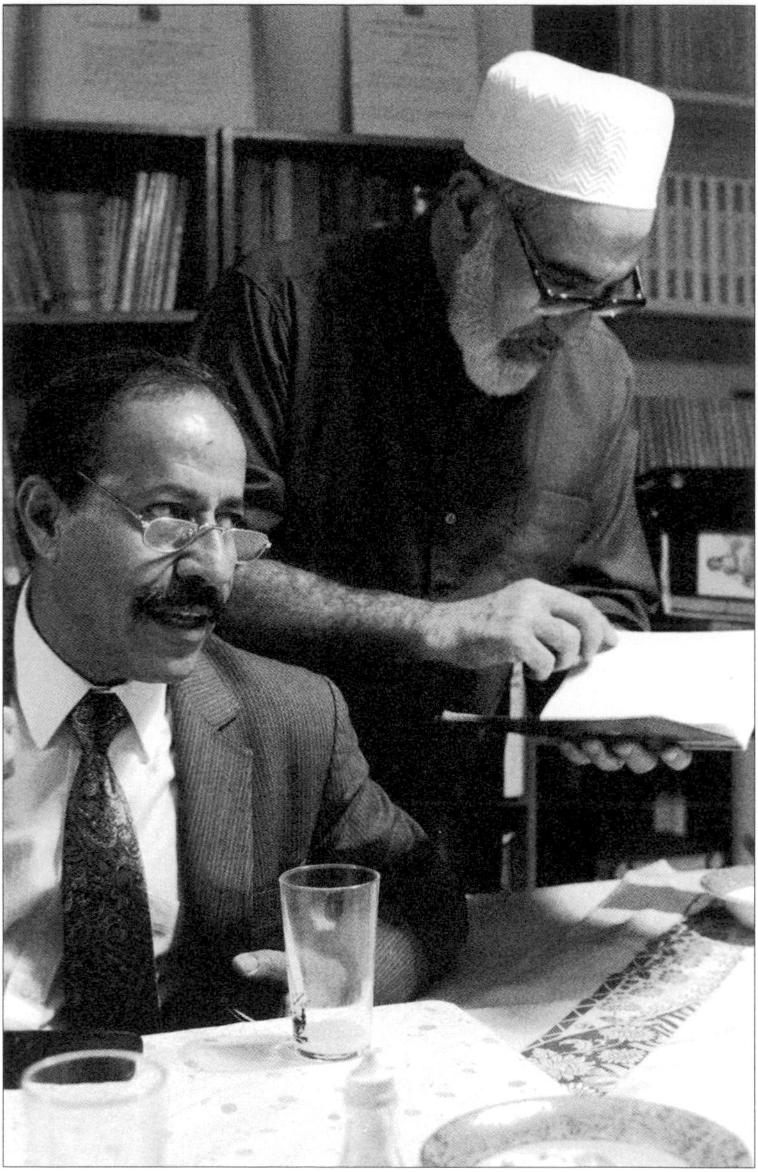

10. The Dilemmas of Civil Society: Black and Ethnic Minority Associations in Wales

CHARLOTTE WILLIAMS

Introduction

The Wales Council for Voluntary Action (WCVA) (2002: 13) report 'A Civil Society Diamond for Wales' suggests that a healthy civil society would be one 'that actively promotes good race relations, equal opportunities and sustainable development within its work and in wider society'. Against this, it finds evidence to suggest that the cultural diversity of Welsh society is not mirrored in civil society, and reports 50 per cent of respondents giving a negative or neutral response to the statement, 'civil society organizations are seen to peacefully promote their interests without promoting intolerance towards other cultural groups'. Overall, the report suggests civil society in Wales to be in 'medium health' (see Nicholl, chapter 4 in this volume, for further details). An immediate conceptual question arises when considering the desired state of health of civil society in relation to black and minority ethnic groups (BMEs). Would a healthy civil society be one in which there existed a distinct, autonomous and vibrant 'black' network of association, or would it be a civil society that reflected cultural diversity, and incorporated into itself the values of equal opportunity and the interests of minority groups? That is, do we aspire to an integrated multicultural civil society or to a model of discrete civil society? Should ethnicity be the basis on which we build associational life at all? This chapter argues that a number of dilemmas are posed for black and minority ethnic groups by the notion of civil society as it is popularly conceived. It explores the concept of an 'uncivil' society. It reviews the existing information on voluntary participation amongst ethnic minorities in Wales and provides a case study to illustrate many of the tensions that characterize this arena of activity.

There are a number of reasons to critically review this terrain from the perspective of BMEs. The concept of civil society immediately raises the issues of membership, identity and participation so fundamental to citizenship of a society. Activity at the level of civil society can serve as a barometer of racial integration and the state of multiculturalism. By contrast, ethnic categorization itself can provide an alternative focus for membership beyond the national collective and serve as an alternative basis for identity, action and aid beyond the boundary of nation. Civil society is a pivotal arena for BME political activity, for the satisfaction of welfare needs, and serves as a source of sanctuary and solidarity beyond mainstream institutions. Traditionally, non-governmental organizations (NGOs) have been the main medium for voicing and influencing the race equality agenda and an important site of resistance and protest to oppressive regimes. The radical potential of this terrain also makes it a key site for coercion and control of minority communities. Many of these dimensions have been extensively theorized and researched in their own terms. They are less understood or empirically tested within the context of Welsh society.

Civil or uncivil society? Conceptual issues

As Day and other contributors to this volume show, the parameters, role and function of civil society are hotly contested. The definition adopted by WCVA presents it in unproblematic and generally optimistic terms; yet the notion of civil society deserves critical exploration in relation to minority communities in as much as it poses a number of particular dilemmas both for BME groups themselves and for the way in which we understand the concept itself. In policy circles, civil society is generally advanced as a locale of mutuality, security, investment and civility. Accordingly, the ideal of civil society commands the moral gain that comes from living in a society that embraces diversity, promotes social justice, stops discrimination and aids social cohesion. Keane (1998) regards civil society as a dynamic and vibrant space with groups in fluid interaction. By contrast, other conceptions (*inter alia*, Gramsci, 1996) reject its harmonizing potential in favour of acknowledging its role as a site of struggle, resistance and protest; a locale for the development of oppositional viewpoints. This perspective emphasizes the autonomous nature of civil society, operating beyond state interference. However, views that stress the progressive potential of an autonomous civil society unregulated by state intervention become more problematic when we consider the emergence of exclusive ethnicities, elites, tribal or caste groupings, bodies such as the British National Party (BNP) based on intolerance, the discrete interests of faith-based groups and so on. Kenny notes:

> the appearance of new movements of a more conservative and reactionary bent – including anti-abortion, fundamentalist Christian and other far right groups. These have also embedded themselves within different societies and seek to enforce particularly exclusive forms of social closure which fly in the face of the benign, pluralistic model of civil society favoured by some on the left. (2001: 21)

In this respect, association on the basis of ethnicity, faith or belief becomes somewhat problematic in relation to ideas of social integration and civility embedded in civil society. From this viewpoint, civil society is characterized not only by disagreement and conflict, but also by lack of trust, lack of tolerance, lack of reciprocity and consequently alienation.

Kenny has also noted the ways in which diversity inevitably brings into question the idea of a consensus of values implied in more traditional visions of civil society:

> The problem for advocates of civil society is that this concept and its related values were first developed by thinkers of earlier eras who were far more confident about the common interests and values which could underpin a model of citizenship which was meaningful to all. These assumptions have been substantially undermined by the complex patterns of differentiation prevalent in late twentieth century life. (2001: 22)

In essence, the various competing locations of identity – national, global, cultural, religious, etc. – can challenge any shared notion of the public good. These identifications also raise critical questions about concepts such as citizenship and community, so fundamental to civil society yet so contested in relation to marginalized groups. The exclusivity of regimes based on ethnic nationhood has long been seen as operating to deny the rights of minority groups.

The conceptual debate between civic and ethnic nationhood has been extensively theorized (Kymlicka, 1995; Nedelsky, 2003). It centres on the potential tension between the universalizing tendencies of the state and the particularistic claims of various communities within it. Modern states invariably face the fundamental issue of how to square the demands of diverse views and interests and the demands for unity and cohesion amongst the national collectivity. They seek to transcend the unity of race, ethnicity, religion and so on, in order to foster loyalties and allegiances based on notions of shared citizenship and rights: civic rather than ethnic affiliation. Modern states, as Parekh has argued, are preoccupied with political and cultural homogeneity and inevitably become 'a deeply homogenising institution' (2000: 184) anxious to communicate shared norms and values and establish civic rights. This signals the limits of civil autonomy based on ethnic cleavage. It is not possible to pursue this debate on the limits of multiculturalism here (see Parekh, 2000; Kymlicka, 1995), but it is important to note the problematic nature of civil society in terms of modern-day diversity and what political theorists call 'the politics of presence' (Phillips, 1995; Parekh, 2000). The dilemma is how to accommodate and nurture diversity and the articulation of specific interests whilst at the same time promoting allegiances and universalizing values and norms that transcend the basis of these groupings.

In many senses civil society demands a permeability of ethnic classification and seeks to foster cross-cultural association: 'linking' and 'bridging' as well as 'bonding' to use Putnam's terms (2000). Similarly, Paul Hirst has argued that essentialist 'communities of fate' stultify democratic participation and produce fragmentation and competition:

> in a multicultural society of conflicting identities, of communities as identities, the public sphere and the freedoms of civil society become nothing more than a medium for different groups to seek to capture the public power for their own purposes. This view supposes that existential communities will predominate and that they will enclose the life of the individual; far from being voluntary associations, they will become communities of fate. Thus to be black, for example, will become an all-defining identity. (1994: 53)

The corollary of 'communities of fate' for Hirst are 'communities of choice' based on a voluntarism that transcends ethnic affiliation. This would imply the need to promote not discrete BME civil activity but a civil society in which black and ethnic minorities associate and participate across many lines of interest. In his focus on the ethnic economy and social capital, Nederveen Pieterse (2003) explores the possibilities of cross-cultural and intergroup relationships between ethnic associations. He argues that significant attention in the literature is paid to group boundaries and antagonisms as opposed to the potentials of cross-group relations. In particular, attention is focused on relationships between minority communities and the majority society and less so on relations between different minority groups. Pieterse does not, however, advocate the abandonment of ethnically based association in favour of total assimilation, but suggests, as do others (for example, Vertovec, 1999), a type of conditional, modified assimilation, with lines of association that value the expression of difference but also integration: 'What matters is neither the situation of full separation behind cultural barriers ("ethnic economy" and multiculturalism as a mosaic of ghettos) nor the situation of full assimilation (cultural boundaries don't matter) but rather the in-between zone that Portes (1996) refers to as "segmented assimilation"' (2003: 46).

Writing about political participation, Vertovec (1999: 30) argues for more differentiated and effective consultative mechanisms – 'an adequate machinery for voicing of interests in the policy process, to allow for self-expression of values and identity based on "ethnic" criteria yet which will also be framed so as to prevent social fragmentation by rigid boundary formation'.

What these debates highlight is whether ethnicity in and of itself should be the basis on which to associate. Arguments in favour of ethnically-based organizations cite their importance in terms of the assertion of difference, identity, the 'politics of recognition' and the lobbying of common interests. Neither is this the whole story of course, because one powerful rationale for ethnically-based affiliation is the historical and sustained exclusion from mainstream institutions. Their evolution and development has often been a response to marginalization and exclusion within the institutions of civil society in situations where the bonds of civil society – trust, reciprocity, mutual concern, security and participation – have not been extended to everyone. In this way civil society has been wholly uncivil.

A second set of questions relates to the definition of minority ethnic association itself. What are minority 'ethnic' associations? What indeed is ethnicity? Jan Nederveen Pieterse has commented on the problem of the ethnic marker in association. He states: 'Ethnicity is a marker of cultural difference, but not every cultural distance qualifies. A country's or a people's location in the hierarchy of power also matters' (2003: 34). Thus in Wales, for example, it is possible to view the English, Polish or Irish as culturally distinct but not axiomatically as 'ethnic' in the same way as Africans, Indians, Bangladeshis or Chinese. In turn, those of mixed descent whose cultural distance or 'difference' may not be so apparent, might be so wholly absorbed into the national collectivity as to become invisible in ethnic terms but yet continue to be regarded as a minority. Diverse ethnic associations also flourish within national groupings. Within migrant communities for example, individuals may associate on the basis of a shared region, a caste or religion, as do tribal associations amongst African migrants. These associations provide continuity and support and continue to prevail in the country of settlement. Not only are ethnic communities internally differentiated but these associations exist alongside other networks of association which may or may not have an ethnic basis – work based, sport based, trade unions, women's groups, political groups and so on. Neither do they respect national boundaries with associations that cross nation-state borders, near and far. The cultural limits of such groups are inevitably fluid and permeable in a way that defies their categorization for the purposes of policy intervention. Assumptions of homogeneity within these communities are misplaced. Migrant communities are ethnically mixed and thus ethnic association itself becomes a narrow basis on which to organize and carries all the risks of exclusion. Ethnic association may well be relevant to 'bonding', but not so helpful to the bridging and linking that Putnam sees as vital to the development of social capital.

What is known about BME voluntarism and how it operates?

The first large-scale study of black and minority ethnic-led voluntary organizations was conducted by McCleod, Owen and Kahamis in

2001. This examined the role and future development of BME organizations in England and Wales. This study suggests there are approximately 5,500 organizations in England and Wales serving a variety of minority ethnic communities. The Council for Ethnic Minority Voluntary Organizations (CEMVO) more recently suggests a figure of 10,000 (CEMVO, 2005). The McCleod et al. study challenges the perception of minority organizations as being small, informal and short-lived bodies, finding in the majority of cases a degree of sustainability and formal legal status. They suggest that BME voluntary bodies perform four major functions: overcoming social isolation, affirming values and beliefs, doing social and pastoral work for their clients and acting as quasi-unions defending the interests of their members. A common finding of this study and others (Davis and Cooke, 2002; Craig et al., 2002; CEMVO, 2005), however, is a continuing concern about levels of core funding, overstretched services and a marked lack of 'joined-up' approaches to capacity building and strategic development. CEMVO, for example, argues that in terms of funding BME organizations capture only 2 per cent of the total funded grants from leading charitable trusts and foundations.

There can be no doubt that a growing 'social policy spotlight' is being turned on to specific types of voluntary organizations, in particular BME organizations and faith-based organizations (Harris et al., 2003: 94). There are increased expectations, for example, in terms of specialist provision for groups such as women experiencing domestic violence, race and community relations, urban regeneration programmes, faith-based schools and other religiously affiliated service delivery. A perennial characteristic of these organizations is that by far the majority provide services to particularized minority ethnic communities. They vary considerably in their internal organization and occupy positions of unequal power and attention vis-à-vis mainstream organizations (Craig et al., 2002). Another important feature is the lack of overlapping membership, integration and coordination between these organizations for the purpose of strategic development.

Some illumination can be gained by considering the motivations of those who participate. Such organizations clearly contribute to the development of civil society by drawing members together around associational activities. But often their special motivations relate in very particular ways to their own ethnic or faith communities, and demands, whether from government bodies, inter-ethnic partnerships or inter-faith councils, that impose different priorities and objectives may result in undermining rather than bolstering commitment. In this respect Harris et al. (2003) warn that the bent of government agendas may actually be inimical to sustaining civil society, social capital and democracy. Similarly, Lukka and Locke (2000) explore religious motivations and voluntary action and note that volunteering in faith-based contexts is seen as an extension of faith beliefs and that there is a strong relationship between belief, participation in religious congregation and motivation to volunteer. Thus the association provides the channel for altruism, and faith-based organizations command an important role in the development of social capital. When religious affiliation and racial and ethnic identities overlap, the ties are even stronger. Lukka and Locke (2000) make the point, however, that, when combined, social and cultural capital can maintain race, ethnic and class barriers.

Lukka and Ellis (2001) contend that the concept of volunteering itself is culturally grounded and that current conceptualizations reflect the dominant Western construct of volunteering. They argue that 'as a cultural construct or an ethical proposition, one word does not fit all cases because the activities and specifics that constitute volunteering vary so dramatically across cultures' (2001, unpaginated). Their overriding observation based on research suggests that BMEs do not see these activities as volunteering but rather as part of self-reliance, community support and helping each other. They posit 'an underlying norm of caring and responsibility' amongst black and ethnic minority communities that is culturally endorsed and a preference for volunteering within their own communities. This is supported by Leigh's study of black elders (2000) which concludes that members of minority ethnic groups do not use the notion of volunteering or the word volunteer to describe their activities.

There is evidently no lack of grass-roots participation and considerable informal involvement amongst BMEs. In addition, although under-researched, the overlap between the 'ethnic economy' and voluntary associational life should not be understated; that is, the twinning of social capital and cultural capital. Business associates in Asian communities may organize along lines of religious affiliation where reciprocal arrangements of trust, voluntary support, self-help and welfare service are communicated. In terms of mainstream charities, however, BMEs are significantly under-represented as volunteers, employees and/or board members. Throughout the voluntary sector there is a notable lack of BME presence, and Wales is no exception in this respect. As the WCVA study accordingly suggests, 'Civil society is not seen to mirror the cultural diversity of Welsh society' (WCVA, 2003: ii).

What do we know about the black voluntary sector in Wales?

The institutions of civil society are not limited to the voluntary sector, although the associational activity in voluntary, non-governmental and non-profit sectors is often seen as synonymous with civil society. The black voluntary sector has a long tradition in Wales, characterized by a high degree of civil autonomy and radicalism and the development of alternative forms of welfare provision beyond the mainstream (see *inter alia* Fryer, 1984; Evans, 2002; Sinclair, 1993 and 2003). Neil Sinclair's accounts of a socially integrated, multi-ethnic, self-supporting community of Tiger Bay filled with clubs and associations is just one example. In his book *Endangered Tiger* (2003: 164) he makes reference to the Neptune Club, the Coloured Brotherhood, the Sons of Africa, the Somali Youth League, the Colonial Club, the Quakers, South Wales Association for the Welfare of Coloured People and many others, pre-dating the turn of the twentieth century. Historically, voluntary organizations have sprung up alongside minority ethnic collectivities creating a particular spatial distribution.

According to the 2001 census, the minority ethnic population of Wales now comprises some 62,000 people or 2.1 per cent of the total population. The main concentrations of minority ethnics by local authority area are in Cardiff (8.4 per cent), Newport (4.8 per cent) and Swansea (2.2 per cent), with the majority of authorities across Wales having minority populations of less than 2 per cent. The ethnic groupings reveal considerable diversity, with people of an Asian background being by far the biggest group, making up 40 per cent of the total minority population. This demographic profile is highly significant to an understanding of BME voluntary activity, organization and capacity across Wales. Spatial embeddedness and uneven development are critical factors in the political mobilization of these groups (Kearns, 1995) and their ability to form communities of interest. By all accounts, the realities are of relatively fragile links between the ethnic communities across Wales, although in recent years a number of umbrella organizations have been established to promote coordination. Little, however, is known empirically about the level of social capital amongst these groups, or the levels of social trust, norms and the nature of networks in the communities. History, culture, social structure and opportunity shape the relationships between the public and private/civil domains. All these factors matter. Lack of political engagement of minority communities and exclusion from mainstream institutions in Wales brings with it a legacy of scepticism and suspicion.

The WCVA figures for 2005 list 354 organizations categorized as 'groups concerned with racial equality, refugees, religious and cultural activities and general activities where the group is run by members of an ethnic minority'. The list necessarily covers a wide and eclectic variety of organizations including mosques, a Greek school, the Asian Cultural Association, the Cardiff Community Gospel Choir, the Filipino Association, the Arab Society, the Wales Gurkha Villages Aid Trust and the Welsh Ladies Indoor Bowling Association, to name just a few. The difficulties of such a categorization are evident when considering the nature, function, constitution and organization of these institutions. Figures provided by CEMVO determine 136 BME organizations across Wales, of which over 17 per cent are focused on faith-based activity (CEMVO, 2005). Minority ethnic organizations form just 1.9 per cent of all voluntary organizations in Wales which, it is suggested, is disproportionately low relative to the BME population (Wales Funders Forum, 2005). In addition to five Race Equality Councils, a number of umbrella organizations and forums exist to link the memberships. These include bodies such as MEWN CYMRU (Minority Ethnic Women's Network), NWREN (the North Wales Race Equality Network), AWEMA (All Wales Ethnic Minority Association) and the Black Voluntary Sector Network that links 120 organizations and CEMVO itself. Following constitutional change, these umbrella organizations now represent an important mechanism for involvement and participation of BME communities in government.

Whilst wider debates offer a case for both vibrant civil society in Wales and/or a decline and loosening of social bonds (Paterson and Wyn Jones, 1999), little specific attention has been given to the 'health' of the black voluntary sector. What evidence exists suggests black voluntary sector activity has a weak organizational infrastructure (Chaney and Williams, 2003; Wales Funders Forum, 2005). In 2005 the Wales Funders Forum and CEMVO published a briefing paper, *Added Value and Added Challenges: Funding the Ethnic Minority Voluntary Sector*, which outlined the particular difficulties this sector faces in attracting funding and made recommendations for change. Interestingly, the report suggests further work needs to be done to profile the sector in Wales in more detail.

Under the policy lens

There can be little doubt that the current rationale for the increased interest in civil society lies not so much in the critical introspection of its nature and organization as in harnessing its potential towards specific political and social policy agendas. The regeneration of civil society is high on the government agenda. The ambitions of New Labour in relation to the third sector extends beyond a reaction against New Right individualism to mobilizing this sphere in the interests of equal opportunity, social inclusion, social stability, trust, active citizenship and accountability in the provision of welfare. In essence, partnership with civil society is regarded as a means of reversing a number of social ills. Social 'goods', it is suggested, can be achieved via a strengthened civil society (Giddens, 2000). A number of developments in Wales reflect this refocused relationship between the state and civil society. Within the context of the devolved legislature, statutory requirements have led to the establishment of the Voluntary Sector Partnership Council which has regular meetings with the minister to promote dialogue and cooperation. Minority ethnic interests are represented on the council. In addition, the Government of Wales Act 1998 places unique equality duties on the National Assembly which have resulted in a whole infrastructure of consultative bodies being established to promote dialogue between the Assembly and grass-roots minority communities (see Chaney and Williams, 2003) and in capacity-building grants and initiatives. The wider impact of the European Union's Race Directive and the Race Relations (Amendment) Act 2000 demands meaningful dialogue between public bodies and NGOs serving black interests. For all these reasons the 'black' voluntary sector in Wales has been launched suddenly and forcefully into the new policy framework. Under this policy lens the visioning of civil society is necessarily increasingly idealized. As the Assembly's Voluntary Sector Scheme states, 'the goal is the creation of a civil society which offers equality of opportunity to all its members regardless of race and colour' (NAW, 2000, chapter 2, para. 2: 7).

The new consultative arrangements driven by these requirements have had a significant impact on BME networks. Expectations within the terrain of civil society have been raised both amongst the minority communities and from policy-makers concerned with driving change towards active citizenship. This has brought in its wake both progressive and regressive developments for civil society. Chaney and Williams (2003) argue that one of the most significant developments in post-devolution Wales is a shift from a laissez-faire approach to racial equality towards a system based on legal duties. There is now considerably more and easier access to decision-makers. Consultative and participatory mechanisms have been put in place to ensure a two-way dialogue and there are dedicated funding flows to support infrastructure capacity building. The impacts are, however, differential. Skills deficits and lack of capacity hinder meaningful engagement between the policy-makers and minority communities. Consultation overload and elite burnout are commonly reported. One activist documents his ill health following multiple commitments:

> Being over a period of a few years Chair of Multicultural Crossroads, a member of the Board of the then Race Equality Council, Chair of both the Norwegian Church Management Committee and the Horn of Africa Charity, Vice Chair of Butetown History & Arts Centre and editor of its magazine The Voice of the Tiger, member of the Waterfront Partners Group, Cardiff Bay Business Forum and the now defunct Cardiff Bay Community Trust and sole proprietor of Dragon and Tiger Enterprises' (Sinclair, 2003: 1)

In addition, no small amount of conflict has been created between BME groups as they grapple for secure funding and attention from the powerful (Williams, 2004). It has also been speculated that the Assembly is actively constructing ethnic categories for the purpose of policy intervention (Williams, 2003). The dangers of top-down intervention, or what Hodgson in this volume calls 'manufactured' civil society, are becoming increasingly apparent through empirical research. A small number of policy entrepreneurs command the field and gate-keep the voice of minority groups; the autonomy of many groups and their agenda are compromised by political funders (Williams and Chaney, 2001). Mouffe (1998) uses the word 'antagonism' as a positive feature of civil society, suggesting that the notion of democracy as dialogue between groups fails to grasp core power relations within society and the inevitable tensions and conflicts between groups. It remains to be seen whether this reshaping of the civic landscape effectively bolsters civil society. A number of writers point to the potential distortions produced by such government orchestration of minority association (*inter alia*, Vertovec, 1999) and its potential to damage spontaneous relationships of trust and voluntarism (Harris et al., 2003). Others argue that you cannot produce social capital from top-down intervention (Mainsbridge, 1992).

Case study: civil society in the making?

Through a sample case study of North Wales Race Equality Network (NWREN) this section illustrates a number of the dilemmas facing black organizations in Wales.[1] It suggests that they do have a newly prescribed and important role to play in influencing policy and that to a limited extent they are showing signs of acting as a forum to stimulate interest in Welsh affairs. However, real issues of capacity challenge their integrity. It is also clear that a number of fundamental issues may be emerging which correspond better to the notion of an uncivil society. NWREN represents an interesting test case in the light of the foregoing discussion. It is not located in an area of minority ethnic density, it did not exist prior to devolution and as a network it embraces the interests of several ethnic groups. Significantly, it also operates in a part of Wales where Welsh nationalist and Welsh-language activist groups are based.

NWREN extends across six local authorities and forms a formal partnership with the North Wales Police Service, North Wales Probation Service and Citizens Advice. The network was formally constituted in 2001, although it began its development in late 2000. NWREN evolved under a Commission for Racial Equality (CRE) initiative to promote race equality in rural areas and was prime-funded by the CRE and sponsored by a branch of MEWN Cymru, a voluntary organization aimed at promoting minority ethnic women into the labour market. MEWN Cymru had existed in the north since 1996 but struggled with a small membership and lack of capacity to undertake any developmental work. NWREN was to benefit from office space, administrative support and the appointment of two full-time members of staff funded for one year. Interestingly, the deployment of the energies of the membership of MEWN into the NWREN development heralded the demise of MEWN Cymru North Wales, currently a dormant minority ethnic organization.

The current membership of NWREN is 180 of which approximately 30 per cent of members are from a minority ethnic background. The membership comprises a number of major voluntary organizations in the area, such as Citizens Advice, and includes the majority of other registered minority associations operating in the north Wales area such as the Black Environment Network, Shekina (an organization aimed at supporting partners of overseas students in the university), the Chinese Association, which includes a Chinese women's association and a Chinese day school, the Filipino Association, which has evolved mainly in response to the needs of Filipino nursing staff in the major hospitals, and an Asian doctors' network. A number of faith groups are also represented in the membership. As such its core membership is extremely ethnically diverse. The web of minority organizations that make up NWREN membership has the potential to form an effective forum for minority interests and a powerful lobby. It is early days as yet to evaluate this potential. However, there is little evidence so far to suggest that beyond information sharing this network has realized its potential in terms of skills sharing or coordinated and proactive lobbying. A number of bids for funding have been submitted but these are used to build the capacity of NWREN as opposed to the associations within its membership. By far the majority of NWREN's work agenda is pitched towards servicing the consultative needs of 'white' organizations rather than responding directly to BME citizenship and participation (BEST Report, 2004). It has no capacity to conduct casework or individual advocacy. In this respect it departs from the traditional remit of the work of race equality councils and their forerunners, community relations councils. In no small measure this orientation has created tension amongst sections of the membership who are critical of the fact that the agenda of NWREN is set largely by responding to the demands of large institutional partners on whom it is reliant for funding.

NWREN serves a minority ethnic population of 7,000 in the north Wales authorities, including a small number of refugees and asylum seekers. An interesting feature of this demographic profile is that, far from reflecting the traditional profile of disadvantaged minorities, the minority population of north Wales as a whole is likely to reflect higher than national averages in terms of employment, employment status, housing status and income (BEST Report, 2004). That is not to say that BMEs do not experience rudimentary discriminations or fundamental social exclusion, but it acknowledges that people may have migrated and settled in the area as a result of small business enterprise or jobs as public service professionals. This is apparent amongst the membership of NWREN, raising key questions as to the extent to which it has been able to include or impact on those most disadvantaged within the community. The main activities of the organization are conducted by a committed core of 'ethnic brokers' whose personal status may leave them somewhat stranded from the rank and file. A study undertaken by the North Wales Registered Social Landlord Partnership in 2004 found only a small proportion of the minority ethnic households they sampled held any affiliation to minority ethnic groups which suggested little active association amongst the minority population. Whilst this committed core is critically comprised of the MEWN Cymru caucus, it is fair to say that a small number of new players have appeared who have seen the potential in the alliance and its links with the NAW consultation framework. These organizations, previously mobilized around a calendar of social and cultural events, are becoming increasingly politically mobilized. An important and noteworthy inclusion is the active commitment of the Chinese community, a minority interest that is relatively neglected in other parts of Wales.

Another key demographic factor that impacts on the organization's ambitions is the dispersal of visible minorities across what is a vast geographic area. The organizational base lies at the centre of the patch, currently in Penmaenmawr. Accordingly, a member from Pwllheli would have at least an hour to travel and a 100-mile round trip to attend a meeting. A member living in the Vale of Clwyd would face an equivalent hurdle to achieve face-to-face contact with the membership. From the outset, the organization accepted this constraint on its activity and thus adopted the word 'network' rather than race equality 'council' as used by other such organizations in Wales. This represents both a potential strength of the organization and a weakness. Face-to-face contact enhances investment and commitment and the building of shared norms and values, yet at the same time the idea of building a loose network of association may leave room for more fluid modes of association and the fundamental permeability that is conducive to the notion of civil society.

In essence NWREN is not ethnically bounded, nor impermeable to overlapping membership. In Putnam's (2000) terms its 'bridging' and 'linking' capacities appear to be greater than its 'bonding'. However, a number of ambiguous statements appear in its constitution document which reflect tensions over its membership and remit. Concerned with the representation of visible ethnic minorities in the make-up of its committees, the constitution states that: 'the North Wales Race Equality Network shall at all times pay due regard to the representation of women and Black and Minority Ethnic people in the composition of the General and Executive committees and any sub-committees established' (constitution document, 2001). Pitched against this is the fact that full membership is open 'to any person who lives within the area of benefit' and 'any corporate body or unincorporated association', thus opening the possibility of a completely white-dominated organization. These issues have been hotly debated during the evolution of the organization. Numerically it is clear that those from the visible minorities are thin on the ground within the membership. Whilst race equality is not the preserve of 'black' people, this nevertheless reflects the issues raised above, namely, what exactly is an ethnic organization? And to what extent is this set of interests being mobilized artificially as a distinctly 'ethnically' based set of interests?

In its short life, its role and remit, title and constitutional framework have all been subject to contestation from both within and outside the organization. Notably, two key Welsh-language groups operating in north Wales have vociferously challenged NWREN's stated remit and aim, albeit in different ways. Cefn, an organization which aims to protect Welsh-language interests, challenged the organization's title and constitutional remit arguing that race equality is not the sole prerogative of visible minorities but critically includes all forms of discrimination and animosities including Welsh/English. This led to a hard-fought defence by members of NWREN for a distinct identity mobilized around the interests of visible minorities. A further conflict arose between NWREN in support of the National Assembly BME Housing Strategy and the organization Cymuned, whose lobby for earmarked Welsh-speaking areas potentially excludes the settlement of BMEs in these areas as statistically few minority individuals speak Welsh (Webb, 2005). These two examples are instructive as they challenge the conceptualization of civil society as harmonious and reflecting an integrative potential. Indeed, they reveal the boundaries of tolerance that state institutions often seek to ignore. More crucially they represent a major tension between the concept of civic and ethnic nationalism that is played out within the arena of civil society (see also Mann, chapter 13 in this volume).

A number of other issues have arisen within NWREN that are of note. Its relationship with the CRE – its core sponsoring statutory body – has not been without tension. For example, at one of the executive meetings of the membership with the director of the CRE, members argued that the core aim of NWREN was 'not serving public authorities, [but] serving our own communities, listening and conveying messages to the statutory bodies', and further stated 'the need for NWREN to develop an independent agenda . . . moving along the 'community development route'. This clearly demonstrated a wish to free up the organization from dominance by the CRE agenda (minutes of 28 February 2002). In the minutes of 5 September 2001 'the low ranking [given to] specialist casework' was noted and it was agreed that for many this reflected a view that such a service could best be delivered 'in partnership with other organizations rather than directly by NWREN'. This document gives high priority to the work of servicing other bodies in respect of race awareness training and working in partnership with other agencies to develop new services. In many respects, therefore, NWREN struggles to bridge total absorption and co-option by major bodies and service to its grass-roots constituency. As a result, in Kearns's (1995) terms, the organization has a 'service orientated' rather than a 'citizen-orientated' modus operandi.

NWREN also experiences the now familiar consultation overload that blights such small but critical organizations. The demands of the National Assembly, local authorities, the police, the health service and a multitude of other public bodies for consultation with minorities is as yet ineffectually managed by the membership. It is doubtful it has the capacity to offer effective consultation within the time-scales expected by such authorities. In addition, as BME organizations in the south mobilize to command funding from bodies like the National Assembly they are required to demonstrate an 'All Wales' remit. As a consequence they place further demands on NWREN to provide representation on their boards and/or consultation. Efforts by AWEMA and the NAW to bolster the capacity of NWREN have been thwarted by the reluctance of secondees to move to the north, or the difficulties in filling posts in the north.

The case of NWREN signals a number of cautionary notes about the notion of spontaneous and autonomous civil society. The heavy demand placed on the core membership may ultimately erode the essence of the spontaneous commitment and trust that is a mainspring of civil society. NWREN potentially challenges the view that social capital cannot be built from top down with concerns about elite burnout and elite gate-keeping countering ideas of civil society as a positive locale of democratic renewal. But perhaps most troubling is the deliberate orchestration of activity in the civil sphere around ethnicity as the basis of association when, particularly in areas of sparse minority population, this may have a very weak foothold. Is this the maintenance of difference for its own sake, an elevation of what Vertovec has called 'the cultural' in multicultural? (Vertovec, 1999) The question of when and how is ethnicity the relevant factor in association/participation needs exploration given the implication that it is not always the key factor.

Conclusion

Ethnic diversity inevitably poses a number of dilemmas for any notion of civil society irrespective of the aspirations of the various commentators. In the normative sense, civil society is associated with integration, social cohesion, trust and reciprocity, and all the securities of citizenship. But even in these terms, association based on ethnic cleavage suggests something of an antithetical tendency. Closure around ethnic boundary necessitates exclusion. It can be speculated that where high levels of investment in community solidarity exist, so also will exist atomization and at times the vociferous targeting of 'the outsider'. The manifestation of racism, tribal and gang warfare, and the resistance of many exclusive communities to integration, testify to these contradictions. As Day points out in this volume, settled, stable and exclusive notions of Welsh community life are fundamentally hostile to outsiderness, diversity and immigration, fostering particular nostalgic versions of social cohesion and insular and regressive tendencies. Thus, too strong a commitment to the assumption of community cohesion means that many diverse voices are not heard at all. In addition there is an assumption that the interests of these associations will not clash with each other or at best that they can be successfully mediated across the space of civil society. As demonstrated in the case study, the demands of different community interests will not necessarily be compatible and may well result in overt antagonism and oppression. Friedman (1998: 28, quoted in Taylor, 2002) points to the potentially destabilizing tendencies in civil society: 'the tragic litany of racism, intolerance, terrorism and persecution of those who are judged to be different from us by some arbitrary distinguishing mark, whether of birthplace, language, skin colour, sexual practice or religious belief'. In addition, civil society itself reflects unequal power relations both within and between organizations. The better-resourced, better-connected and better-networked organizations can command greater positions of power and a louder voice. Further, the internal workings of organizations too frequently produce oligarchies far removed from the rank and file of the constituencies they purport to serve.

Taylor summarizes many of these conflicting tendencies when he argues that civil society seeks to straddle what are often irreconcilable demands: 'between universalism and particularism, between individual and the collective, between public and private, between heterogeneity and equality, democracy and agency, formality and informality, reflexivity and order, enthusiasm and rules' (2002: 60). Recognition of the politics of difference gives rise to the very difficult issues of how links can effectively be made across communities of interest and of how to engage with and stimulate activism in minority communities without disregarding the essence of their constituency.

This exploration of the issues within the context of Wales has raised a number of questions about Welsh society and multiculturalism. Within the new constitutional framework many of the issues of equality of opportunity, citizenship and social inclusion have come to the fore at least in the political rhetoric, and great store is placed on the ability of civil society to progress these ambitions. A by-product of attempts to harness black organizations to the newly devolved state may, however, be the distortion of grassroots interests and the dissipation of naturally occurring/existing voluntarism around bottom-up interests. Institutionalization of the BME constituency is necessarily a deradicalizing force, as formalization brings with it co-option and the suppression of diverse voices. Remoteness, scarcity, capacity and the demographics of association prompt questions about ethnic category as a basis for mobilization in some parts of Wales. It is also pertinent to note that ethnic mobilization is not confined to the Welsh borders and operates across geographical boundary and interest in Welsh affairs to wider communities of interest. Participation and engagement in the institutions of civil society remain the luxury of the few in a society that has for too long excluded attention to diversity. These are some of the key dilemmas and challenges for the regeneration of civil society that embraces cultural diversity in Wales.

Notes

1. This forms of an ESRC-funded project (2001–4) 'Social capital and the participation of marginalised groups in government', led by Professor Ralph Fevre of Cardiff University, ref: R000239410. The case study relies on meeting attendance and participation in the network over a period of two years, an examination of the networks documentation and discussions with key actors. It also draws on interviews with members of associated groups in the north Wales area and on an associated study 'North Wales BME communities research' (the BEST Report) 2004, carried out by the Department of Social Sciences, University of Wales, Bangor.

References

BEST Report (2004). 'North Wales BME communities mapping', prepared by North Wales Race Equality Network in association with the Department of Social Sciences, University of Wales, Bangor.

Chaney, P. and Williams C. (2003). 'Getting involved: civic and political life in Wales', in C. Williams, N. Evans and P. O'Leary (eds), *A Tolerant Nation: Exploring Ethnic Diversity in Wales*, Cardiff: University of Wales Press.

Chaney, P. (2002). 'Social capital and the participation of marginalised groups in government: a study of the statutory partnership between the third sector and devolved government in Wales', *Public Policy and Administration*, 17, 4.

Council for Ethnic Minority Voluntary Organizations Wales Office (CEMVO) (2005). *http://www.cemvo.org.uk*.

Craig, G., Taylor, M., Wilkinson, M. and Bloor, K., with Munro, S. and Syed, A. (2002). *Contract or Trust? The Role of Compacts in Local Governance*, Bristol: Policy Press, for the Joseph Rowntree Foundation.

Davis, S. and Cooke, V. (2002). *Why do Black Women Organise? A Comparative Analysis of Black Women's Voluntary Sector Organizations in Britain and their Relationship to the State*, London: Policy Studies Institute.

Evans, N. (2002). 'Immigrants and minorities in Wales 1840–1990: a comparative perspective' in C. Williams, N. Evans and O'Leary, P. (eds), *A Tolerant Nation: Exploring Ethnic Diversity in Wales*.

Evers, A. (2003). 'Social capital and civic commitment: on Putnam's way of understanding', *Social Policy and Society*, 2, 1.

Fryer, P. (1984). *Staying Power: The History of Black People in Britain*, London: Pluto Press.

Giddens, A. (2000). *The Third Way and its Critics*, Cambridge: Polity Press.

Gramsci A. (1996). *Prison Letters*, Pluto Classics, London: Pluto Press.

Harris, M., Halfpenny, P. and Rochester, C. (2003). 'A social policy role for faith based organizations? Lessons from the UK Jewish voluntary sector', *Journal of Social Policy*, 32, 1.

Hirst, P. (1994). *Associative Democracy: New Forms of Economic and Social Governance*, Cambridge: Cambridge University Press.

Keane, J. (1998). *Civil Society: Old Images, New Visions*, Cambridge: Polity Press.

Kearns, A. (1995). 'Active citizenship and local governance: political and geographical dimensions', *Political Geography*, 14, 2.

Kenny, M. (2001). 'After the deluge: politics and civil society in the wake of the New Right', *Soundings*, 12.

Kymlicka, W. (1995). *Multicultural Citizenship: A Liberal Theory of Minority Rights*, Oxford: Clarendon Press.

Leigh, R. (2000). *Black Elders Project*, Leicester: Leicester Volunteer Centre.

Lukka, P. and Ellis, A. (2001). 'An exclusive construct?: Exploring different cultural concepts of volunteering', *Journal of the Institute of Volunteering Research*, 3, 3, 87–109.

Lukka, P. and Locke, M. (2000). 'Faith, voluntary action and social policy: a research review', *Journal of the Institute for Volunteering Research*, 3, 1, 25–41.

Mainsbridge, J. (1992). 'A deliberative perspective on neo-corporatism', *Politics and Society,* 20, 4, 493–505.

McCleod, M., Owen, D. and Kahamis, C. (2001). *Black and Minority Ethnic Voluntary and Community Organizations: Their Role and Future Development in England and Wales*, London: Policy Studies Institute.

Mouffe, C. (1998). 'The radical centre: a politics without an adversary', *Soundings*, 9, 11–23.

National Assembly for Wales (NAW) (2000). *Voluntary Sector Scheme*, Cardiff: NAW.

Nedelsky, N. (2003). 'Civic nationhood and the challenges of minority inclusion: the case of post communist Czech Republic', *Ethnicities*, 3, 1, 85–114.

Nederveen Pieterse, J. (2003). 'Social capital and migration: beyond ethnic economies', *Ethnicities*, 3, 1, 29–58.

NWREP (North Wales Registered Social Landlord Equality Partnership) (2004). *The Housing Experience and Related Experiences of Black and Minority Ethnic Communities in North Wales*, Caernarfon: NWREP.

Parekh, B. (2000). *Rethinking Multiculturalism: Cultural Diversity and Political Theory*, Basingstoke: Palgrave.

Paterson, L. and Wyn Jones, R. (1999). 'Does civil society drive constitutional change?', in B. Taylor and K. Thomson (eds), *Scotland and Wales: Nations Again?*, Cardiff: University of Wales Press.

Phillips, A. (1995). *The Politics of Presence: Issues in Democracy and Group Representation*, Oxford: Clarendon Press.

Portes, A. (1996) in Nederveen Pieterse, J. (2003). 'Social capital and migration: beyond ethnic economies', *Ethnicities*, 3, 1, 29–58.

Putnam, R. D. (2000). *Bowling Alone: The Collapse and Revival of American Community*, London: Simon & Schuster.

Sinclair, N. (1993). *The Tiger Bay Story*, Cardiff: Butetown History & Arts Centre.

Sinclair, N. (2003). *Endangered Tiger: A Community Under Threat*, Cardiff: Butetown History & Arts Centre.

Taylor, M. (2002). *Public Policy in the Community*, Basingstoke: Palgrave Macmillan.

Tester, K. (1992). *Civil Society*, London: Routledge.

Vertovec, S. (1999). 'Minority associations, networks and public policies, reassessing relationships', *Journal of Ethnic and Migration Studies,* 25, 1, 21–42.

Wales Council for Voluntary Action (WCVA) (2002). *The Civil Society Index*, Cardiff: WCVA.

Wales Funders Forum (2005). 'Added value and added challenges: funding the ethnic minority voluntary sector', briefing paper, Cardiff: Wales Funders Forum.

Webb, T. (2005). 'Y Fro Gymraeg declaration: Cymuned fight back', *Planet*, 169, February/March, 63–7.

Williams, C. (2003). *Colour Coded Devolution*, Cardiff: Institute of Welsh Affairs.

Williams, C. (2004). 'Passions and pathologies in the politics of minority ethnic participation in governance', *Wales Journal of Law and Policy*, 3, 2, 157–73.

Williams, C. and Chaney, P. (2001). 'Inclusive government for excluded groups: ethnic minorities', in P. Chaney, T. Hall and A. Pithouse (eds), *New Governance, New Democracy?*, Cardiff: University of Wales Press.

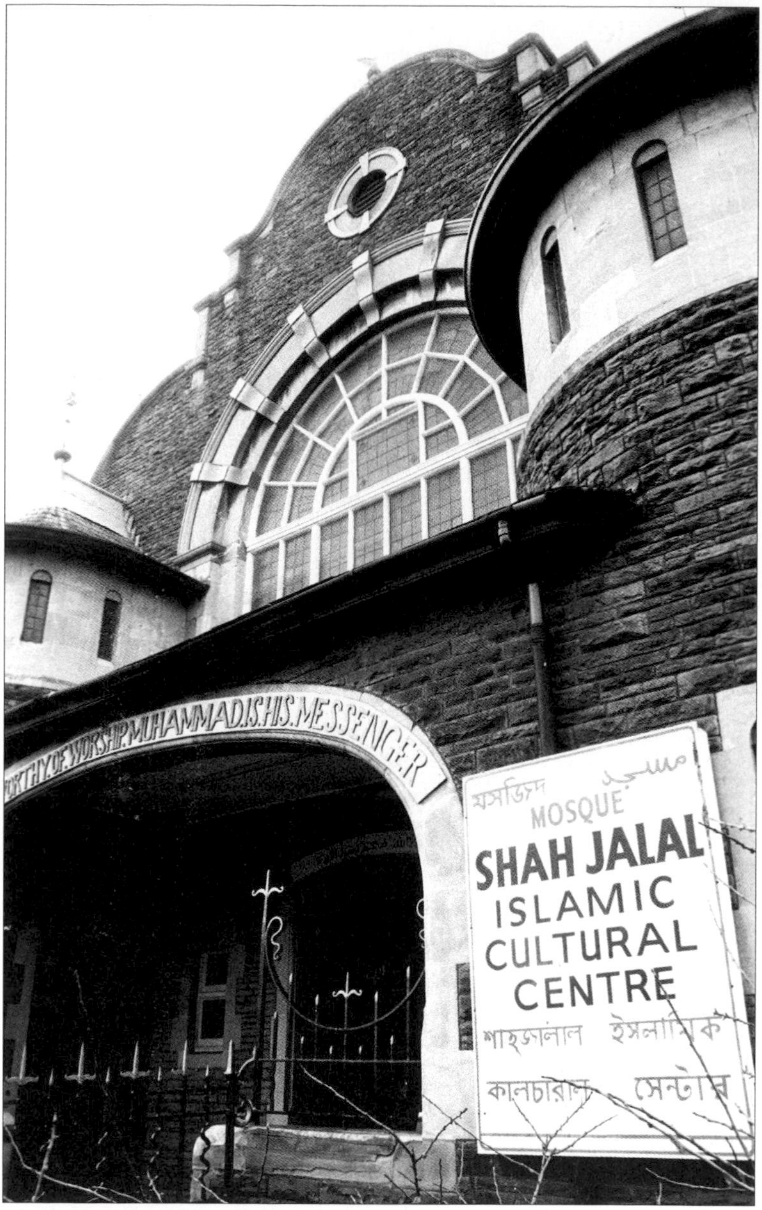
ORTHY.OF.WORSHIP.MUHAMMAD.IS.HIS.MESSENGER
মসজিদ
مسجد
MOSQUE
SHAH JALAL
ISLAMIC
CULTURAL
CENTRE
শাহজালাল ইসলামিক
কালচারাল সেন্টার

11. Public Religion and Civil Society in Wales

PAUL CHAMBERS AND ANDREW THOMPSON

Voluntary associations are an important component of civil society and religious institutions are an inescapable part of this sphere. Indeed, it might be said that to some extent the health of civil society can be measured by the health of its religious institutions. This chapter outlines and explores the contribution of religious organizations and institutions to Welsh civil society. Adopting an inclusive orientation which seeks to address the views of both traditional Welsh religious institutions and newly arrived religious groups, it will describe the various networks operating within the religious sphere, how they are formed, what barriers exist to communication, and the ways in which these organizations cooperate (or not) to formulate and convey their concerns through political institutions like the National Assembly. The chapter draws on data gathered in the course of interviews with forty faith group leaders in Wales.

Religion and civil society

At its simplest 'civil society' has been seen as a particular form of society, celebrating social diversity and capable of limiting potentially despotic forms of government (Hall, 1995) and, as that public space, often understood as situated between market and state, that is the province of voluntary associations and the site of active citizenship (Wuthnow, 1996). More specifically, Shanks (1995) writes of *self-conscious* civil society, the province of intellectuals, engaged in critiques of the state and market, and *unself-conscious* civil society, the sphere of professional expertise. In the latter, voluntary associations, both religious and secular, dominate, providing both a space for politics independent of the state or political parties and fora in which awkward questions can be asked about state and society. Shanks characterizes this activity as 'anti-politics' and its practitioners as uninterested in gaining political power for themselves but concerned with questions of morality and ethics, the defence of freedoms and the promotion of social justice. Faith groups, as voluntary associations, are both an integral part of civil society and the theory of civil society and can therefore legitimately contribute to discourses surrounding morality, power and ethics.

The idea that religion might have a place within civil society has been met variously with enthusiasm in some quarters and with suspicion or indifference in others. Within many European societies, religion is seen as primarily a private affair or, if public, then properly restricted to a limited range of state-sanctioned activities such as parades, processions and civic ceremonies. Within British sociology and political science, where religion is treated at all in discussions of politics, it tends to be in negative terms and as an exotic species, employing labels such as the 'New Moral Right' (Thompson, 1997).

The literature emanating from the USA is rather more positive about faith group involvement in civil society. In part this reflects the fact that faith communities and religious institutions play a greater part in American society, both in terms of the sheer number of their adherents and in their power to influence moral and political debates. Thus, Parker (2000) points to the sizeable contribution of faith groups to public policy debates in the USA, from the public support of the 10-million-member United Methodist Church for higher taxes on the wealthy through to the work of groups such as the Greater Boston Interfaith Organization on urban regeneration. For writers like Parker and Wuthnow (1996) there is no question that faith groups are at the forefront of efforts to address questions about the nature of civil society and morality. Key questions revolve around the decline of voluntary associations (Putnam, 2001), the decline of ethics and civility in moral discourses, notably within the abortion debate (Wuthnow, 1996) and the nature of social bonds within a highly egoistic and individualistic society (Bellah, 1991). Lovelace (1995: 69) highlights the still strong relationship between faith and public life in the USA: 'It is certainly not an America gripped by religious decay, indifference and relativism . . . it is not a post-Christian society in any sense that reverses de Tocqueville. Any political landscape with this much God talk going on may be divided, but it is religiously alive.'

Parekh (2000: 235) suggests that even within a highly secularized Britain 'faith communities and religious organizations play significant roles in civil society'. These roles include voluntary activity at the local level, partnership with government in regeneration programmes and also their capacity to inform and sensitize their own members to issues of social justice. Parekh also suggests that public life should both recognize a wider range of cultural (including religious) identities and realize that faith groups represent a valuable resource of ethical arguments that might inform public discourses on morality and ethics. The key question here is how realistic is it to expect, and to what extent *can*, faith groups influence public moral debates? From the standpoint of faith groups, it is clear that, compared with the religious situation of America, faith groups in Europe have become progressively marginalized in these debates as religious institutions have suffered that loss of social significance associated with secularization.

In his book *Public Religions in the Modern World*, Casanova (1994) calls into question some of the assumptions about the impact of secularization on religious institutions operating within the public sphere, arguing that religion in modern societies is now undergoing a process of 'deprivatization' leading to re-engagement with the world of public affairs and issues. For Casanova, 'public religion', the active involvement of faith groups in public affairs, has historically taken three broad forms. The first is 'established' public religion at the state level. The second is where religious institutions use their influence and connections to defend their particular privileges. These forms of public religion correspond largely to pre-modern social and political arrangements. With regard to the first this was largely about the imposition of the Church's will on the population through the legislative arms of the state. Although state religions still exist in some European countries, this all-encompassing power is a thing of the past. In terms of the second form, this was primarily about religious institutions using their influence within political society both to defend their interests and to uphold their vision of society. This is best exemplified by the relationship in Britain between the Liberal Party and Nonconformity, or in continental Europe between the

Catholic Church and Christian Democratic parties. For Casanova, only a third type of public religion, in which faith groups are concerned with the defence of the human person and rights of all people, is truly consistent with the principles of structurally differentiated modern societies and the open discursive sphere of civil society.

Religion and social change in Wales

In the modern period there have been strong connections between religion, notably Nonconformity, and political and social life in Wales. The rapid spread of Nonconformity throughout Wales from the mid-eighteenth century onwards was a key development in this process and by the mid-nineteenth century Nonconformity was a pervasive influence throughout Welsh society. In this respect, nineteenth-century Welsh Nonconformism bears the hallmarks of a public religion. While some ministers of religion opposed the participation of clergy in political activity, increasingly Nonconformism was becoming associated with political radicalism. Opposition to the Anglican Church was a central tenet of the Free Churches, but its ministers were also increasingly active in many areas of rural politics and wider issues such as the campaign for franchise reform. By the end of the nineteenth century, Nonconformism was part of the political establishment and a pervasive influence in Welsh society. A flourishing Welsh-language press played an important role in this respect. Nonconformist clergy utilized the newspaper to carry their message to the public. Among the most important of these publications, in terms of those responsible for their production, were *Y Diwygiwr*, *Y Cronicl* and *Yr Amserau*. The common ground shared by these papers is that they were published by radical independent ministers who were vociferous supporters not only of disestablishment but also of the demands made by social reformers. In other respects Nonconformism constituted a powerful moral community, whether within or outside of the orbit of the chapel. To transgress against the strict moral codes of the chapel was to be placed outside of respectable society (Welsby, 1995; Chambers, 2005). The combined influence of Nonconformism and Liberalism was evident in 1881, when the first legislative act specific to Wales was passed: the Sunday Closing Act. By this period, too, public religion was part of an emergent Welsh nationalism. The influence of the Nonconformism/Liberalism axis in Wales continued into the twentieth century, until the Labour Party became the political choice of the mass of the Welsh electorate, but the seeds of its demise were planted earlier.

The factors taken to have contributed to the demise of Liberal Nonconformism are numerous, but arguably one of the most significant is that the issues most concerning the nonconformist churches, chief among them disestablishment, increasingly failed to resonate with those of the industrial working classes. As one commentator remarks:

> The concentration of Welsh nonconformity on disestablishment during and after the 1880s became less and less relevant to the problems of an industrial society. By the end of the century, workers concluded that they could best achieve their aspirations through their own industrial and political organizations, and they ceased to look to the chapels as their political allies. (Lambert, 1976: 14)

The Nonconformist churches were certainly not unaware of the need to develop a social gospel that reflected the changing social and economic conditions in Wales, especially in its industrial areas. Indeed, in his study of the relationship between Nonconformism and the labour movement in the first half of the twentieth century Pope (1997) claims that the chapels continued to play an important role within local communities.

Even allowing for Pope's argument, the fact remains that from a position of considerable influence over social and political life in Wales, throughout the course of the twentieth century, and especially in the post-1945 era, the purchase of Nonconformism has gradually waned. In this respect, Wales has not been exempt from the patterns of secularization that have swept Europe in the twentieth century. The most recent survey of religious worship in Wales, which estimates that fewer than 9 per cent of the population still regularly attends Christian places of worship, demonstrates graphically this loss of the social significance of religion in Wales (Bible Society, 1997). Numerical decline has been accompanied by a weakening of the purchase of organized religion over political and social affairs in Wales. Though the historic Welsh denominations (Baptists, Independents and Presbyterians), and the Church in Wales, retain personal links into the political establishment in Wales, there is little doubt that the influence they exercised over the population even as recent as the 1950s has weakened markedly (Chambers and Thompson, 2005).

It is possible to overstate the hegemony of Nonconformity during this period, not least because the Roman Catholic Church and various newly arrived English faith groups were becoming a visible force in the industrialized regions of Wales. The story of religion in the twentieth century, therefore, is not just about declining attendance figures and diminishing public influence; it is also about increasing religious diversity and pluralism. Unsurprisingly, these groups have also sought to extend their influence into the public sphere. Disestablishment in 1920 paved the way for the reinvention of the Church in Wales as a major Welsh institution (Harris and Startup, 1999). The Roman Catholic Church, despite encountering continuing prejudice, also established itself as a Welsh institution, eventually winning social and cultural acceptability (Hughes, 1999). The evangelical sphere, both within the mainstream churches and among the sects, also continued to grow throughout most of the twentieth century. Among the mainstream Christian churches, from 1950, their energies were largely taken up with coming to terms with their past and in trying to stem numerical decline. Among these churches, this growing sense of crisis led to the gradual embracing of ecumenism, of which CYTÛN (Churches Together in Wales), a loose partnership arrangement among the mainstream churches established in 1956, is the most visible and successful example.

Outside of the Christian sphere many world faiths are now present in Wales: Bahaism, Buddhism, Hare Krishna, Hinduism, Sikhism and, most visibly, Islam. While it would be misleading to suggest that these non-Christian religions constitute a numerically significant presence in Wales, nevertheless, with the notable exception of Judaism, which has been in decline since the 1960s, they constitute a growing sector within the religious sphere (Davies, 1990). The 2001 census shows that Islam constitutes the largest non-Christian faith group in Wales, with 20,301 people, or 0.7 per cent of the Welsh population, defining themselves as Muslim. Cardiff (Butetown and Riverside) and Newport (Corporation Road) have long been home to significant Muslim populations and in recent years Swansea (St Helens) has also developed a vibrant and visible Muslim community. While these populations have until recently been associated with cities, within the last year new mosques have been established in the county boroughs of Bridgend and Rhondda Cynon Taff. Rather like the role of the chapels in the nineteenth century, the mosques provide the focus for public life within these localities, often mediating between the local population and government and other public bodies. In 1997 a Welsh-based Association of Muslim Professionals was established, furthering the institutionalization of Islam within Welsh society.

It is therefore important to acknowledge that, although discussions of religion in Wales have almost invariably, and perhaps understandably, concentrated on the decline of Nonconformism, the last century has seen a proliferation in the types of faith groups. It would also be erroneous to underestimate the continued role of religious institutions, notably the mainstream Christian faith groups, within Welsh society. Throughout the twentieth century these organizations have retained personal links with key figures in the political sphere. The media attention given to the appointment of Rowan Williams as archbishop of Canterbury in 2003 illustrates the way in which religion continues to attract interest within the public domain. While there can be no doubt that sections of the faith community have experienced decline, they retain their presence within localities and are an important resource for local populations both in terms of social capital and the various welfare related and associational activities they provide. As with so many areas of life in Wales, the key question is whether devolution has provided faith groups with an opportunity to increase their contribution to the public life and raise their national profile.

Religion and civil society in Wales

When we consider civil society and the role of voluntary associations within it, we cannot ignore the contribution of faith groups and institutional religion. There are, however, clearly some elements of religious moralizing that sit uneasily with the population of many contemporary European societies. Questions of sexuality, abortion and contraception are perhaps the main areas of contention. For example, the rhetoric and activities of some pro-life groups has sometimes spilled over into direct action of a violent nature. The Rushdie affair raised serious questions about both the limits of free speech and the right of faith groups to impose their beliefs on others who do not hold to those belief systems. In the matter of personal and privatized morality, much of the discourses on Clause 28 have again been highly proscriptive. Some of the representatives of faith groups to whom we spoke expressed open opposition to any policies seen to encourage what they viewed as immoral behaviour.

On the other hand, faith group representatives also expressed opposing views, which affirm personal liberty. What many had in common was a defence of the individual person against materialist currents present in modern societies. In their differing ways all the faith groups we talked to seek to affirm the dignity and self-worth of the individual and, by extension, communities. For instance, when asked about the contribution that faith groups make to society, the mainstream churches' National Liaison Officer to the National Assembly told us:

> I think the most valuable thing that we can offer is an understanding that people and communities matter. And that people have an intrinsic value that sees them as more than voters and consumers. And I think that is the one perception, the one aspect of our life that we can't really abandon. And that's what we can offer to people, is that intrinsic sense of value. That community value is important. That the individual is important . . . and that people are more than things.

This was not merely the view of the mainstream churches but was expressed by all faith groups. This idea of individual self-worth was communicated to us as being an integral element of religion. Further, religious belief itself was viewed as a bulwark against the intrusion of what one senior member of Cardiff's Muslim population called 'materialistic passions'. In a similar vein, a representative of the Presbyterian Church, when asked how religion responds to the intrusion of market values into morality, commented that what religion represented is a 'spirit that puts society before self. Where you give not because you're getting anything back, but because you want to help the common good.'

For faith groups, it is important that this general ethical stance should be expressed in social action, particularly action within localities. This notion of putting faith into practice was perhaps best expressed by an evangelical Christian youth worker, who remarked that his religious calling was summed up as being to 'work with people where they're at . . . one-to-one in the local community'. Nearly all groups spoke directly about the centrality of social responsibility in the religious imperative and the importance of deeds as well as words within the public arena. A leading Methodist, when asked what right faith groups have to speak on moral or ethical issues, said: 'we're speaking out of our concern . . . I want us to exercise social responsibility. I want us to do it in word and I also want us to do it in action.' A representative of an evangelical Christian voluntary sector organization similarly linked faith with social action when, in the course of talking about the difference between the Christian and secular voluntary sector, remarked that 'there is no special difference in terms of the nature of the product provided. Obviously, Christians have a different motivation I guess because their motivation is to provide an active demonstration of God's love to people.' Indeed, a common theme that emerged in discussions about morality was the need to lead by example, demonstrating in practice a moral orientation towards others.

Such sentiments are illustrative of the idea of a 'public religion'. In terms of the active participation of faith groups in public affairs this was not restricted to merely advancing their own interests. For example, CYTÛN was instrumental in bringing the plight of asylum seekers lodged in Cardiff Prison to the Assembly's attention. The south Wales Hindu community (assisted by other faith groups) organized extensive relief materials for victims of the recent Indian earthquake. All the main faith groups in Wales were vociferous in their opposition to British involvement in the war in Iraq in 2003. On a more localized level, all faith groups are to some extent actively involved in schools work and projects related to local community development, including services for the homeless, the unemployed, pensioners, parents and young people. In some senses this kind of work is not new but recent years have undoubtedly witnessed renewed efforts by faith groups to address some of the negative impacts of socio-economic change in Wales. Moreover, whereas before a good deal of this work happened within faith communities, now this work is increasingly taking place within the wider society.

These developments can perhaps be seen as part of a wider process of adaptation on the part of religious institutions, especially among Christian groups wherein anxieties about declining attendance have forced them to reassess their role within what appears to be a post-Christian society. For example, a leading Anglican commented:

> Deindustrialization means that we can no longer afford now to ignore employment issues and we have got to find a new model of engagement both strategically and structurally and to help reconstruct the future of Wales. The challenge for the churches is whether they can play a role, a distinctive role, in facilitating a new approach to civil society. Citizenship participation, leadership, partnerships, regeneration schemes, local community projects . . . and by being there, by being supportive, by demonstrating a genuine interest in these things . . . and an ability to engage with the nation.

The ongoing rural crisis and the conditions in post-industrial localities have challenged Christian faith groups to engage with communities in a practical way and in doing so to develop a wider theology of social engagement. With the Muslim community this 'theology' is already an integral part of Islamic religious teaching. For the churches, and particularly the evangelical community, this has meant developing a theology of social engagement that resonates more clearly with the people of Wales.

An important element of this development has been the move towards greater cooperation between faith groups. To date, this has largely been between Christian groups. Since 1950 the evangelical community has produced a number of associations, such as the Evangelical Movement of Wales and the Associating Evangelical Churches in Wales. During the same period the mainstream churches moved towards ecumenicalism, of which CYTÛN, as we have noted, is arguably the most effective such entity. This period has also seen localized efforts towards dialogue between faiths, such as the Cardiff Council of Christians and Jews established in 1948 and Cardiff Interfaith. There is little doubt that the impetus for and profile of inter-faith work has increased in recent years. Devolution has played its part here, culminating in 2002 in the formation of the Interfaith Council for Wales as a subcommittee of the National Assembly, and through which faith leaders liaised directly with AMs. In 2004 the council was replaced by the Faith Communities Forum. The forum is not an Assembly body in the way that the council, as it was, sat within the formal Assembly structure. The presence of the forum allows faith groups to directly to lobby the Assembly within the context of an Assembly 'partnership', replicating the former role of the council but within a slightly different structural context. The Interfaith Council now operates as an ecumenical forum for the mainstream world faiths based in Wales.

Despite these efforts towards cooperation, boundaries remain. Evangelical groups are reluctant to work with their mainstream counterparts and again there is little or no visible cooperation between Christians and other faith groups on substantive issues. For example, although evangelicals and Muslims share similarities on moral issues, particularly those relating to sexuality and gambling, there have been no moves to pool resources or cooperate in lobbying appropriate bodies. Even within CYTÛN, which represents liberal mainstream Christian groups, differences in theological emphasis and denominational integrities sometimes make achieving consensus difficult.

Perhaps the changing face of Welsh religion is best captured through the notion of a multi-faith Wales, even if this is at present still largely restricted to the south. The decline of Nonconformism, and the weakening of religion generally, and the increasing fragmentation of the religious sphere highlight the way that spaces have appeared for multiple expressions of religious faith. Indeed, the Wales of a monolithic Nonconformist hegemony was to some extent an illusion fostered by the strength of Nonconformism. It could be argued that Anglicanism and Roman Catholicism were as much expressions of an indigenous Welsh identity, but it is only now, as the gaps appear, that these institutions can be seen for what they are: indigenous to Welsh society. In the same vein, non-Christian faith groups are increasingly seeking to stake their claim as Welsh institutions. As the public role of these faith groups grows, an ethno-religious vision of Wales becomes increasingly anachronistic, out of step with the realities of modern Welsh life. Nevertheless, part of the process of coming to terms with the past still necessarily involves a place for religious institutions and faith. Especially in the case of sections of Wales's ethnic minority populations religious faith is an integral element of their ethnic identity and of their Welshness. If the early twentieth century was marked by the reinvention of the Church in Wales as a Welsh institution and the gradual acceptance of the Roman Catholic Church as a Welsh institution, then the current period is witnessing the beginnings of a recognition of non-Christian faiths as also Welsh. Indeed, as faith groups increasingly seek to engage with the project of redefining Welsh public culture, religious diversity in itself becomes a reflection of an increasingly diverse Wales. This is more than a passive reflection, however, as faith groups actively seek to engage with public institutions and public life to further what they perceive as the common good.

The impact of devolution

Many of the Christian denominations and their members were vocal supporters of devolution. The preservation and protection of the Welsh language and culture was a key issue among those denominations and groups who operate largely through the medium of the Welsh language, but there was also much more to recommend devolution to religious institutions in Wales. Not least was the government's stated intention to narrow the democratic deficit through more inclusive and consensual government and a commitment to tackle some of Wales's most pressing social and economic problems through the greater use of partnership arrangements with the voluntary sector, including faith groups. Central to this project was the establishment of the Voluntary Sector Scheme, with a remit to develop better channels of communication between the state and the voluntary sector and to formalize arrangements for consultation and partnership. These channels follow both formal and informal routes and both have been utilized by faith groups, if somewhat patchily, to share ideas, make representations and generally raise their profile in Welsh policy debates.

In terms of policy issues, in a recent document CYTÛN has identified four evolving areas of concern for Christian faith groups. These are: greater access to the National Assembly; an emphasis on better directing available funding to deprived communities; the development of policies concerned with addressing social exclusion and vulnerable sections of society; and working through the Assembly to tackle matters over which it has no direct influence but which through its offices it has the ability to lobby on, such as the Jubilee 2000 'drop the debt' campaign and transnational environmental concerns. CYTÛN itself has, among other things, submitted evidence to the Assembly on the conditions of asylum seekers placed in Cardiff Prison as indicated above and made representations to the Assembly regarding Objective One funding for Wales. For the Evangelical Alliance, devolution: 'provides more interfaces for us to engage with than there were before, and a greater incentive to engage in them . . . an opportunity to have the potential to shape some of the values of nation and government policy'. Other faith groups share these concerns, though the matter of gaining greater access to the Assembly in order to voice their concerns understandably has a different resonance for minority groups. Indeed, individual faith groups also have specific issues they are keen to pursue in the Assembly. For example, Clause 28 has been a particular focus of lobbying for evangelical groups, as have racially motivated attacks for Muslims, Hindus and Sikhs, most notably in the wake of the events of 11 September 2001.

In terms of links into the Assembly, the mainstream Christian groups were the only faith groups to be directly represented on the Voluntary Sector Partnership Council (VSPC) before the creation of the Interfaith Council for Wales, a representative from which now speaks on behalf of all faith groups on the VSPC. Welsh Christian denominational leaders also meet the first minister on a biannual basis. The churches have also sought to voice their concerns and extend their influence through informal channels and face-to-face contact with Assembly ministers. In this they are helped by both the small size of the National Assembly and the historic contours of Welsh civil society, both of which contribute to an ease of access not yet found in Westminster or Edinburgh. The churches' own liaison officer contrasted the favourable Welsh experience with that of other UK faith groups with whom they are in contact, commenting:

> Yes, we are in dialogue with our partners in Scotland. They have a far more formal response to the legislative process in the new parliament, for example, and they notice our way of dealing with things in Wales is far more intimate and hands on. That refreshing day-to-day dialogue is something that I think we can offer for the future . . . In the case of the Assembly, through my office particularly, you can get very, very hands on . . . and because you have a one-to-one level of dialogue with politicians with something that is just Welsh, then you can have an indigenous dialogue developing.

However, in contrast to the degree of 'intimacy' with the Assembly experienced by mainstream Christian groups, other faith groups have struggled to achieve recognition based on their religious identity rather than their ethnic identity, something that Weller (2001) has noted is found in England as well as Wales. As we have noted, however, since early 2002 the Interfaith Council for Wales member on the VSPC has represented all faith groups.

The latter development illustrates the way in which faith groups have adapted to the opportunities presented by devolution. A further development among those faith groups operating in Wales but with their principal base in England has been to refashion themselves much more as specifically Welsh institutions. Thus, the Methodist Church has instituted a Gymanfa, or General Assembly, which operates as the forum for the various circuits based in Wales and which acts as the focus for a specifically Welsh Methodist identity. In a slightly different manner, the Salvation Army has for the first time adopted a Welsh-language policy in recognition of the changing political culture in Wales. The changes within CYTÛN provide another interesting example of the galvanizing effect of devolution. Though CYTÛN has existed since the mid-1950s, its organizational remit was primarily to foster closer relations between mainstream Christian faith groups. Since devolution it has established a full-time liaison officer based at the Temple of Peace in Cardiff with the task of informing the churches about Assembly affairs and also giving them a presence in the Assembly. Before the advent of the Interfaith Council for Wales, CYTÛN was the sole faith body present on the VSPC. The Interfaith Council and the Faith Communities Forum are the most recent manifestations of the impact of devolution on the religious sphere in Wales.

There are, then, a number of both institutional and informal means by which faith groups can access the Assembly and its politicians. When we undertook our interviews in 2001/2 the general perception, from the Church in Wales to the Commission for Racial Equality and from the Union of Welsh Independents to Cardiff Interfaith, was that the Assembly is keen to work with faith groups and they, in turn, with it. Of all the reasons cited perhaps the one expressed most widely was the view that the Assembly was more 'accessible', both in the sense of being in south Wales and in being approachable and receptive. Thus, a senior member of the Church in Wales's Church and Society Board told us that 'because the Assembly has deliberately espoused higher access than Whitehall, and because we're smaller, there is a much greater chance, in theory and practice, of influencing the Assembly'. A leading member of Cardiff's Hindu population similarly remarked that 'we find that since they're in Cardiff, the Assembly, then the chances for us to talk is more nearer for us and it's more convenient for us to talk to them than when they were in Westminster'. Christian faith groups were more upbeat about their links with the Assembly due to relations with politicians pre-dating devolution, though even representatives of other faith groups remarked that they expected that they would see an improvement in their relations with government because of devolution.

To what extent faith groups are finding receptive ears within Cardiff Bay is, however, difficult to discern. The direct intervention of the first minister in enabling the creation of the Interfaith Council in 2002 would certainly seem to be a step forward for faith groups. Yet, the impetus for this development came not from within Wales but rather from New York, or more precisely the attacks on the World Trade Centre. Nor, arguably, was the creation of the council a direct response to faith issues, but instead to concern about racism and racial violence in Wales following 9/11. As the first minister remarked on the occasion of the inaugural meeting of the council,

> There has been overwhelming support and enthusiasm for the Interfaith Council across all religious groups in Wales and a very deep commitment to working together to eradicate the scourge of religious and racial intolerance from Wales . . . The terrible events of September 11th have drawn people together in an unprecedented spirit of unity and cooperation and I am confident that we can build upon this so that people in Wales can go about their daily lives without fear of abuse and violence.

The existence of the Interfaith Council, and subsequently the Faith Communities Forum, has nevertheless given faith groups an institutional presence in the Assembly. If for Christian faith groups this is a welcome development, its establishment is potentially of greater significance for other faith groups. Though at the time of writing the representative of the Interfaith Council on the VSPC is the same individual who had previously represented CYTÛN on this body the involvement of the Interfaith Council is intended to ensure that representation of a broader range of views from within Wales's religious sphere. At present it is too soon to make any assessment of the impact of the Interfaith Council or the Faith Communities Forum. However, for faith groups the future clearly lies in cementing firmer institutional links with the Assembly. One Welsh Baptist leader succinctly summed up this dilemma, saying:

> I think the influence we have is on a personal level rather than on a general level. The fact that Rhodri Morgan was brought up a Baptist. The fact that the leader of Plaid Cymru [then Dafydd Wigley] is a Baptist, a Deacon of the Church, that is important. That many of the AMs are church members. Paul Murphy [then Welsh Secretary] again, is a Catholic and a devout Catholic. So it's on that kind of level, but what happens then, the fundamental question is, what happens in 5 or 10 years' time, when those in leadership, when those in [political] leadership will have no belief? Who will want to listen to the churches? The question then, is what influence remains when the personal contact has gone?

Others similarly added that the days when certain Christian denominations exercised political influence 'are gone', as one leading Methodist commented: 'Churches don't have an absolute right to be heard just because they are Churches.'

Nevertheless there are obstacles to the participation of faith groups within civic life, arguably the most significant one of which is the general difficulty facing faith groups wishing to voice their concerns within an increasingly secular society. Ironically, in spite of the concerns voiced by some that members of non-Christian faith groups struggle to have themselves heard as members of faith groups rather than as members of an ethnic minority, it is the desire to embrace multiculturalism that has been behind the most significant political development for faith groups, the Interfaith Council. There are also a number of institutional barriers. For example, Christian faith groups, with more conventional organizational structures, are better equipped in terms of resources and structure to engage with the Assembly than faith groups, such as Hindus and Muslims, that do not have comparable types of national or even regional structures. The mainstream Christian churches are especially well-served by the offices of their Assembly liaison officer. The operation of CYTÛN nevertheless brings its own difficulties, perhaps part and parcel of any ecumenical organization charged with acting for a diverse range of denominations.

Conclusion

The nature of public religion in Wales remains fluid and, in the case of the mainstream, is largely tied into the project of political devolution. This has not always been the case. In the late nineteenth century and early twentieth century, Nonconformity could with some justification point to its pervasive influence throughout Welsh society. However, under the conditions of marked secularization and a declining religious constituency that have characterized the past five decades, religious institutions have become increasingly resigned to speaking from the margins. While political devolution and the creation of new democratic structures have facilitated the emergence of a renewed prophetic religious voice, it is only one among many competing organizations seeking to disseminate their views. From the perspective of the Assembly, faith groups are merely one species of voluntary association, albeit with a significant historical tradition in Wales that cannot yet be discounted. In essence, religious institutions, while demonstrating a renewed confidence in their ability to contribute to the moral and ethical debates surrounding a 'new' Wales, are highly dependent for this on the goodwill of the political architects of civil society in Wales. In this light, this is certainly not a case of resurgent religious institutions forcing their way back into the public sphere but is more an unintended consequence of the impact of political devolution on many areas of public life.

References

Bellah, R. (1991). *Beyond Belief: Essays on Religion in a Post-traditional World*, Berkeley: University of California Press.

Bible Society (1997). *Challenge to Change: Results of the 1995 Welsh Churches Survey*, Swindon: Bible Society.

Casanova, J. (1994). *Public Religions in the Modern World*, Chicago: University of Chicago Press.

Chambers, P. (2005). *Religion, Secularization and Social Change in Wales*, Cardiff: University of Wales Press.

Chambers, P. and Thompson, A. (2005). 'Public religion and political change in Wales', *Sociology*, 39, 1.

Davies, D. P. (1990). 'A time of paradoxes among the faiths', in D. Cole (ed.), *The New Wales*, Cardiff: University of Wales Press.

Hall, J. A. (1995). 'In search of civil society', in J. A. Hall (ed.), *Civil Society: Theory, History and Comparison*, Cambridge: Polity.

Harris, C. and Startup, R. (1999). *The Church in Wales: A Sociology of a Traditional Institution*, Cardiff: University of Wales Press.

Hughes, T.O. (1999). *Winds of Change: The Roman Catholic Church and Society 1916–1962,* Cardiff: University of Wales Press.

Lambert, W. R. (1976). 'Some working-class attitudes towards organized religion in nineteenth century Wales', *Llafur*, 2, 1.

Lovelace, R. (1995). 'The Bible in public discourse', in R. Petersen (ed.), *Christianity and Civil Society*, New York: Orbis Books.

Parekh, B. (2000). *The Future of Multi-Ethnic Britain*, London: Profile Books.

Parker, R. (2000). 'Progressive politics and, uh, . . . God', *The American Prospect Online*, 11, 5, 17 January.

Pope, R. (1997). *Building Jerusalem*, Cardiff: University of Wales Press.

Putnam, R. (2001). *Bowling Alone*, New York: Simon & Schuster.

Shanks, A. (1995). *Civil Society, Civil Religion,* Oxford: Blackwell.

Thompson, W. (1997). 'Charismatic politics: the social and political impact of renewal', in S. Hunt, M. Hamilton and T. Walter (eds), *Charismatic Christianity: Sociological Perspectives*, Basingstoke: Macmillan.

Weller, P. (ed.) (2001). *Religions in the UK: A Multi-Faith Directory*, Derby: The Multi-Faith Centre, University of Derby.

Welsby, C. (1995). '"Warning her as to her future behaviour": the lives of widows of the Senghenydd Mining Disaster of 1913', *Llafur: Journal of Welsh Labour History*, 6, 4.

Wuthnow, R. (1996). *Christianity and Civil Society*, Valley Forge: Trinity Press International.

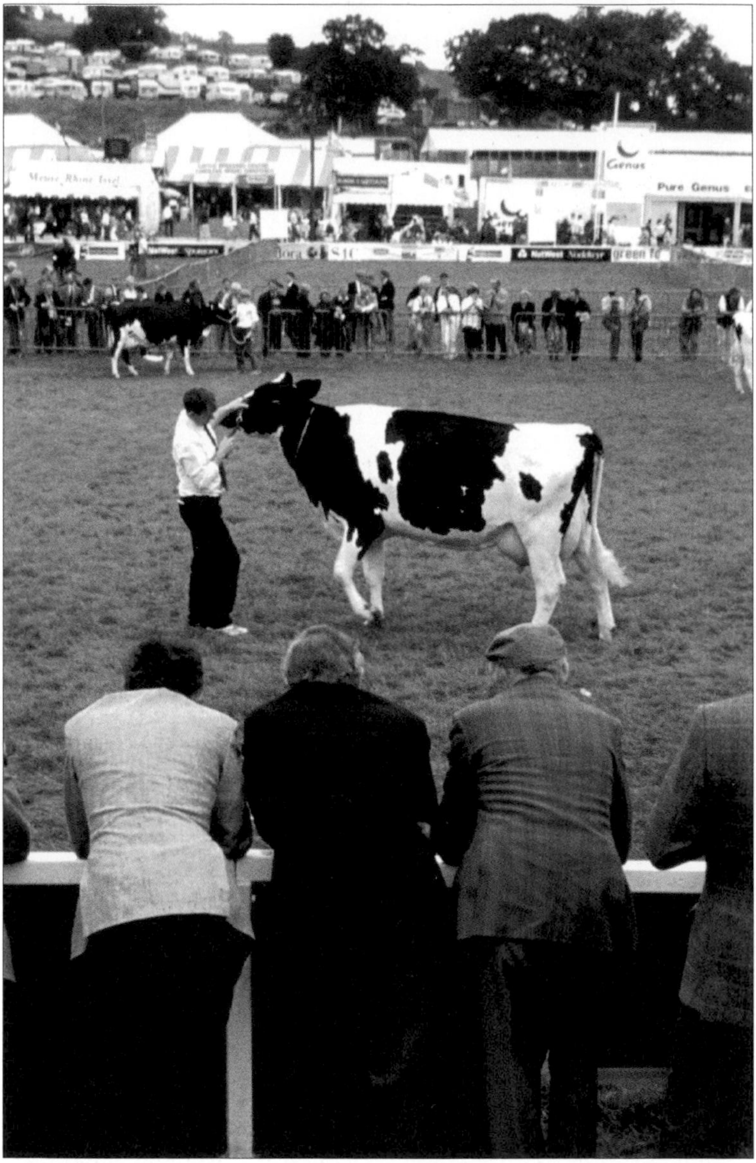
Genus
Pure Genus

12. A Community of Communities? Civil Society and Rural Wales

GRAHAM DAY

Introduction

Like other rural areas, across Britain and indeed most of Europe, rural Wales has been going through some difficult times. Those industries which traditionally provided its economic and social foundations have been in long-term, continuous decline. Changing perspectives and values have brought into question old assumptions about the nature and purpose of country living, and helped challenge established patterns of social power and interest domination. Particular crises, associated with BSE and foot and mouth disease (FMD), have shaken people's faith in the groups trusted with 'stewardship' of the countryside and led to vigorous debates about the relative merits of productive, environmental and consumer uses of rural resources. FMD finally drove home the message that country districts no longer revolve around farming, and that, whatever rural economy and society today is about, it does not begin and end at the farm gate. As a result, there has been a sense of confusion and disarray, as politicians and decision-makers make long-overdue adjustments to these changes, which has encouraged some major rethinking about rural policy. In England, a seminar series promoted by the newly reorganized DEFRA (the Department for Rural Affairs) and the Countryside Agency has tackled a range of new concerns and concepts, such as the value of the 'countryside capital', new interests in community capacity building, forms of social enterprise, and questions of local empowerment and exclusion (see, for example, Countryside Agency, 2003). Interestingly, these all highlight the importance of the 'social' dimensions of rural living, and blur quite considerably the boundaries between the social, the political and the economic.

These preoccupations are echoed in much of the policy framework and debate in Wales. As part of its vision for 'a sustainable, inclusive and equal Wales' (NAW, 2001), the National Assembly for Wales (NAW) has set as its objective the maintenance of 'viable and balanced' communities in rural Wales. While this means doing what is necessary to support and maintain traditional rural industries, especially agriculture, it also involves responding to the impact of major change and restructuring which has transformed the nature of rural Wales. Following NAW's lead, the Welsh Development Agency (WDA) document *Supporting Rural Wales* (WDA, 2001) refers to the region's 'traditional community strengths' and states that: 'The traditional close knit communities of Rural Wales with their unique culture and heritage are a resource to be built upon. We need to harness the enthusiasm and enterprise of these communities to enable them to play a significant part in shaping their future.' (p. 8) According to the Rural Partnership for Wales in its report on *Rural Wales* (2002), 'The communities of rural Wales provide a solid foundation for social and cultural life and a springboard for economic regeneration'.

More locally, the same message comes over from the agencies, in a statement of aspiration as much as fact. For example, the North Wales Economic Forum *Rural Recovery Plan* notes how '(f)lourishing, vibrant and culturally strong communities attract and retain people; they have the potential to provide areas of economic growth'. The recovery plan incorporates the rural 'communities' of north Wales into its vision statement, which aims to 'create a rural economy in North Wales which is vibrant, sustainable and resilient, that builds on its unique culture, gives people a pride in their communities and motivates them to live and work here' (*http://www.llandrillo.ac.uk/host/nwef*).

The stress on creating 'thriving' or 'vibrant' local communities, as the key to successful rural development, is not peculiar to Wales – it has been a theme of successive English rural White Papers – but there is a tendency to assume that Wales has a head-start in this respect, because it is already the home of the strong, integrated, rural community. At the same time, 'really existing' rural communities are expected to *prove* that they deserve this reputation; if not, then they must work to remedy the problem. So the bidding document for support under the Assembly's Rural Community Action programme (NAW, 2002) states that 'it must be demonstrated that a broad cross-section of the community are actively engaged in the planning and decision-making process' (p. 2). Development strategies are expected to 'take into account community consultation to establish what measures are necessary to foster a strong sense of community cooperation, participation and cohesion, and remove barriers to participation, particularly for women, young people and the elderly' (p. 6). There is a recognition here that communities may not live up to their image, and may need encouragement to do so. The expectation is that, by engaging in these processes of consultation and participation, new ways of working in partnership will be found that will 'genuinely empower communities'. If successful, the main outcomes will be

- more effective, better-skilled, empowered self-confident communities;
- more inclusive communities, a stronger sense of community and local pride;
- wider range of people involved;
- better appreciation of local skills and experience;
- better understanding of issues and development needs. (NAW, 2002, p. 7)

This checklist of what could be achieved is also an indication that all may not be well as things stand – that without support and direction rural communities may lack confidence, exclude sections of their population, undervalue local skills and experiences, and misunderstand development needs. The message about community seems ambiguous: it is the source of both energy and action, but also in need of guidance and direction.

The state of rural civil society

The question of the fortunes of civil society in rural Wales is hardly new. It preoccupied the minds of the pioneer generation of social scientists who put rural Wales firmly on the mid-twentieth-century sociological map. Their accounts of traditional Welsh rural society added greatly to the impression of Wales as a land of 'social cooperation and associative effort' (I. B. Rees, cited in Carter, 1996: 9). But they were also agitated by the breakdown of social cohesion and community in a way that foreshadowed the more contemporary concerns of writers like Putnam and Etzioni. According to Alwyn D. Rees (1951), the village of Llan (Llanfihangel-yng-Ngwynfa) was 'one of the most sociable and friendly places imaginable', its communal character heightened by close physical proximity and daily face-to-face contacts among its inhabitants. Life in the more remote countryside surrounding it was less visibly sociable, but nevertheless social intercourse and hospitality were inseparable aspects of the daily round. The organization of social life revolved around the twin centres of the hearth (meetings in and around the home and farm) and chapel. These were the focal points for the diffuse society of *cefn gwlad* (the neighbourhood in the countryside), which supported an 'essentially rural culture', opposed to all forms of centralization, and without a 'civic' (urban) heritage. Because rural Wales was sparsely populated, and had few significant towns, it was even more dependent than other rural areas on the intricate network of personal connections which existed between neighbours and relatives. At the time when Rees was researching this society, it was being squeezed by the encroaching pressures of the market, as farming became more commercialized and integrated into the wider economic system, and the state, with the beginnings of government regulation and direction of agricultural production. These developments were seen to be undermining the traditional web of local reciprocities which bound people together, while at the same time separating out the economic from the social and cultural domains. The self-contained and largely undifferentiated life of rural Wales and its communities was waning.

A symptom of this transformation was the appearance of new kinds of formal organization, introduced into the locality from outside. Examples included the Women's Institute, the Mothers' Union, the *Aelwyd* (hearth) of the Urdd, the Workers Educational Association, and presumably the university extramural classes run by Rees himself. Rees and his colleagues (Jones, 1962; Owen, 1962) described these as 'intrinsically non-traditional' or intrusive societies, which betrayed their urban origins in the way that they catered for the specialized interests of women, or youth, rather than for the community as a whole. Previously everyone had been able to take part in the local eisteddfod, *gymanfa ganu*, and *noson lawen*, while even the young people's societies attached to the chapels were attended by adults as well as children. The newer organizations took their agenda from outside, were responsible to centralized and remote authorities, and bore no particular relation to activity on the land. In many cases, they were also vehicles for the intrusion of the English language into a Welsh-speaking universe, Anglicizing as well as urbanizing influences. At the very least, these authors believed that the shape of Welsh/rural civil society was being changed, dramatically, but they were fearful of something worse – its destruction, through the weakening of social ties, and the impoverishment of social life. Hence, according to Rees, 'the little community in Llanfihangel, through accepting current values and becoming part of the contemporary economic system, is already in the initial stages of the social atomisation which is general in Western Civilization' (Rees, 1951: 168).

It is easy to place this argument sociologically in the broader framework of the shift from *gemeinschaft* to *gesellschaft*, from community to association (Tönnies, 1955; Murdoch, 2003), with all the consequences that go with it. Except for the organization of religious denominations and the educational system, 'traditional' community life in rural Wales appears to have been self-organized, organic and (in modern parlance) holistic. It was a society with strong social conventions and moral norms, backed by effective local social sanctions. It was also imbued with a fund of social capital, resting on extensive relations of generalized reciprocity and inclusiveness – 'the doors of the homes remain wide open to welcome those who have come from afar' (Rees, 1951: 100). Social relationships were dense and many-stranded. This was helped hugely by social homogeneity – a population tied to the land, united in its liberal Nonconformity, predominantly speaking Welsh, and gathered together in a 'continuous network of solidarities'. According to Putnam (2001: 19), it is in such conditions, when 'embedded in a dense network of reciprocal relations', that civic virtue flourishes. Clearly Rees himself would endorse such a conclusion, since he attributed to the social relationships of rural Wales an ethical and spiritual depth that was missing from modern, 'urban'/English alternatives.

Yet such a society conforms well to Tom Nairn's category of 'the ancient *gemeinschaft* of *pre-civil* society' (Nairn, 1997: 77, my emphasis), of the type that formed the historical background to Adam Ferguson's coining of the term 'civil society' (Ferguson,

1767). It also meets Bauman's test of authenticity, in which 'community' signifies shared understandings of the 'natural' or 'tacit' kind which are not self-conscious, nor loudly proclaimed (Bauman, 2001). The people studied by Rees and his associates did not need to formalize their relationships or express them through officially organized bodies and frameworks, let alone produce 'vision' and mission statements. They came to them 'naturally', in ways that were rooted in their culture and everyday interdependence. Rural Wales as a whole was a 'community', in the sense that these shared ways of thinking and behaving were common to all the various local communities – the details might be particular to a given locality, but were 'characteristic, *mutatis mutandis*' of all comparable places (Davies and Rees, 1962: x). Hence the familiar shorthand description, a 'community of communities'.

Against this background, Alwyn D. Rees provided plenty of ammunition for a critique of social change, with his references to remote control, superficiality, specialization, rootlessness and a future lacking in social wholeness. Again this matches Tönnies's analysis of how 'society' destroys 'community', with the aid of the modern market economy, rational calculation, individualism and competition. Others, however, would see the emergence of 'civil society' in its modern meaning – the appearance of sets of relatively formalized, specialized 'voluntary' organizations and institutions – not as the problem, but as a solution to the kind of social collapse portrayed by Rees. It could be seen, as indeed it was by Adam Ferguson, as part of the civilizing process which accompanies the modernization of rural societies. In Wales, this came relatively late.

Reality and perception: from 'old' to 'new' communities

For more recent critics (Harper, 1989; Wright, 1992; Day, 2002), the Welsh studies have come to represent, in an almost clichéd fashion, typical examples of an ideologically driven, 'common sense' version of rural community. Although this still has a hold over the popular mind, it has been discarded among social scientists, who now bring to their investigation of rural places an expectation that there will be social divisions, conflict and disagreements, and that competing versions of 'community' and belonging will be found among different social actors (Cohen, 1985; Cloke and Little, 1997). This is highly probable, given that rural areas have been subjected to extensive social change and recomposition during the intervening period, resulting in a far more diverse social structure, reflecting among other things the relative decline of the agricultural base and the development of new and alternative forms of employment and occupation. Furthermore, improvements in transport and communications, and in market linkages, as well as increased state intervention, have broken down any pretence that local communities are isolated or self-contained. Virtually all rural settlements now contain a more pluralistic set of inhabitants, and are influenced by substantial patterns of population movement, both inward and outward.

In the Welsh context, this has contributed to the blurring of the boundaries around 'Welshness', the intermingling of groups and factions from widely differing backgrounds and with differing relationships to rural economy and society, and the weakening of the Welsh-language culture. Secularization has also undermined the religious basis of 'traditional' community. This poses significant questions about what, in the twenty-first century, constitutes a 'Welsh' rural community, or even a Welsh 'rural' community. More generally, what does it really mean to talk about 'community' in modern rural conditions, and to what extent are people able to erect and maintain boundaries around their space and place? The contemporary countryside of rural Wales is altogether more complex and variegated than that described by the early geographers and sociologists. The 'traditional' foundation in land-based industries (farming, forestry, horticulture and animal industries, such as horses) no longer provides the depth of shared experience and interests which once pervaded rural life. Indeed, most of those living in the Welsh countryside now have only an indirect connection to the land, and the numbers of those who do work on it is continually shrinking. If we consider the nature of the contemporary rural economy alone, as the basis on which rural society rests, it is not about agriculture or even tourism (Countryside Agency, 2003; Jones and Day, 2003). Important though these industries are, the reality is much more complex, with more than 80 per cent of the rural workforce in England and Wales employed in other activities. The majority work in manufacturing, wholesale and retail, public administration, business and financial services. For more than half a century, the thrust of economic change in the countryside has been *diversification*, with all the ensuing differences of orientation and attitude which this produces.

This diversity is further complicated by marked demographic changes. As real incomes have risen, car ownership has spread and roads have improved; more people have been willing to live in rural areas and travel longer distances to work, often in more urban locations. Others have seen the countryside as an attractive place for retirement, or for the realization of some other version of a rural dream. Wales has shared in the above average growth of rural population, and has also experienced some expansion in rural employment. However, the shift from town to country has been geographically uneven, contributing to new types of problems in different communities and growing disparities between rural areas. Many districts, especially those which are more 'remote', continue to face problems of economic and demographic decline and over-dependence on the primary sector, whereas others experience population pressures as new, more mobile and usually more affluent social groups move into areas considered to be desirable places in which to live and work. Needless to say, much of this movement originates outside Wales, creating additional disruption to established cultural patterns. Additionally, parts of rural Wales continue to harbour significant social deprivation, though this is often concealed behind a dominant image of prosperity and contentment. Overall, the variety of lifestyles and social conditions which coexist in the Welsh countryside today is considerable (Cloke et al., 1997), as is the range of meanings which people bring to 'rurality' and country life.

In many ways, this means that the social nature of rural community is less distinctive, and certainly less uniform, than it was previously – leading to a febrile debate among the academic and policy community about the meaning of the 'rural'. Keeping to a view of the rural as something which is really a 'world apart', as it might once have been, forces us to focus on progressively more remote, inaccessible, and indeed, people-less places, or else to prescribe an unduly restrictive, and normative, definition of what the rural 'ought' to be, regardless of what it actually is. Hence there is increasing agreement that no single theme captures the diversity of social, economic and environmental challenges for people living and working in rural areas, except perhaps the very idea of growing heterogeneity.

The implications for 'community' are summed up by Jonathan Murdoch (2003) as follows:

> We witness then the emergence of 'new' rural communities. These are not the closed timeless entities that we saw in the earlier community studies; rather they are some kind of mixture of urban (or ex-urban) and rural ways of life. In comparison to traditional communities they are dynamic, open and diverse. These are also *constructed* rather than *natural* communities (and less 'communal' in the traditional sense).

Bauman (2001) might regard communities of this type as 'inauthentic' simulations of the 'real' thing.

This means that the social base and conditions for the construction of a rural civil society are something quite different from what they were. Nevertheless, the traditional account of rural Wales casts a long shadow, and exerts an undue influence upon policy and perceptions, while the idea of rural community continues to play a critical role in analyses of rural changes. This is evident, as already noted, from the many statements, plans and strategies which have emanated from the National Assembly and its various agencies, both before and after the FMD crisis threw the spotlight onto the question of what the contemporary countryside and its future represented. To take one obvious example, for reasons that are understandable, given the context, though questionable, the National Assembly's statement on *Farming For the Future* (2001: 7) asserts that 'socially, the family farm defines the character of Welsh rural society, and its sense of identity. The numbers directly and indirectly employed in farming make a crucial contribution towards sustaining rural communities.' Christine Gwyther, when she was agriculture secretary in NAW, somewhat tempered this claim, while reiterating that farming remained a 'substantial proportion of employment in rural areas; it shapes the appearance of the countryside and the pattern of wildlife; and it helps define a strong sense of identity in rural communities'. However, even in Powys and Ceredigion, the most rural counties of Wales, agriculture's share of full-time equivalent employment had fallen to 13 per cent by 1996; Pembrokeshire was the only other county where it reached 10 per cent. Furthermore, research carried out in rural Wales reveals a considerable disjunction between the social world of farming and the remainder of the rural population. For example, although farmers in the Ithon Valley could be shown to be well integrated into extensive networks of work and familial ties, extending across much of mid Wales, others living in the valley only touched these networks at their edges (Day and Murdoch, 1993). While in that instance farmers and their local organizations remained strong enough to set the terms on which others could participate in local life, the trend has been to weaken the hold of these traditional elements, and marginalize them to some extent. Certainly, as indicated by the very limited part they play in Cloke et al.'s 1997 study, farmers and farm families no longer carry the social or economic clout they possessed in the past, and this contributes to anxieties about the future of farming and the wider rural society captured in moments like the fuel protest of November 2000, and the wider formation of the Countryside Alliance. While these represent outbursts of activity and organization around specific rural interests, they leave other sections of the rural population unaffected, or even antagonistic. At best, one could say that farming, and the farm family define the identity of rural Wales for some of its inhabitants, or provide one among several competing definitions of its nature. It is still helpful to think in terms of Massey's metaphor of the different 'layers' of rural economy and society that are superimposed upon one another by successive rounds of social change and economic investment (Massey, 1984; Day et al., 1989). These layers interact with one another at certain points, but may remain disconnected at others. Although originally developed to refer to the impact of economic restructuring, the metaphor captures well enough the fragmented and overlapping nature of contemporary rurality, and the differences of perspective and interest which compete and coexist within it.

To recapitulate, I have been describing the dissolution, over a substantial period of time, of the traditional framework of rural Wales, and its relegation to a subordinate position within a much more varied, and complex, contemporary reality. Consequently it is no longer possible to take social integration, and local ways of doing things, for granted, as they were within what Wittel (2001) terms the 'sociality of communities'. Nor are they unchosen or 'instinctive'. Instead, we find a much greater level of reflexivity in the ways in which rural society is constituted. As Wittel remarks, even in country districts, individuals now must actively construct their social bonds. In a context increasingly marked by a 'higher degree of mobility, by translocal communications, by a high amount of social contacts, and by a subjective management of the network' (Wittel, 2001: 65), they must make decisions and order preferences. In contrast to the stability, coherence and embeddedness previously attributed to rural communities, this implies a far more active, fluid, kind of social reality framed around shared interests and shared identities. It represents a movement to 'networked rurality' (Murdoch, 2005) or 'network sociality' (Wittel, 2001), which is bound to influence the shape taken by rural civil society. Patterns of association will be influenced by particular arrangements of interests, shared among different groupings. Hence, very often, 'people will be simultaneously participating in one "community", as a local network of interaction, whilst also being located in networks and "stretched out communities" of many other kinds' (Liepins, 2000: 30; see also Day, 1998; Day and Murdoch, 1993).

For critics of the older style of rural community, this represents a liberation from the coercive pressures of uniformity and stagnation, which held back rural development. In Putnam's terms, the traditional social order of rural Wales was strong on social bonding, but weak (though not entirely lacking) in bridging connections. Maybe the emphasis has switched now, with networks providing forms of bridging capital to replace the old exclusiveness. If so, Putnam would presumably welcome the change, as generating broader identities instead of narrower selves (2000: 23). For admirers of the old ways, who adopt a more communitarian stance, individuals have been set free to pursue their own narrow interests, without duly respecting 'country' values and traditions, or the legacy of the Welsh rural heartland. Country people find 'townies' in their midst, while Welsh communities are infiltrated by 'English newcomers'. Faced with such challenges, 'locals' may unite around the defence and reassertion of the old order; on the other hand, they may resign themselves to seeing 'their' town or village mutate into something completely different.

Implications for civil society in rural Wales today

Whereas the classic studies mention no more than a handful of clubs, organizations and activities, mostly in the realm of leisure and entertainment, it is an impossible task to enumerate, let alone describe all those institutions, organizations and relations which have developed since in rural areas to fill up the space between the economy and the state, and which have substituted, to a large extent, for the older connections of family, neighbouring and mutual cooperation. In a recent review of rural communities and the voluntary sector focused mainly on England, Blackman et al. (2003) found that virtually nothing was known in any detail about the dimensions of such voluntary activity except that it showed enormous diversity, had wide-ranging impact and was impossible to delineate with accuracy because there were no unique authority or reliable data sets. Their working definition of the voluntary sector embraced the 'totality of organizations and groups characterised by an altruistic or mutual support ethic', made up mainly of non-profit elements. Although a powerful force, the sector consisted of a vast number of independent bodies, ranging from organizations with incomes in the millions of pounds and substantial permanent staff (BTCV: £23 million and 1,043 permanent staff) to tiny groups with a few thousand pounds and part-time staffing. They suggested that rural groups were more likely to be smaller, less well resourced and without effective support systems. One would expect the pattern in rural Wales to be broadly similar, with many of the same UK 'national' and interest-focused organizations performing much the same role (like the National Trust, RSPB, Conservation Trusts, Ramblers etc.).

According to the *Wales Voluntary Sector Almanac* for 2003, rural areas in Wales have higher numbers of voluntary organizations than urban districts – about double the ratio (19 per thousand as opposed to 10 per thousand). The same source claims that as many as 57 per cent of adults in (predominantly rural) north and mid Wales 'volunteer' compared to 45 per cent of adults in the (more urbanized) south (WCVA, 2003). The basis for these figures, and their reliability, is unclear, but it is evident that there is no shortage of social groups and organizations available in rural places to soak up the voluntary time and effort of individuals, if they so choose. Some impression of their range and diversity can be gained from a look at the websites put up by the local authorities in two of the rural counties of Wales, Gwynedd and Powys.

- The Gwynedd Community Website (*http://cymuned.gwynedd.gov.uk*) lists some 622 clubs and societies. The list is by no means exhaustive, but indicates the range of groups and associations which can be found in most local towns and villages. It includes local branches of national organizations, such as Caernarfon Lions Club, the RSPB North Wales Local Group, or the Royal Naval Association Blaenau Ffestiniog; local clubs and groups – Shekina Multicultural Women's Group (Bangor); Snowdonia Canoe Club; Brythoniad Male Voice Choir; and welfare organizations and development bodies, like the Special Children of Gwynedd and Ynys Môn, or the Slate Valleys Skills Initiative Community Ltd, Felinheli.
- Powys Communities Online Listing (*http://www.pco.powys.org.uk*) covers 60 groups and bodies ranging from Builth Wells brownies and scouts, via the Llanwrtyd Model Railway Society to the Montgomery County Recreation Association and the Radnor Valley Link, a community-based project to introduce local people to computer technology. Each listed site takes the visitor 'in' to learn about the particular concerns and activities of the varied organizations.
- The Powys County Council site on 'community issues' includes Builth Wells YFC ('a highly sociable website for a highly sociable young farmers' club from mid-Wales'); CARAD (Community Arts Rhayader and District); Ecodyfi (sustainable community development); and the Glasbury Scout Group.
- Under Community General Links the Powys Gateway (*http://www.powysweb.co.uk*) lists 91 sites, some of which have no business being there (Crux Press, a publisher of Christian books, or the Pearls Trust, a charity restoring a property in France for young homeless people), but including Rural Futures, a Britain-wide initiative; the Powys Regeneration Partnership, made up of 165 organizations dedicated to maximizing the uptake of European Funding in Powys; Sennybridge.org which acts as a shop window for the Upper Usk Valley; and the Talgarth Community Forum, 'Talgarth's

> first electronic discussion board' for 'anyone who ever wanted to have your say about Talgarth but were too shy to say [it] in public'.

No doubt this is only a tiny fraction of all the many groups, clubs and societies which could be gathered up by a diligent researcher, especially as the countryside is said to be the locus of the 'micro-organization', very local and very specific in its interests (Blackman et al., 2003). These many different groupings could be organized in a variety of ways. As in the last entry above, they could be placed in a hierarchy descending from the national (rural) through regional or county levels down to district and local. One could also separate out those which address specifically 'rural' or village concerns, like the Young Farmers' Clubs, WIs and Merched y Wawr's, from organizations which are 'spatially indifferent' like Masonic Lodges or Citizens' Advice Bureaux. The preponderance of organizations are very limited in their social range – recreational or hobby groups – or specific to a given locality, such as the many local flower shows, amateur drama groups, community hall management committees and so on. Others are considerably more ambitious in their reach. It is an eclectic mix, which corresponds to the fundamentally chaotic nature of the concept of a 'civil society'. The whole set would fit comfortably within the loose definition offered by Nairn, as 'the diffuse assemblage of anything and everything which can be located somewhere in between politics and state power on the one hand, and the family on the other' (Nairn, 1997: 77).

Nairn is sceptical about the value of such a category, with good reason, asking in what sense it composes a corporate or overall entity deserving a title of its own. The same question has been raised about the closely associated idea of the 'voluntary sector' (see Drakeford, chapter 6 in this volume, with reference to Chaney et al., 2001). We have the added problem of trying to decide whether there is a distinctively 'rural' component or version of this 'entity'. Nairn's usage comes close to the definition adopted by the CIVICUS project in its work on Wales (WCVA, 2003), which delineates civil society as 'the sphere of institutions, organisations and individuals located between the family, the state and the market, in which people associate voluntarily to advance common interests'. The difference is that Nairn's definition would include activities directly related to the economic/market sphere; his conception of civil society therefore would certainly embrace the various quasi-economic community development bodies which appear on the rural listings, like the Slate Valleys Initiative, the Radnor Valley Link, or Menter Waun Fawr, a social enterprise organization which provides paid work and training for individuals with learning difficulties. However, these types of organization are very unlike those groupings which are 'about' enjoyment, relaxation, or pure sociability (and which may, incidentally, like Putnam's bowling leagues, build valuable social capital). As the name implies, development bodies are 'about' making a change; they serve a purpose beyond the immediate context of association, and this may be a crucial observation in helping us move beyond the mere listing of social groups, to get some purchase on the very slippery idea of a civil society.

In classifying rural voluntary bodies in England, Blackman et al. suggest a typology based on degree of formalization, local/national identity and engagement with statutory bodies. During a seminar presentation of their ideas, the latter assumed a special significance, since they argued that DEFRA stood to gain much from greater engagement with the voluntary sector, with respect to having a vehicle for service provision and delivery, a sounding board for policy and programmes, as well as an ability to contribute directly to community well-being. Alun Michael (then minister for Rural Affairs at Westminster), who was present at the seminar, applauded the idea of rural communities as 'mechanisms of delivery'.

In a similar way, the WCVA/CIVICUS study makes a subtle but very important shift from its broad definition of the field, when it spells out the nature of civil society involvements in such terms as: taking responsibility; finding solutions for problems; managing services and facilities; workplace organizing; and lobbying. These are normative, 'civic' activities, which serve interests *beyond* those of the people immediately concerned. They form part of the public realm, of 'active citizenship' and social responsibility. They do things, not just for those who belong to civil society organizations, but for the wider society. Hence the selective principle used to define the 'content' of civil society does not come from *within* the social relationships and networks of the people themselves, but from outside. This may help explain why informants in the study had some difficulty interpreting what was meant by 'civil society'. A comparable sleight of hand seems to be true of the majority of definitions of civil society – the descriptive content of the realm of 'free association' or non-market/non-state relations is intersected by assumptions about the motivations and purposes of those involved, so as to emphasize some activities and organizations while setting others aside. Hence perhaps the common and problematic elision of the 'civil' with the 'civic', referred to in the introduction to this volume.

Conclusion: civil society from below or above?

The attempt to mobilize civil society relations on behalf of external objectives and in the 'societal' interest has been very evident in rural contexts in recent years. This represents an interesting reversal of earlier approaches. Although conscious efforts have been made to combat and reverse rural decline in Wales from the late 1960s onwards, early policy efforts were premised on the *lack of ability of local people* to do much for themselves. The reports and proposals of the time are full of descriptions of rural people as unenterprising, 'traditional', conservative, stuck in the past and in need of a kick to make them change their ways. The thrust of development policy during this period was about introducing more 'modern' values, attitudes and activities into the area from outside. Rural communities were to be energized by inward investment, along with the infusion of new kinds of people and motivations (Day, 2002). The experiences and power relations of this period have led to rural Wales being classified by rural sociologists as a prime example of 'clientelist' dependence (Murdoch et al., 2003). However, inspired in part by examples and arguments from within Wales, later years have seen the emergence of 'neo-endogenous' theories of development, which favour the mobilization of local energies and efforts (Ray, 1999; Shucksmith, 2000; Edwards and Woods, 2004). This takes us back to the start of this chapter.

To an increasing extent, from the late 1980s onwards, rural communities have been *expected* to engage with policy development and delivery. They have been built into policy directives as key collective actors, and their performance has been judged accordingly, and employed as a tool in the allocation of resources.

In England, indicators of community 'vibrancy' have been developed which position different local communities as 'vibrant', 'active', 'barely active' and 'sleeping' (Department for Transport, Local Government and the Regions/Ministry for Agriculture, Fisheries and Food, 2000; Countryside Agency, 2001). Similar steps are being taken in Wales. The North Wales Economic Forum has commissioned a set of monitoring indicators, including one for community vibrancy, which recommends a process to record the number of 'activity groups' for all ages, by function and location; their membership levels, and numbers of active members; and also the number of local community enterprises (Datris, 2003). Communities which do not have the right kinds of groups, and levels of involvement, risk being seen as failing. Through this extension of an audit mentality, practices like community appraisals and consultation, which have been developed and disseminated as part of a grass-roots, ground-up participatory practice, can be translated into top-down measures of community viability, and incorporated as conditions for receipt of grant. To qualify for support, communities must match up to the image of an active, inclusive, responsible local society, with plenty of dynamic clubs and associations. Measured in this way, Llanfihangel, described so positively by Alwyn D. Rees, would probably have been declared dead.

Advocates of the newer approaches argue that there are some obvious differences from the older style of development, which are better attuned to contemporary rural conditions. Rather than looking to outside support and inward investments, it is the internal strengths of the community and the local society, with its history and culture, which are highlighted as the 'glue' that holds effective development together. The mobilization of an active civil society is regarded as key to overcoming past limitations, enabling the interactions between different activities and sectors to be understood and handled better than in the past. Rather than being overtly 'top down', local involvement and participation is favoured. It is claimed that this will ensure a more balanced perspective on rural needs, which 'naturally' not only takes into account the range of different economic interests and activities, but also brings social, political and cultural considerations more fully into the picture. Greater consideration for, and consultation with, local people should create a stronger sense of ownership, and encourage a shared vision and commitment, which will increase the sustainability of interventions, so that in the end 'communities' can be left to get on with more of the work themselves, without the need for expensive support, and constant regulation and guidance. In summary, according to the Community Affairs section of the WCVA, local involvement and the participation agenda is held to produce a wide range of potential benefits – for example:

- establishing processes for sharing power and responsibility;
- increasing local commitment and sense of ownership;
- releasing community resources;
- adapting services and facilities to local needs and circumstances;
- improving cooperation and wasting less effort on conflict resolution;
- increasing goodwill and trust;
- increasing the knowledge base of communities.

From this perspective of participation and empowerment civil society is *put in charge*.

At the same time, to ensure that all these worthy aims are met, a variety of mechanisms and devices have been put in place to make sure that the whole process does not run riot. Chief among these is 'partnership', whereby agencies and local authorities are built into positions which give them leverage and control over community initiatives and activity. The list of 'community' groupings above included one, the Powys Regeneration Partnership, a mini-civil society in its own right, made up of no less than 165 organizations with a shared goal. In their research on rural governance, a team of geographers from University of Wales, Aberystwyth found that there were over 150 such rural regeneration partnerships operating in the three counties of Ceredigion, Powys and Shropshire; two-thirds had been formed since 1996 (Goodwin, 2003; Edwards et al., 2001). There were no less than 25 strategic partnerships in Ceredigion and Powys concerned with health and well-being alone. In other words, there is an intricate and rather sophisticated structure, fitted like an armature around rural civil society, to hold it in shape. At its apex it has the Rural Partnership for Wales, established in 1998 and charged with writing strategy documents mapping out the future, on behalf of the Welsh Assembly. At county level, processes of community planning are designed to produce the 'local' strategies and commitments which fit within the overall strategic direction decided in Cardiff. In short, there is a high degree of orchestration and management, which invites people in through recognized channels of participation and consultation, while ignoring or sidelining 'non-approved' groups and interests.

Rose (1996) has noted the extent to which government now operates through 'community'; individuals are governed through their freedom as members of heterogeneous communities of allegiance, as 'community' emerges as a new way of conceptualizing and administering moral relations among persons. On this account, civil society has been *taken into charge*. No sooner do notions of civil society, social capital, 'trust' and so on rise to prominence, than government and authority moves in to capture them for its own ends. In his massive work on the network society, Manuel Castells (1997) sees civil society as an arena within which dominant institutions will seek to extend and legitimize their power. Thus he defines it as 'a set of organizations and institutions which reproduces (albeit sometimes conflictually) the identity that rationalizes the source of structural domination' (1997: 8–9). Among other things, this would include the identity of the active, engaged, socially responsible citizen. Ironically, in view of the preceding discussion, Castells sees the main source of resistance to this as coming from a second kind of identity, often tribal in form, rooted in 'community' and organized around self-definitions based in history, geography, or even biology. He suggests that this type of resistance may be the most important type of identity-building in our society. However, we see from this account of changing civil society in rural Wales that the phenomenon is not as new as might be supposed, and that, like the BME networks Williams describes in her contribution, 'community' is far from immune to being seized within an agenda that is decided elsewhere, and which may distort the voluntary commitments willingly undertaken by individuals and groups.

References

Bauman, Z. (2001). *Community: Seeking Safety in an Insecure World*, Cambridge: Polity.

Blackman S. P., Skerratt, S. J., Warren, M. F. and Errington, A. J. (2003). *Rural Communities and the Voluntary Sector: A Review of the Literature*, Plymouth: University of Plymouth, report commissioned by DEFRA.

Carter, H. (1996). 'Foreword: life in a Welsh Countryside: A Retrospect', in A. D. Rees, *Life in a Welsh Countryside*, Cardiff: University of Wales Press.

Castells, M. (1997). *The Power of Identity*, Oxford: Blackwell.

Chaney, P., Hall, T. and Dicks, B. (2001). 'Inclusive governance? The case of "minority" and voluntary sector groups and the National Assembly for Wales', *Contemporary Wales*, 13, 203–29.

Cloke, P., Goodwin, M. and Milbourne, P. (1997). *Rural Wales: Community and Marginalization*, Cardiff: University of Wales Press.

Cloke, P. and Little. J. (eds) (1997). *Contested Countryside Cultures*, London: Routledge.

Cohen, A. P. (1985) *The Symbolic Construction of Community*, London: Tavistock.

Countryside Agency (2001). *The State of the Countryside*, Cheltenham: Countryside Agency.

Countryside Agency (2003). *Rural Economies: Stepping Stones to Healthier Futures*, Cheltenham, Countryside Agency.

Datris (2003). *Rural Indicators Count: Socio-economic Indicator Model for North Wales*, Datris, Bangor, report to the North Wales Economic Forum.

Davies, E. and Rees, A. D. (eds) (1962). *Welsh Rural Communities*, Cardiff: University of Wales Press.

Day, G. (1998). 'Working with the grain: towards sustainable rural and community development', *Journal of Rural Studies* 14, 1, 89–105.

Day, G. (2002). *Making Sense of Wales: A Sociological Perspective*, Cardiff: University of Wales Press.

Day, G., Jones, D. and Morris, E. (2001). *The Dynamics of Demographic Change and Migration in North West Wales*, report to the North Wales Local Employment Observatory.

Day, G. and Murdoch, J. (1993). 'Locality and community: coming to terms with place', *Sociological Review*, 41, 1, 82–111.

Day, G., Rees, G. and Murdoch, J. (1989). 'Social change, rural localities and the state', *Journal of Rural Studies*, 5, 3, 227–44.

DETR/MAFF (2000). *Our Countryside: Our Future – A Fair Deal for Rural England*, London: Department of the Environment, Transport and the Regions.

Edwards, B., Goodwin, M., Pemberton S., and Woods M. (2001). 'Partnership, power and scale in rural governance', *Environment and Planning C: Government and Policy*, 19, 289–310.

Edwards, B. and Woods, M. (2004). 'Mobilising the local: community, participation and governance', in M. Kneafsey and L. Holloway (eds), *Geographies of Rural Cultures and Societies*, Basingstoke: Ashgate, pp. 173–96.

Ferguson, A. (1767). *An Essay on the History of Civil Society*, Edinburgh: Miller & Caddel.

Goodwin, M. (2003). 'Partnership working and rural governance: issues of community involvement and empowerment', DEFRA/ESRC seminar paper.

Harper, S. (1989). 'The British rural community: an overview of perspectives', *Journal of Rural Studies*, 5, 2, 161–84.

Jones, D. and Day, G. (2003). *North Wales Rural Skills Audit*, report to the WDA, Cardiff: Welsh Development Agency.

Jones, E. (1962). 'Tregaron: The sociology of a market town', in E. Davies and A. D. Rees (eds), *Welsh Rural Communities*, Cardiff: University of Wales Press.

Liepins, R. (2000). 'Exploring rurality through "community": discourses, practices and spaces shaping Australian and New Zealand rural "communities"', *Journal of Rural Studies*, 16, 3, 325–41.

Massey, D. (1984). *Spatial Divisions of Labour: Social Structures and the Geography of Production*, London: Macmillan.

Murdoch, J. (2003). 'Reflections on the changing nature of rural communities', paper presented to DEFRA/ESRC seminar on rural communities and demographic change.

Murdoch, J. (2005). 'Networking rurality: the growing complexity of rural space', in P. Cloke, T. Marsden and P. Mooney (eds), *Handbook of Rural Studies*, London: Sage, pp. 171–200.

Murdoch, J., Lowe, P., Ward, N. and Marsden, T. (2003). *The Differentiated Countryside*, London: Routledge.

Nairn, T. (1997). 'From civil society to civic nationalism: evolution of a myth', in *Faces of Nationalism: Janus Revisited*, London: Verso, pp. 73–89.

National Assembly for Wales (NAW) (2001). *Farming for the Future*, Cardiff: NAW.

NAW (2001). *Plan for Wales*, Cardiff: NAW.

NAW (2002). *Rural Community Action: Strengthening Living and Working in Rural Wales*, bidding document, November.

North Wales Economic Forum, *Rural Recovery Plan. http://www.llandrillo.ac.uk/host/uwef.*

Owen, T. M. (1962). 'Chapel and community in Glan-Llyn, Merioneth', in E. Davies and A. D. Rees (eds), *Welsh Rural Communities*, Cardiff: University of Wales Press.

Putnam, R. (2000). *Bowling Alone: The Collapse and Revival of American Community*, London: Simon & Schuster.

Ray, C. (1999). 'Endogenous development in the era of reflexive modernity', *Journal of Rural Studies*, 15, 3, 257–67.

Rees, A. D. (1951). *Life in a Welsh Countryside*, Cardiff: University of Wales Press.

Rose, N. (1996). 'The death of the social? Re-figuring the territory of government', *Economy and Society*, 25, 3, 327–56.

Rural Partnership for Wales (2002). *Rural Wales.*

Shucksmith, M. (2000). 'Endogenous development, social capital and social inclusion', *Sociologia Ruralis*, 40, 2, 208–18.

Tönnies, F. (1955). *Community and Association*, London: Routledge & Kegan Paul.

Wales Council for Voluntary Action (WCVA) (2003). *Wales Voluntary Sector Almanac*, Cardiff: WCVA.

Welsh Development Agency (WDA) (2001). *Supporting Rural Wales*, Cardiff: WDA.

Wittel, A. (2001). 'Towards a network sociality', *Theory, Culture and Society*, 18, 51–76.

Wright, S. (1992). 'Image and analysis: new directions in community studies', in B. Short (ed.), *The English Rural Community: Image and Analysis*, Cambridge: Cambridge University Press, pp. 195–217.

ARDAL
GYMRAEG
WWW.CYMUNED.ORG

13. Between Consent and Coercion: Civil Society, Bilingualism and the Welsh Language

ROBIN MANN

Introduction

It has been argued that through the establishment of the National Assembly for Wales a distinctively *Welsh* civil society, based upon the production of a civic conception of Welsh national identity, can be seen as coming into fruition (Osmond, 1999; Paterson and Jones, 1999). The Assembly, it is believed, 'will reinforce and give substantive *civic* meaning to the national dimension of the country's identity' (Osmond, 1999: 1, my emphasis). Similarly, Paterson and Jones (1999) state that 'devolution in Wales may be best understood as part of the process of creating and animating a Welsh civil society' and that 'while Welsh civil society was not the precursor of devolution, it may yet be among its progeny' (1999: 182). Such a collective identity implied within the notion of a *Welsh* civil society, however, assumes a certain consensus over its cultural content. As such it may result in downplaying the presence of divisions and conflicts which would question such a consensus.

The Assembly and its constituent political parties have brought with them an apparently mutual agenda of partnership and engagement and the attempt to establish an inclusive civic culture. What is also clear, however, is that such a process will continue to be influenced by the number of divisions and boundaries within Wales and the ability of both government and groups within civil society to negotiate and accommodate such differences, not least those between Welsh speakers and English speakers.[1] Before investigating these dimensions of conflict and consensus within civil society, it is necessary briefly to account for the historical and contemporary relationships between national identity, the Welsh language and a Welsh civil society.

Civil society, national identity and the Welsh language: historical transformations

It is widely accepted that the roots of Welsh civil society stem from the emergence of a Nonconformist indigenous bourgeoisie in the second half of the nineteenth century (Adamson, 1991; Paterson and Jones, 1999; Williams, 1985). In this context, the Welsh language along with religious difference, was central to the contestation which drove the development of Welsh civil society. This contest was essentially between the existing hegemonic feudal/landed gentry and an emergent autonomous bourgeoisie which provided the material basis in order to act not merely in its own particular interests but to make appeals to common interests with the working and rural classes. It is in this appeal to common interests that the Welsh language and religious difference in Wales were important: 'Nonconformity provided at various times ideological cement for alliances between objectively antagonistic classes' (Adamson, 1991: 115). Such a Welsh civil society, however, was necessarily short-lived, as the Nonconformist middle class came to be seen not as 'radical dissenters' but as 'owners of capital and direct exploiters in their own right' (Adamson, 1991: 117). Subsequently, it was through the discourses of British and international socialism that the interests of the Welsh working class were best articulated. As Adamson concludes, 'Nationalism as an ideological cement between an indigenous bourgeoisie and working class was redundant: nationalism was no longer articulated with class struggle' (1991: 123).

The re-emergence of Welsh nationalism in the 1960s, constituted in the main by the twin political forces of Plaid Cymru and Cymdeithas yr Iaith Gymraeg (The Welsh Language Society), came from the resurgence of ethnicity and nationalism within the wider context of the rise of political protest and 'new' social movements. In emanating from such particularistic or single-issue standpoints, however, it became apparent that emphasizing the connections of language and nation could no longer serve as the same cultural articulation of a collective national identity. As a result, much of the opposition to devolution in 1979 resulted from fears surrounding the Welsh language and its attachment to the nationalist cause. On one hand, it was feared that a Welsh Assembly would be dominated by a Welsh-speaking elite, solely concerned with issues surrounding the promotion of the Welsh language. For the Labour Party and other prominent forces in south Wales, the language movement, led by a middle-class minority, represented a potential 'denial of Welshness to the English-speaking Welsh' which led inevitably to 'a bitter self-exclusion of the English-speaking Welsh from the Welsh people and the nation' (G. A. Williams, 1985: 293). On the other hand, it was feared that the hegemony that 'south Walian Labourism' had over Welsh political culture would result in a marginalizing of the issues that concerned the nationalists and Welsh-language protagonists. The result of these combined fears was a wholehearted rejection of devolution.

It is ironic, therefore, that through a number of legislative developments in the 1980s and 1990s aimed at promoting its status within public life, the language has received increasing support within English-speaking Wales. Of particular importance here has been the establishment of the Welsh-language channel S4C in 1982 and the Education Reform Act (1988) which, somewhat inadvertently, led to the compulsory teaching of Welsh, to varying degrees, throughout all state-funded schools in Wales. More important still has been the 1993 Welsh Language Act which sets out the requirement for all public bodies in Wales to provide a bilingual service. As a result of these institutional developments, the promotion of the Welsh language is seen to have detached itself from its nationalist origins (Aitchison and Carter, 1997; C. H. Williams, 1994).

Clearly, therefore, the institutionalization of the Welsh language has contributed to the endorsement of devolution in Wales. As Osmond contends, 'By 1997, however, the language had been swept away as an issue. Instead of a negative force it had become a positive impulse' (1998: 2). Paterson and Jones (1999: 184) make a similar point, indicating 'a paradigmatic example of civic activism whereby non-Welsh speakers have consciously embraced the language either for themselves or their children'. Widespread support or 'goodwill' towards the language is evident in the results of the Welsh Language Attitude Survey carried out on behalf of the Welsh Language Board in 1995 (NOP, 1995). However, in light of more recent political and media debates, this perceived consensus over the Welsh language appears somewhat premature, to say the least; for the first term of the Assembly has been punctuated by not only a series of antagonistic interventions regarding the future of the language but also the founding of a 'new' radical pressure group, Cymuned, to act on behalf of the majority Welsh-speaking communities.

The repoliticization of the Welsh language?

In January 2001, the issue of (English) migration into the majority Welsh-speaking communities was raised on a BBC Radio Wales talk show by one Plaid Cymru councillor, Seimon Glyn, chairman of Gwynedd County Council's housing committee. As he states 'if they [the English] were coming here under strict monitoring and control, were made aware of the cultural aspects and made to learn Welsh there wouldn't be a problem . . . They're coming here and you know frankly, they're telling us "listen we're the new kids on the block and you do as we say now"' (cited in Lamport, 2001: 1). Such comments led not only to a split in the apparent consensus between Plaid Cymru and New Labour but also to numerous accusations of 'anti-English' racism. Prior to this particular event, the establishment of the National Assembly for Wales, it was argued, had brought with it a 'new politics' based on a shared agenda between political parties, particularly Labour and Plaid Cymru. As Osmond (2001) points out, terms like 'inclusivity' and 'consensus' featured prominently in Assembly rhetoric, an important part of which included the neutralization of the Welsh language as a party political issue. It would now appear, however, at least with regard to the language debate, that this depoliticization was only temporary, to ensure a successful devolution referendum campaign. This would appear to break down the perceived consensus between Labour and Plaid Cymru which had so epitomized the positive 1997 referendum result. If anything, the establishment of the National Assembly has led to an intensification or *repoliticization* of the 'language debate' in Wales. There are, however, two reasons why conflict rather than consensus was more likely within the post-devolution context.

First, many of the main enactments in favour of the Welsh language occurred within a 'democratic deficit' and the unique political relationship between Welsh-language lobbyists and the Westminster Conservative administration. Naturally, the coming of a more democratically accountable Assembly was likely to bring with it greater public debate and representation of the opinions – particularly those of majority language speakers in Wales. Some have even questioned whether S4C or a Welsh Language Act would ever have materialized under a devolved administration (Thomas, 1997), the suggestion being that the Welsh-language lobby group had benefited from a democratic deficit and the Westminster government's desire to temper more 'extreme' nationalist agitations. Secondly, the Assembly was also likely to bring with it heightened expectations from the Welsh-language movement itself regarding the possibility of further concessions, particularly in the form of a new Welsh Language Act, the granting of official status to Welsh in Wales, and also the bilingual nature of the Assembly itself.

The contemporary debate, however, took another turn when BBC's *Question Time* took place in Caernarfon in February 2001. During the programme the long-standing antagonism between the Labour Party in Wales and Plaid Cymru, not least on the question of the Welsh language, also seemed to re-emerge when Glenys Kinnock, a Labour member of the European Parliament, challenged the then Plaid Cymru leader, Ieuan Wyn Jones to dismiss Seimon Glyn from the party. The 'Seimon Glyn affair' was not the first occasion that the accusation of 'racism' had been applied to the Welsh speaking community (see also Denney et al., 1992; G. Williams, 1994). What was particularly significant about the Seimon Glyn incident was that it was followed by the establishment of a 'new' Welsh-language pressure group, Cymuned.

Historically, Plaid Cymru and Cymdeithas yr Iaith Gymraeg have represented the main political voices of the Welsh-speaking communities (Rawkins, 1979). With Cymuned a new group has come to the fore, which threatens to emerge as the most prominent agitator. At the same time, it is against specific members of Cymuned that accusations of racism have been most fervently raised. In particular, the *Welsh Mirror* and its editor Paul Starling (2001) have taken it upon themselves to alert the people of Wales to what is believed to be the 'racist' intentions of the group. In a number of its documents, Cymuned sets outs its task as 'to act on behalf of Welsh-speaking communities' (Cymuned, 2002: 1), an important aspect of which is that 'newcomers in Welsh-speaking communities have a civic responsibility to learn Welsh' (Cymuned, 2001: 13). It also states its campaign aims as, amongst other things, 'controlling in-migration into Welsh-speaking areas' and 'assimilating in-migrants linguistically' (Cymuned, 2002: 2). Such rhetoric places the moral boundaries of civil and uncivil society in quite distinct terms whereby 'incomers' who 'learn the Welsh language and contribute to social and cultural life' are part of civil society while those who 'refuse to learn the Welsh language' or 'refuse to respect the existence of a minority culture' (Hunter, 2002: 3) are placed outside – as uncivil society. Such a claim to a moral monopoly is also evident in an article by Mike Parker who states that 'many English immigrants into rural Wales are out-and-out racists' and see Welsh culture 'as just another "minority" to be ridden roughshod over' (Parker, 2001). Yet such arguments would seem to deny the above claims that the promotion of Welsh and bilingualism are widely supported by non-Welsh speakers. In light of such statements, it is necessary to examine the boundaries between Welsh and English speakers within civil society around which consensus and conflict tend to emerge.

Investigating consensus and conflict between Welsh and English speakers

Within the last few years, the future of the Welsh language and its place in Wales have been subjected to more public and political debate than perhaps at any other point in its history. This is evident not only in terms of the National Assembly's language review and subsequent policy recommendations but also in a number of academic contributions and televised debates on both BBC and S4C. In one case, BBC Cymru/Wales had gone to the length of commissioning a large-scale questionnaire of the adult population in Wales for its 'Fate of the Language' debate in November 2001. Significantly, this questionnaire provides a useful insight into the 'quality' of the relationship between the Welsh- and English-speaking groups. In particular, because it distinguishes the responses between Welsh and English speakers it gives an indication into the degrees of accommodation made by respective groups to each other. It will therefore be worthwhile to outline some of the findings of this survey.[2]

Accommodations by English speakers

To begin with, the responses of English speakers towards the Welsh language appear mixed. For instance, when asked 'To what extent do you support or oppose the use of the Welsh language?' only a small majority (53 per cent) stated that they either strongly or mostly supported its use. That said, only 5 per cent returned a distinct opposition (strongly or mostly oppose) to this statement. Again similar results were found in regard to questions such as 'How important is the future of the language to you?' and 'Do you believe that the Welsh language is gaining, declining or about the same in strength and status?'. In these cases, 48 per cent considered the future of the language as either very or fairly important to themselves while 22 per cent considered the Welsh language to be declining in terms of strength and status. More specifically, when asked 'Would you like to be able to speak Welsh yourself?', English speakers were evenly divided, with 43 per cent stating 'yes' and 41 per cent stating 'no'.

While none of these responses demonstrates conclusively high levels of accommodation, they do contest the notion of an *overwhelming* negativity of English speakers towards the Welsh language. Moreover, the question 'Would you like to be able to speak Welsh yourself?', 66 per cent of English-speaking respondents in north-west Wales,[3] where language issues are perhaps more pervasive, answered 'yes', while only 32 per cent stated 'yes' in the Cardiff and south-east Wales area.[4] Significantly, the more *conclusive* levels of linguistic accommodation were on the question of whether English-speaking parents would like their children to learn Welsh. In this regard, 37 per cent stated they would while 41 per cent stated that their children were already doing so. In other words, 78 per cent of English speakers had accommodative responses in relation to their children learning Welsh in school. Likewise, 61 per cent believed that 'all children in Wales should be able to receive education entirely in Welsh'.

Accommodations by Welsh speakers

As one might expect, Welsh speakers demonstrated far more convincing levels of support towards the Welsh language and its promotion. For example, when asked, 'How important is the future of the Welsh language to you?' 89 per cent stated that it was either very or fairly important. Similarly, 89 per cent of Welsh speakers stated that they either strongly or mostly supported the use of the Welsh language. High levels of support were also reported with regard to the future of the language. For example, 65 per cent thought that 'the Welsh language will be a living language in daily use in 40 years' time', although responses were more mixed with regard to the use of Welsh within their 'Local Area' where only 30 per cent of respondents considered the use of Welsh to be on the increase.

Of equal significance were accommodating responses regarding English speakers within Welsh-speaking communities. For example, when asked whether 'incomers to Welsh-speaking communities make a valuable contribution to the local economy', 60 per cent either slightly or strongly agreed. Moreover, this figure was 69 per cent within the more linguistically aware north-west region. Likewise, only 25 per cent of Welsh speakers thought that 'new laws are required to control immigration into traditionally Welsh-speaking communities'. What is also significant about such responses is that they appear to question Cymuned's claims to *represent* the voice of the Welsh-speaking group. This appears to be the case not only in terms of the contributions made by 'incomers' to the local communities but also on whether new laws on restricting inward migration would be widely supported.

In both groups there is a tendency towards convergence as opposed to polarization. For example, on the issues of whether 'introducing measures to protect the Welsh language in Welsh-speaking communities would be racist', both Welsh and English speakers seemed in agreement. In this case only 31 per cent of English speakers and 29 per cent of Welsh speakers thought that the introduction of such measures would be racist.

Boundaries of accommodation

Thus far, there appears no small degree of accommodation by both Welsh and English speakers towards each other, which suggests a consensus over the language. However, there are two issues, crucial to civil society, surrounding which more conflictual attitudes emerge. These are *individual citizenship rights* and *equality of opportunity*. In particular, is a concern with how these principles were seen to be contravened through notions of *social responsibility* and *minority group rights*. For instance, as was shown above in the case of English speakers, the most positive responses were found on the question of the right to receive education in Welsh. When asked 'should it be *compulsory* for every child in Wales to be taught Welsh in secondary school?' (italics added), clear differences between English and Welsh speakers emerged. While 64 per cent of Welsh speakers agreed that it should be compulsory, this figure was only 31 per cent for English speakers. When asked 'should there be an expectation on non Welsh speakers to learn Welsh in Welsh-speaking areas?', only 18 per cent agreed that there should be an expectation. Yet in north-west Wales 60 per cent of Welsh speakers agreed that 'non Welsh speakers who move into Welsh-speaking communities should learn Welsh'.

It becomes apparent that attitudes to the Welsh language modify when its promotion is seen to *contravene* principles of individual rights. In other words, as the focus shifts from notions of individual entitlement and choice to questions of social responsibility, expectation or compulsion, so conflict tends to emerge. Similar boundaries and divisions between Welsh and English speakers are also found on the issue of 'equality of opportunity'. For example, when asked whether 'local people in Welsh-speaking communities should be able to buy subsidized housing', 53 per cent of Welsh speakers either strongly agreed or agreed that they should. In contrast, only 26 per cent of English speakers stated that they supported (either agreed strongly or agreed with) this. Similar responses were also found when asked whether 'a person who has lived in an area for 10 years+ should have priority when buying a home'. While only a quarter (27 per cent) of English speakers supported this, this figure was over half (57 per cent) for Welsh speakers in north-west Wales.

To summarize these findings, we can state that both Welsh and English speakers demonstrate levels of consensus and of accommodation towards each other but that divisions tend to emerge when principles of individual choice and equality of opportunity are perceived to be contested. The boundaries of accommodation would tend to be based on the shift from notions of opportunity, choice, and entitlement to expectation, responsibility or compulsion. Although, this boundary itself reflects the way minority language policies may contest individual rights, as May (2000) argues, it is questionable whether, without a degree of compulsion, such equality of opportunity would be available in the first place.

Criticisms of large-scale language surveys

The degree to which we can take such quantitative research as evidence of consensus or accommodation is questionable. Clearly such research was motivated by a politically polarized climate that saw the emergence of Cymuned receiving regular media coverage. It is not surprising that neither Welsh speakers nor English speakers should wish to demonstrate feelings or views that may be perceived as hostile, politically incorrect or deviant. That respondents would unintentionally converge towards the other is a potential weakness of this kind of quantified research. There is also the question of the reliability of language attitude research in general. Williams and Morris (1999: 153–8) question whether attitudes can be considered in behavioural terms – as predispositions to act. As such, accommodative attitudes cannot be concluded to mean active support. To this the reverse should also be stated: that non-action cannot be read as a *lack* of principled agreement or respect. The biggest potential weakness of such surveys is raised by May (2000) in his argument that because of their objective/positivist nature they are more likely to extract cognitive (reason and thought) as opposed to affected (emotion and feeling) responses. In other words, respondents would tend to reply to statements in terms of universal principles as opposed to feelings from particular experiences. While I do not wish to dismiss such findings or the political importance of consensus, they give us 'little indication of either the effects of certain language policies or the remaining obstacles to bilingualism' (May, 2000: 112). My own research with adult learners of Welsh in Bangor found, for instance, that while principles of minority language rights were widely supported, distinct concerns about the particular institutional manifestations of such principles were also evident. I shall now draw on some of the interviews conducted with learners to illustrate this.[5]

Adult learners of Welsh: A case study in civic activism

In attempting to gauge the specific concerns of non-Welsh speakers, learners were asked to respond to certain statements made by Cymuned regarding the monitoring of levels of in-migration into Welsh-speaking areas. The majority of the learners interviewed supported or were at least sympathetic to some of these ideas and agreed that incomers had a responsibility to learn Welsh. As some learners stated:

> Well I have a lot of sympathy with them [Cymuned]. I think when you go into someone else's country you should do your best to learn the language in which you are living. I think it's important. I think it's ignorant not to at least learn the basics.

> Oh I definitely agree with that, I mean from living somewhere like Llŷn and seeing places like Llanbedrog and Abersoch and seeing how those communities have pretty much died, I mean there's not an awful lot of Welsh people who live there who speak Welsh there, mainly holiday homes and things like that so I think the emphasis should be placed on people to make an effort to learn and its difficult and I think when you get like migration of people coming over here it's very difficult to persuade people to speak Welsh, I mean you know some people will but I'd say the majority won't and I think it's up to us – I mean I've got no excuse born Welsh, I am Welsh and I should speak Welsh you know.

Within the first statement here is the argument that the Welsh language should be given parity with official state languages. In other words, if you move to the UK it is expected that you learn English, if you move to France it is expected that you learn French and therefore, if you move to Wales you should learn Welsh. The second statement raises the distinct concerns surrounding the perceived threat posed to the language by in-migration into Welsh-speaking areas. Other learners, however, were slightly more critical of the idea that everyone should learn:

> I sort of appreciate that it's important not to lose the language but I feel if there's people like us who are trying our best to fit into society, we're not coming here and refusing to fit in with how things are, if we're trying to learn the language then that's fair enough as well. Although I don't think you should expect everybody to learn because people have different reasons for doing it. I think in Menai Bridge and Bangor you don't notice it but as soon as you go into rural areas like

> Bethesda and small villages you really do notice it and it does become Welsh speaking country.
>
> Well I've lived in Wales now for seven years. I haven't learned before now because I was waiting for my daughter to go to school so that I could have the time to do it. Otherwise it was baby sitters and I didn't think it was fair with her being so young. So I waited until she was in school full time and then decided to do the course. It's been going on now since last September just over a year . . . what motivated me? Because I felt around here no one would employ me without a second language which is fair enough you know and my children are obviously learning it in school so that helps as well. Whereas when my son was bringing home books from school I couldn't understand them I couldn't help him whereas now I'm at my daughter's reading stage you know so I can help her along. So it was sort of 50–50 I wanted to stay around here and I wanted to be employed.

In this last statement it is important to point not only to structural factors such as 'lifecycle' or work intentions which motivate learning but also to the degree of differentiation within the so-called Welsh-speaking heartland. Both of these points are reiterated by another learner who states:

> I live in Llanddaniel on Anglesey. We live in a row of cottages and nobody speaks Welsh. Maybe it's because it's so close to Menai Bridge and the University. So I find the idea of a 'Welsh speaking community' a bit difficult because I don't know if I feel part of a community yet because I haven't actively joined things in my area. But I don't think you can force it. I think perhaps *there are certain things in life that make you become involved in a community* such as having children. Definitely when I have children I would become more involved in the community and things like that. (my italics).

However, as has been pointed out, 'community sanctions' can be no less coercive than legal restrictions. As some other learners state:

> Are *you* going to tell me that I *should* and make sure that I speak it? Are you going to watch over what I do and don't do? That's a very dangerous thing if that's what the majority of people think. The whole basis of adult learning is that it's voluntary and anything other than that isn't right.
>
> I'm always really uncomfortable with this kind of 'outsider thing' with the awareness of being an 'outsider'. I think that creating that kind of thing can be a bit negative. I think that as long as people who move

> here and are willing to accept where they are moving to and to actually learn Welsh and to use it when they can then you can't ask anymore.

What is interesting about this last statement is how being a non-Welsh speaker in an area like Gwynedd constitutes being an 'outsider' or even an 'other'. Further, that the presence of an 'other' is acceptable only on the basis that they try to integrate and conform to certain cultural norms. In other words it is because they are recognized as 'Welsh learners' rather than 'English' that they feel accepted. As one learner states:

> Yeh well I live in Bethesda which is quite a Welsh speaking area so I do feel very English when I go down to the shop for a pint of milk. So yeh I try little things like saying 'diolch' instead of thank you so yeh, when I first moved there I did feel really English I suppose a bit like an outsider. But I'm glad I'm learning and I feel more at home as a 'Welsh learner' rather than an English person not making any effort. When I talk to members of the public through work and I say I'm learning Welsh they say oh very good and they're quite impressed that I'm making the effort so I do feel that it's appreciated.

On the other hand, others felt that even learning Welsh would not get them accepted by some:

> I think by and large people are pleased that I'm learning and I can't say that I have ever been made to feel unwelcome or unaccepted. However there are those who are supportive and are committed to having as many others as they possibly can speak their language but there's another group who see it as a badge of exclusion, and would be quite happy if no one else ever learned the language like a way of deliberately excluding. For some I don't think anything would be good enough . . . it's basically an exclusive band who have an interest in keeping you excluded.

In sum, while the majority of learners agreed in *principle* and sympathized with the concerns of groups like Cymuned, there were enough ambiguities in their responses regarding the implications of actual policy implementation to suggest that some of the issues are more complex and less clear cut than is suggested, in particular, concerns about how Welsh-born English speakers might also come to be considered as outsiders. Significantly, the National Assembly has also begun to address some of these issues.

The National Assembly and the Welsh-language movement: new directions or old ground?

Colin Williams asks, 'how far will the Assembly be part of the process of creating (or re-making) Wales as a bilingual country as opposed to one comprised of two relatively discrete linguistic communities?' (C. H. Williams, 1998: 113). Clearly, the establishment of the National Assembly for Wales (NAW) brings with it questions over the *direction* that Welsh society will take over bilingualism in the coming years. Will there be *one bilingual Welsh civil society* or *two Welsh civil societies* made up of majority and minority linguistic groupings? During 2001 the NAW conducted a review of the Welsh language, based primarily on invited consultations from a range of individual experts, public bodies and civil society organizations. Following this, the NAW has since produced a number of policy documents outlining its commitment to promoting bilingualism throughout Wales, the most important of these being *Iaith Pawb: A National Action Plan for a Bilingual Wales* (NAW, 2003). Although questions do remain over whether the goals and targets stated within these documents can actually be achieved (see C. H. Williams, 2005, for a critical appraisal) there are perhaps two significant points to make: first, is the emergence of a Labour government within the Assembly that is 'wholly committed to revitalizing the Welsh language and creating a bilingual Wales' (NAW, 2002a); and, second, recognition of the threats posed to the use of Welsh:

> Whilst several factors have contributed to the decline in the use of the Welsh language, two of the most influential factors which have hastened this decline, particularly in rural communities, are the in-migration of non Welsh speakers and the out-migration of local people due to the lack of affordable housing and of local employment. (NAW, 2002b: 24)

Undoubtedly, the inclusion of this last statement reflects not only the input of Plaid Cymru but the involvement of Welsh-language pressure groups within the review. On this point it can be argued that the National Assembly has changed the relationship between the language movement and government for the better. As a former chair of the Welsh Language Society explains:

> I think they [Assembly Members] are quite open because for us between 1987 and 1997 the government would not speak to us at all. So

> this is a massive change for us. In the period between 1987 and 1997 the Welsh Office, the various Conservative Secretaries of State, had refused to hold any discussions with Cymdeithas because we were a law-breaking organization. Along with Sinn Fein we were the only two organizations that the Conservatives refused to discuss anything with us. So really there was no relationship whatsoever with one major exception really – in the early 90s when there was no dialogue at all between Cymdeithas yr Iaith and the government. The exception was when two of our members were imprisoned in 1991 during a campaign for a Welsh Property Act one of the members went on a hunger strike. So there was absolutely no relationship between Cymdeithas yr Iaith and the Welsh Office up to 1997.[6]

Since the establishment of the Assembly a considerable focus of the Welsh Language Society has been on the Assembly itself, particularly in terms of their lobbying, their communications with Assembly members, and monitoring and presenting of papers at various subject committees. It is undeniable that the Assembly represents a more inclusive approach to governance in terms of its impact on the position of the Welsh-language movement within the political structure. What also remains to be seen is how the language movement itself is affected by the new institutional reality whereby the production of policy documents and briefing papers along with lobbying the Assembly, as opposed to direct action, form the main points of political action and pressure. On the one hand, Cymuned represent a retreat from a 'national' language framework to one based on historical division between Welsh-speaking and English-speaking Wales. On the other hand, it is questionable whether a language review would have taken place without the pressure applied by civil society and pressure groups such as Cymuned and Cymdeithas yr Iaith Gymraeg in particular.

Conclusion

The aim of this chapter has been to investigate both consensus and divisions within civil society over the Welsh language and bilingualism. The attitudinal data provided give an indication into how both Welsh speakers and English speakers do accommodate each other in a number of ways. As has been shown in the case of

English speakers, there is considerable active support through their being either Welsh learners themselves or parents who send their children to Welsh-speaking schools. To this it should be added that there are distinct boundaries to such accommodation. As was illustrated through the research with adult learners of Welsh, despite overall support for bilingualism, distinct divisions emerged around notions of a social responsibility, expectation and compulsion to learn Welsh.

There would also appear a certain consensus within the Assembly government regarding its commitment to creating a bilingual Wales. Such a commitment is perhaps even more significant given the way in which party-political divisions over the language re-emerged during the middle of its first term (Osmond, 2001). If such a commitment is to manifest in the form of bilingual society it will require the consent and participation of the majority English-speaking group. This in turn will require the Assembly government and the associated public sphere to *confront* rather than *downplay* the divisions surrounding the specific institutional developments pertaining to the language, divisions that are at present so hotly contested within civil society in Wales.

Notes

1. While it is acknowledged that this is not an accurate description, I shall for the sake of clarity be referring to the bilingual Welsh/English-speaking minority and monolingual English-speaking majority language groups as Welsh and English speakers respectively.
2. This study was conducted by Beaufort Research Ltd on behalf of BBC Cymru. A total of 1004 interviews were conducted with a representative sample of Welsh speakers between 1 and 20 November 2001. A further 992 interviews with a representative sample of the total adult population of Wales were also conducted between 21 and 30 November 2001. I would like to thank both Beaufort Research and BBC Cymru for permission to reproduce the findings of this study.
3. North-west Wales consists of the counties of Anglesey, Conwy and Gwynedd.
4. Cardiff and south-east Wales consists of Cardiff, Vale of Glamorgan, Monmouthshire, Torfaen and Newport.
5. The data presented here is based on twenty qualitative interviews carried out with adult learners of Welsh based at the Centre for Continuing Education, University of Wales, Bangor, between June and October 2002.

6. Interview with Dafydd Morgan Lewis, Cymdeithas yr Iaith, Aberystwyth, March 2001.

References

Adamson, D. L. (1991). *Class, Ideology and the Nation: A Theory of Welsh Nationalism*, Cardiff: University of Wales Press.

Aitchison, J. and Carter, H. (1997). 'Language reproduction: reflections on the Welsh example', *Area*, 29, 4.

BBC News (2000). 'Call for a new language movement', *BBC News*, *http://news.bbc.co.uk/1/hi/wales/871220.stm*.

Beaufort Research (2002). *BBC Wales [Fate of the Language] Report*, Cardiff: Beaufort Research Ltd, BBC Cymru/Wales.

Cymuned (2001). 'Submission by Cymuned to the Culture Committee', Cymuned, *http://www.penllyn.com/cymuned/papurau/cym2.html*.

Cymuned (2002). The resolutions adopted in Cymuned's Annual General Meeting at Harlech, 20 April 2002, Cymuned, *http://www.penllyn.com/cymuned/papurau/resolutions.html*.

Denney, D., Borland, J. and Fevre, R. (1992). 'The social construction of nationalism: racism and conflict in north west Wales, *Contemporary Wales*, 4, 149–65.

Hunter, J. (2002). 'What is Cymuned?', Cymuned, *http://www.penllyn.com/cymuned/papurau/saesneg.html*.

Lamport, J. (2001). 'Voice of hate', *Welsh Mirror*, 18 January.

May, S. (2000). 'Accommodating and resisting minority language policy: the case of Wales', *International Journal of Bilingual Education and Bilingualism*, 3, 2.

National Assembly of Wales (NAW) (2002a). *Bilingual Future: A Policy Statement by the Welsh Assembly Government*, Cardiff: NAW.

NAW (2002b). *Our Language: Its Future, Joint Report of the Culture and Education Committees*, Cardiff: NAW.

NAW (2003). *Iaith Pawb: A National Action Plan for a Bilingual Wales*, Cardiff: NAW.

NOP (1995). *Public Attitudes to the Welsh Language*, a research report prepared by NOP Social and political for the Central Office of Information and the Welsh Language Board, London: NOP Social and Political.

Osmond, J. (1998). 'Introduction', in J. Osmond (ed.), *The National Assembly Agenda*, Cardiff: Institute of Welsh Affairs.

Osmond, J. (2001). 'In search of stability: coalition politics in the second year of the NAW', in A. Trench (ed.), *The State of the Nations 2001*, Thorverton: Imprint Academic.

Parker, M. (2001). 'Loaded dice', *Planet*, 148.

Paterson, L. and R. Wyn Jones (1999). 'Does civil society drive constitutional change?', in B. Taylor and K. Thomson (eds), *Scotland and Wales: Nations Again?*, Cardiff: University of Wales Press.

Rawkins, P. (1979). 'An approach to the political sociology of the Welsh nationalist movement', *Political Studies*, 27, 3.

Starling, P. (2001). 'Language of hatred', *Welsh Mirror*, 7 November.

Thomas, A. (1997). 'Language policy and nationalism in Wales: a comparative analysis', *Nations and Nationalism*, 3.

Welsh Language Board (1999). *The Welsh Language Fact-File*, Cardiff: Welsh Language Board.

Williams, C. H. (1994). *Called Unto Liberty: On Language and Nationalism*, Clevedon: Multilingual Matters.

Williams, C. H. (1998). 'Operating through two languages', in J. Osmond (ed.), *The National Assembly Agenda*.

Williams, C. H. (2005). 'Iaith pawb: the doctrine of plenary inclusion', *Contemporary Wales*, 17.

Williams, G. A. (1985). *When Was Wales?*, Harmondsworth: Penguin.

Williams, G. (1994). 'Discourses on "nation" and "race"', *Contemporary Wales*, 6.

Williams, G. and Morris, D. (1999). *Language Planning and Language Use: Welsh in a Global Era*, Cardiff: University of Wales Press.

VALLEYS KIDS
PLANT Y CYMOEDD
B175 FF

14. Community Regeneration Policy, the State and Civil Society

DAVID ADAMSON

The concept of civil society has enjoyed increasing currency in both political and academic discourses in recent years. Fuelled partly by the rise of new social movements and partly by the increased role of voluntary agencies in contemporary governance, the term has emerged to describe a complex array of socio-political processes operating in contemporary society. The term has experienced an enthusiastic take-up by a wide range of actors and characterizes debates on both the left and right of the conventional political divide, if such a division has survived the 'reinvention of politics' (Beck, 1997). There is a sense in which the term civil society represents one of those uniquely malleable terms which can transcend political ideologies and reside comfortably in all political perspectives. However, it is a feature of such terms that their meaning is rarely specified or elaborated on and there is an assumed but artificial consensus on their use. In reality the terms exist within competing discourses and there is no commonality of meaning across discourses. The malleability of the terms is such that they can be employed without detailed delineation of their meaning.

Civil society is one such term. Its contrasting deployment in the New Right and libertarian philosophy of, for example, Hayek and Nozick respectively (King, 1987), alongside its use to describe anti-globalization and anti-capitalist organizations, points to a complex significance in contemporary political discourses: 'deployed by conservatives, liberals and radical utopians alike, by oppositional movements and by international aid donors, civil society has become an ideological rendezvous for erstwhile antagonists' (Khilnani, 2001). Nor is the academic community free from ambiguity in its application of the term. Variously, it is used to describe a range of actions in society by disparate groups of social movements and organizations. It crosses disciplinary boundaries with immunity and is of interest to political theorists, sociologists, philosophers and political economists. In reality, there are competing usages of the term, which vie for incorporation into broader discourses of social change. Some attempt will be made here to delineate current usages.

Two political traditions have influenced recent Conservative thinking on the role of civil society, although neither tends to use this specific term. The first is the neo-liberalism associated with political philosophers such as Nozick and Hayek. Both are characterized by an extreme opposition to the role of the state in contemporary society. Both see individual liberty as best protected by voluntary association without the need for state coercion (King, 1987). Their influence on Thatcherism is well recognized (Faulks, 1998) and, whilst recent Conservatism is most associated with Thatcher's assertion that 'there is no such thing as society', it is civil society where the market operates and where individual freedom is guaranteed. For Hayek, civil society is a spontaneous order which develops in the absence of a strong state. Nozick's concept of the 'night watchman state' further minimalizes the state's role and asserts that liberty and freedom are best guaranteed by free association, the market and free choice: 'It is Nozick's utopia which will provide the basis for mutual respect, voluntary action and ethical behaviour' (Faulks, 1998: 63).

The second philosophical strand within contemporary Conservatism is the surviving elements of classical Conservatism. Core values focus on a contract to obey the rule of law and to fulfil our obligation to the state as citizens. This includes a degree of voluntary acceptance of rules and a participation in the implementation of those rules. Thus, the citizen will be expected to uphold the rule of law, firstly, in his or her own behaviour, secondly, as a member of a family and a community, with a responsibility to promote and enforce codes of behaviour, and, thirdly, by participating in specific voluntary associations such as neighbourhood watches and other community-based activities. Such patterns are seen as the core of the morality of contemporary society. They maintain a culture that is seen as best protected by citizens acting in association, rather than by the state. This usage is a return to Locke's conception of a 'civil society' of good manners and a social contract to limit the excesses of individualism whilst protecting individual rights.

In contrast to this usage within Conservative discourses, the term civil society has also recently been employed to describe a plethora of organizations that wish to place pressure on the state for a wide range of reforms or to promote special interests. Derived from the usage of the concept of civil society developed to explain the popular revolts of the Soviet bloc in the mid to late 1980s, civil society is perceived as the terrain of popular protest and insurrections against the state machinery of communism (Seligman, 1993). In the fall of communist states, civil society created a cultural space for dissent and ultimately revolt (Hall, 1995). The academic and political interest in these processes and the perceived role of civil organizations has ensured that the concept of civil society has become a central issue in describing and analysing similar dissenting social and political movements in all contemporary societies and also in the wider context of globalization and resistance to it.

Such groups range from voluntary/interest groups with mass membership such as Greenpeace, to international campaigns challenging the very basis of capitalism. This application of the term civil society often mobilizes around issues of civil rights and articulates demands from the state around a range of sectional interests best represented by anti-capitalist and anti-globalization organizations; there is no organizational orthodoxy evident. Organizations range from loose Internet-based affiliations of anarchist and socialist groups to environmentalists and political opponents of the world's harshest regimes. This radical sector has given us the 'reclaim the roads' model of activities at the local level and international campaigns to reduce the debt burdens of third world countries at the international level.

More evident in UK politics than either this Conservative or oppositional view of civil society has been the articulation of the concept of civil society with the centre-right programme of social reform pursued by the Labour administration since 1997. Personified by the Blairite vision of a nation of self-regulated communities where individual liberties are balanced against community liberties, the 'third way' brings communitarianism to the heart of UK politics. Clearly influenced by Etzioni's vision of revitalized communities (Etzioni, 1995 and 2000) this perception of civil society has become firmly established in contemporary social policy. It welds social responsibility and civic duty to a discourse of rights which challenges the centrality of individual liberties in Western political culture and asserts communal rights as a critical aspect of the moral and social order. For example, the right to communal freedom from antisocial behaviour manifests in Anti-Social Behaviour Orders and an increasingly punitive legal code, providing an innovative response to conflict at the local and neighbourhood level.

The Blairite vision of civil society is one in which labour market participation will reintegrate the socially excluded who wish to rejoin mainstream society. Their part of the bargain is to accept an obligation to enter the lower levels of the labour market and be 'flexible' in their employment expectations and the associated need to retrain as the economy moves their labour power to new uses. In social policy and welfare provision, stakeholder partnerships operate complex models of service delivery which blur the lines between the state, the voluntary sector and the citizen. Multi-agency partnerships are engaged in attempts to restructure local democracy and bring service providers into greater public accountability. Through renegotiating the level of community participation and control in decision-making in the local state, such groups are unravelling the municipal model of public service and replacing it with a more participative form of civic structure. For those not willing or able to enter this new contract there is an increasingly punitive welfare regime and 'abusive' social security system (Jones and Novak, 1999: 91) and a penal code which increasingly centres on incarceration and related patterns of social control such as tagging. It is this latter model of civil society that this chapter explores, along with its implications for the development of the relationship between the individual citizen and the state.

In delineating these current uses of the term civil society we see that all employ the same terminology but refer to very different outcomes and visions of civil society in practice. However, they all share a desire to redefine the relationship between the individual and the state. In the Conservative model it is an attempt to roll back the state and recover a civil society in which individuals respect the needs and wishes of others without a requirement for undue state intervention. It is the freedom espoused by Hayek to establish common association without state interference and to derive full benefit from labour without undue taxation and welfarism. It is a return to a simpler sense of freedom that predates welfare rights and develops an independent citizenry that does not expect to be bankrolled by the state. For the centre-right it is the middle way of welfare for those who need it and independence and self-reliance for all those who are competent and able to work. The social contract is one of rights and obligations and civil society is where the negotiated boundaries are drawn.

Both versions share a perception of civil society as the social terrain which lies between the state and the private lives of individuals. For Deakin it is the realm of voluntary action and 'association'. It is variously perceived as charity, mutual aid or voluntarism (2001: 9). For Walzer, it is the 'space of uncoerced human association' (Walzer, 1995: 7), again stressing the perception that civil society is where voluntary association underpins the moral and social order. For Neilsen it is located between the state and the 'supposedly private sphere of the family and spousal arrangements and the like' (1995: 42). For the initial purposes of this chapter the notion of civil society adopted will reflect this dominant usage which sees civil society as the realm of private association, separate from the state. Particular reference will be made to a neo-Gramscian perspective which sees civil society as standing between the economy and the state.

Emerging from the internecine warfare in Marxism of the 1980s over the relationship between the economic relations of the mode of production and the nature of the state, the concept of civil society was drawn from Gramsci's work to resolve the tensions between economic reductionists and autonomists. The former believed the state superstructure to be a direct reflection of the economic base whilst the latter view argued for complex mediations which in effect create either a 'relative autonomy' or complete autonomy for the state. Formulated by Urry (1981) and others, this conception of civil society developed to express a sphere of individual, communal and socio-cultural relationships which were independent of the direct class relations of capitalist society and independent of the state itself. In civil society gender, ethnic, sexuality and other identity issues were resolved without undue levels of interaction with underlying class identities. A perception of civil society emerged which saw it as the realm of voluntary actions based in individual choice but which became institutionalized in various forms, one of interest to this chapter being the voluntary sector or 'third' sector.

The crisis of capitalism and the new social policy

Despite the triumphalism of the victory of capitalism over communism and the end of the Cold War there are other views assessing the state of contemporary capitalism. A strong theme is the notion of a 'victory crisis' (Beck, 1997) which sees capitalism as almost as badly damaged as the communist system over which it has triumphed. Whilst 'reflexive modernity' can be seen as an end of the dichotomous East/West distinction, it is also the beginning of an unknown settlement of current contradictions. For Beck, 'The European project of democratically enlightened industrialism is disintegrating and losing its foundations' (1997: 13). All the old labels and structures no longer apply. In parts of the developed capitalist world such as south Wales, modernist industrialism has been 'tested to destruction' just as communism was tested in the Soviet Union and Eastern Bloc. Beck's notion that capitalism is damaged is self-evident in localities like the south Wales Valleys where it cannot sustain any reasonable quality of life for a significant proportion of the population (Adamson, 1995). Damaged by the impact of globalization and economic decline, the region experiences some of the worst poverty in Europe. However, this experience is evident everywhere in the post-industrial economic order and poverty and social exclusion derive from a wide range of social experiences of economic restructuring throughout Europe (Chamberlayne et al., 2002). For Beck, the triumphalism of capitalism after the collapse of the Iron Curtain has disguised its own 'loss of substance' (Dubiel, cited in Beck, 1997: 178). That loss of substance has ensured that welfare capitalism does not deliver on its promise of security and prosperity for all. The civil rights of liberal democracy are irrelevant compensations for the loss of economic rights to work and income experienced by the poor throughout Europe.

In the face of this localized failure of capitalism communities have (re)discovered their ability to self-organize (Adamson, 2001). Local community responses echo the embryonic welfare provision that emerged in the late nineteenth century as communities organized to meet the needs forced on them by the privations of the new industrial order. As the twentieth century progressed, this active civil society was slowly absorbed into municipalism as the housing, health and educational services they provided were gradually brought under central and local state control. By the second half of the century clientelism and dependency characterized the relationship of the citizen with the state. However, in the 1980s the practical withdrawal of the welfare state from marginal communities triggered a similar ethic of mutualism to that of the nineteenth century, to create a survival mechanism in the face of major social deprivation. In south Wales and other parts of post-industrial Britain and Europe this emerging practice was facilitated by a local culture where individualism had always been weak, and supported by a culture which possessed a natural immunity to the appeals of the New Right in the 1980s and 1990s (Adamson, 2001).

Community organizations that emerged in response to the social conditions arising from the effective withdrawal of the welfare state were based on an ethic of resistance that did not accept the marginalization and social exclusion which the restructuring of global capitalism was imposing on their lives from outside. Communities began to self-organize to provide youth services, leisure activities, training opportunities, environmental improvement and housing renewal (Adamson, 1997). This indigenous, 'bottom-up' development was often based on a conscious recognition of the desertion of such 'poor places' by the state. 'Transformation from within' was a slogan of the community regeneration movement in the Rhondda Valleys during the early 1990s, in recognition that help was not forthcoming from any external source.

The community associations formed were embedded in local civil society. They were self-funding, populated by volunteers and managed by committees of community activists. Funding was secured from a wide range of semi-independent sources including the European Union Structural Funds, Lottery Commission, private trust or charitable funds and local fund-raising (Adamson, 2001). The organizations were locally controlled, often by community membership or 'share issue'. Organizations such as the Rhondda Arts Factory, Blaenllechau Bell Centre, Penywaun Partnership and Bryncynon Community Revival Strategy developed significant funding portfolios and provided major levels of service to the local community. They became significant local employers and registered as companies limited by guarantee and as charities.

By the end of the 1990s organizations promoting community-centred regeneration were a feature of the south Wales coalfield region (Adamson 2001). Development was not uniform in scope and scale or spatially and there were areas in the coalfield where community development initiatives failed to emerge. However, the successes of the sector were increasingly recognized as they improved their ability to deliver a range of services which local government had significantly failed to provide. In developing social policy to promote social inclusion, government has sought to emulate the successes of this 'bottom-up' pattern of regeneration initiatives by introducing a wide range of policy streams that promote community-centred solutions.

Conventionally, community regeneration has been seen as an oppositional activity, staffed by community activists working against the state for the benefit of the community. In the 1970s, community regeneration in the UK was weakly supported by state programmes and secured little real effect in improving life in Britain's disadvantaged communities (Popple, 1995). The Community Development Programme of the early 1970s created an antagonism between those in the community work profession and the state (Mayo and Robertson, 2003) and, following the widely recognized failure of this community development policy, British urban regeneration was rarely targeted at the community level. During the Conservative years, key projects were delivered through private sector development corporations which brought together statutory and private sector organizations in partnership to develop local areas in what was generally described as 'property-led' regeneration. Focusing on infrastructural developments, such urban development partnerships rarely directly involved communities beyond a limited degree of consultation about the character of the developments proposed. Community organizations were outside the partnership structure and did not exert any degree of control over development plans. This was certainly the case in the early Single Regeneration Budget (SRB) projects and Urban Development Corporation programmes. Where exceptions existed they were to provide early proof of the value of community involvement which would be recognized in later SRB and City Challenge projects, especially following the election of a Labour government in 1997.

By the mid-1990s the self-generating practice of community regeneration outlined earlier was beginning to prove its effectiveness at combating social exclusion. There is a gradual evolutionary process of change, which was rapidly accelerated by the election of the 1997 Labour administration, which developed a communitarian set of influences to become a core strand of New Labour's 'middle way'.

> What was emerging under Conservative governments in the UK over the last decade using pro-market rhetoric, and what is being developed further by New Labour using communitarian rhetoric, could be described as a new kind of work and welfare regime, a new accommodation between state, market and civil society. (Roche, 2002: 76)

Kendall (2000) additionally identifies a number of 'policy entrepreneurs' who were influential in developing Labour Party thinking in this direction. From individuals such as Andrew Deakin (the Deakin Commission) and Alun Michael who created the compact between government and the voluntary sector to key think tanks such as Demos, there was a growing orthodoxy suggesting that the 'third sector' could play a major role in delivering the Labour vision. There was additional pressure emerging from the evaluation of a number of City Challenge and Single Regeneration Budget programmes which demonstrated the effectiveness of community involvement in tackling urban decay, social exclusion and community regeneration. Finally, considerable evidence for the value of the approach was emerging from extensive research conducted by the Joseph Rowntree Foundation (JRF) Neighbourhood programme. A plethora of JRF reports from the mid-1990s onwards substantiated the perception that community- and partnership-based approaches to social policy and welfare provision had a clear potential to solve some of the most intractable social problems which had confounded the policy community throughout the Conservative era.

All these factors promoted a strong practice-based 'push' to develop policies that promoted the perceived advantages of community-based approaches. Manifested in a wide range of policy domains, community-based strategies have become the norm in contemporary social policy.

> The governmentalism of community facilitates this [linking of citizens to the state] by the creation of a whole array of discourses about

> community, for instance community regeneration, community experts, local community initiatives such as community policing, community safety and community development. (Delanty, 2002: 167)

Delanty sees this as a move towards 'government through community'. One of the primary policy streams in which this has emerged is in various attempts to promote social inclusion. All devolved regions of the UK have established area based anti-poverty programmes which are grounded in communitarian perceptions of social capital, community empowerment and direct participation of community organizations in the delivery of services for social inclusion. The Strategy for Neighbourhood Renewal In England, Social Justice in Scotland and Communities First in Wales have all centred on highly participative delivery mechanisms which place 'ordinary' citizens at the heart of community regeneration partnerships. Following seventeen years of a policy desert in relation to anti-poverty policies this emerging practice has offered an attractive alternative model of policy provision, standing some way between conceptions of a failed centralized welfare state and a highly localized provision of services at community level. Supported by both the traditional left and New Labour, the attraction of the concepts of empowerment, participation and social inclusion have offered a convincing alternative to the absence of anti-poverty policy of the Conservative years.

As well as these practice-based pressures to develop a community basis for social policy there are ideological pressures which integrate various aspects of communitarianism, the legacy of Thatcherism and new conceptions of welfare to work. The process described above represents a considerable reworking of the relationship between Britain's poorest communities and the welfare state. It demonstrates a change from the Marshallian conception of the 'welfare citizen' to a more collective provision of welfare policy that engages the welfare recipient in collaboration with state agencies. Thatcherism to a considerable extent delegitimized the orthodoxy of welfarism, making it impossible for any government to follow with a traditional approach to welfare provision. The formulation of an alternative pattern had become essential by the time of the 1997 Labour victory.

The communitarian influence is evident in perceptions that communities have rights over individuals who reside in them. Individual rights are decentred to provide a balance between collective and personal rights. Emphasis is placed on social institutions such as family and marriage to provide a basis for a moral and social order. Infringements of that order are dealt with by a wide range of initiatives that firstly attempt to resolve the behaviour within social programmes (in which community regeneration approaches play a major part). The emphasis is on attitudinal change as demonstrated in welfare-to-work programmes such as New Deal, including the New Deal for Communities Programme. Social inclusion is seen as deriving from labour market inclusion (Levitas, 1996) and more peaceful neighbourhoods are derived from engaging and involving delinquent groups in community renewal activities to promote 'stakeholding'. For those who continue to violate the rights of the community, increasingly coercive and punitive measures are applied, culminating in the Anti-Social Behaviour Order with its risk of imprisonment for behaviours which are not in themselves illegal.

Continuities with Thatcherism are thinly disguised in the structure of the welfare-to-work policy which has emerged. Considerable emphasis is placed on challenging the dependency culture of the long-term unemployed and addressing the attitudinal patterns that are seen to underpin economic non-participation. Early approaches triggered by key thinkers such as Frank Field were redolent with elements of theories of the urban 'underclass' which had enjoyed currency through Charles Murray's influence on Conservative thinking (Murray, 1990 and 1994). Challenging the dependency culture was as important to the first approaches of New Labour as it had been to the Conservatives. The language employed was one of social inclusion and the policies lacked the coercive elements of the early job seeker's allowance but the target was similar. It was to return the long-term unemployed to the labour market.

New Deal advisers and Department of Employment Action Teams for Jobs have relocated themselves within marginal communities and work in very close relationships with clients to develop attitudinal change and skills acquisition that favours labour-market re-entry. Much of that emerging labour-market re-entry is in the lower reaches of the labour market where wage levels and employment conditions do little to challenge the poverty of those making the transition. However, arguably their self-esteem and confidence are raised and will in many instances permit advancement within the labour market. In all this there is little attention paid to structural causes of unemployment.

The consequence of both the practice 'push' and the ideological influences detailed above is the emergence of two policy streams running in parallel, with connections between them. Welfare-to-work policies are promoting a return to employment of the long-term unemployed, whilst community regeneration programmes are tackling the residual populations where spatial and cultural characteristics combine to render welfare to work approaches ineffective. The former demonstrate a fairly conventional 'client'-based relationship between beneficiaries and service providers. In contrast, key features of the community regeneration policies have implications for an analysis of contemporary civil society in the UK. Roche sees this as an emerging form of 'social contractualism': 'the development of the role of key forms of civil society [i.e.] voluntary and community organisations in work and welfare policy necessarily involving principles and practices of 'associationalism' between citizens and 'contractualism' between citizen organisations and the state' (2002: 75).

Community regeneration and civil society

In all the devolved policy streams that have emerged to promote state-sponsored community regeneration, the central tenet is one of community participation delivered through membership of multi-agency partnerships. Community organizations and community members are provided with equal status with statutory organizations on regeneration partnerships that make the key decisions about strategy and resource allocation. Major emphasis is placed on deriving community definitions of social problems and in implementing solutions favoured by the community. In England the Strategy for Neighbourhood Renewal has established local strategic partnerships (LSPs) at local authority level to bring statutory organizations together with the private sector, the voluntary sector and community organizations. It extends the involvement of the voluntary sector, which has been incorporated into the provision of statutory services since the 'contracting out' approaches of the mid-1980s. Additionally, it creates a space for a major influence by the community sector that is being increasingly identified as distinct from the voluntary sector. In thirty-eight of those LSPs in England characterized by extreme deprivation an additional £1.2 billion has tackled social exclusion and disadvantage. Community membership of the LSP is determined by local elections of representatives.

In Wales, the Communities First Programme has identified 142 communities for support. The spatial targeting is generally at electoral division level but thirty-two communities have been identified at sub-ward level, the remaining ten interventions are communities of interest that are not spatially targeted. This is a more localized delivery model than in the English LSPs with some Communities First partnerships entirely focused on a single local authority estate or sub-ward-sized community. The potential for very direct local involvement and engagement of community members is therefore considerably greater than in England where the LSPs are dominated by county-level voluntary groups.

Each identified area is required to establish a partnership based on the 'three-thirds' model in which membership is one-third statutory sector, one-third voluntary/business sector and one-third drawn from the target community. Community membership is not formally determined by election as in England but is promoted by community development teams established by the first round of funding. Considerable emphasis is placed in the programme on 'capacity development' to enable local residents to take part in the policy process. All partnerships have been required to produce a 'community capacity plan' which identifies skills gaps and methods of filling them. Additionally, each partnership has been required to complete an audit of community issues, problems and opportunities which is directly derived from community participation. Theoretically, each partnership moves forward into the delivery phase of the Communities First programme with a community action plan grounded in community consultation and to be delivered through community participation. The projected expenditure for the first three years of the programme is £83 million with other spending programmes being required to 'bend' their allocation clearly towards the Communities First programme.

Both these examples demonstrate that such area-based regeneration approaches place community members alongside representatives of statutory providers within key decision-making partnerships. Furthermore, they are externally validated to ensure that community participation is genuine and not tokenistic. In England the LSPs are subject to a registration process and in Wales the community can formally appeal if it believes that the partnership is not providing it with the leading role. These patterns of participation theoretically place beneficiaries of major spending programmes in the lead position in determining the detailed pattern of spending at community level. It significantly alters the relationship between service providers and their client groups and should ensure that the community representatives lead the decision-making process. This chapter will not comment on the extent to which these objectives are realized or the nature of the implementation barriers which exist (see Adamson, 2003; Hodgson, 2004) but does note that the achievement of these objectives and the overcoming of institutional resistance in statutory organizations will require major cultural and institutional change which will take several years to mature.

The implications for an understanding of the role of civil society are considerable. These processes of engagement of beneficiaries in the delivery of services and policies instigate a two-way transfer of function in the traditional relationship between citizen and the state. Firstly, many of the actions being undertaken by community regeneration organizations within these frameworks were conventionally provided by the local and central state. Control and delivery of services such as housing, health promotion, family planning, environmental improvement, training, adult education, job creation and job placement services have passed into local control. The partnership model of public service delivery effectively places community members, who have traditionally occupied a 'client' role, in direct partnership with the state. Secondly, many social processes conventionally defined as being in the realm of civil society are passing to the partnerships, thereby engaging the representatives of state agencies in activities it has not traditionally been expected to provide. Issues of social capital, mutuality, volunteer action, personal development, empowerment and participation in community organizations are now in the remit of the multi-agency partnerships in which local and central state organizations have a clear role. This two-way flow of function is creating a convergence of activities conventionally seen as belonging to the different domains of civil society and the state.

This blurring of the state and civil society can be interpreted in a number of ways.

Firstly, the position accepted at the opening of this chapter is that civil society is a separate realm where independent voluntary associations are established and maintained by a range of social institutions over which the state has little or no influence. In this model, the contemporary practice of community regeneration suggests a new dimension in policy which is bringing about a merger in the functions, if not the form, of civil society and the state to promote a combination of state-led and centrally funded policy which is directed and delivered by community-led organizations. It is a partnership in which the state is placed at the service of the beneficiary in an unprecedented reversal of the conventional welfare state relationship with its 'clients'. It reverses the dependency traditionally associated with welfare receipt and attempts to create a pool of active citizens involved in the management of their communities and in the delivery of locally determined solutions to locally identified problems. In communities with advanced regeneration infrastructures, community-led organizations are in direct receipt of government funding, thereby removing the local state completely from the equation. It is perhaps ironic that these developments are occurring in locations characterized by social exclusion, low electoral turnout and disengagement from the conventional mechanisms of civic life.

This is clearly a potentially radical model of change with clear processes of stakeholder empowerment, localization of control over major spending programmes and the creation of new levels of accountability of statutory organizations such as local government and the health service. The approach can be seen as creating active citizens capable of challenging long-standing power structures and overturning the subservience of clients of a wide range of public services. In England the electoral process to determine LSP membership is providing an additional and alternative route to local democracy that is challenging the local government electoral process and anecdotally achieving higher levels of voter turnout. In broader terms this interpretation suggests that the state is subordinated to a local delivery mechanism grounded in civil society but that nevertheless they remain separate entities. Clearly, it is this view which underpins the Labour Party commitment to this approach and it represents a fundamental component of the Third Way.

However, this apparent partnership between state and civil society can be interpreted differently. Rather than a radical transformation of the influence of civil society over the state it can be seen as a process of incorporation. For Delanty, it is difficult to discern whether we are observing 'empowerment for ethico-practice' or innovative mechanisms of social control (2002: 167). The demonstrated successes of 'bottom-up' community regeneration programmes were beginning to establish a model of community organization over which the state had no control. In the early experience of community regeneration prior to the election of the 1997 Labour administration, community regeneration initiatives were largely independent and self-funding. They had established clear domains where the state had no formalized influence or control. Relationships with local government were particularly uneasy and in many localities conflictual. Local authority members have often seen local community organizations as a challenge to their community leadership role. Legitimized by ballot, councillors' antagonism can be seen to derive from both a loss of local control and opportunities for patronage as well as a perception that important community processes were being controlled by individuals with no formal mandate or legitimacy. The emergence of state-promoted community regeneration policy can be seen as an attempt to regulate and control this emerging community-based practice.

The advent of state-sponsored community regeneration has challenged the independence and integrity of long-standing community-based organizations. They have become harnessed to the regeneration timetables and priorities of a national programme with targets and milestones determined by government rather than local will. The very existence of many such organizations has been challenged by the development of state-sponsored strategies and many have simply been incorporated into the new policy structures with a resulting loss of independence. Hodgson refers to this as 'manufactured civil society' in which the state re-establishes control over civic organizations and community groups:

> Manufactured civil society can be viewed as a means of controlling what happens within the community and civil society more broadly. Rather than a redistribution of power and influence, what we may be

> witnessing is the extension of state power via a range of social actors. (2004: 157)

At a more fundamental level we could see the pressing need to address the actual and potential social disruption caused by Britain's 'dangerous places' (Campbell, 1993) as requiring an innovative strategy to incorporate and diffuse negative expressions of civil society. Increased organization of crime, potential and actual civil unrest and ever lower engagement with the wider social normative structure has placed up to a quarter of the population in potential conflict with the wider social order. Populations with no stake in society, the labour market or the social system, and who are marginalized and increasingly excluded, are a potentially dangerous presence in any society. Policies for finding a solution to this situation and promoting public order could be seen as essential in much the same way that embryonic welfare provision was at the turn of the twentieth century. In this sense, the programme of state-sponsored community regeneration in the UK can be seen as an element of a wider 'hegemonic project' to protect social order and promote social cohesion. Muir suggests that area-based regeneration initiatives have to be understood within a complex arrangement of local networks and national policy frameworks. They constitute a key component of the state 'hegemonic project' to regulate the conditions of capital accumulation. Area-based regeneration initiatives are hegemonic because

> The effectiveness of participation is not questioned (even when the practice leaves participants dissatisfied); participation structures have secured 'relative unity' between the state and civil society through contributing to an ideology of common interests; and because participation, through partnership structures, has provided an arena for the management of social conflict. (2004: 962)

However, these interpretations of the role of community regeneration policy imply a regulated regime of social policy delivery in which active citizens and community organizations become entirely subordinated to the state and in which civil society becomes artificial and illusory. Indeed, these views suggest a passivity on the part of communities and a lack of agency through which to achieve any community-based objectives. They suggest a powerlessness which is the complete antithesis of the claims made by the policies, which are rich with terms such as empowerment and participation. It is difficult to imagine a hegemonic project which is so complete and successful in disguising reality from its civil society participants. Such a view is reminiscent of the 'false consciousness' debates of the 1960s in which the working class was seen as entirely subordinated to the needs of capitalism through the actions of the dominant ideology. Such views were replaced with a more realistic formulation that 'hegemonic projects' are sites of struggle where all parties are collectively engaged in the creation of a dominant ideology which reflects hegemony as a negotiated outcome of class relations.

More realistically, the pattern of community regeneration and its mode of delivery discussed in this chapter can instead be interpreted as a body of evidence to suggest that the perception of civil society as separate and distinct from the state is mistaken. The chapter commenced with this view in recognition of a long pedigree of analysis of the relationship between civil society and the state. This perception has particularly come to characterize debate since the mid-1990s when the Eastern Bloc experience suggested that civil society was the location of resistance to the state and was beyond its control. Such a view could also draw on earlier discussions and particularly key interpretations of Gramsci's views on civil society referred to earlier. However, within the writings of Gramsci, other interpretations are perfectly possible. It is possible to argue that the state and civil society have never been separate but are different realms of the same process of coercion and control in society. The distinction employed by Gramsci was for analytical purposes rather than recognition of clear space between civil society, political society and the state (Neilson, 1995). Neilson suggests instead a complex articulation of different spheres of the social formation constituting a 'continuous whole' (1995: 44). The understanding of that articulation is critical to developing not just a map of civil society but also a political praxis for progressive change.

> The stark polemical opposition between civil society and the state can only be a slogan, a starting point for analysis or for mobilization against statist regimes, but it is certainly not adequate for serious analysis or politics within civil societies. (Cohen, 1995: 35–6)

The early distinction between the state as the locus of coercion and civil society as the locus of consent or hegemony is not as clear cut as that. Althusser's perception of key civil society organizations such as the family and trade unions as 'ideological state apparatuses' is one key interpretation which sees a historical melding of the function of the state and of civil society (Althusser, 1971).

Rather than a binary formulation, this suggests that state and civil society lie along a continuum of mechanisms of domination and control in which there is contest for dominance. This is not to suggest that both state and civil society are crude instruments of class domination but rather to suggest that the state intervenes in civil society and that civil society in turn exercises influence over the state. Both political society and the market provide mechanisms for this two-way flow of influence. At different points in history the balance of influence will move between civil society and the state. Civil society offers space for voluntary action and oppositional formulations but the state also exercises influence or even control over the boundaries and rules within which civil society actions take place.

> We believe that more progress can be made in assessing and scaling 'civil society' by considering it in relation to state institutions and by regarding this term as an adjective more than as a noun. It refers not to a single, homogeneous thing which can be larger or smaller, stronger or weaker, but rather to networks of relationships between state institutions and the citizens within a society who are subject to state authority as well as among those citizens. This balance of power and influence can favour the state more than citizens, or vice versa; but it is important to bear in mind that it is the balance that varies, not some thing called 'civil society' that stands between citizens and the state. (Uphoff and Krishna, 2004: 358)

This formulation of a more unified conception of civil society and the state also suggests that citizens who engage with the state may derive benefit from that relationship and achieve the inherent potential to realize their objectives. Rather than an entirely incorporated and disempowered praxis of participation it is a praxis of contest and struggle in which the gains of the citizen and the state push and pull at each other but are able at times to harmonize and achieve common objectives. If we consider this in the context of community regeneration it suggests that even in the realm of 'manufactured civil society' identified by Hodgson there is scope for active citizens to exercise control over the state and influence policy outcomes, at least at the level of their own community. The relationship between citizen and the state is not simply one where citizens are subordinated to the hegemonic project identified by Muir (2004) and discussed earlier. Nor is it a relationship characterized only by co-option and subordination to state objectives, timetables and funding requirements within the regeneration partnership as suggested by Hodgson. Both these formulations imply a zero-sum relationship where state and civil society are separate and opposed and locked in a struggle for power which is perceived as a finite resource. Uphoff and Krishna's discussion implies a more complex 'positive-sum relationship' between state and civil society where 'the latter gives citizens greater capacity to engage with the state in mutually agreeable endeavours rather than just oppose the state or retain complete autonomy from it' (2004: 358). This is not to deny the existence of a 'hegemonic project' or processes of domination in citizen/community/state partnerships. However, it does recognize that there are socio-political spaces where public participation derives public benefit and shapes the actions of the state more closely to the desires of community members and organizations.

Some evidence for this latter view can be derived from experience within some of the Communities First partnerships in Wales. Whilst the general model has been for the relevant local authority to receive Communities First funding, employ the community workers and host the partnerships, in some areas existing community organizations have been given Grant Recipient Body status and perform all these functions. Additionally, some of the more flexible local authorities have provided considerable autonomy to the local partnerships and have even reorganized their own organizational structures to reflect the increased localism in service delivery suggested by the Communities First approach. Consequently, within the Communities First programme for Wales we can see evidence of 'manufactured civil society' (Hodgson, 2004) alongside partnerships where citizens are achieving significant levels of control over local services, securing empowerment within partnerships and providing a clear lead to the actions of the partnership. This was clearly illustrated in 2004 when the Welsh Assembly Government announced funding for play and transport schemes with a six-week deadline for submission of plans. Three communities with which the Programme for Community Regeneration has contacts rejected the funding in the belief that they could not adequately involve the community in the identification of what the funding should be used for. As Communities First partnerships throughout Wales move to the next stage of the programme which will fund the community action plans derived from community participation, we will be provided with empirical tests as to whether the 'mutually agreeable endeavours' envisaged by Uphoff and Krishna (2004) can be realized in practice.

In summary, this latter discussion suggests a rethinking of the relationship between state and civil society to identify a unity with internal domains which shift and change. Recent policies of community regeneration represent a major shift which melds both social processes and organizations, conventionally seen as firmly rooted in civil society, with a more flexible and inclusive state. This represents a mutation of the welfare function of the state to provide new patterns of poverty alleviation. This change in the very nature of welfarism is as important historically as the 1945 settlement with which it breaks. It will not be recognized as a historical event in the same way, but as a process which began with the Conservative Party's promotion of the voluntary sector as a solution to specific service delivery problems in the 1980s. It currently culminates in policy models in which citizens effectively co-manage state interventions. This new welfare model is driving change in the wider set of relations between citizen and the state. It is promoting more direct forms of democratic practice and developing citizen engagement in the most marginalized social locations. It is involving and delegating to civil society organizations the achievement of policy objectives and the delivery of services. In this process the state is emerging as more responsive to the beneficiaries of social policy and its recent characterization as the 'interactive state' (O'Donovan, 2000) more clearly reveals the unity of state and civil society.

References

Adamson, D. (1995). *Living on the Edge: Poverty and Deprivation in Wales*, Llandysul: Gomer Press.

Adamson, D. L. (1997). *Social and Economic Development in Wales: The Role of Community Development*, Merthyr Tydfil: Community Enterprise Wales.

Adamson, D. (1999). 'Poverty and social exclusion in Wales today', in D. Dunkerley and A. Thompson (eds), *Wales Today*, Cardiff: University of Wales Press.

Adamson, D. (2001). 'Social segregation in a working-class community: economic and social change in the south Wales coalfield', in G. V. Guyes, H. D. Witte and P. Pasture (eds), *Can Class Still Unite. The Differentiated Workforce, Class Solidarity and Trade Unions*, Aldershot: Ashgate.

Adamson, D. (2003). 'Communities First: contemporary community regeneration policy in Wales', *Journal of Community and Development Work*, 1, 4.

Althusser, L. (1971). 'Ideology and ideological state apparatuses. (Notes towards an investigation). January–April 1969', in L. Althusser, *Lenin and Philosophy and Other Essays*, London: New Left Books.

Beck, U. (1997). *The Reinvention of Politics: Rethinking Modernity in the Global Social Order*, Cambridge: Polity.

Campbell, B. (1993). *Goliath: Britain's Dangerous Places*, London: Methuan.

Chamberlayne, P., Rustin, M. and Wengraf, T. (2002). *Biography and Social Exclusion in Europe: Experiences and Life Journeys*, Bristol: Policy Press.

Cohen, J. (1995). 'Interpreting the notion of civil society', in M. Walzer (ed.), *Toward a Global Civil Society*, Oxford: Bergahn Books.

Deakin, N. (2001). *In Search of Civil Society*, Basingstoke: Palgrave.

Delanty, G. (2002). 'Communitarianism and citizenship', in E. F. Isin and B. S. Turner (eds), *Handbook of Citizenship Studies*, London: Sage.

Etzioni, A. (1995). *The Spirit of Community: Rights, Responsibilities and the Communitarian Agenda*, London: Fontana.

Etzioni, A. (2000). *The Third Way to a Good Society*, London: Demos.

Faulks, K. (1998). *Citizenship in Modern Britain*, Edinburgh: Edinburgh University Press.

Hall, John A. (1995). 'In search of civil society', in John H. Hall (ed.), *In Search of Civil Society: Theory, History, Comparison*, Cambridge: Polity Press.

Hodgson, L. (2004). 'Manufactured civil society: counting the cost', *Critical Social Policy*, 24, 2.

Jones, C. and Novak, T. (1999). *Poverty, Welfare and the Disciplinary State*, London: Routledge.

Kendall, J. (2000). *The Mainstreaming of the Third Sector into Public Policy in England in the late 1990s: Whys and Wherefores*, Civil Society Working Paper 2, London: LSE, Centre for Civil Society.

Khilnani, S. (2001). 'The development of civil society', in S. Kaviraj and S. Khilnani (eds), *Civil Society: History and Possibilities*, Cambridge: Cambridge University Press.

King, D. S. (1987). *The New Right: Politics, Markets and Citizenship*, Basingstoke: Macmillan.

Levitas, R. (1996). 'The concept of social exclusion and the new Durkheimian hegemony', *Critical Social Policy*.

Mayo, M. and Robertson, J. (2003). 'The historical and policy context: setting the scene for current debates', in S. Banks, H. Butcher, P. Henderson and

J. Robertson (eds), *Managing Community Practice: Principles, Policies and Programmes*, Bristol: Policy Press.

Muir, J. (2004). 'Public participation in area-based urban regeneration programmes', *Housing Studies*, 19, 6.

Murray, C. (1990). *The Emerging British Underclass*, London: Institute of Economic Affairs.

Murray, C. (1994). *The Underclass: The Crisis Deepens*, London: Institute of Economic Affairs.

Neilson, K. (1995). 'Reconceptualizing civil society for now: some somewhat Gramscian turnings', in M. Walzer (ed.), *Toward a Global Civil Society*, Oxford: Bergahn Books.

O'Donovan, O. (2000). 'Re-theorizing the interactive state: reflections on a popular participatory initiative in Ireland', *Community Development Journal*, 35, 3.

Popple, K. (1995). *Analysing Community Work: Its Theory and Practice*, Buckingham: Open University Press.

Roche, M. (2002). 'Social citizenship; grounds of social change', in E. F. Isin and B. S. Turner (eds), *Handbook of Citizenship Studies*, London: Sage.

Seligman, A. B. (1993). *The Idea of Civil Society*, New York: The Free Press.

Uphoff, N. and Krishna, A. (2004). 'Civil society and public sector institutions: more than a zero-sum relationship', *Public Administration and Development*, 24.

Urry, J. (1981). *The Anatomy of Capitalist Societies: The Economy, Civil Society and the State*, London: Macmillan.

Walzer, M. (1995). 'The concept of civil society', in M. Walzer (ed.), *Toward a Global Civil Society*, Oxford: Berghahn Books.

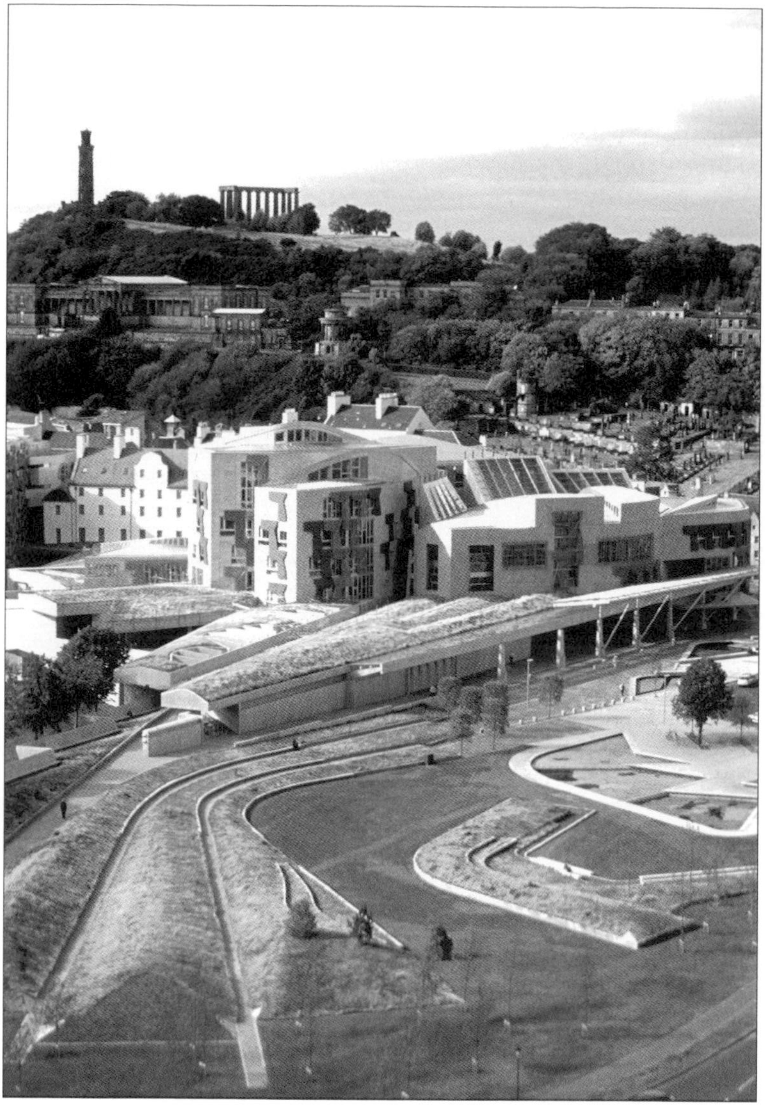

15. Civil Society in Scotland

ISOBEL LINDSAY

The outcome of the 2003 Scottish Parliament elections brings to mind the civil society equivalent of the patients taking over the asylum! 'Taking over' is an exaggeration but there has certainly been a minor invasion of groups who have been more commonly associated with campaigning than legislating. The Greens won seven seats, the far-left Scottish Socialist Party won six, the recently formed Scottish Senior Citizens' Party gained one as did a campaigner against a local hospital closure. Two independents rejected by their parties also won. The interface between the executive and the institutions of civil society has settled into a conventional pattern of formal consultation exercises and lobbying. But the Parliament has had a more innovative relationship with developments like the Petitions Committee and the growing number of cross-party groups with non-parliamentary participants. The success of minority parties with strong links to campaigning organizations has also created more fluid boundaries.

This chapter will examine the current direction of civil society in Scotland in the context of its historical background. There have been very marked changes in its role. The themes emerging are of a very central position in the eighteenth and nineteenth centuries that was crucial in sustaining Scottish distinctiveness. A much diminished role after the First World War until the end of the 1970s was followed by a significant period of coalition-building and social and political leadership in the 1980s and 1990s. The post-devolution period is a paradoxical one for civic institutions with opportunities both gained and lost and a more complex interrelationship between them.

The historical background

The wider political implications of civil society in Scotland have a long and very significant history. Scotland's incorporation into the English Parliament in 1707 was the outcome not of conquest but of a deal between political elites. Although unpopular among the wider public, it offered access to the English economy and colonies in return for neutering a long-standing threat to the security of the English state. The Scottish negotiations put paid to the prospects of a federal solution but did gain protection within the Treaty of Union for certain institutions – the Scottish legal system, the Presbyterian religion, the education system and the local system of burgh administration, for example. If we add to this the fact that most economic, cultural and charitable developments were indigenous, it has been argued that Scotland had a very substantial degree of civil autonomy despite the loss of its position as an independent state.

The importance of this civil autonomy has been stressed by several writers. Harvie (1977: 193), for example, explored its relationship with nationalism and national identity: 'The institutions of Scottish civil society – Kirk, law, local government and education . . . had traditionally provided the means of bringing national consciousness before the public.' Paterson makes this the central theme in explaining the absence of a strong nationalist movement in Scotland in the nineteenth century when such movements were prevalent throughout Europe:

> Civil society was autonomous from the state in Scotland as throughout Britain. Its Scottish character derived from its roots well before the Union, and above all from the legal system and the Presbyterian Church. When civil society was regulated at all, that happened from a Scottish centre which, in these functions, retained much of the symbolic significance of sovereignty and majesty that it had always had. (1994: 45)

It can certainly be argued that the absence of a government/Parliament focus in Scottish society gave high status to institutions of church, education and the professions, especially law. Religious institutions had a particularly powerful role, both integrating and dividing society. Scotland, by the late nineteenth century, had also developed an increasing range of its own 'modern' civic organizations such as the Scottish Trade Union Congress established in 1897, the Scottish Football League in 1890, cultural organizations, medical charities, mutual societies etc.: 'In the voluntary sphere the Scottish urban middle class, in particular, created an intricate web of active institutions, the apex of which were the voluntary hospitals of the four cities.' (Morgan and Trainor, 1990: 130).

The overall picture at the start of the twentieth century was one of a strong civil society that was in most respects distinctly Scottish and acted as a counterbalance to the inevitable English dominance of the British state. Although much of the twentieth-century story was different there were still important elements of that strong distinctive civil society playing a central role at the end of the century and acting as one of the midwives of constitutional change.

The First World War and its aftermath were a particular disaster for Scotland. Scotland lost a higher proportion of men than any other part of the UK: 26 per cent of the men who served died in comparison with 12 per cent for the rest of Britain. This was followed by a huge outflow of population through migration in the following decade – a net loss of 390,000 in ten years (Devine, 1999: 309). This greatly undermined confidence and initiative in many areas of social and economic life. Economic recession, failure to invest in new industries, appalling housing conditions, political disillusion, sectarian tensions, the perception of failure and decline and the scale of socio-economic problems left people looking towards the state for amelioration. The voluntary association route was marginal to the extent of the problems.

Although the traditional civil institutions continued to be significant and the churches and trade unions had a period of growth in the two decades following the Second World War, the focus during this period was overwhelmingly on the state. For social and economic change, Scotland looked to the Scottish Office, Westminster and to local authorities. As in other parts of the UK, the 1950s and 1960s were periods of substantial change but it is difficult to think of any examples where these changes were initiated or driven by civil society. Innovations in Scotland such as regional economic development policy, the Children's Panel juvenile justice system, the Highlands and Islands Development Board, the New Towns programme, the radical Wheatley regional local government reforms, the Scottish Special

Housing Association and educational change were largely driven by Scottish Office civil servants and politicians in that order. There were pressure groups like the Scottish Council (Development and Industry) but their impact on policy was not profound. The state was powerful and could deliver change. The challenge was to control the state through the direct route of political parties. This was especially so in Scotland since it was assumed that on the whole the Scottish Office would 'bat for Scotland' whichever of the two parties was in power.

On the campaigning front in this period Scotland was more of an imitator than an innovator. Pioneering groups like Shelter, CND, the Child Poverty Action Group and New Left groups, had their origins in the south and were then 'imported'. The civil society role was still quite strong on the traditional front – churches, trade unions and professional associations, employers' associations, 'old' charities – but it was weak on new campaigning and charitable organizations. Scottish civil society could be summarized , for much of the two decades following the end of the war, as reinforcing rather than changing the structures and values in Scottish society.

What role did the institutions of civil society play historically in the specific context of constitutional reform? There was a crucial period in the 1880s when growing discontent with the inefficiency, corruption and unaccountability of government in Scotland led to the campaign for the establishment of the Scottish Office and the position of Scottish secretary. This was a genuine example of civil society in action. Sections of the Liberal Party, emerging socialist groups, churches, the burghs, newspapers etc. worked together to mobilize public opinion on constitutional reform issues, challenging a largely indifferent or hostile Westminster. The Scottish Home Rule Association was formed in this period. Eventually the demand for a Scottish secretary was reluctantly granted and, although the substance of the change was very limited at the time, it was a crucial campaign and outcome since it established a basis for public policy decision-making in the following century that was distinctive from the rest of the UK.

The late 1920s and early 1930s saw another time of focus on the Scottish constitutional agenda with the formation of the Scottish National Party, but it was the cultural turn that was as significant in this period with the emergence of a range of writers asserting and exploring Scottish identity. Hugh MacDiarmid, Eric Linklater, Compton McKenzie and Neil Gunn were prominent examples. Many of them had specific links with political nationalism. The National Trust for Scotland and the Saltire Society were examples of cultural organizational initiatives at this time.

The later 1940s saw another attempt to mobilize the wider institutions of Scottish society for the establishment of a domestic legislature. The Scottish Convention was initiated by people who had given up the nationalist political party route in favour of wider civic and cross-party cooperation to achieve change. It launched the National Covenant in 1949 and was very successful in the mobilization process with a large number of organizations giving support and gathering 2 million signatures. But delivery was a different matter. The Labour government rejected it while the Conservatives in opposition offered a Royal Commission. This was established when they returned to power in 1951 and this took the steam out of the movement. When the commission reported in 1954, it recommended only modest changes in the Scottish Office. By this point the wider home rule movement was considered to be on the fringes.

We can see from this that civic mobilization was used on a significant scale during two periods specifically on the issues of constitutional reform. In the first in the 1880s it was successful. In the second in the 1940s, with a more ambitious agenda, it was not. In addition, there were party political initiatives in the inter-war period and a loose cultural network seeking to focus on the Scottish dimension.

Coalition-building: the response to the New Right

If we define this contemporary period as from the end of the 1970s to the establishment of the Scottish Parliament, we can see significant changes in many aspects of civil society in Scotland. Many of these changes are shared with other developed societies; some are more specific to Scotland. The feature that marked the period was a response to the emergence of what was perceived as an intransigent and unrepresentative political system after Margaret Thatcher took over as prime minister. There were unlikely to be many who were familiar with Antonio Gramsci's writings but what happened in practice in Scotland was a good example of his prescription for the development of intellectual and moral leadership in civil society bringing together alliances for radical change. Certainly civil society played a key role in this period.

Some of the cooperation over these two decades 'emerged' rather than was the outcome of conscious planning. The various organizations and sectors reflected the concerns of their own members and the communities from which they came. The traumatic loss of 40 per cent of Scotland's industrial base in the 1979–94 period affected most civic organization and crossed social class lines (see Brown et al., 1998, ch.4). Similarly, the government's hostility to the welfare state had greater implications for Scotland than most of the UK. Scotland had a much higher proportion of housing in the public sector than any other region, a lower proportion of private health and education provision, and the very low population density of much of rural Scotland has required greater state support. It was predictable that churches and unions and voluntary organizations would express many similar concerns and those in cultural networks would reflect the dominant mood. In the comparatively small Scottish society, many activists were already known to each other.

However, it may be questioned why this led to increased cooperation on the issues of constitutional change. There were bitter divisions around this in the 1970s and the divisions between supporters of independence and devolution were still live but largely concentrated in the political parties. The core party politicians were still divided but for many others the common enemy of Thatcherism was a source of unity.

After the third Conservative victory in 1987, the concern about the democratic deficit reached a peak. There were groups which had been consciously promoting civic and cross-party cooperation as the best route to resist the government's agenda and to promote change. It was at this point that the idea of a Constitutional Convention, which had been around since the failure of the 1979 referendum, became viable. A related development was the campaign by women's groups for radically improved women's representation in Scottish public life. The fourth successive Conservative election victory in 1992 produced a new range of civic initiatives – Scotland United, Common Cause, the Civic Assembly – in an attempt to counter the political depression and build some new momentum. The following examines some of the developments in the period in the churches, trade unions, voluntary sector and the cultural sphere.

The churches

Secularization is one of those trends associated with advanced industrial societies and Scotland broadly fits the pattern. Yet ironically there is a case for arguing that decline in membership and in social role has been accompanied by an increase in the political role. As we have seen, the story of church membership is not one of straight decline. The period after the Second World War saw a resurgence in membership and a substantial role in the provision of recreation. The Church of Scotland had over 1 million members and the Catholic Church had almost half a million regular attenders. In 1956 the Church of Scotland had 325,000 enrolled in Sunday school but this had declined to 61,000 by 1994 (Brown, 2001). By the end of the 1960s, the decline had set in and the recreational role of the churches as well as their spiritual and social control functions were moving from centrality to the margins. Churches are still among the largest of the voluntary organizations. A survey in 2000 found that 35 per cent claimed an attachment to the Church of Scotland and 12 per cent to the Catholic Church (Curtice et al., 2002: 95). They have a presence in most communities and a cultural role in rites of passage. But this cannot disguise substantial contraction. However, where the churches at earlier periods were very limited players on the political scene, their significance in the political arena broadened and deepened during the 1980s and 1990s. Before that, the Church of Scotland at formal national level would have been seen as reflecting typical middle-class Scottish opinion. This would have been even more so at local level. It made a more radical stance on anti-colonial issues with its overseas missionary background. It was broadly sympathetic to 'Home Rule'. It would actively lobby on such issues as alcohol licensing laws and Sunday observance. It was bitterly divided for years on nuclear weapons policy. Until the Thatcher period the Roman Catholic church was even narrower in its political focus. On issues like separate Catholic schools, divorce and abortion legislation, the Scottish bishops would lobby very strongly but, apart from advising against voting for Communists, it limited its political activities.

The Thatcher period radicalized the churches but in this they reflected the trend of opinion in Scottish society. The rapid deindustrialization in Scotland combined with the loss of many established companies through closure or takeover, affected the middle class as well as manual workers. The Scottish churches individually and together through Action by Churches Together in Scotland (ACTS) became regular participants in protest coalitions. Against industrial closures and unemployment, against nuclear weapons and war, against the Poll Tax, for constitutional change – these were some of the issues that brought churches into formal and informal coalitions. ACTS formally participated in the Constitutional Convention and played an active role through its representatives in sustaining the convention and influencing its outcome on such issues as proportional representation.

There was also greater identification on the part of the Catholic Church with the Scottish dimension rather than Irish ethnic subculture within Scotland. Cardinal Gray was a member of the Campaign for a Scottish Assembly. Cardinal Winning, who succeeded him, was involved in a wide range of social and economic causes. The Scottish bishops took a stronger anti-nuclear position than those in England. The Pope's visit in the period was seen by many as a recognition of Scottish identity.

The Church of Scotland had always had a loose left/right division among clergy and lay representatives and this was expressed in often strongly contested General Assembly debates. The Thatcher period moved the Church to the left but this was a reflection of wider opinion in Scottish society. The prime minister's controversial speech to the General Assembly in 1988 and her very critical reception, when she was presented with a Church report on poverty, was a clear indicator of the predominant mood of the period.

The voluntary sector

It was the Thatcher period that brought expansion, sectoral identity and greater radicalism to the voluntary sector in Scotland. Before that period there was work going on that was worthy but quite limited in scale and not notable for its pacemaking. The sector's nineteenth century buoyancy and sense of purpose had not been replicated in the twentieth century. The public looked to the state to initiate and deliver, and did so with some confidence in the post-war period.

The combination of Thatcher's hostility to state provision and the 'democratic deficit' in Scotland created a climate more conducive to the third sector. However, outcomes were complex. On the one hand, the Conservative government and its supporters were ideologically quite sympathetic to the idea of the voluntary sector as an alternative to the state where the private sector could not be used (Green, 1993). On the other hand, the kind of people who were drawn to much of the work of voluntary organizations were 'pro-underdog'. They were inclined to social justice values. They were pushing for better services for the vulnerable and more public expenditure to achieve this. They were generally in favour of greater state regulation on, for example, environmental, animal welfare and disability issues. If one thinks of a social Darwinian spectrum, much of the voluntary sector was at the opposite end from the Thatcherite Conservatives. One study of chairs and chief executives of organizations affiliated to the Scottish Council for Voluntary Organisations found in 1994 that only 13 per cent identified with the Conservatives (Lindsay, 1995: 328).

A range of new or intensified social problems emerged during this period: high levels of unemployment, community breakdown, more lone parents, the emergence of AIDS, a sharp increase in illegal drug use, more rough-sleeping. In addition there was more assertiveness by groups subject to prejudice on grounds of sexual orientation, gender, race, mental illness and disability. Environmental issues moved towards the mainstream and in the early 1980s proposals for nuclear waste stores in Scotland gave these a particular edge. There was also a period of strong peace movement activity in response to the Reagan–Thatcher Cold War strategy. While little of this was unique to Scotland, most of the organizational initiatives were now either entirely Scottish or had a strong Scottish dimension.

The sector became more organized and cohesive during this period with the development of intermediate structures to encourage cooperation and a substantial expansion of networking through training courses and conferences. There was probably some expectation on the part of government, when they promoted the market-testing, contract culture approach that involved not-for-profit organizations competing for public sector contracts, that this would create a sector more sympathetic to market values and be more compliant. However, there were too many factors pulling in other directions. Most of Scotland's voluntary sector during this period fitted comfortably into the centre-left anti-Conservative consensus that typified most of Scottish society.

By the end of the 1990s there were an estimated 44,000 voluntary organizations with an annual income of £2.2 billion, around 4 per cent of Scottish GDP, and 100,000 employees (see Scottish Executive, 2001). There was substantial sectoral infrastructure – a strong Scottish Council for Voluntary Organisations, a network of local Councils for Voluntary Service and a range of intermediaries like Children in Scotland, Youthlink and Environmentlink. The concept of the social economy was just about emerging into the mainstream and had some recognition from the economic development agencies, Highlands and Islands Enterprise and Scottish Enterprise. There was also an active range of campaigning groups at the radical end of the spectrum involved in direct action on anti-nuclear and environmental issues. As the larger political parties declined in active membership, it appeared that it was the campaigning/voluntary sector that were more likely to attract those concerned with social change.

Trade unions

The trade unions in the 1980s and 1990s in Scotland had certain similarities to the churches – declining membership combined with an increasing political significance. The trade unions before the 1980s had much greater workplace influence and their relationship to the Labour Party appeared to provide political influence. In practice the latter was often more illusory than real. There are some examples, but not many, where union intervention in Scotland was significant during a period when Labour was in office. One example of this was between the two general elections in 1974 when the role of the unions helped to shift Labour policy on devolution but that was in a situation of strong divisions within other sections of the party. During the years of Conservative government after 1979, the trade union role was more influential in Scotland despite its increasingly weak industrial position. To be more precise, it was not so much the unions in general but the Scottish Trade Union Congress. Although Scotland had few remaining independent unions (most had been incorporated into UK structures), the existence of the STUC gave the trade union movement in Scotland a distinctive voice. Its role was especially important since it had organizational resources that could provide some logistical support for campaigns.

This, of course, depended on there being the political will. The STUC had generally been to the left of the Labour Party leadership over a long period and had been accustomed to take its own initiatives. Its role became more focused when a new general secretary, Campbell Christie, took over in 1985 and he started his period in office by developing a policy of alliance-building. This was not new to the STUC but he pursued it with greater enthusiasm. The STUC had a history of support for devolution and had given some backing to the cross-party Campaign for a Scottish Assembly after its establishment in 1979. The STUC played a central role in the formation of the Constitutional Convention and later in the other initiatives that followed the failure of Labour to win the 1992 election, such as the Scotland United group that organized mass demonstrations and the Scottish Civic Assembly. Earlier the STUC had helped coordinate the anti-Poll Tax campaign. In 1986 it brought together opposition parties, local authorities, churches and academics in the Commission on the Scottish Economy to prepare strategies for economic regeneration. This was in addition to its role in coordinating campaigns against the closure of the steel industry and many other specific industrial closures. It also promoted a range of cultural and anti-racist initiatives.

One of the few successful examples of union activity forcing a change in government policy in Scotland was in relation to the introduction of primary pupil testing and league tables. In this case one of the few independent Scottish unions, the Educational Institute of Scotland, together with some support from local authorities, succeeded in mobilizing parents to withdraw their children from testing and forced the Scottish Office to abandon its proposals and negotiate a different assessment programme. Although this was a good example of successful individual union action working together with the wider public, it was not typical of the period. The strength of the unions in the post-1979 period was that they had the STUC structure in place and there were some leading figures in the movement who had an ideological perspective committed to the strategy of alliance-building.

The cultural dimension

At the start of this 'contemporary' period there were still concerns about a rural romanticism and a Kitsch Scottishness, Kailyard and Tartanry, dominating Scottish culture. The Edinburgh Festival of 1981 had an exhibition of the worst of tartan artefacts and debates on the Brigadoon-style portrayal of Scotland on film, raising concerns that Scottish culture was failing to engage with the real world. How justified these concerns were is a wider debate. There were changes already taking place in the 1970s with such drama as John McGrath's *The Cheviot, the Stag and the Black, Black Oil* and John Byrne's *The Slab Boys*. Thirty years later it is difficult to imagine a similar debate taking place. Even if one took a narrowly structural interpretation of civil society, many of the cultural developments in Scotland in the 1980s and 1990s were linked with the social/political developments taking place in the period. Most of the major writers (Alasdair Gray, Iain Banks, A. L. Kennedy, William McIlvanney, Irvine Welsh, Edwin Morgan, James Kelman and Liz Lochhead) were not only part of a broad Scottish consensus on social and economic justice issues and constitutional reform, but were in many cases happy to give their names to or participate in political action. A new element was the Scottish popular music scene, most of which was also explicitly political like Runrig, Deacon Blue and Hue and Cry. The Scottish film output was small but also recognizably radical in its values with the involvement of people like Peter Mullen and Lynne Ramsay. There were some differences between the devolution and the independence supporters but the similarities were much more important than the differences. Leading cultural figures were very much part of a coherent network. As the poet, Edwin Morgan (2002: 18) has commented: 'There has always been argument about whether cultural change should precede, accompany, or follow political change. In this case, the outburst of good writing in the 1980s . . . clearly presaged the 1997 referendum with its overwhelming endorsement of a Scottish Parliament' (2002: 18).

Post-devolution

Civic institutions in Scotland entered the new Scottish Parliament era with a very positive inheritance. They had played an influential role in sustaining morale and cohesion in Scottish society during the difficult years of deindustrialization and the attack on the social democratic consensus. They had asserted their 'Scottishness' in opposition to the Thatcher promotion of Great British patriotism. In particular, they had been significant participants in the process of shaping and delivering the new constitutional settlement. With the exception of some of the organizations representing business, civil society formally supported the Yes vote in the referendum. Despite the very wide variety of organizations it represented, the Scottish Council for Voluntary Organisations took a decision to support the Parliament on the specific grounds that it would be good for the sector in providing more legislative time, greater access and accountability. This did not prove to be a controversial decision.

The civic role was recognized in the make-up of the Consultative Steering Group, established by the new secretary of state to prepare recommendations for the internal structures of the Parliament. The steering group recommended strong specialist Parliamentary committees that, among their other roles, would be expected to offer a direct route to dialogue with MSPs for many organizations. It recommended a Public Petitions Committee to which any organisation or individual could raise any issue and which would ensure that there was an appropriate response by referring the topic to the specialist committees or the executive. It also gave its support to the establishment of the Scottish Civic Forum, not in statute as in Northern Ireland, but receiving recognition and financial support from the executive (Lindsay, 2000: 404).

So the constitutional reforms offered the prospect of new influence on public policy. There were early positive developments. Having taken the decision in principle to end university tuition fees, the task of producing a specific scheme was given to an advisory committee whose chair and members had a strong civic sector background and carried out very extensive consultations (Scottish Executive, 1999). A similar approach was taken in relation to teachers' pay and professional development. A Social Inclusion Network was established with broad civic representation to work with the minister (since disbanded in June 2003).

However, political life in Scotland was no longer the same. The old democratic deficit was not there. There were 129 elected members together with their staff to offer leadership and anxious to be seen to do so, and it has been argued that it is right that civic leadership should play a lesser role (Paterson, 1999). So, while the institutions and values of the new political landscape should have ensured an increasingly influential civic sector engaging in the process of policy development, what so far has the outcome been? It is a short period in which to pass judgement but there are several factors that signify some of the pluses and minuses of change. These are the consultation overload, some cynicism about the quality of engagement, exposure of divisions within civil society, and the decreasing presence and quality of the political party in the community.

The number of formal executive consultations has doubled, comparing the annual average of 132 in 1999–2001 with 76 in 1993–6 (Scottish Civic Forum, 2002: 38). This might be expected to be seen as an advantage but, for many organizations with small staff numbers, it means so much reactive work that the time available for the proactive has diminished. Yet, if they choose not to respond, it becomes difficult to intervene or criticize at a later stage. An organization like the STUC with a broad range of interests has experienced great work pressures as a result of this. The Civic Forum's Audit of Democratic Participation found in its survey of its own members that there was by 2001 still on balance a positive view of consultation, with only 20 per cent saying it was poor and 52 per cent claiming that there had been some changes to executive policy as an outcome of the consultation process (Scottish Civic Forum, 2002: 72). But a cynicism about the influence of consultation, the very short periods in which it is conducted and the lack of feedback is quite commonly heard.

One positive development has been a system of cross-party groups on specific topics of public interest (Scottish Civic Forum, 2003). These are made up of MSPs from different parties along with interested groups and individuals. They have to be approved by the Parliament's Standards Committee. There are now over forty of these on, for example, animal welfare, epilepsy, nuclear disarmament, Scottish music, sexual health and Palestine. They range beyond devolved functions and, of course, have no power but they offer dialogue and networking. This does not involve executive ministers and is, therefore, several stages away from the decision-taking structures.

One predictable development in the current scene is that the unifying factor of the 1980s and 1990s – the 'external enemy' – is no longer there and this exposes divisions that were kept muted in those earlier decades. The abolition of Clause 28 (it had a different number in Scottish legislation) that had prohibited the 'promotion' of homosexuality by public authorities, created a very bitter period in which churches were divided as were political parties and some other organizations, although the outcome was in many ways a tribute to civil society. Belatedly, the minister established an advisory committee with the usual variety of civic representatives to produce an alternative statement of guidance for schools. This was a sensitive and broadly liberal statement that was widely accepted. MSPs voted for the abolition of the clause and the storm disappeared as quickly as it had arisen. This did, however, illustrate the diversity rather than the familiar coherence of civil society to which Scotland had become used. Other legislation on land reform, fox-hunting, housing, as well as policy initiatives on transport and roads, were examples of civil diversity. While this pluralism is normal and desirable, it has required some adjustment. Civil alliances have to be more complex and variable than they might have been in the past. Also, because the larger organizations felt, at least to begin with, that they had more of a direct route to the new executive, there may have been some feeling that alliances were less important.

One element of civil society that devolution might have been expected to strengthen was that of the political party. The transfer of greater power to Scotland and the establishment of a democratic legislature should have given some stimulus to political parties at the Scottish and the local community level. Yet the paradox has been that this greater power to deliver social change has been accompanied by a decline in membership in all the larger parties and, although not measurable, a general acceptance that most party political activity at community level has been in decline. While the explanations can only be speculative and this is not a trend unique to Scotland, the lack of internal democracy within parties, disempowering activists and focusing politics on national leaders and national media, has some plausibility as part of the explanation. But, while the established parties have not been invigorated at their grass roots by the Parliament, what has happened with potentially important implications is that small parties and campaign groups have succeeded in getting elected and, in doing so, they have set an example for others. Given the likelihood that coalition government will be the norm in Scotland and so will the election of MSPs from a variety of small parties and campaigns, the movement in and out of the conventional categories of civil and state institutions may become more fluid.

References

Brown, A., McCrone, D. and Paterson, L. (1998). *Politics and Society in Scotland*, 2nd edn, London: Macmillan.

Brown, C. (2001). *The Death of Christian Britain*, London: Routledge.

Curtice, J., McCrone, D., Park, A. and Paterson, L. (eds) (2002). *New Scotland, New Society*, Edinburgh: Polygon.

Devine, T. (1999). *The Scottish Nation*, London: Penguin Press.

Green, D. (1993). *Re-inventing Civil Society*, London: Institute of Economic Affairs.

Harvie, C. (1977). *Scotland and Nationalism*, London: George Allen and Unwin.

Lindsay, I. (1995). 'The voluntary sector: on whose side?', *The Political Quarterly*, 66, 4, 328–35.

Lindsay, I. (2000). 'The new civic forums', *The Political Quarterly*, 71, 4, 404–11.

MacCormick, J. (1955). *The Flag in the Wind*, London: Gollancz.

Morgan, E. (2002). 'Scottish fiction', *Scottish Left Review*, 12 September/October, 18–20, http://www.scottishleftreview.org.

Morgan, N. and Trainor, R. (1990). 'The Dominant Classes', in W. H.Fraser and R. J. Morris (eds), *People and Society in Scotland*, vol. 11, Edinburgh: John Donald, pp. 103–37.

Paterson, L. (1994). *The Autonomy of Modern Scotland*, Edinburgh: Edinburgh University Press.

Paterson, L. (1999). 'Why should we respect civic Scotland?', in G. Hassan and C. Warhurst (eds), *A Different Future*, Glasgow: The Big Issue/Centre for Scottish Public Policy, pp. 34–43.

Report of the Consultative Steering Group on the Scottish Parliament (1999). London: HMSO.

Scottish Civic Forum (2002). *The Audit of Democratic Participation*, Edinburgh: SCF.

SCF (2003). *Briefing Paper: Scottish Parliament Cross-Party Groups*, November.

Scottish Executive (1999). *Report of the Independent Committee of Inquiry into Student Support*, Edinburgh, December.

Scottish Executive (2001). *Review of Funding for the Voluntary Sector*, Edinburgh, April.

Woman's Claim of Right Group (1991). *A Woman's Claim of Right in Scotland*, Edinburgh: Polygon.

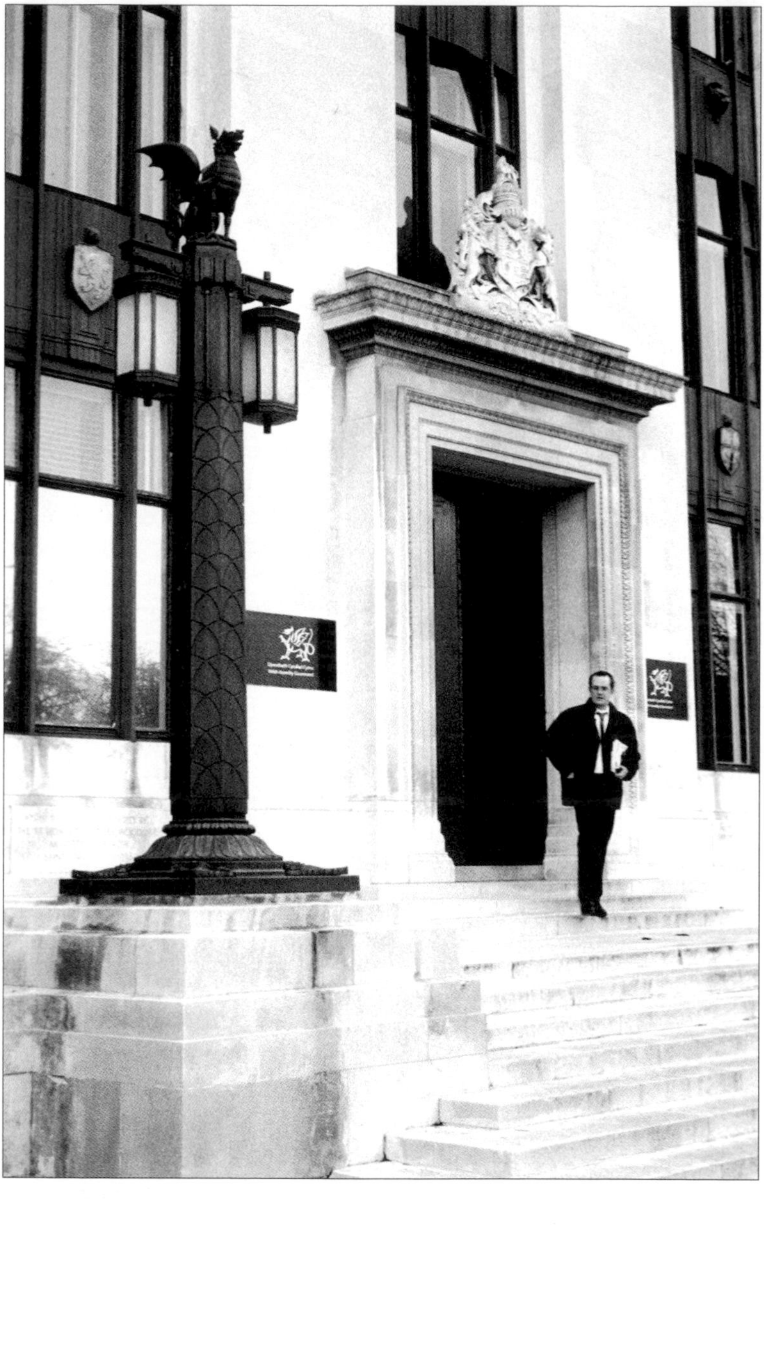

16. Evaluating Policy Initiatives to Enhance Civil Society

SARAH BATTERBURY

Introduction

Almost all the chapters in this volume touch on issues of policy and its intersection with civil society. The policy world is generally acknowledged as seeking to control and manage civil society. This has become a central focus of current policy initiatives in Wales, heightened by the process of devolution and also by the parallel emergence of theories of social capital indicating a potential link with economic and community development. Throughout this book a key theme has been the way in which the Assembly has sought to influence civil society through a variety of policy interventions.

Thus actions by the Assembly in the area of civil society are both overtly interventionist and responsive at the same time. There is a cyclicity between policy interventions and the shape and nature of civil society. This is hardly surprising when we realize that civil society in Wales is a dynamic construct, which changes in character over time. The main force for change in the character of civil society comes not from policy interventions aimed at civil society per se, but from global forces changing the economic configuration of the country and the demographics of place as people move into and around the country. The very fluidity of civil society also enables it sometimes to elude state control and policy direction. Assembly funding for particular groups has inevitably recast some aspects of civil society, bringing them into partnership with local authorities and the Assembly itself. This process has been occasioned by raising the stakes (offering funding) and imposing eligibility criteria, thereby inducing change within some civil society institutions, interest groups and communities.

However, in this very process the state merely shifts the focus of its support. It is engaged in simultaneously supporting some aspects of civil society whilst also re-creating groupings of those considered ineligible.

Given the dynamic nature of civil society in Wales and the multiple influences on its character, it is hardly surprising that attempts to *evaluate* civil society have not been very successful. This is especially the case as evaluative efforts to date have been concerned with measuring civil society as a precursor to policy formulation intended to capture civil society and to harness its potential to achieve policy objectives. As most students of methodology will know, the quantitative measurement of a non-static, dynamic phenomenon is a particularly difficult, if not mistaken, enterprise. Charlotte Williams demonstrates this problem very well in this volume where she outlines how a tendency not to use the term 'volunteering' by black and ethnic minority groups has led to the mistaken impression that they are not active in these kinds of activities (see also Leigh, 2000). The more recent attempt by the CIVICUS project to measure civil society was also problematic, as shown by Nicholl in chapter 4. Indeed, Williams confirms that the CIVICUS finding that black and ethnic minority groups are not active in civil society masks a more complex reality of engaged activity that eluded the rather crude measurement criteria employed.

This chapter suggests that we need to turn the tables on this evaluative approach. Instead of evaluating civil society (a somewhat ethically dubious and normative notion), it argues that effort is better directed to the evaluation of policy initiatives intended to enhance and develop civil society. The realistic evaluation approach offers a useful way of grounding our understanding of what we expect policy to achieve (policy theory) in the policy context to ensure that the implications of the intersection between context, mechanism (policy intervention) and outcomes are more clearly understood. The contextualization of our understanding of policy is of particular importance where the object of evaluation (that is, the policy) is needing to respond to a shifting context (civil society).

Evaluating policy initiatives to foster civil society is no easy task as there is a myriad of policy interventions which have some bearing on supporting the development of civil society in a large variety of domains including education, vocational training, voluntary activities, strategies for community regeneration and partnership governance in Wales. This chapter presents just one case study, that of a volunteering scheme currently being sponsored by the Assembly. The case study is useful as it demonstrates the utility of the realistic approach in helping to formulate policies that are more contextually responsive. The chapter concludes with an overview of the ways in which the realistic approach may also be utilized in the different policy arenas discussed in the book, focusing on the difference between contextually appropriate programme theory and *conviction politics* (Nutley et al., 2002 and 2003) which lacks the analytical rigour of programme theory. Looking at the different policy approaches discussed through the book, the ways in which context interacts with policy mechanisms to produce both desired and unanticipated (less hoped for) outcomes is reviewed.

Employing a realistic approach to evaluating policy

The utility of the realistic approach to evaluation was expounded by Pawson and Tilley (1997) when they published their (already seminal) text on *Realistic Evaluation*. This approach relies on understanding the relationship between the context within which policy initiatives are carried out, the mechanism of the initiative, and the outcomes that ensue. As they have commented, the realistic approach can 'give us an initial explanatory 'fix' on any social program' (1997: xv). It is the explanatory potential of this approach which makes it of particular use for understanding why things work (or do not work) in particular contexts.

The realistic approach to evaluation draws on earlier work from the realist school recognizing the open systems character of research in the social sciences generally (Sayer 1984). This implies an acceptance that not everything can be controlled as in a scientific experiment, given that the social world consists of a number of cross-cutting variables which are difficult to isolate and interrogate. This description applies very easily to civil society. In evaluation the realistic approach focuses on the links between context, mechanism and outcome – this provides a useful way to understand why things work (or do not work). Ensuring desirable policy outcomes entails the development of middle range theory that explains this dynamic. This approach has particular utility for evaluation as it identifies causality and contextual linkages, enabling policy improvement to take place as the result of the emergence of grounded understandings about the interaction between context and policy interventions. Although Pawson and Tilley make no reference to the work of Glaser and Strauss (1967) and grounded theory, the approach they advocate builds on the need to ground theoretical understandings in empirical data.

In order to utilize the realistic approach we need to understand the hypotheses and policy rationale held by policy-makers which shape the formulation of the policy interventions. From this it is possible to develop theories about the way in which policy interventions interact with their contexts to create the outcomes that we can observe. Pawson and Tilley write of this process that 'theories must be framed in terms of propositions about how mechanisms are fired in contexts to produce outcomes' (1997: 85). This provides a way of examining the existing policy approaches being adopted in Wales, to examine and understand the specificities of the Welsh case and why particular outcomes are visible.

Evidence-based policy-making (EBP) based on the synthesis of evidence from different sources holds greater prospect of success than policies built purely on an ideological vision. Here evidence must be seen as the outcome of analysis rather than just a collection of data. Pawson (2002a, 2002b) argues in favour of drawing together disparate sources of evidence (perhaps from the realistic evaluations of different programmes) to build a better understanding of the likely intersection between context and policy mechanism. This entails the interrogation of the potential ramifications of particular policy mechanisms and the way in which they are likely to operate in different situations and contexts. In March 2003 the Assembly launched an evidence-based policy-making seminar series designed to reflect on how best it can apply notions of EBP to its activities.

Building civil society: the policy rationale

Policy-makers and academics increasingly see the existence of dynamic civil society and social capital as a prerequisite to the development of entrepreneurial, learning and successful regions (Putnam et al., 1993; Asheim, 1995 and 1998; Cooke, 2003). The emergence of a connection between civil society, social capital and development has led to the formulation of a policy theory that civil society must take a particular form (have partnerships, have lots of associational activities, be 'inclusive' and so on).[1] This theory is buttressed by the work of academics such as Cooke (2003: 2) who observes that 'social capital is a missing ingredient of economic development, and that it can be built up through the efforts of policy makers'. This approach dates back to debates about social capital and civil society in the work of Coleman (1988) and later Putnam et al. (1993). The much quoted study by Putnam et al. argued that civil society, rather than either institutional structures or policies, was to blame for difficulties in institutional performance in southern Italy. Making a specific link between civic virtue and economic development they observe: 'when we use both civic traditions and past socioeconomic development to predict present socioeconomic development, we discover that civics is actually a better predictor of socioeconomic development than is development itself' (1993: 156). This study has been heavily criticized for its potential for racist use by those arguing in favour of some form of innate superiority of northern Italians over those from the south of Italy, and for its failure fully to understand the context within which the southern regional institutions operated (Bagnasco and Putnam, 1996, Grote, 1996, Batterbury, 2002). Bagnasco and Putnam, referring to the problem of the particularistic Northern Leagues in Italy, goes so far as to say of the study that it 'remains to be said that this book is not an explanation of the backwardness of the south, [and] that it is in danger of being misunderstood' (1996: 365). The work of Putnam et al. arguably directs inadequate attention to understanding the socio-cultural and historical context shaping the performance of their case study regions. This lack of detailed empirical investigation of the context creates some difficulties for understanding the real links between socio-economic development and civil society. This reaffirms the importance of the realistic approach with its pursuit of middle range theory explaining the intersection between contextual specificity, policy/institutional mechanisms and outcomes.

Putnam famously published a subsequent book in 2000, *Bowling Alone: The Collapse and Revival of American Community,* where he defines social capital as bridges and bonds between groups of people. At the same time the concept of social capital found favour with policy-makers ranging from the World Bank and other multinational organizations to regional authorities. For example, the World Bank's Social Capital Initiative has led to a stated wish for further research to unpick the interaction between social capital and 'the social dimensions of development' (Francis, 2002: 17). Putnam's definition places attention on the associational elements of social capital. If we accept this definition then it is easy to conceive of civil society as being a much richer concept that also entails the whole range of global and multi-tiered elements of a fluid, hybrid and porous area of human interaction.

At the regional level, and certainly in Wales, the philosophy of the 'learning region' has become a key component of contemporary policy-making. In Wales the plan for the 'Learning Country' was launched in 2001 in recognition of the links between training and education and 'community development, social inclusion, wealth creation and personal fulfilment' (NAW, 2001: 7). The notion of the learning region is more closely related to the desire to bring about economic development than policies that simply focus on building social capital through volunteering schemes or support for particular services. For Cooke, the learning region and social capital are interrelated (2003: 2). The spread of knowledge and learning that forms the basis of a learning region relies on dense social networks and linkages between people and the capturing and embedding of learning to ensure that innovation and economic growth results. Strong social capital is the bedrock of civil society where groups cooperate and interrelate and the antithesis of atomistic welfare-dependent cultures.

Civil society and social capital are therefore considered by policy-makers to be essential components of economic development and the emergence of learning regions. Arguably, it is this link which makes actions in support of civil society most attractive to the policy world. However, the empirical research to support this link is sparse and at times over-theorized, lacking important grounding in empirical data (Bagnasco and Putnam, 1996; Grote, 1996; Batterbury, 2002). The hypothesis ignores the role played by social stability, education, urbanism, personnel stability, the prevailing party of government, globalization and the political economy in explaining institutional performance and ultimately socio-economic development.

Inevitably the rapid acceptance of the concept of social capital by the policy world and the design of policies to capitalize on its potential is problematic. While the bonding and bridging elements of social capital are important, this provides only a partial understanding of the forces of change within the area of civil society. A more holistic understanding of civil society which also recognizes the contextual specificity of arenas of policy intervention is more likely to yield successful policies. This supports the need for a systems approach to understanding policy interventions in civil society. If you change one aspect of civil society this may have an impact on a number of elements; similarly, if global forces induce the collapse of an industry this will have significant knock-on implications on the character of civil society. For this reason policy interventions need to pay due cognizance to context and to understanding the way in which different, superficially unrelated, policies impact on one another.

In terms of policy formulation and evaluation, specific links between context, mechanism and outcome require further attention to determine the way in which economic development can be enhanced by measures to support the growth and development of civil society and social capital. Realistic evaluation provides us with a useful explanatory device for assessing these linkages. In what follows the policy theory/mechanism, context and observed outcomes for one of the Assembly's interventions is analysed. This exemplifies the way in which realistic evaluation can illuminate our understanding of the links between context, mechanism and outcomes. This case study is a fairly simple one, focusing on a scheme to promote volunteering in Wales with a specific focus to build up social capital and the use of partnership as a governance strategy.

Building social capital in Wales: the Volunteering Scheme

The Volunteering Scheme (not its real name) is just one example of a policy intervention in Wales developed to promote citizenship and help build communities. There are many other policy initiatives in Wales which also strive towards this kind of outcome,

Sustainable Communities, People in Communities, the Active Community Initiative, the Voluntary Sector Scheme and Communities First to name but a few. In what follows I apply a realistic evaluation to the Volunteering Scheme by way of illustration of how this approach can reveal both strengths and weaknesses in the mechanism given the contextual circumstances prevailing in Wales.

The Volunteering Scheme was intended as an explicit contribution to building civil society and reducing social exclusion. It set out to encourage volunteering and to enhance institutional capacity. Anticipated outcomes included reduction of social exclusion and addition of value to the lives of those participating. This is consistent with the approach taken by the Welsh Assembly Government in tackling social exclusion, building capacity and developing communities.

At the same time the Volunteering Scheme also sought to empower communities by enabling them to take responsibility for the development of social linkages and support mechanisms. The development of dynamic social activities would also ensure that costs would be reduced for local authorities and the Assembly, who could then direct their limited resources to other areas. As an Assembly report observes, the ethos behind supporting volunteering in Wales is based on 'increase in participation in community life . . . integral to the strengthening of civic engagement, the development of dense networks and social capital necessary for regeneration of marginalized and deprived communities' (WAG, 2003: 25). This applies equally to the Volunteering Scheme. The Volunteering Scheme supported a number of projects aimed at increasing access to volunteering by developing capacity, bringing together volunteers and those responsible for working with volunteers and increasing funding for these schemes.

If we examine the complex intersection between mechanism, context and outcome for the Volunteering Scheme we gain some interesting insights into the way in which outcomes were shaped. Figure 16.1 details some examples of these links. The Volunteering Scheme borrowed an 'off the shelf' design, a mechanism that had been conceived centrally in Whitehall and was then applied in Wales. It is clear that the mechanism operated as a fairly blunt instrument to deliver the aims and objectives of the programme. Its principal component was a degree of financial support for the project coupled with support for measures aimed at increasing participants' access to volunteering opportunities. In addition, the participating organizations were also encouraged to form partnerships with each other and to raise the profile of volunteering though use of media and promotion.

As the result of lack of clarity over the likely interactions between context and mechanism, the mechanism was not assessed in the light of an understanding or theory about the relationship between context and mechanism. A number of difficulties resulted (see figure 16.1 for a detailed assessment). Although it is easier to identify the likely impact of context and mechanism on outcomes with the benefit of hindsight, a policy system that routinely assesses these implications as well as the likely impact of other policies should be better able to ward off undesired outcomes. This is why evidence-based policy-making requires an analytical focus, rather than a simple collection of data.

Problems with the stated aim to encourage more volunteers were met as the result of a reduction in the numbers of participants from the student population (the end of student grants saw students seeking paid rather than voluntary work, for example). As a result, projects needed to recruit participants from harder-to-reach populations but chose instead to prioritize retention of existing volunteers. Although, on the face of it, this seems a perfectly reasonable approach to the problem, it misses the point of the scheme which was to build social capital through volunteering not simply to maintain existing levels. Lack of detailed understanding of the socio-cultural dynamics of Welsh communities meant that sums of money were also invested in media and promotion: however, we know that the word of mouth was the most successful way of attracting new volunteers. Problems in recruiting qualified staff due to low salaries in the sector and geographical remoteness of some of the projects was not remediable by the financial support provided by the Volunteering Scheme. The provision to encourage the formation of partnerships with other projects did not adequately address the need for opportunities for organizations to meet and exchange policy learning.

The scheme was, however, particularly successful in building the self-confidence of participants, in providing a service and in equipping volunteers with useful skills. This is an important aspect of maintaining employability of individuals as well as for bringing together communities and building social capital.

Figure 16.1. Volunteering Scheme – policy rationale, policy delivery mechanism, contextual circumstances and resultant outcomes.

Programme theory	**Mechanism**	**Context**	**Outcome**
Increase and sustain greater numbers of volunteers in Wales. Support for volunteering a good thing because it increases social capital and therefore economic development.	• Financial support to volunteering organizations to increase the numbers of volunteers. • Ensure access to potential volunteers through internet sites and physical infrastructure.	• Reduction of student numbers for summer volunteering due to abolition of student grants. • Increase in the number of women in full-time employment.	Perception by some projects of a reduction in the pool from which volunteers could be drawn. Shift in focus towards retaining volunteers not just encouraging new ones.
	Raising the profile of volunteering through media and promotion.	Some of the target communities have high levels of unemployment and higher than average illiteracy. Existing social networks operate by word of mouth.	Word of mouth found to be the most successful means of increasing numbers of volunteers. Existing volunteers recommending participation to potential participants.
		Promotional activities undertaken by the projects but not by WAG.	Opportunities for raised profile for the initiative lost. Inadequate public accountability.
	Financial support to volunteering organizations to increase the numbers of volunteers.	Ongoing need for additional services over and above that provided by statutory authorities (e.g. care of elderly, support of minority groups etc.).	Benefits made available to communities as the result of services provided at limited cost to the state.

		Delays in criminal record checks resulting in delays in recruiting volunteers to work with children.	No provision in the initiative for dealing with this kind of externality.
		Disaffected youth, social deprivation, widespread social exclusion.	Engagement with community leading to increased confidence, social integration and feelings of self worth for volunteers. Increase in social capital.
		Negative perceptions of some minority groups (e.g. disabled people) Negative perceptions challenged by participation in the volunteering scheme. Increase in social capital.	Negative perceptions challenged by participation in the volunteering scheme. Increase in social capital.
		Widespread unemployment.	Retention of work-based skills and employability of participating volunteers. Increase in potential for economic regeneration.
		Lack of trust in communities.	Trust developed as the result of volunteering and increased reciprocity among communities. Increase in social capital.
		Barriers to communication between generations.	Emergence of intergenerational links breaking down barriers, reducing isolation of the elderly and disaffection of youth. Increase in social capital.

Programme theory	Mechanism	Context	Outcome
		Post-retirement life without structure and purpose for the elderly.	Increased health and social well-being for elderly volunteers experiencing a reason to keep active and a focus for energies and talents. Increase in social capital.
Support capacity development of volunteering organizations so they can deliver the objectives of the initiative.	Financial support to volunteering organizations to increase the numbers of volunteers.	Continued capacity problems for volunteer organizations due to lack of human resources and knowledge.	Strategies focusing on retention of volunteers fail to build new social capital when not accompanied by a drive to recruit volunteers from some excluded groups (e.g. little focus on attracting volunteers from ethnic communities).
		Inadequate skill base in some areas a problem for recruitment, lack of human resources within volunteer organizations and projects.	Need for increase in vertical partnership between WAG and voluntary sector bodies and for wider field of potential recruits not really met by the financial support mechanism.
		Inadequate skill base, lack of human resources within volunteer organizations and projects.	Training programmes on volunteer management, customer service and monitoring for learning have led to an increase in capacity by those organizations focusing on these elements.

		General low level of salaries across the sector.	Unresolved problems in retraining qualified staff in the organizations.
		Uncertainty over long-term funding arrangements.	Provision of financial support not enough unless accompanied by some clarity in procedures enabling forward planing by volunteering organizations.
	Encouragement to volunteering organizations to form partnerships with each other.	Insufficient opportunities for organizations to meet and exchange policy learning.	Umbrella organizations and coordinating bodies perform a useful role giving technical advice and bringing together the projects periodically to enable exchange of lessons learned and best practice. Reinforcement of this role could ensure increased capacity.
		Lack of knowledge about what other projects in the initiative do.	Need for increased knowledge management inadequately met by simply encouraging organizations to form partnerships.

Source: author's elaboration from evaluation report.

Figure 16.1 charts the evolution of the Volunteering Scheme from formulation of the original programme theory through to the design of the project mechanisms through which the programme theory would be implemented. The important contextual features are also set out along with the actual outcomes achieved.

The analysis in figure 16.1 shows where problems occur as the result of a mismatch between the design of the mechanism and the contextual specificities in the implementation environment for a specific initiative. The relatively simple mechanism of providing financial support, some limited media and promotion support and encouragement to work in partnerships had a number of desirable outcomes, as we can see, ranging from increased health and well-being for the elderly to increased engagement of socially disaffected youth with the communities and confidence building. However, the mechanism was not able to address some of the structural problems common across Wales, including inadequate numbers of available volunteers, insufficient numbers of skilled staff and consequent lack of institutional capacity. The shift in focus towards retaining volunteers induces a substantial move away from the desired outcome of building additional social capital. Part of the problem lies in the widespread structural features (economic and demographic) which lie outside the remit of a relatively small project such as this one. This highlights the need for a more integrated polity able to recognize where policy intentions are likely to be tripped up by prevailing contextual dynamics. In planning new policies and projects there is also a self-evident need for greater complementarity in policy approaches.

The analysis presented above is fairly simple as it relates to just one project. The task of understanding the systemic implications of policy intervention become more difficult once comparison between related (and even unrelated) policies is added in to the analytical process. Pawson and Tilley (1997) term this 'cumulation of evidence'; similarly, Glaser and Strauss (1967) spoke of the critical importance of comparative research. Thus, a comparative approach combined with realistic evaluation techniques is an important means of grounding our emergent understandings of the impact of particular policy interventions on civil society in the supporting empirical data (Glaser and Strauss, 1967; Eisenhardt, 1989). Inevitably, the policy world needs to find strategies for undertaking this form of comparative analysis of policies as part of a broad systems approach to policy-making.

Other policy interventions in the civil society arena in Wales

The chapters of this book provide a number of illuminating examples of policy interventions which have been thrown off-beam by the unanticipated impact of the socio-economic context within which they have been implemented. In addition there are good examples of problematic programme and policy theory – where ideology rather than sensible interrogation of the likely intersection between context and mechanism has been responsible for policy choices. If we look back we find evidence in many of the chapters that policy or programme theory is often only partially developed or even wholly lacking among the policy decision-makers. Very often conviction politics has held sway rather than the development of incisive theories about why particular policies are likely to impact in particular ways. This is most evident where policies produce unanticipated outcomes.

For example, Williams notes in chapter 10 that 'consultation overload and elite burnout are commonly reported' – hardly the intended outcomes for a set of policies aimed at increasing participation and being inclusive. With regard to Assembly efforts to improve access to decision-makers for black and ethnic minority groups, she also notes that the 'impacts are, however, differential'. This differential impact is rooted in capacity issues, in spite of funding flows for capacity enhancement being put in place. This reminds us of the temporal factor associated with all policy interventions – a vital consideration for any evaluative enterprise. It is a commonplace that some change must be sustained over a medium- to long-term period to have effect and evaluation needs to bear in mind the need for adequate time for the achievement of desired outcomes.

Williams also raises concerns about the 'deliberate orchestration of activity in the civil sphere around ethnicity as the basis of association when, particularly in areas of sparse minority population, this may have a very weak foothold' (p. 203). This is a classic case of failure to appreciate adequately the positive dynamics of particular contexts when formulating policy. It confirms the need for a better evidence base. An effective realistic evaluation of this form of policy initiative should reveal that the mechanism is inadequately tailored to the socio-cultural characteristics of its implementation context, and that the outcomes will potentially artificially reinforce perceptions of difference in this way.

Similarly, Hodgson in chapter 9 also outlines the potential for policies to produce undesired outcomes. She describes the widespread emergence of a culture of partnership and networking, an increasing requirement for securing funding. Partnership is regarded as an important mechanism for 'including' civil society in the process of government, though, of course, inclusion is always on the terms set by the host organization (Skliar, 2002). It also saves money as many social partners contribute their time for no remuneration. Partnership is also perceived to be a mechanism for controlling civil society (but only those aspects willing to participate). Hodgson reports that compulsion to work in partnership can sometimes lead to the undermining of 'the independence, the ethos, and the modus operandi of civil society'. She notes, further, that an increase in competition between different groups is having a negative impact on social cohesion by pitting one against the other in pursuit of funding. This atomizing process hardly achieves the goals of inclusivity, developing civil society, nor of cost saving. These unintended negative outcomes are suggestive of an inadequately grounded programme and policy theory and of a need for the policy world to rethink its approach to policy formulation. Hodgson's (2002) study uncovers the detailed contextual circumstances within which partnership policies are being implemented as well as the resultant outcomes observed.

Mann discusses the way in which the Assembly has sought to depoliticize the Welsh-language issue. Behind this lay the need to gain a successful result from the referendum on devolution. Given the significant mismatch between the drive for depoliticization and the actual circumstances for Welsh speakers, this approach unsurprisingly proved difficult to sustain – particularly in the middle of the Assembly government's first term of office. Contextual factors have had a critical role to play: language issues are almost always political. The minority status of Welsh speakers has a number of important implications (protection of the language, the need to develop a collective voice to lobby for group interests, displacement of individual rights for English speakers in favour of collective interests etc.) making political activity around language issues very likely.

Drakeford notes the strong convictions which led the first minister to call for a close engagement between the voluntary sector and the Assembly. This was predicated on his personal belief in giving as many citizens as possible a continuing stake in the social welfare services. It is difficult to ascertain from this the extent to which a strong evidence base may have influenced these policy approaches, a certain involvement of ideology and personal conviction is clearly evident. Unless a strong understanding of the contextual features within which this intervention is taking place is maintained any change to the context may result in problematic outcomes. Drakeford has observed that many in the voluntary sector feel obliged to take on public sector responsibilities in return for proximity to government – a loss of this proximity under these circumstances could have a number of negative consequences.

For Thomas and Taylor in chapter 5, civil society is portrayed here not as the object of policy but as an instrument for influencing hearts and minds about the process of devolution. Alongside the economic development objectives for policy involvement in civil society (discussed above), they offer another rationale for the adoption of policy interventions to 'support' the development of civil society (or, perhaps, as Adamson and Day have suggested in chapters 12 and 14, to control it). Thomas and Taylor also note that the small electoral margin achieved in favour of devolution in 1997 reinforced the drive for public legitimacy to be achieved, in part, through the adoption of notions of *inclusivity*. This provides the context within which actions to build legitimacy have been developed. A low level of political trust (referred to by Thomas and Taylor, and by Davies and Dunkerley in chapter 8) also sets the context for political actions to improve relations with civil society.

The shift in discourse towards inclusivity and partnership therefore has an element of self-interest behind it. This highlights an important assumption behind the realistic approach to evaluation – that programme theories are necessarily developed with the interests of the programme beneficiaries in mind. Thomas and Taylor remind us that there are multiple stakeholders and an unequal distribution of power within the system that can exert a distorting impact on rational analytical realistic policy-making and evaluation. It has long been recognized, of course, that the whole evaluation enterprise is itself political and takes place in a politicized context (Palumbo, 1987; Weiss, 1998). Where the self-interest of the political elite coincides with that of the broader stakeholder constituency, there is little problem. We need to be aware, however, of the potential for this happy consensus to diverge.

Discussing the Blairite policy vision, Adamson (in chapter 14) sets out the rationale upon which many policy initiatives are now being constructed. He notes that the *inclusive* vision is a conditional one which imposes obligations as well as benefits on those within the social welfare system. Adamson unpicks the discourse behind much contemporary rhetoric, highlighting here (with Skliar, 2002) the conditionality of the discourse of 'inclusion'. This perspective tailors well with suggestions by Drakeford (in chapter 6) and Thomas and Taylor of a degree of political ideology behind current policy interventions in the civil society arena in Wales.

When advocating the realistic approach to the evaluation of policies (with Pawson and Tilley, 1997) we find ourselves with a dilemma. Effective policies require a rational, outcome-focused orientation which is rooted not in *conviction* but in a genuine attempt to expend policy energies on things that work. The evidence-based policy-making initiative of the Assembly has a heightened importance in this context as it offers the prospect of a move away from politicized decision-making towards the emergence of grounded programme theories and mechanisms designed with contextual specificity in mind. It is likely that a large-scale organization culture shift lies in front of the Assembly as it seeks to move towards learning-focused, evidence-based policy-making.

Adamson also highlights the tradition of community regeneration in Wales as an oppositional activity. Its demonstrated success provided an important indication to the policy world that community-owned processes could work. Understandably, the Assembly sought to replicate this approach through a variety of WAG supported initiatives (Communities First, People in Communities, etc). The oppositional culture of community regeneration work was, however, an important aspect of the recorded success. The Assembly will need to be aware of the risk of 'death by legitimacy' for the schemes it sponsors – ensuring that genuine community ownership and tangible results (real employment prospects) are at the centre of these kinds of initiatives. The phenomenon comes up every so often in the evaluation of social programmes. It amply demonstrates the need to understand the detailed processes that underlie particular phenomena in civil society, and the problematic outcomes from inappropriate state encroachment in the civil society arena. Adamson terms this 'incorporation' and the tension is also identified by Hodgson.

Conclusions

A number of chapters in this book provide a historical glimpse of the shifting character of civil society in Wales as it changes through time from a Nonconformist eighteenth-century phenomenon to something differentiated across different localities in Wales, simultaneously courted and rejected by the state authorities depending on its particular characteristics in different places. We should perhaps speak not of one 'civil society' in Wales but of many 'civil societies'. This chapter opened with the observation that civil society was a fluid, dynamic, multi-layered construct that was not amenable to measurement or even substantial policy direction. We have seen, however, that policy intervention in the civil society domain is an often explicit and prioritized objective in Wales.

A number of the chapters have highlighted the selectivity of public sector support for civil society. Williams notes in chapter 10 how black and ethnic minority formations are increasingly the focus of consultation exercises, Chambers and Thompson in chapter 11 describe the creation of the Interfaith Council to provide a forum for consultation with different faith groups, and Davies and Dunkerley in chapter 8 recount the attempts being made to reach out to young people in Wales, for example. Conversely, Day in chapter 12 shows how contemporary support for rural communities would now exclude the very communities held up as beacons of strong civil society in the past. If civil society represents all communities and groups that are not part of the state then this policy approach of determining of 'who is in' and 'who is out' is puzzling. We have seen, above, that the policy rationale is not as simple as 'let's support civil society', there are distinctive political as well as economic theories for policy actions.

However, the policy redefinition of civil society represents a normative approach, evaluating civil society according to certain predefined criteria. As noted at the beginning of this chapter, it makes more sense to evaluate the policy mechanisms rather than civil society itself.

In proposing a realistic approach to evaluating civil society initiatives this chapter has advanced the idea that it is possible for policy-making to be grounded more effectively in empirical reality and to be more complementary and cohesive. Civil society can be seen as a series of overlapping systems so that a change in one area will have implications for another. Policy initiatives to support civil society are also impacted upon by external structural impacts and shocks that can induce significant change in the demographic character of civil society and in the needs of its constituency. A greater evidence-based orientation to policy-making will recognize the systemic interrelatedness of policy interventions. The way in which context and policy mechanisms interrelate to produce particular outcomes was illustrated at the level of an individual project (for the sake of simplicity). Given the overlapping nature of policies, the task of using realistic evaluations entails the ability to manage complexity and multiple information flows as well as to have a strong and in-depth knowledge of contextual dynamics within Wales. The rewards of better, more effective, policy will come if the Assembly is able successfully to implement its evidence-based policy strategy, invoking a change in its organizational culture to prioritize a learning focus rather than the adoption of ideological approaches.

In thinking about civil society as a number of overlapping civil societies with different constituencies, we find that there is some overlap between notions of civil society and new theories of identity and hybridity. Williams has hinted in chapter 10 at the complexity surrounding attempts to speak either of a single civil society and the possibility of groups and individuals simultaneously belonging to more than one group or community. She writes: 'The cultural boundaries of such groups are inevitably fluid and permeable in a way that defies their categorization for the purposes of policy intervention. Assumptions of homogeneity within these communities are misplaced.' This statement may well be applied not only to black and ethnic minorities but to all the other communities, groups and individuals who form collectively what has been described as the civil society of Wales. As Whatmore in her study of hybridity has observed, mapping hybridity entails: 'Emphasising the multiplicity of space-times generated in/by the movements and rhythms of heterogeneous association. The spatial vernacular of such geographies is fluid not flat, unsettling the coordinates of distance and proximity; local and global; inside and outside' (Whatmore 2002: 6). This serves to remind us that civil society in Wales is also hybrid, a place where multiple layers of identity overlap within individuals and within groups, both inside the physical territory of Wales and beyond it. There are many civil societies within Wales (and beyond). Individuals may be part of more than one civil society in the same way that they may lay claim to multiple identities (constructed around ethnicity, religious orientation, community identity, age, class, interest groups and so on).

At the level of policy, understanding this complexity of inter-relationships is likely to prove critical in achieving a series of policies that work and policies that are cognizant of the implications that policy activity in one domain may have on another. Realistic approaches to evaluating these civil society interventions are likely to prove useful in providing evidence about how policy mechanisms interact with the context, so that policy formulation may be more closely aligned with evidence about what works and why.

Note

1. It is perhaps worth pausing to reflect on the meaning of the word 'inclusion'. Carlos Skliar (2002), in his research on deaf and other minority groups, has observed that inclusion is a term that in fact requires change by those being included and is anything other than a genuine acceptance of our mutual diversity. He has noted that inclusion is about inviting 'the other' in but only on our own terms. This effectively perpetuates on going exclusion and division.

References

Asheim, B. (1995). 'Industrial districts as "learning regions": a condition for prosperity?', *European Planning Studies*, 4.

Asheim, B. (1998). 'Learning regions as development coalitions: partnership as governance in European workfare states', paper presented at the Second

European Urban and Regional Studies Conference, University of Durham, UK, 17–20 September.

Bagnasco, A. and Putnam, R. (1996). 'Making democracy work', *International Journal of Urban and Regional Research*, 20, 2.

Banfield, E. (1958). *The Moral Basis of a Backward Society*, New York: The Free Press.

Batterbury, S. C. E. (2002). 'Evaluating policy implementation: the European Union's small and medium-sized enterprise policies in Galicia and Sardinia', *Regional Studies*, 8, 36.

Coleman, J. (1988). 'Social capital in the creation of human capital', *American Journal of Sociology*, 94.

Cooke, P. (2003). 'Social capital in the learning region', published on the Internet at *http://www.rtsinc.org/learningnow/cooke.doc* (accessed 18 June 2003).

Eisenhardt, K. M. (1989). 'Building theories from case study research', *Academy of Management Review*, 14, 4.

Francis, P. (2002). 'Social capital at the World Bank: strategic and operational implications of the concept', 31 March, Social Development Strategy: report (accessed 18 June 03) available at: *http://lnweb18.worldbank.org/ESSD/essdext.nsf/62DocByUnid/859A26E9E5E3400B85256C5500534E34/$FILE/Francis4.pdf.*

Fukuyama, F. (1996). *Trust: The Social Virtues and The Creation of Prosperity,* New York: The Free Press.

Glaser, B. and A. Strauss (1967). *The Discovery of Grounded Theory*, Chicago: Aldine.

Grote, J. R. (1996). 'Cohesion in Italy: a view on non-economic disparities', in L. Hooghe (ed.), *Cohesion Policy and European Integration: Building Multi-Level Governance*, Oxford: Oxford University Press.

Hodgson, L. (2002). 'Experiencing civil society: the reality of civil society in post-devolution Wales', unpublished Ph.D. thesis, Pontypridd: University of Glamorgan.

Jacobs, J. (1961). *The Life and Death of Great American Cities,* Harmondsworth: Penguin.

Leigh, R. (2000). Black Elders Project, Leicester: Leicester Volunteer Centre.

National Assembly for Wales (NAW), (2001). 'The Learning Country, a paving document: a comprehensive education and lifelong learning programme to 2010 in Wales', available on the Internet at: *http://www.wales.gov.uk/subieducation-training/content/PDF/learningcountry-e.pdf* (accessed 18 June 2003).

Nutley, S., I. Walter and H. Davies (2002). 'From knowing to doing: a framework for understanding the evidence-into-practice agenda', discussion paper 1, March 2002, available on the Internet at *http://www.st-andrews.ac.uk/~ruru/KnowDo%20paper.pdf* (accessed 22/ March 2003).

Nutley, S., Davies, H. and Walter, I. (2003). 'Evidence based policy and practice: cross sector lessons from across the UK', keynote paper for the Social Policy Research and Evaluation Conference, Wellington, New Zealand, available on the Internet at *http://www.st-andrews.ac.uk/~ruru/NZ%20conference%20paper%20final%20170602.pdf* (accessed 23 March 2003).

Palumbo, D. J. (ed.) (1987). *The Politics of Program Evaluation*, London: Sage.

Pawson, R. (2002a). 'Evidence-based policy: in search of a method', *Evaluation*, 2, 8.

Pawson, R. (2002b). 'Evidence-based policy: the promise of "realist synthesis"', *Evaluation*, 3, 8.

Pawson R. and Tilley, N. (1997). *Realistic Evaluation*, London: Sage.

Putnam, R. (2000). *Bowling Alone: The Collapse and Revival of American Community*, New York: Simon & Schuster.

Putnam, R. D., Leonardi, R. and Nanetti, R. (1993). *Making Democracy Work: Civic Traditions in Modern Italy*, Princeton, NJ: Princeton University Press.

Sayer, A. (1984). *Method in Social Science: A Realist Approach*, London: Hutchinson.

Skliar, C. (2002). *¿Y Si El Otro No Estuviera Ahí?*, Buenos Aires: Miño y Davila.

Welsh Assembly Government (WAG) (2003). *Evaluation of Wales Active Community Initiative: First Tranche of Projects, Final Report for the Welsh Assembly Government*, Cardiff: WAG, 7 February, Mimeo.

Weiss, C. (1998). 'Have we learned anything new about the use of evaluation?', *American Journal of Evaluation*, 19, 1.

Whatmore, S. (2002). *Hybrid Geographies: Natures, Cultures, Spaces*, London: Sage.

17. Civil Society in Wales

GRAHAM DAY, DAVID DUNKERLEY AND ANDREW THOMPSON

As we have noted elsewhere (Day et al., 2000), the devolution of decision-making powers to the National Assembly for Wales (NAW) signifies political recognition of the distinctiveness of Wales as a place that merits independent representation, which has its own 'voice' and which has its own problems and concerns. In other words, it is accepted as forming a distinct, although not wholly separate, society with its own particular history, identity and institutional structure. The arrival of the Assembly has been accompanied by numerous expressions of hopes and predictions about the dawn of a new and stronger Welsh civil society, the hope being that it will work to strengthen democratic engagement. It has also precipitated, to a limited extent, a discussion of what it is that makes Wales different in terms of the nature of its existing civil society.

Like 'inclusion' and 'partnership', the term 'civil society' has become part of the post-referendum Welsh political lexicon. Rhodri Morgan's hopes on this subject are shared by a wide range of academics and politicians. Osmond, for example, holds that the development of a more active civil society is a vital element of the 'new politics' emerging in Wales. Writing after the 1997 referendum, he argued that a 'new and interactive network of policy communication will be a building block of a new dynamic civil society' (1998b: 3). Many of the initiatives of the NAW incorporate ideas about how a stronger element of public participation and involvement can be built into future arrangements, and treat this as an essential step towards more effective economic and social performance.

The various contributions to this volume amply demonstrate that the nature, operation and effectiveness of civil society in Wales require more detailed investigation and discussion. Broadly, it is the case that knowledge is more developed with regard to work dealing with the economic aspects of Welsh development and analysis of the institutions of economic governance, and in relation to changes in the political sphere leading up to devolution and beyond, than with respect to the wider terrain of the 'social' – those institutions, networks and relationships that make up the substance of Welsh civil society. Useful assessments are provided by Osmond (1998b), Dunkerley and Thompson (1999), Chaney, Hall and Pithouse (2001), Day (2002) and the journal *Contemporary Wales*, but there are few in-depth studies that provide anything like a comprehensive and systematic evaluation of civil society in Wales. Thus many of the claims have to be regarded as no more than plausible interpretations. The contributions to this volume go some way to addressing this lacuna.

So, what of the existing civil society in Wales? Why the need for it to become more 'dynamic' as Osmond (1998a) suggests? There are indicators suggesting that, in fact, large parts of the Welsh population at present do have little more than a vestigial engagement with public and civic life. These 'excluded' elements include inhabitants of public housing estates and derelict industrial locales, substantial sections of the rural population, the elderly and very young, in some situations those who are primarily speakers of Welsh, or English (non-Welsh) and ethnic minority migrants, and those located in parts of Wales that are either geographically remote or viewed as essentially 'British' rather than Welsh in orientation. These exclusions and separations mean that, in reality, it may be only a minority that is fully connected and conscious of its involvement in Welsh society. This might go some way towards explaining the low turnout and vote in both the devolution referendum and the two elections for the National Assembly.

At the same time, it would be wrong to be overly pessimistic. It may be argued that we have seen the development of a new kind of civil society in Wales. Today, we can point to a wide range of institutions that function as autonomous actors within the Welsh context, including educational institutions, churches, community groups, voluntary organizations, trades unions, cultural organizations, pressure groups, civil rights and equal opportunities organizations, youth groups, as well as organizations representing local and regional commercial interests. Many of these organizations directly lobby policy-makers, in Wales and elsewhere, and now take a keen interest in monitoring the activities of the National Assembly on behalf of their members. Moreover, through these organizations many individuals throughout the country are involved in civil society, although not necessarily always as active participants. The role of the National Assembly as one of the primary sources of funding for a range of programmes, such as community regeneration or education and training initiatives or giving young people a voice, undoubtedly ensures that in future such civil society institutions will advance under the shadow cast by the progress of the National Assembly.

It is now possible to see the development of a Welsh civic society through the links between the National Assembly and its civil society 'partners' in the voluntary sector, but it remains to be seen what impact the latter will be able to exert over policy-formulation. Even if these developments succeed in fostering stronger civic networks between civil and government institutions in Wales, it is still questionable whether the former will necessarily view themselves in explicitly Welsh terms. Institutions, such as the Wales TUC or the Commission for Racial Equality in Wales, may operate as Welsh institutions in a territorial sense, but on the whole it is unlikely that they will be dealing with matters that are distinctively or peculiarly Welsh. While there are civil society institutions that operate as uniquely Welsh institutions, notably those organizations that exist to promote, in various ways, the Welsh language, in most cases, right down to the level of local community groups, the issues they deal with will be common to other areas of the United Kingdom and beyond.

Civil society institutions in Wales are undoubtedly coming to work with a more explicitly Welsh agenda. Already, there are signs of this activity in that numerous institutions, particularly the larger, more experienced operators, such as the higher education institutions, the Wales TUC, the WCVA, the churches and some sections of the media, are taking a keen interest in the policy-making of the National Assembly. Moreover, many of the chapters in this volume have documented how the Assembly is becoming more of a focus for and, to some extent, organizer of civil society in Wales. As networks proliferate and intensify, and as institutions come to orient themselves more towards Welsh policy matters, so the direction of civil society in Wales will change. In all of this, there is a role for the NAW in promoting both civil and civic activity in Wales (where the latter is more explicitly connected to political life).

A Scottish comparison is interesting in explaining both why more powers have been devolved to Scotland than to Wales and why they have been received there with apparently greater local enthusiasm. Such comparisons presuppose that there is a problem about the present state of affairs, in that Wales has a form of civil society that is somehow less effective than can be found elsewhere.

The very brevity of the now infamous entry in the 1888 edition of the *Encyclopaedia Britannica* – 'Wales, see England' – said much about the state of the union between England and Wales, and especially about its consequences for the junior partner, in the past. As Paterson and Wyn Jones have commented, 'even if reducing Wales to England is grotesquely misleading, little in Welsh history can be understood without reference to the relationship with the English neighbour' (1999: 171). In particular, Paterson and Wyn Jones suggest that the absence of separate and distinctive Welsh social institutions until the late nineteenth century can be attributed in large part to the consequences of union. However, if the effects of integration with England go some way towards explaining the past and even the present in Wales, in a number of respects it is Scotland that has become the model for thinking about how Wales might develop in the future. This is largely because devolution has gone further and been embraced with greater enthusiasm among the Scots. Scotland is a useful point of comparison for thinking about, and evaluating, the condition of civil society in Wales.

The devolution process has been the principal catalyst for discussions of how political devolution might unfold from now on, specifically with regard to the powers exercised by the NAW. This has been a central theme of many of the contributions to this book. If we think of civil society as referring to that wide range of activities and institutions that exist beyond the limits of the state and, in the Welsh context therefore, outside the domain of the National Assembly, then it is alleged that comparison with Scotland will serve to expose the *weakness* of civil society in Wales. Even after the 1707 Act of Union, Scotland managed to retain a range of important and independent civil institutions, including its own education and legal systems. More recently, through the work of the Constitutional Convention, the institutions of Scottish civil society were able to play an influential role in pushing for a Scottish Parliament, as Lindsay highlights in chapter 15 in this volume. In contrast, though the situation improved considerably around the turn of the twentieth century, with the establishment of bodies like the University of Wales, a National Library and Museum, the Welsh League of Youth (Urdd) and women's organization (Merched y Wawr), distinctively Welsh civil society institutions appear to be comparatively thin on the ground. Moreover, in Wales, civil society institutions seem to have had relatively little bearing on the move towards devolution, except perhaps for the period immediately preceding the 1997 referendum (Osmond, 1998a; Wyn Jones and Lewis, 1998). For this reason, much has been made of the capacity and need for the Assembly to transform this situation. As Rhodri Morgan remarked on the eve of his election as first secretary of the Assembly, 'getting this idea of a civic society in Wales, where autonomy is regarded as the most natural thing in the world, was actually the predecessor of devolution in Scotland. It may be the successor to devolution in Wales' (2000: 19).

There are good reasons, then, for making comparisons with Scotland when thinking about civil society in Wales, or more precisely, the nature of a *Welsh* civil society. However, there is also a danger that such comparisons can distort our perceptions. Wales certainly lagged behind Scotland in the growth of urban and intellectual centres and elites, especially during the eighteenth century, when the chief cities of Scotland could justly claim to be at the heart of the European Enlightenment. Even if some of the great figures of the Scottish Enlightenment, like David Hume, themselves believed that Scotland in turn lagged behind England, and especially London (see Porter, 2000), Wales produced no equivalent of thinkers like Hume, Adam Smith, Adam Ferguson and John Millar. Yet, despite the absence of the kind of urban civil institutions that thrived in Scotland, it can hardly be said that Wales has lacked altogether its own historic civil society institutions. During the nineteenth century from within the ranks of Welsh Nonconformism there came preachers and teachers who engaged not only in profound theological and ecclesiastical matters but also in a range of significant social issues and reforms. Arguably, it was Wales that took the lead in the development of British trade unionism in the late nineteenth and early twentieth centuries: by the early 1890s, union membership in Wales far exceeded that in England or Scotland (Williams, 1985). Nonconformism and the labour movement did much to transform the country's political culture, and to create a framework of organizations and associations with which large numbers of Welsh people were able to identify. These have had deep effects on the shape of Welsh social life, and its prevailing values and attitudes. The biographies of currently serving Assembly Members (AMs), as set out in successive volumes of the *Wales Yearbook*, serve to illustrate the continuing links between the structures of civil society and political representation and power in Wales. The majority are drawn from backgrounds in which involvements in education, the voluntary bodies and the labour movement, broadly defined, feature prominently.

Nevertheless, the contrasting accounts of the relationship between civil society and political culture in Wales and Scotland, offered by Lindsay and by Thomas and Taylor in this volume, demonstrate the greater capacity of Scottish civil society to speak out on and to influence national, political issues while succeeding still in standing apart from political society. However, the argument that civil society in Wales is comparatively weak because its key institutions do not wield the same clout as equivalent organizations elsewhere, or fail to speak adequately as Welsh institutions, can serve to detract from the level of activity, diversity and impact of the civil society that actually exists in Wales, and obscures just how much of social life in Wales is managed and organized through it.

Rhodri Morgan (2000: 19) argues that, in contrast to Scotland, in Wales 'we don't think autonomy' so that, consequently, civil society is not distinctively Welsh. The activities of the National Assembly are helping to ensure that this changes. Certainly, it is to the advantage of the Assembly that it does change, since the transformation from civil society in Wales to a Welsh civic society may help to give additional legitimacy to the process of devolution. Legitimizing devolution is not, however, the function of civil society. Distinguishing between supporting civil society so as to improve conditions in Wales and providing support for the purpose of buttressing the Assembly should be to the fore of the minds of politicians and researchers alike as devolution progresses.

Yet, whether or not devolution is making civil society more consciously Welsh is only one element of what is in effect a much wider debate about social life and organization in contemporary Wales. As many of the contributors to this book make clear, the Assembly obviously has an important bearing on civil society in Wales, and thus it is necessary to explore the relationships between them. As is very apparent from several of the chapters in this volume, the Assembly is becoming a focus for civil society in Wales, perhaps even to some extent fostering a truly Welsh civil society, in that its advent has meant that bodies are integrated more firmly into a national system of rules, funding and governance. However, to make the Assembly the sole focus of an understanding of civil society in Wales would be to misunderstand the idea, and possibly the function, of civil society. Civil society is a thoroughly sociological phenomenon for in essence it refers to the many diverse forms of human association that constitute 'society' and the values and forces that inform them. To enquire into civil society is therefore to consider broader matters about why and how individuals get involved in activities that are intended to help others as much as, or more than, themselves, what principles shape these actions, how conflicts arise as well as how agreements are reached and what the consequences are of such voluntary activity. In effect, then, to think about civil society is to explore how society 'happens'. More specifically, in terms of the focus of this book, it is to continue the sociological analysis of Wales that has been given such a boost in recent years by the process of devolution. The issues with which individuals and organizations are concerned today are difficult to contain comfortably within a national framework, as indeed are the larger networks within which increasingly they participate. Nevertheless, by putting the spotlight on civil society in Wales the purpose has been to show that public spiritedness – a civic culture – exists, indeed thrives in Wales, in spite of the pessimism bred by the evident disaffection with formal party politics, and the supposed weaknesses of civil society in this country. In order to explore the relationship between public and social policy and civil society, it is important not only to ask what constitutes civil society in Wales today but also to ask whom it should serve and how it might look in the future. The various contributions to this volume go some way to answering these central questions about contemporary civil society in Wales.

References

Chaney, P., Hall, T. and Pithouse, A. (2001). *New Governance – New Democracy?*, Cardiff: University of Wales Press.

Day, G. (2002). *Making Sense of Wales*, Cardiff: University of Wales.

Day, G., Dunkerley, D. and Thompson, A. (2000). 'Evaluating the "New Politics": civil society and the National Assembly for Wales', *Public Policy and Administration*, 15, 2.

Dunkerley, D. and Thompson, A. (eds) (1999). *Wales Today*, Cardiff: University of Wales Press.

Morgan, R. (2000). *Variable Geometry UK*, Cardiff: Institute of Welsh Affairs.

Osmond, J. (1998a). *New Politics in Wales*, London: Charter 88.

Osmond, J. (1998b). *The National Assembly Agenda*, Cardiff: Institute of Welsh Affairs.

Paterson, L. and Wyn Jones, R. (1999). 'Does civil society drive constitutional change?', in B. Taylor and K. Thomson (eds), *Scotland and Wales: Nations Again?*, Cardiff: University of Wales Press.

Porter, R. (2000). *Enlightenment*, Harmondsworth: Penguin.

Williams, G. A. (1985). *When was Wales?*, Harmondsworth: Penguin.

Wyn Jones, R. and Lewis, B. (1998). *The Wales Labour Party and Welsh Civil Society: Aspects of the Constitutional Debate in Wales*, paper delivered at Political Studies Association Annual Conference, University of Keele, April 7–9.

Index